The Promise of Beauty

Mimi Thi Nguyen

the promise of beauty

DUKE UNIVERSITY PRESS
Durham and London
2024

© 2024 DUKE UNIVERSITY PRESS
All rights reserved
Project Editor: Michael Trudeau
Designed by A. Mattson Gallagher
Typeset in Minion Pro and Poetica
by Westchester Publishing Services

Library of Congress Cataloging-in-Publication Data
Names: Nguyen, Mimi Thi, [date] author.
Title: The promise of beauty / Mimi Thi Nguyen. Description: Durham : Duke University Press, 2024. |
Includes bibliographical references and index.
Identifiers: LCCN 2024003240 (print)
LCCN 2024003241 (ebook)
ISBN 9781478030973 (paperback)
ISBN 9781478026761 (hardcover)
ISBN 9781478060000 (ebook)
Subjects: LCSH: Aesthetics—Political aspects. | Aesthetics—Philosophy. Classification: LCC BH301.P64 N48 2024 (print) |
LCC BH301.P64 (ebook) | DDC 111/.85—DC23/ENG/20240604
LC record available at https://lccn.loc.gov/2024003240
LC ebook record available at https://lccn.loc.gov/2024003241

Cover art: Illustration by Nicole Gomez.

Everything for everyone

CONTENTS

Preface ix
Acknowledgments xi

Introduction. Small Art and Love and Beauty 1

1 The Beautiful, Finding Itself in Danger, Desires Its Copy 37

2 An Education in Beauty (and the Necessity of Lawlessness) 70

3 The Right to Be Beautiful without Guarantee 103

4 Beauty's Ruin at the End of the World 139

5 Living Beautifully, or Resilience 171

Epilogue. In Conclusion, Crime Is Beauty 199

Notes 209
Bibliography 251
Index 287

PREFACE

The presence or absence of beauty might trace, among other things, the relationship between a structure and a subject, a history and a biography. And so I admit that throughout the course of writing, I have at times felt unmoored emotionally from a sense of ongoingness, let alone the ongoingness of this scholarly inquiry, because all I could perceive about the world was not beauty, but ruin. The attenuation of a livable life, and the accelerating destruction of what remains, found in an intensifying detention and deportation regime funneling humans into an archipelago of private prisons and concentration camps; the normalization of endless war through the specter of terror; anti-Muslim travel bans and anti-immigrant rancor heightening our security theater at all points of crossing; the criminalization of refugee aid at land or sea; the immense accumulation of wealth for private equity built on others' impoverishment and indebtedness; moral crusades masquerading as "pro-life" or antitrafficking or "pro-children" legislation, while creating new categories of crime and criminality; a global pandemic that demonstrated the complete and utter negligence of governments toward mass death; and an ongoing genocide of an occupied people unfolding on our phones. Even though I have been with this book for over a decade, I still have wondered if beauty could only be a distraction from the horrors promised as bulwark and revenge against others—the refugees, queers, feminists, freaks, outcasts, criminals, sex workers, and asylum seekers among us. I knew this to be a banality, yet I felt it to be true.

But we are also inundated with calls to create and nurture beauty in dark times. Even as state violence and its sanctioned counterparts proliferate deathliness, and climate science locates the extinction horizon closer and closer (fifty years to twelve years to ten years to next year when the permafrost is thawed and the coral reefs are dead and . . .), we cling to BTS's back catalog, young adult fantasy novels, ten-step skin-care routines, the guidance of tarot and celestial bodies, a well-formed sourdough loaf, and other sources of what we call *beauty* to help us endure another day. We are encouraged to combat political ugliness with art as affective contagion, and to organize mutual aid, but also to rest in times of uncertainty, because *resilience is beautiful*. This is also a familiar story. These pleasures and reminders to find them in the midst of crisis and cruelty insist that our moment requires a promise to bring about another way of life, one that is not yet known in all its dimensions but is nonetheless accessible through aesthetic possibility. In this case, beauty promises its presence as a necessary mnemonic for the lives we must imagine living, if we are to go on at all.

The historical present sees still other gestures to the beautiful marshaled to call for harmony, equilibrium, or a return to the status quo against the disruptions that threaten law and order. Even as the administration of Donald Trump cobbled together policies that contravened constitutional and international conventions, and embraced the virulent racisms that animalize populations, Democratic congresswoman and House minority leader Nancy Pelosi scolded her colleague Maxine Waters for the latter's calls to confront publicly, openly, the architects of family separation that caged migrants at the US-Mexico border. Drawing on centuries-old correspondences (going back to Pythagoras and Plato) to lend structure to a feeling, Pelosi called on a collectivity to "make America beautiful again" through a "return" to a more genteel civility. While Waters identified complicity with law and order as a moral and political crisis, Pelosi sought to secure social cohesion against another crisis, named as the absence of harmony—for her, shared by Trump as well as Waters in a zero-sum equivocation—which is also the absence of beauty, jeopardizing "America." Beauty is recruited here as a psychological-affective imperative to support a governing order against the chaos of its principled refusal.

Beauty as distraction, as balm, as harmony—the promise in each of these alignments toward our historical present is about what forces are considered responsible for the presence, or absence, of something that could be called a life worth living.

On whose side is beauty, anyway?

ACKNOWLEDGMENTS

For almost twenty years, the Department of Gender and Women's Studies at the University of Illinois, Urbana-Champaign, has been my scholarly home, and I have learned important lessons from my departmental colleagues about how to build and sustain community and collaboration. I owe extra thanks to the staff, Jacque Khan, Tasha Robles, Virginia Swisher, and Erin Smith, who kept me going during my stints in (too much) administration. The Department of Asian American Studies also provided much-needed support, and I would not be who I am today without it. I received generous support from Antoinette Burton at the Humanities Research Institute as a faculty fellow and collaborator, while Cynthia Oliver and Maria Gillombardo supplied invaluable encouragement at the Office of the Vice Chancellor for Research and Innovation. As faculty affiliated with the OVCRI, Craig M. Koslofsky, Shelley E. Weinberg, and Carol Symes read multiple drafts of grant proposals and gave enthusiastic feedback and guidance.

I have benefited tremendously from opportunities to share this project throughout its conception and completion at multiple forums, including the University of Texas at Austin; Brown University; Colorado College; Dartmouth College; Harvard University; the University of North Carolina at Asheville; the University of Hartford; Davidson College; Tufts University; George Washington University; the Center for Humanities at Wesleyan University; the annual symposium of the IUB Asian American Studies

Program at Indiana University; Miami University; the biennial meeting of the Canadian Association of Cultural Studies in 2014; the LCSL Graduate Student Conference in Literature and Cultural Studies at the University of Illinois Chicago; for the *Journal of Narrative Theory* at Eastern Michigan University; Johns Hopkins University; the Colloquium for Critical Asian Studies and Critical Ethnic Studies, Northwestern University; the Ray Warren Symposium on Race and Ethnic Studies at Lewis and Clark College; the Biopolitical Afterlives Symposium at California State University, Los Angeles; Vassar College; Purdue University; the University of Arizona; the University of Michigan; the Graduate Center at the City University of New York; and the University of Cambridge. My thanks to those who organized these events and those who engaged so generously with the work in progress.

Earlier and substantially different portions of *The Promise of Beauty* appeared elsewhere. From "The Beautiful, Finding Itself in Danger, Desires Its Copy," the section on the *Ao Trang* calendar appears in a longer essay called "Diasporic Erotic," published in *Camera Obscura* (2013). "An Education in Beauty (and the Necessity of Lawlessness)" draws on the first seed of this work, "The Biopower of Beauty," published in *Signs* (2011).

For everything from conversation to support (scholarly and otherwise), I am grateful to friends and colleagues, including Tonya Abernathy, Patty Ahn, Aren Aizura, Jennifer Allen, Grace Ambrose, Inez Anderson, Paul Michael Atienza, Osa Atoe, Aimee Bahng, Vivek Bald, Sarah Banet-Weiser, Terri Barnes, Shuli Branson, Ruth Nicole Brown, Keva X. Bui, Long Bui, Lawrence-Minh Bui Davis, Cristy Road Carrera, Sarah Cervenak, Karma Chavez, Christina Chin, Michelle Cho, Kandice Chuh, Brian Chung, Genevieve Clutario, Arwen Curry, Jenny Davis, David Eng, Tommy Falk, Jonathan Beecher Field, Stephanie Foote, Tanisha Ford, Jenna Freedman, Elizabeth Freeman, Emi Frerichs, Zach Furness, Tait Graves, Eva Hageman, Cookie Hagendorf, Christina Hanhardt, Kathleen Hanna, Jillian Hernandez, Nels Highberg, Hua Hsu, Ming-Wei Huang, Zalika Ibaorimi, Doug Ishi, Hellen Jo, Simi Kang, Maryam Kashani, Sawyer Kemp, Mahruq and Sonia Khan, Mimi Khuc, Farah Kidwai, Ava Kim, Yvette Koch, Rachel Kuo, Leopold Lambert, Beck Levy, Mireya Loza, Dana Luciano, Erica Dawn Lyle, Vicki Mahaffey, Bruce Manning, Blake Manning Wong, Anita Mannur, Sarah McCarry, Nick Mitchell, Isabel Molina-Guzman, Nadine Naber, Lisa Nakamura, Rani Neutill, Trung Nguyen, Erin O'Brien, David Palumbo-Liu, Christopher Patterson, Kimberly Rose Pendleton, Curtis Perry, Janice Radway, Junaid Rana, Sarah Roberts, Gilberto Rosas, Anna Rosenwong, Sasha Sabherwal, Ellen Samuels, Ahalya Satkunaratnam, Emi Sawada, Preeti

Sharma, Elena Shih, Chad Shomura, Arabelle Sicardi, Siobhan Somerville, Christian Sorace, James Spooner, Jon Strange, Thea Quiray Tagle, Kyla Wazana Tompkins, Karen Tongson, Angharad Valdivia, Ma Vang, Emma Velez, Damian Vergara Bracamontes, Anuradha Vikram, and Deke Weaver.

Former and current undergraduate and graduate students have buoyed me through the years with their brilliant company, especially Silas Cassinelli, Meg Cornell, Eman Ghanayem, Max Grogan, Catalina Hernandez, Kyli Kleven, Sabrina Lee, Jody Stokes-Casey, and Liz Verklan. Eman in particular is my refugee-for-refugee ride-or-die through grief, love, and life-living.

For their continued mentorship, I am forever grateful for Caren Kaplan, Inderpal Grewal, and Minoo Moallem, who taught me that being a feminist in the imperial university means building and transforming the infrastructure within these institutions that will never love you—and nor should you expect it to, for that way lies danger—to carve out other possibilities for being within it, around it.

Ever a patient interlocutor and catalyst, Ken Wissoker at Duke University Press has believed in my work since I was a graduate student with an "online journal." I model some key parts of my own engagement with others' intellectual labors after his example. I am also grateful to the anonymous readers for their insights, and to Shuli Branson and Sabrina Lee, whose efforts on behalf on this manuscript (as developmental editor and research assistant, respectively) helped me to let it go. At Duke, Kate Mullen, Michael Trudeau, and Mattson Gallagher stewarded this book to its completion, while Diana Witt indexed this behemoth like a beast. Finally, Nicole Gomez promised a prophetic dream of roses for the cover, and I am grateful for the art she makes in a world on fire.

To punk, but also Kim Namjoon, Kim Seokjin, Min Yoongi, Jung Hoseok, Park Jimin, Kim Taehyung, and Jeon Jung Kook, I owe immeasurable joy in the midst of ongoing catastrophe. As Kim Taehyung put it, when asked what his favorite lyrics are, *All fire, bow wow wow*.

Yumi Lee, Golnar Nikpour, and Thera Webb make up the greatest group text chain of all time; old punks FTW. Toby Beauchamp, Cyn Degnan, and A. Naomi Paik are my Illinois family, sharing love, rage, and much-needed sustenance in equal measure. Toby especially is my accomplice and anchor; together, we are every hilarious meme about a dear friend who is also a co-worker. Vernadette Vicuna Gonzalez has been an indispensable presence in my life since graduate school, providing even-keeled insight and impromptu haiku. Yutian Wong is the truest friend and most stalwart heart whose generosity and myriad hobbies have led me to try *a lot of things*. Toby, Dette, and Yutian all share with me the same orientation to scheming and getting shit done, which has led to so many fruitful (and fun) collaborations both in and outside the academy.

My brother, George, is my first best friend, supporting every unhinged and off-the-wall idea I have ever had, while my niblings, Maggie and Sally, remind me of when we were dragons. Thomas Falk kept all our emails and messages from decades ago to remind me that I should have dumped all those zeros to get with a hero already.

At last, this book is for my mother and father. My mother showed me how to be stubborn, loving, and proud, especially in the face of terror and hardship, which means it is her fault I am punk. My father taught me to be curious, broad-minded, and playful, which means it is his fault I am a scholar. On weekends, when I still in high school, he would bring me to the downtown San Diego public library, where we would pursue our separate research—his on the latest discoveries in pharmaceuticals, colonialism, and the war that forced us to leave home, mine on histories of feminism, protest, and the war that forced us to leave home—before visiting thrift shops, surplus warehouses, and hole-in-the-wall record stores. He passed away during the COVID-19 pandemic, months before the vaccine was available, which meant that I could not be there with him. I keep an altar to him in my living room, stocked with flowers, chocolates, and incense, because his presence reminds me that I am well-loved and that I too must love well—I hope very much that this book is that evidence.

introduction

Small Art and Love and Beauty

As we come marching, marching, unnumbered women dead
Go crying through our singing their ancient song of Bread;
Small art and love and beauty their drudging spirits knew—
Yes, it is Bread we fight for—but we fight for Roses, too.

James Oppenheim, "Bread and Roses"

Anybody who thinks that they can understand how terrible the terror has been, without understanding how beautiful the beauty has been against the grain of that terror, is wrong.

Fred Moten, "The Black Outdoors"

In June 2016, "Emily Doe" read a twelve-page victim impact statement at the sentencing hearing of Brock Turner. The college athlete had been convicted of sexually assaulting her after a party while she was unconscious, slumped on the ground next to a dumpster, on the campus of Stanford University. Standing before the court, Doe began her statement, "You don't know me, but you've been inside me, and that's why we are here today," before recounting the harrowing violence of the assault, the investigation, and the trial.[1] In response, the judge spoke sympathetically of Turner's unrealized potential (*for what, though—more violence?*) and sentenced him to just six months in county jail and probation. So, Emily published her statement, a clear-eyed account of self-shattering violence—by rape, by law. Three years later in the memoir *Know My Name*, Emily, or Chanel Miller, reflects on these compound traumas and the unbending apparatuses that doubted her, and others like her and unlike her—the gymnasts, the actresses, Andrea Constand, Philando Castile, Christine Blasey Ford, all the ordinary people who are forcibly unhomed from spirit, flesh, or future. As she claws back some trick for living, she absorbs a lesson from her Chinese immigrant mother: "You have to hold out to see how your life unfolds because it is most likely beyond what you imagine. It is not a question of if you will survive this, but what beautiful things await you when you do."[2]

I start with a simple proposition: beauty is often a habit, instance, property, or force through which we engage narratives of crisis in our time. Crisis is one name for an ongoing condition that coheres or collapses into an intensified situation in which the threat to survival dominates the preservation of life. Such life is often the life of the beautiful, whether children, birds, coral reefs, art, communion, or human rights, and the discrepancy between the world and what ought to be, fundamental to an idea of historical consciousness, so often unfolds through their recitation. On these grounds, the meeting with beauty in a bad situation lends itself to thoroughly political observations. Beauty is often assigned a sanctified power to name a feeling of life being furthered, and for life-living itself, where beauty withers under such conditions we too fight to survive or overcome; or, where beauty endures and, in our attachment to it, fosters our own perseverance; or, where beauty eases a truth or opens a rift in a moment of danger. But beauty might also sustain the social order through its long-held consonances with symmetry, proportion, and harmony (none of which are neutral properties) at the expense of all that lies outside of it. Or beauty might assist a deception or lie, a covering-over as obstacle to living on, the floodlit grove that aims to disguise a terrible violence that lingers still. In the midst of an ongoing negotiation with Stanford and its poor attempts at resolution (installing a contemplation garden at the site of the dumpster), Miller asks, "What do you do when you're invited to your own rape garden ceremony, that's been scheduled to last twenty minutes?"[3] Just like that, beauty might lay bare a contradiction, untruth, or failure at the heart of an enterprise that fails to sustain or nurture it, or beauty might precipitate a crisis, rendering some understatedly awful condition recognizably, finally unbearable. When this occurs, crisis and beauty activate each other as capacity and concept. Turning to beauty's promise tells us quite a lot about just how messy this historical project of being or becoming alive truly is, because even if we do survive (which *is* still a question), what can beauty do? How can it put the world to right after all that has gone wrong?

At the center of this book is an inquiry into the promise of beauty. Hoping to capture something of the dimensions of our historical situation, I turn to aesthetic responses to scarcity, precarity, and uncertainty, during and "after" (an uneasy temporality) crises of war, capital, and colony, in order to understand the promise of beauty as a world-building engagement. Promise establishes beauty as an object, a scene, a reason, or a ritual for living on and through such crises, as the sometime name through which our attachments unfold into futures that crises threaten to foreclose. In "small art and love and beauty," such a promise might be a balm, a habitus, or a critique—perhaps an ordinary pleasure, or an ontological flourishing. It might be found in an instance, a movement, or an opening toward what one desires as beautiful and wishes to make present or proximate, or it might be perceived as an enclosure, a limit, a boundary, an allegiance, or a horizon. But the promise is not necessarily optimistic; a promise could be made because of appreciation, devotion, or love but also fear, calculation, or greed. The promise might be broken, or altogether illusory, and that is also part of its animating power. Seeking out those objects, habits, properties, and forces that pledge themselves to the transformation of that which cannot sustain life otherwise—a structure, a way of being, a world order—this book asks, how and why is the promise of beauty so portable across a spectrum of political claims, imperial or insurgent? What is promised by beauty, to beauty, in a given historical situation? How are competing principles, causal relations, or criteria for beauty assembled such that we might perceive the presence of beauty and also the threat *to* it—and sometimes the threat *of* it? My hope is to raise these and other questions about the promise of beauty to order social arrangements and political structures and render them intelligible, perceptible, and sensible as scenes of dispute or comparison about the *beauty we deserve*.

Because it often accompanies narratives of redemption, justice, or hope that attenuate disaster, injury, and grief, and that are the consequence and also the compensation for capital or colony, beauty inhabits this book as a multisensory history of the present. In this I follow scholars and artists who have long observed the political mattering of aesthetics as infrastructure, consciousness, or a feeling for life. Jacques Rancière defines political subjectivity as "an enunciated and demonstrative capacity to reconfigure the relation between the visible and the sayable, the relation between words and bodies: namely 'the partition of the sensible,'" and Kandice Chuh observes that "aesthetics may be recognized as simultaneously political (that is, conditioned by relations of power and their material manifestations) and the grounds upon which the political is constituted and perceived."[4] Sylvia Wynter argues for the aesthetic as a Foucauldian "dense transfer point ... of power" where the senses meet those "'discourses' whose codings in our 'nervous system' regulate our response and sentiments"; she continues, "Each mode of the aesthetic is isomorphic with a specific mode of human being or 'form of life.'"[5] More, as Kyla Wazana Tompkins insists, it is through the aesthetic as a "processual doing in time, in space, in a field of sensory possibility" that "the human is a life 'form' in the sense that to be human is to be made."[6] And as Lauren Berlant and Kathleen Stewart note together, "It was as if whatever there was to notice was already scored onto matter."[7] From Rancière, Chuh, Wynter, Tompkins, and Berlant and Stewart, among others, this series of propositions articulate aesthetics as a politics of meaning-making that includes the historical partition of sense and matter. Beauty is one such partition, not just as the form its promise takes through which expression and experience is felt, but also the manner in which its promise cuts into time to manifest life-living.

The Promise of Beauty gathers genres that mark a conceptual history of beauty as a proposition and a politics, or, in the words of modernist poet Mina Loy, how the "flux of life is pouring its aesthetic aspect into your eyes, your ears."[8] As a *processual doing in time*, beauty is a living form for the schooling of the senses as a historical project, a flux and a frame through which we might understand the *human*, *history*, and *life*. When beauty is promised at the threshold where the desire for the good and the true (love, hope, kinship, freedom, and care, among others) collides with mechanisms of interference and control in the name of improving life chances, or altering the quality of existence, the promise of beauty is a proposition and a politics of intervening in history (or the conditions under which beauty endures) and life itself (or what meaning beauty lends to it). For us right now, these thresholds are the inheritance of capital and colony, otherwise known as our engines of emergency. Beauty enters as response to and respite from these engines—sometimes a chance encounter, sometimes a transformational habit, weighed against the scale and feel of the violence. Considering that which might hold out to us clusters of real or ideal formations such as romantic love, spiritual transcendence, economic mobility, or political renewal, this book is a historiography of a concept of beauty as an imperative discourse, one that determines what conditions are necessary to live; what forms of life are worth living; and what actions must follow to preserve, secure, or replicate such life that the beautiful promises to us.

In other words, beauty is an empty space overfull with those things that we conceive as necessary for a historical sense, or a consciousness of life, and this is its crucial conceptual power to manage or resolve or survive it. This introduction (and this book) is an incomplete (though fit-to-burst) list of those things, whether as events of knowing or intuitions or feelings, as pressures of form or releases from them, that interrupt or intrude on the labor of being in a sometimes drowning, sometimes burning world. In short, beauty is a practical concern about an imprecise formation—life, and how to live it. This animating power, with its adaptations, correspondences, and schemata for absorption and comparison, can reorder our spaces, times, desires, and sensations toward whatever is to come. *Between promise and presence, beauty makes history appear.* To this end, beauty is also a method, a method that invites us to trace its ebb and flow through visions of life-living and projects of power, archives of memory and resources for possibility. And it is in those instances where beauty is ameliorative—either as process or outcome—to a life that is not quite good and even very awful that I follow how *small art and love and beauty* suggest something vital about beauty as a method for asking why, and what now.

Genres of Beauty

Beauty is all around us (it is said), but there is no unity or truth to beauty. It is not an essence, property, or given, and yet there are those who nevertheless wish to collect, to own, or to hoard it. Beauty does not exist in an object, person, or scene until another perceives it, or it is wholly autonomous, independent of our observation or judgment.[9] We apprehend beauty through such things that fill its form, whether a lovely face, a painting, a harmony, or a shout ("Palestine will be free"), and which are not identical to it (beauty) or each other; or "we agree that beauty exists but disagree about its examples."[10] In *Symposium*, Plato argues that beauty is a principle of the eternal that follows from a body to the soul to a law and onward, "mounting the heavenly ladder" to "the special lore that pertains to nothing but the beautiful itself."[11] For Immanuel Kant, beauty is not a property of objects but a relation between those who might share pleasure (derived in part from judgment) in a sensus communis.[12] Iris Murdoch takes issue with those who say there is nothing moral about beauty; instead, "goodness and beauty are not to be contrasted, but are largely part of the same structure."[13] Toni Morrison insists beauty is not a privilege, an indulgence, or a quest, but a necessity: "I think it's almost like knowledge, which is to say, it's what we were born for."[14] Still others argue, as Vanita Reddy does, that beauty occupies "a regime of value with material effects" encompassing labor, care, pleasure, and capital.[15] And Michael Taussig supposes in his ethnography of body modification, "Surely beauty is as much infrastructure as are highways and bridges, storytelling and the Internet, rainfall and global warming."[16] Beauty resists utility, or follows from function; induces an aptitude for living, or supplies the illusion of solace. Some presume the truth of beauty's nature, the content of which might bind us to a situation of plentitude or profound scarcity; some accuse it of failure, circumscribing the grounds of a given universal to a narrow understanding of the life worth living, or even the species category of the human. Beauty is a dense palimpsest, a premature closure, and an anarchic faculty; its promise is a knife that cuts through the liveliness of the world, or is the hand that binds the wound.

It is as an unruly multitude that the promise of beauty permeates as a habit, object, property, instance, concentration, or force, unfolding through space and time as a transmission from beheld to beholder. *The Promise of Beauty* starts here in the reflection about beauty as a case of x, where x is whatever is made known as beautiful in the meeting of judgment with a perceptual order, and a study of y, where y is whatever follows the promise to secure beauty's presence. To paraphrase Michel Foucault, awkwardly, beauty might be nothing more or less than the relation between the beholder and the world and how it might be made sensible or perceptible, which is already quite a lot.[17] With attention to beauty as an axiological problem for the epistemological or ethical grounds of certain domains of life and knowledge, I am trying to do something unfaithful yet true in tracing the promise of beauty as an argument for freedom and also an archive of violence, as a multisensory history of how we experience continuity or rupture. Through beauty as method, we can make sense of the fungibility of beauty and its claims, and our claims, which will not be the same. This book dwells here in the productive unease between claims about ontological being, forces of history, and habits for living, through which the promise of beauty poses questions *and* answers for how we survive or thrive—or not. I am less interested in what beauty *is*, and more in what beauty *does*.

Many genres of beauty appear throughout the book, whether as an emergent authenticity, a false idol, or a fascist country.[18] What the genres of truth and possibility have in common is beauty as an elaboration of a good life. There are echoes of Plato, who surmised that whether there is an immortal realm or no, the brush with beauty leads "to a more capacious regard for the world," found in Elaine Scarry, who posits that beauty calls forth in a beholder a wish to preserve and even to provide to others the benefit of beauty, soliciting an ethic of care for life itself.[19] The art critic Arthur Danto argues beauty as a "necessary condition for life as we would want to live it," while Denise Gigante observes that the "sense of beauty defined scientifically as life—and life defined aesthetically as beauty" informs all rationalist arguments about its necessary functionality.[20] But while beauty might be "a feeling of life being furthered," per Kant, determinations must be made about the status of beauty, the qualification of life, and the grounds of their fastening together. In *The Human Condition*, Hannah Arendt describes Aristotle's account of the three ways of life that men might choose in freedom. All labor and "ways of life chiefly devoted to keeping one's self alive" are inimical to such a life, "exclud[ing] everybody who involuntarily or voluntarily, for his whole life or temporarily, had lost the free disposition of his movements and activities." The life that can be lived, in other words, can neither be circumscribed by the needs of survival nor exist alongside the cruelties of dominion or dispossession. Only in freedom might one commune with the beautiful, threefold: "the life of enjoying bodily pleasures in which the beautiful, as it is given, is consumed; the life devoted to the matters of the *polis*, in which excellence produces beautiful deeds; and the life of the philosopher devoted to inquiry into, and contemplation of, things eternal, whose everlasting beauty can neither be brought about through the producing interference of man nor be changed through his consumption of them."[21]

Beauty's judgment, as we can see, concerns much more than the truth or being of an object, scene, person, or lifeworld. It is also a judgment about the grounds for beauty's flourishing or fading, which is a judgment about a historical situation. After all, as Kandice Chuh argues, the conditions of history "are also themselves fundamentally aesthetic in that they are brought forward to be sensed by (historiographic, archival, methodological) practices that (re)shape the sensibilities held in common."[22] So, for Eve Sedgwick, writing about "comfort" and "nourishment," beauty is one of "the many ways selves and communities succeed in extracting sustenance from the objects of a culture—even of a culture whose avowed desire has often been not to sustain them."[23] The artist behind *My Favorite Thing Is Monsters*, the richly illustrated graphic novel about a young Latina werewolf in 1970s Chicago whose upstairs neighbor, a beautiful Jewish woman with a mysterious past in wartime Nazi Germany, is murdered (which is not enough to even begin to capture the experience of this dark, luminous tale), Emil Ferris (citing painter Susanna Coffey) said, "Beauty is the thing that allows us to wrap our minds around even the worst."[24] Fred Moten credits beauty as a bulwark "against the grain of the terror," while Ocean Vuong observes, "How valuable beauty is for a world on fire."[25] Even the iconic denim retailer Levi's agrees. In 2021, the company's "Beauty of Becoming: Fashion a New World Forward" campaign for Women's History Month launched with a series of short videos featuring Naomi Osaka, Willow Smith, Jaden Smith, Leyna Bloom, Dolores Huerta, and others. In the inaugural short, each athlete, artist, or celebrity delivers variants on a promise: "Become something we've never seen before, fashion a new world, forward, better than how we found it."[26] And where liberal empire imposes the gift of freedom as sanctioned violence or indebtedness, beauty slips in as an endurable form for aliveness in a wrecked world. Indeed, the promise of beauty seems at times inseparable from such a gift, whether in the scene of a parade float riotously blooming with carnations and refugee thanksgiving to "America," or in the fervently whispered wishes of a napalm victim for her scars to disappear, and for beauty to rescue her from loneliness and communism.[27] Here the ideal presence of beauty is found in pursuit of an arrangement for its flourishing, or at least as some relief from the pressure of a terrible form bent toward its (or our) annihilation.

But we are also intimate with the violence and terror deemed necessary to make beauty present in a given historical situation, like civilization; and we know beauty as violence and terror in itself. Critiques of beauty as a judgment that secures a racial divide animate those accusations not just that beauty is inadequate for a historical sense of the present, or an ethical alignment toward others, but that the whole enterprise is faulty. These critiques establish claims to the beautiful, in both its singularity and its universality, as damaging, decrying its abuses on behalf of imperialism and colonialism, white supremacy, racial capitalism, and compulsory normalization of a body. Such harms are not in dispute (for me, at least). A brute and terrible history of violence operates, insidiously and insistently, through colonial cartographies and racial classifications that sort and grade stages of human and other existence. The body that is proportionate, symmetrical, or fair (in all senses) is just one threshold of such a determinate concept. The faculty for judgment *as* a property, which is also a faculty *for* property (including self-possession as the foundation for action), in communion with others, is another; the Arab, the African, and the "Oriental" have all been deemed historically deficient in this faculty. Consider Kant's atlas of Chinese grotesqueries and African foolishness ("still not a single one was ever found who presented anything great in art or science or any other praiseworthy quality"), or the Islamophobe's accusation that hijab disturbs or diminishes feminine beauty.[28] Such cartographies of aesthetic philosophies have too often cohered through what

Ruth Wilson Gilmore calls "the state-sanctioned or extralegal production and exploitation of group-differentiated vulnerability to premature death"; as so many observe, such as Anne Anlin Cheng in her study of ornamentalism (what she calls orientalism's cousin), or Toni Morrison in *The Bluest Eye*, or Kara Walker in her monumental installation *A Subtlety, or the Marvelous Sugar Baby*, racial schema are aesthetic schema.[29] Tressie McMillan Cottom avows, "For beauty to function as it should, it must exclude me," while Monique Roelofs puts it simply. "Whiteness... presents aesthetic promise that blackness withholds; blackness constitutes an aesthetic threat."[30] Any forensic investigation of beauty thus contains a record of injury.

Such grievous harm is not cosmetic, incidental, or of second-order consequence. The charge of beauty's deception has everything to do with an onto-epistemological failure to know truth about the world. Its ornamental nature, we are warned, distracts from faithless monstrosity. As Shakespeare's Juliet cries, *O serpent heart, hid with a flow'ring face? Did ever dragon keep so fair a cave?*[31] The mortifications of beauty, she laments, are disguised by the sweetness of its visage and easy pleasure. It could be a lover, a flower, or a state that wears a pretty face to hide an ignoble heart. Disability activist and writer Mia Mingus, in her keynote address at the 2011 Femmes of Color symposium, declares, "There is only the illusion of solace in beauty. If age and disability teach us anything, it is that investing in beauty will never set us free. Beauty has always been hurled as a weapon. It has always taken the form of an exclusive club; and supposed protection against violence, isolation and pain, but this is a myth."[32] Chasing *Orwell's Roses*, Rebecca Solnit notes that the laborers in the Colombian flower industry, who raise 80 percent of the roses sold in the United States, cannot dwell in their crops' beauty—that occurs elsewhere, for others: "The idea of an immense plane whose sole freight was roses burning its carbon and rushing high over the Caribbean to deliver its burden to people who would never know of all that lay behind the roses they picked up in the supermarket was maybe as perfect an emblem of alienation as you could find."[33] *O, that deceit should dwell in such a gorgeous palace.*[34]

The crisis of beauty is also a problem of scale or balance. Even as beauty is censured as deceptive, it is just as often disowned as cheap, weak, irresolute, superfluous, and even pornographic. Beauty is shelved as placid or plainly inadequate against the sublime and its emphatic monumentalism (the latter more appropriate to terror or justice, per Mark Canuel).[35] Theodor Adorno famously stated, "To write poetry after Auschwitz is barbaric."[36] Decades later, Hamid Dabashi asks, "Is writing poetry after Gaza also barbaric?"[37] Likewise, beauty might appear inappropriate for the affectively weak aestheticization of everyday life that Sianne Ngai observes at the dead-end of capitalism; or it is made too banal, diffuse, or indistinct from the clutter of aesthetic categories.[38] No longer novel, singular, or untouchable, beauty becomes a monotonous gesture soliciting a shrug or an eye roll.[39] The meme that exhorts you to post a beautiful piece of art to affectively shift our social media feeds, or to remind you to gaze at your own reflection and say to yourself, "You are beautiful," might be received as poor defense against depression, loss, or grief. To what extent can beauty respond to the manifold terrors of being alive?

At the same time, it is a commonplace that even the briefest meeting with beauty renders a dire state of being more bearable. We see this in narratives about wars or camps, in the smuggled plant carried from a lost homeland, the love found in time's suspension, or a child's compact rescued from the rubble after an airstrike, each of which assures us that life can still be beautiful.[40] In these situations, "beauty is something we can control, love, and celebrate. It is, at some of the worst times, all we have left."[41] In a Reuters photograph of a present-day Syrian refugee encampment, a bride-to-be in a rhinestone-encrusted dress sits in a plastic lawn chair, her eyes closed as another woman in T-shirt and jeans carefully applies frosty blue eye shadow. What frames this photograph is the promise of what is not yet present: a loving marriage, or a prosperous life after catastrophe, whatever nourishes a feeling of life being furthered. Particularly meaningful in these accounts is an economy of impossible equivalence. What beauty might give is too often eclipsed by what threatens the survival of it, and us, and yet—. Artist and activist David Wojnarowicz said to Zoe Leonard, when she worried about making beautiful images during the AIDS crisis, "Zoe, these are so beautiful, and that's what we're fighting for. We're being angry and complaining because we have to, but where we want to go is back to beauty. If you let go of that, we don't have anywhere to go."[42] Martin Manalansan formulates *biyuti* as a queer analytic of the life that can be lived for queer Filipino men; it is a fluctuating quality and also its measure. "*Biyuti*, which is a loose transliteration of the word 'beauty,' is used not only to talk about the aesthetic qualities of things, people, and objects, but is also used to talk about the flow of daily life, countenance, feelings, and self (e.g., *Kumusta ang biyuti mo?* How is your beauty today? *May sakit ang biyuti ko.* My beauty is sick.)"[43] *Biyuti* is thus found in the drama of survival against those "routine oppressions and violence" that queer brown persons endure every day.[44] And as Robert Diaz asks, "What does it mean to commit to articulations of *biyuti* even when such a commitment seems frivolous and risky to do so?"⁴⁵ Despite this incommensurability, can we call it living if a life is without beauty? Is there a future without it?

Beauty coexists alongside destruction, horror, and despair, even unlife; its promise is experienced as arrestingly transcendent *and* as woefully inadequate within the sensual registers that impact our historical sense of the world as it is, and as it could be. In the words of W. E. B. Du Bois, "Here, then, is beauty and ugliness, a wide vision of world-sacrifice, a fierce gleam of world-hate. What is life and what is death and how shall we face so tantalizing a contradiction?"⁴⁶ Beauty secures but also disturbs life's description, evaluation, argument, and historicity. *The Promise of Beauty* embraces this contradiction not as contradiction but as a method for tracing the unities, tensions, and pressures of its forms—between what is promised and what is present, between the order and the reorder of things, between life and how we live it.

To ask how beauty is political is to presume to know in advance what the sphere of the political is, whereas we might instead consider how the political is circumscribed and at what cost. This book argues that, in the broadest sense, beauty is a politics because there is no agreement on what beauty means, and because it requires a calculation of presence—this might be a capacity, a law, a habit, a scene, an instance, a ritual, or a crime, for example— and this is always political. That is, if politics constitutes a disagreement about whose representation of an object or event will secure value for some claims and grievances over others, as Rancière has it, then beauty is long one such disagreement.⁴⁷ For some, beauty might evoke the prepolitical premise of a foundational truth or universality beyond contestation, or a new, postpolitical consensual space emptied of debate. For others, the promise of beauty might describe the limits of a structure or practice, because such a structure or practice cannot (or will not) sustain life; or such a promise might ease our distress in our cognizance of those endings. It is a disaster, or it is not. In a best-selling memoir (later, an immensely popular prestige-television series), a heart-shaped cosmetic compact passed from one prisoner to another is borne as a talisman of humanity in a place of its suspension.⁴⁸ Such fugitive beauty serves as a measure of sovereignty against the experience of its foreclosure, tied to historical material circumstances (the drug war or mass incarceration) that produce captivity as "justice." Or, as Arabelle Sicardi observes so well, "Beauty is a tool that tends to serve those in power . . . and, at the same time, it fundamentally involves acts of witnessing the body, helping it to endure its conditions."⁴⁹ To argue that beauty makes *no* difference because it is trivial or ornamental, as some do, precludes the possibility of politics, since *any* difference requires the undecidability of politics as the condition for history itself. The promise of beauty is always a partisan one, but there is no predicting on whose side it might be found.

Instead of conceiving of beauty as a scene or surface of study, as an object or a theory (one that seeks its law in a social structure, or a collective unconscious), I turn to beauty as a method to think and also act with—as a life force, a world-making vision, a record of history, or a habit of being in the world. The task ahead for tracing the difference that beauty makes is, after Kandice Chuh, "to think/work aesthetically, which is to say, of and through perception and persistently attuned to the conditions that prioritize and legitimate certain modes of knowing by the subjugation of others; and by acknowledging how questions of artistry and artistic value are also always questions of politics and history."[50] In this way, beauty as method illuminates certain epistemological and ontological claims about the history and the human, where beauty's promise diagnoses a situation in order to act in time, and beauty's presence exists not as itself but as a question mark, a constellation of contingencies, that might guide us closer to a life we deserve. Rather than a predictable expression of social infrastructure or transcendental universal, a banal countenance or a deceptive detail, the promise of beauty is more expansively an accessible concept to make claims about our *ideal* relations to objects, persons, scenes, habits, or concepts (such as freedom, or proportion, or democracy) in the world.

To this end, beauty is no more or less than a feeling about life-living, through which its promise and presence foster wonder—or collapse.

Beauty's Promise

In tribute to the love between a teenage human and a centuries-old vampire, someone sings, "Time stands still / Beauty in all she is."[51] Elsewhere the camera slows to capture the sensation of time's dilation as we perceive for the first time—or again—someone or something beautiful (sunlit horses galloping across a mountain stream, a young woman amid a fall of petals, Keanu Reeves). Beauty here is an intensity, an irruptive event that stretches out, out of sync with continuous normative time. Sarah Nuttall observes that its apprehension propels "a politics of hope and anticipation, a surge of feeling beyond the merely given present moment," while Mila Zuo writes that as a consequence of "its breathtaking effect perforating our mundane rhythms," "beauty throws us into small crisis."[52] It is as a concept of threshold time that beauty is poised between continuity and rupture, whether fostering a sense of aliveness or jarring a viewer to regard the world anew, or isolating a moment as eventful, after which we are returned to an established timeline, albeit with an altered consciousness that might be the origin of something else.

This sensorium of beauty and its multidimensional apprehension of time (or in time) cannot be reduced to positive forms (it is *this*, or *that*) even though it has a necessary relationship to them. The nineteenth-century French author Stendahl writes simply about its infinite expansiveness, "Beauty is only the promise of happiness."[53] And Adorno notes that "the unstillable longing in the face of beauty" fosters "the longing for the fulfillment of what was promised," whatever this might be.[54] In another iteration, beauty is a genre that promises to us another world is possible; as the poet June Jordan put it, "To tell the truth is to become beautiful, to begin to love yourself, value yourself. And that's political, in its most profound way."[55] Similarly, and against the argument that our regard acts on beauty to trap or capture it (simplified as "objectification"), Elaine Scarry proposes that beauty acts on the beholder, arousing the desire for and the creation of new things in the world, such as "infants, epics, sonnets, drawings, dances, laws, philosophic dialogues, theological tracts."[56] But such infinitude is necessarily delimited by our desires and historical circumstances. Not everyone wishes an infant or a law; one might want instead other beautiful things, perhaps unthinkable or unsayable under such a regime that loves infants or laws. (And, of course, to disagree about what *is* a beautiful thing is no small matter.) In this way, beauty might fashion a philosophical and experiential awareness of a historical formation, even as our knowledge of beauty disavows its own historicity at times in order to claim for itself a universal applicability. Where beauty might open us to a moment of truth, or give notice that something is lost, stolen, or gone missing, attachments to beauty arrange the grounds for conjuring a being, a substance, or a subject to come.

It is as a promise that beauty moves from a descriptive category (not a simple thing as is) to a diagnostic criterion, inasmuch as it gestures toward those conditions that render beauty possible and perceptible, at the same time it is directed toward a future tense, in which an object, project, person, habit, or world imparts a sense of life being furthered. And where the promise promises the survival of someone or something such as a painting, or a poet, or a political project, it becomes a specifically interventionist concept for life. We can see this in the refugee camp, where makeshift beauty parlors might be described as interrupting an ongoing state of despair, holding out as lifesaving those conventions of an ordinary good life. On a designated Beauty Day at the women and children's center at the now-destroyed Calais, France, encampment, volunteers offered massages and nail treatments to refugees, "to keep them feeling human" against the deprivations of statelessness.[57] If beauty designates that which is required to live ("feeling human") through a historical conjuncture, beauty also solicits a commitment to *act*. Or, as Toni Morrison put so well, with all necessary ambivalence, "Beauty was not simply something to behold, it was something one could do."[58]

As such the promise *of* beauty is also about the promise *to* beauty, or *about* it, which *we* make. As Rita Barnard observes, we do not just look at beautiful objects, persons, or scenes, but "we judge them, we sell them, we wear them, we display them, we court them, we collect them, we smuggle them, we forge them, and so on."[59] We also replicate them, preserve them, perfect them, and recommend them to others to ensure their longevity *as* beautiful (consider the canon or the museum). This is the second sense of promise I consider here—the promises we make on beauty's behalf so that it can continue to move us.

A promise is at the heart of most any concept of politics, ethics, law, economy, language, friendship, and love. It underscores such capacities as gift, hospitality, apology, forgiveness, secrecy, order, and amnesty; without promise, these are signs without substance. The forms for promise are not singular; it might be made as a prophecy, for instance, or a prescription. What these forms hold in common is the promise as their foundation for subjectivity and sociality, also known at times as a contract. For instance, the origin of liberalism is premised in part on the capacity and right to make promises for "buying, selling, barter, trade, and traffic," and to submit these to the rule of law; in the enforcement of contractual agreements, legislation and forms of police arose to regulate the obligations between creditor and debtor, owner and laborer.[60] It is toward such determinate forms as credit, debt, marriage, and inheritance that the promise, as Sara Ahmed notes, is often an imperative to orient oneself toward certain outcomes and not others.[61] But the promise might also conjure those more hazy or ideal forms, such as care, mutual aid, and reparation, that are hard or even impossible under conditions or attachments that might instead favor credit, debt, marriage, and inheritance. The promise is the scene and the consequence of a social or political order; some structures must be in place for the promise to be met, or proposed to replace those that cannot guarantee it, which is to say that the promise relies on preceding promises (some of which are ossified into institutions, arrangements, or, as Ahmed puts it, orientations) for its power—whether to shore up an existing order or to pull it apart.

The promise is a cut into time, encompassing risk, speculation, and capture; it is a narrativization that orders and arranges our sense of history and our capacity to act on it. To bring to fruition that promise, one must be able to conceive of the future in terms of its difference from the past, by way of a normative or teleological concept of progress, perfectibility, or redemption. It is through this conception of time and narrative that *crisis* is a founding term for the elaboration of history through the promise of beauty. Here I build on the work of Janet Roitman, who observes that crisis (as a narrative) incites forms of critique that entail suppositions about how categories should function, evaluations of the conditions for their decay or disintegration, and conjectures about the world as it could be otherwise.[62] Naming a situation a *crisis* requires reference to a comparative state of judgment based on knowledge claims, and to a norm or an ideal that requires certain arrangements be in place for whatever is in peril—democracy, beauty, hope—to flourish, or to persist in time. Likewise, as a response to crisis (or its narrativization as such), the promise also promises the capacities for prognosticating or producing history anew, which might include the promise of another social or political order. Such capacities are the historical forms with which sovereign acts negotiate the sensual experience of consciousness and distinguish between past and future. The promise thus necessarily solicits judgment or critique about latencies, absences, and errors that must be overcome, and in doing so provides meaning or a sense of possibility at or beyond the limit of the present. And, while sometimes abstract and speculative in nature, the promise further requires a consciousness that posits that we can act on history itself, or what Foucault called "the entry of life into history."[63]

The promise as such is multiply binding. First, the promise binds historical consciousness to knowledge. It gathers together multiple tenses, in which a philosophical and experiential awareness of a historical formation (such as a formation of possibility, or one of failure) and the historical quality of our knowledge about a situation or a structure (even where such knowledge disavows its own history) are brought to bear on the calculative reason of a collective faculty. Second, the promise binds that knowledge to the commitment to act. The one who promises proceeds through such self-referential enclosure—aware of their own historicity—as a precondition for bold action. For Nietzsche, this capacity to think causally about the future is the origin of humanity ("To breed an animal *with the right to make promises*—is this not the paradoxical task that nature has set itself in the case of man?").[64] Such responsibility requires "this emancipated individual, with the actual *right* to make promises, this master of a *free* will, this sovereign man," who is regularized and desires to regularize what is and what is *not yet* under their control.[65] To put it bluntly, the promise makes a person out of you.[66]

To become a person, conventionally, is to possess the capacity to reason and to act on that reason to change the course of history. Furthermore, per Arendt, the promise creates certainty, and conviviality, from chaos. "Binding oneself through promises . . . serves to set up in the ocean of uncertainty, which the future is by definition, islands of security without which not even continuity, let alone durability of any kind, would be possible in the relationships between men."[67] The one who promises claims, *I can make this happen*, but these capacities for sovereignty, appointed unevenly, haunt the promise binding oneself to another, as islands in an ocean. (We know, of course, that not all genres of the human can become persons and that not all persons—especially those who carry a debt, including debt as a remainder of gender or race—can promise and be believed.)[68] Third, the promise binds the one who promises to the obligation to remember to what, and to whom, they are bound. In its aesthetic dimension, the promise is grounded in forms of address and those arrangements that make it recognizable, or credible, between us. Such an address and arrangement must be shared in order to be perceived as binding between persons or parties, whether as an utterance ("I do"), a signature, or a gesture (a spit-handshake). As Jacques Derrida argues (though I depart from his discussion of its messianic nature), "a promise must promise to be kept, that is, not to remain 'spiritual' or 'abstract,' but to produce events, new effective forms of action, practice, organization, and so forth."[69]

That the experience of promise necessarily includes the interval during which the promise is not yet met, and might still never be, is crucial. Such a *meanwhile* consists not only of the lengthening moments that must be endured with the hope for another ending, but also the continual iteration of the promise. To sustain critique or power, a promise must repeat the distance between what is and what could be, between history and its representation, between life and its maximalization. In this way the promise is made in relation to an as yet uncertain fate; Derrida defines "the structure of the promise" as "the memory of that which carries the future, the to-come, here and now."[70] The cosmetics industry, in what might be construed as the promise's most banal invocation, cannot guarantee rescue from critical or compulsory conditions of historical being—aging, for instance—but promises to prolong the interval between youth and inevitable decline. *Maybe she's born with it, maybe it's Maybelline.* Another such interval might be the occasion for the intensification of powers, as in liberal war and its promise to usher in a more beautiful country. Opening a school amid the US occupation to teach Afghan women "the art and commerce of beauty" as a precursor for self-sovereignty is, for example, one such capture. In this way, the interval bears its own temporal power, delaying, drawing out, or forestalling an outcome.

Likewise, a promise can be broken, suspended, empty, or deferred; a promise might beget a cruel optimism, per Berlant, as promises maintain our attachments to forms of life that might be utterly impossible, especially during crises without foreseeable endings.[71] We might argue that this structure is the object of critical inquiry for so much feminist scholarship about beauty in the last few decades; such cruelty is part of the injurious properties of beauty, and its promise that is not kept might be condemned as a lie, or a trap. This accusation is also at the heart of the sinister "trans panic" defense; a beautiful woman is "revealed" to be trans, and her "deception" becomes the source of violence for which she is disappeared, or made to die.[72] Derrida continues, "A promise must *be able not to* be kept, it must risk not being kept or becoming a threat to be a promise." Thus, "the possibility of failure must continue to mark the event, even when it succeeds, as the trace of an impossibility, at times its memory and always its haunting."[73] Indeed, where the content of the promise is presence, its achievement is continually deferred because full presence is impossible. (But also because, as Adorno and others argue, the promise cannot be carried out in the world *as it is*—a point to which I return.) This interval is critical as the precondition or condition of possible crisis; it holds open the contingency that might lead on the one hand to a broken promise or worse and further devastation, and on the other, a demand for more than these known forms or claims on us (laws, contracts, covenants) for being together. Finally, it might be that the broken promise is a relief, unburdening you of becoming human in a historical project that is itself a curse, or a debt. As the graffiti says, *Be gay, do crime.*

Throughout this book, the promise of beauty is addressed to multiple times and temporal politics—from continuity, rupture, threshold, deferral, crisis, endurance, progress, and metamorphosis. Promises serve as distinctions that carve out an inviolate transcendental realm (the promise of beauty being "nothing more than happiness," for instance) in order to make historically contingent claims about relations between objects, scenes, persons, and worlds. In doing so, the promise blurs the distinction between ethics and politics, wherein the subject who must consider their relations to others specifically, and to alterity generally, is caught up in the constitution of a presence and, by necessity, a polity. Furthermore, the aesthetic lives within and even politicizes the political in the genre of promise itself, rendering observable the distinctions between categories (aesthetics and politics, politics and ethics) and in doing so undermining these distinctions. The promise of beauty establishes among these elements a contingent relation of *a feeling of life being furthered* in a historical formation, which can be changed or undone. But just as much as it might restore you to something that you sense is otherwise fraudulent, missing, or in parts, the promise of beauty might radically misrecognize that which you need. What else is promised by the presence of whatever claims to sustain us?

Beauty's Presence

In T Fleishmann's *Time Is the Thing a Body Moves Through*, a personal essay and unfinished meditation on Felix Gonzalez-Torres's artworks, they recount a meeting with a young child in their neighborhood. Fleishmann is asked, as bold children will do, whether they are a boy or a girl; they answer that a person does not have to be either. In response, the child gaily shouts, "Hey! I live in a house with a door!" Later, Fleishmann reflects on this encounter with friends over blunts and tropes. "She says to me that she actually thinks what the kid said is more beautiful if it isn't metaphor, anyway. I had shared some information about the world and then the kid wanted to share some information about the world, and if I get all loopidy-loo about what the kid said, I'm probably missing the whole message, which is just, 'Hey, I live in a house with a door.' And really, she reminds me, isn't some information about being alive beautiful enough? That we dry forks and touch hair and throw away a sock?"[74]

There is a house with a door, a fork, a touch, a sock, a person who is not a boy or a girl, a heap of cellophane-wrapped sugar candy in the corner; here beauty is *some information* that moves between us, whatever shapes or sharpens our sense of being alive. But its presence is confounding, elusive. In the most commonly understood sense, presence denotes a thereness, the affirmation of an existence "here now." More complexly, it is as an index of a historical circumstance or substance (Charles Sanders Peirce names a footprint, a weather vane, thunder, the word *this*, a pointing finger, and a photograph as indices) that presence traces, an emptiness that can only be filled in specific dependent situations. Presence does not come from nowhere; it requires certain grounds for its own possibility (and impossibility). Presence might take the form of an object, a habit, a structure, a feeling, or a force—and each of these forms is always an arrangement of tense and locality, bound pragmatically to its circumstances to make the eventfulness of it possible. *I perceive this* _____ *here and now*. Or as Steven Shaviro writes, in *Without Criteria*, "The orchid is not beautiful in itself: but something *happens* to the wasp, or to the gardener, who encounters the orchid and feels it to be beautiful."[75] For this reason, presence is at once material and worldly, transcendent and fleeting. It is the compact that makes one more day of crushing boredom or deep despair seem livable; it is the house with a door that promises safety, for a while.

But presence is an undecidable concept. It is not so much a property of an object, person, scene, or world ("She has such presence!") but a set of conditions as both circumstance and stipulation. Some constellation of variables in space and time must be in place for its recognition, for our sense-making, but beyond this is inconstancy. Derrida knew that full presence is an aporia, and yet presence permeates the spaces between you and me and others as an intensity, a mood, a body, a principle, or its index ("this is it"). Under the law, a percipient witness is able to share direct knowledge obtained through the senses; but hearsay, or testimony under oath about an out-of-court statement, is inadmissible as evidence. Affect theory locates presence as a phenomenological substance in gestures, sounds, tensions, and other atmospherics; the electric charge those in a room might share when someone, someone terrifying or beatific, for instance, enters. But while *a body occupying space* seemingly secures presence, and thereby truthfulness, her avatar's evidentiary status is more complexly wrought.[76] Photography, film, and the MP3 are among those technological forms that claim to deliver presence—bearing the imprint of a singular moment, person, object, or history—even as that presence is immediately divided from itself (*it has been there*). And when we encounter or even collect the representation of a thing (such as the love song), as a conduit to access a relation to the thing (love of another), does the representation also become lovely? What about the recording or the photograph of a beloved body? Can information be beautiful without becoming a metaphor? The duplication of presence "as" something else—the photograph, the love song, the metaphor—is presence of another order; something is there through reference to what is not. This puzzle can be put to all sensible forms that claim to produce presence, including states, laws, education, rights, or houses with doors. These forms are divided from the beautiful thing itself—democracy or safety, for example—but muster attachment anyway. We might hang on to romance, though disappointing, or rights, though imperfect, as palimpsests for what might be possible or yet to come.

If presence is undecidable at the best of times (whenever this might have been or will be), how much more so in crisis, when beauty might be the one resonant note in a tuneless or noisy thrum? The difficulty is not in observing that this might be true, but in observing how or what the promise of presence looks like, feels like. The promise proposes to manufacture beauty, to arouse it, and protect it, where presence is the sensation of movement and opening toward what one deems beautiful and wishes to be closer, and a measure of greater or lesser gradations of intensity, duration, or quantity. In other words, promise is both a historical narrativization and the determination of what is necessary for life-living, and presence, constituted through forms of circumscription (this *not* that) or opening (this *and* that) that establish criteria and produce the conditions of its own possibility, is its actualization. But while the promise attempts to make operational such criteria and conditions, presence might yet evade capture. It is undecidable because immediate presence, unmediated presence, is an impossibility; because absence haunts it; and because there is no agreement about its disposition. (Is presence an immersion, an awareness, an abundance, or the sensation of their lack?) This is why the promise of presence is political because what causes being, and gives it time to be, is never not a partisan argument about the flux of life and its living.

To observe presence at the meeting of aesthetics and politics is thus to observe an economy of form, not just content. Though the capacity to perceive beauty is so often imagined as an intuition, a phenomenological alignment, or a gut feeling, we can understand each of these as a "trained thing," to follow from Berlant, "where affect meets history, in all of its chaos, normative ideology, and embodied practices of discipline and invention."[77] Or, after Foucault, presence, "like every event, . . . is unique, yet subject to repetition, transformation, and reactivation."[78] It is as such that where the promise vows to sustain or manufacture beauty's presence, it must also *organize* it, and ceaselessly subject it to review and regulation *as* presence. Mina Loy argued for the recognition of beauty in lowly, contemporary objects away from *the picture gallery, the museum, the library, the frame, the glass case, the tradition*. All of these are static forms that police presence, barricaded against what she calls the flux of life. "Would not life be lovelier if you were constantly overjoyed from the sublimely pure concavity of your wash bowls?"[79] Indeed, our attention oftentimes yields the reorder of such things. Other repeatable forms are the heart of Judith Butler's performativity for creating presence on a physical body in space and time, and in Arabelle Sicardi's observation, "When we learn beauty rituals, share them, and celebrate them with each other, we're recognizing the work it takes to be OK with being alive."[80] When Elaine Scarry states, "Beauty is, then, a compact, or contract between the beautiful being (a person or thing) and the perceiver," she argues that presence is sensible in the form of the contract, as a structure for evoking it.[81]

But though she heralds beauty as a highly particular experience (a specific owl in a tree, for instance), Scarry also names the museum and the assembly as ideal forms for its presence and what she considers its corollary, justice. Yet none of these are natural or obvious forms; our recognition of them follows from an intelligible historical relation *to* them. (Gender is a historical sediment, and makeup routines are a bodily discipline; the museum and the assembly—in the United States, at least—are built on a philanthropic foundation and the three-fifths compromise. None of these are aesthetically or politically neutral.) So, what beauty is, how it is known, and what it does are all implicated in contingent arrangements of variables, including space, time, material, and sensation. We (or some and not others) become attached to certain rituals, contracts, museums, or assemblies, among other things, as historical situations that refer to or foster the presence of beauty and its erstwhile companions—justice, freedom, security, or life.

These structures and situations sometimes assure presence consistently, or continuously. It could be a skin-care routine, or the founding of a new regime. Underwriting the gift of freedom, for instance, imperial formations "grant" to those racial, colonial others certain political or institutional norms (constitutions, assemblies, trials by jury, among them) that are promised to manufacture freedom. Likewise, certain historical arrangements that claim to foster beauty might be taken up in order to regularize presence, which might include interference and control. The United Nations Educational, Scientific, and Cultural Organization (UNESCO), as one example, designates sites of "world heritage" considered to be valuable to all humanity (nonetheless a preferential proposition) to protect them from threats such as environmental degradation or asymmetrical warfare. At the same time, its promise might be comfortably subsumed into an instrumentalist calculus, seized as a divine or timeless form to secure capital or colony (such as a lovely young woman in a beautiful dress), or its presence usably lauded in what lies between a worker, a machine, and their movements. Andrew Ure, in his 1835 treatise *The Philosophy of Manufacturers; or, an Exposition of the Scientific, Moral, and Commercial Economy of the Factory System of Great Britain*, praised industrialism's beautifying effects for those who found themselves the grist in its mills: "Their light labour and erect posture in tending the looms, and the habit which many of them have of exercising their arms and shoulders, as if with dumb-bells . . . opens their chest[s], and gives them generally a graceful carriage . . . and . . . not a little of the Grecian style of beauty."[82] The work ethic as a moral good in turn becomes a promise of beauty, even as its manufacture breaks you, or at the least wears you out.

The presence of beauty might therefore be secured through biopower, bringing together the disciplinary power operating on bodies with the exercise of power over populations, especially in their shared capacity to "make live." Recruited as physical fitness, emotional well-being, or cultural competency, beauty might be directed at purposes as specific as eliminating welfare dependency and as comprehensive as nurturing whole personhood, whether providing business-appropriate attire for low-income jobseekers; wigs and beauty supplies to chemotherapy patients; or job training for women in prisons, camps, and war zones. A promise of beauty as the American Dream informs the apocryphal story about Hollywood actress Tippi Hedren, who flew her personal manicurist Dusty to a refugee camp in Sacramento, California, to train Vietnamese refugee women in nail technology.[83] At the same time, a concession to beauty might be presented as a boon from its administrators to mediate state violence; after scandals of deprivation and abuse, US commanders built a basketball court and a salon for Haitian detainees with HIV/AIDS held at a so-called humanitarian camp at Guantánamo.[84] These promises have in common the schooling of the senses to address, if not social harms and structural violence, then at least our conduct and capacities for their endurance. Since the 1980s, in another example, nonprofit initiatives have enlisted beauty salons as partners for Black women's health advocacy. Campaigns such as Stay Beautiful / Stay Alive and Beauty and the Breast staged salons as scenes for breast and cervical cancer screening and health education.[85] The trial North Carolina BEAUTY ("Bringing Education and Understanding to You") and Health Project trained cosmetologists as peer educators for "behavioral health outcome interventions" aimed at Black women, who are among those most at risk for preventable cancer deaths.[86] BEAUTY's interventions included "strategies on eating at least five servings of fruits/vegetables per day, reducing calories from fat, and increasing moderate physical activity among customers," their achievement becoming an object of self-discipline.[87] Through beauty and all it stands for ("education and understanding," among other things), the future is conceived here through the calculative capacity to summon its presence through practice.

Just as beauty's promise inaugurates a certain coming together, so too does presence require such forms, or such forms that those who come together consign to themselves, from within a time and place in the world. Citing Derrida, Miranda Joseph argues the romance of community is a supplement that "intervenes or insinuates itself *in-the-place-of*," filling a void at the core of capital.[88] Sitting in a hotel room, I flip through channels and land on a brief CNN report about a Filipino hairstylist who walks the streets of

New York City to give haircuts to the unhoused every Sunday afternoon.[89] Certainly, this is the scripted circulation of a human-interest story (one of thousands like it) that tells us nothing about capitalism's violence. Why not seize homes from the banks and the municipalities (or simply seize the banks and municipalities) that leave them empty, lifeless? I know I would find this beautiful. But watching this stylist gently touch an elder's paper-thin scalp (just *there* at the temple to brush away cut stray hairs), we may not be able to (or want to) deny roses, a sock, or a soft caress—those things that avow presence, aliveness, right here and now, between you and me. This is a difficulty at the threshold of sensory aesthetics and biopolitical governance where a longing for beauty—as touch, for instance, or feeling—collides with the forces that render material the vitality of a body, a people, or a planet. The promise is addressed to a specific situation or site for intervention, where the desire for presence is opened up to the inscription of the conditional—for instance, a historical consciousness of loss or catastrophe, the political economy of extractivism, or the longing for intimacy under the shadow of capital—as its guarantee. In documenting health advocacy campaigns at Black salons, Tiffany M. Gill notes, "Beauty salons, where touch and care of the body are high priorities, provide a place for black women's bodies to be dignified and find a safe place for care and exploration."[90] Such a place (despite whatever discipline it requires) might make a claim on you by sharing freely (or less miserly) what is scant or otherwise withheld.

Here beauty also promises the pleasures and risks of being present inside a relation with another. Kant distinguishes the agreeable from the beautiful, inasmuch as the beautiful is an invitation (which might shade and slip into a demand) to others to participate in a collectivity, a sensus communis.[91] After Kant, and others who follow, Alexander Nehamas suggests, "Far from being selfish or solipsistic, the desire beauty provokes is essentially social: it literally does create a new society, for it needs to be communicated to others and pursued in company."[92] Beauty desires society; its judgment tests our aliveness with and against others. But who belongs to the company we might keep? Who is included by nature of the form of the *we*; who is able to give form to itself; and what molds or mandates such a form, which might be an act, a structure, or a dream? What presence is possible with those with whom we might not share a common experience of beauty, but nonetheless share a biome, a world, a cosmos? What is the "we" given the schemes that sanction a "we"—one that can speak a promise, to make present or absent beauty and its cousins, including ugliness? Though Kant argues that the judgment of beauty makes no recourse to the law or proceduralism, it is through such an invitation—that others find as you do a thing beautiful—that beauty and also "correct" communion with it might become a norm, or a rule. In Lauren Berlant's words, "The concept of the 'we' is itself aesthetic evidence of the process in which affective response becomes form."[93] On the one hand, James Thompson, writing about participatory theater as one avenue for reconciling victims and perpetrators after wartime, suggests that the urge to share beauty with others across divides acts as a "universal claim to some form of good."[94] On the other, the "we" invoked by First Lady Barbara Bush when she appeared on the talk show *Good Morning America*, on the eve of the war on Iraq, is a "we" who both wages war and will not "waste" a moment on its devastation. "Why should we hear about body bags and deaths? . . . It's not relevant. So why should I waste my beautiful mind on something like that?"[95] She solicits those *like her* with beautiful minds, while blithely assuming that those who die are radically separate from "us." The bodies of the dead ("ours" or "theirs") are not relevant to her politics of life—even though the dead sanctify and otherwise ordain this empire.

This "we" is a lethal fault line, when and where beauty depends on resemblance to solicit sympathy, harmony, or order.[96] It brings up iterations of beauty in a moralistic tenor that renders it apolitical, prepolitical, or antipolitical, whether in glossing "America" or a whole humanity. Through beauty such coercive collectivities established through aesthetic and other norms become obligatory forms that permit little or no dissent, and assume social unities that are false, if not outright violent. Or as the Beat poet Lawrence Ferlinghetti writes:

    The world is a beautiful
place

to be born into
if you don't mind some
    people dying

all the time
    or maybe only
starving

some of the time
    which isn't half so bad
       if it

isn't you[97]

In circumscribing the forms through which "we" come together, the promise of beauty might bind a universal history of the human—and also occasion a sectarian history of its other. "O beautiful for spacious skies" (from the hymn "America the Beautiful") is the violent dispossession of Indigenous peoples; so too is the museum, the national park, and the land-grant university, each heralded as a preserve of the beautiful that depends on its insidious enclosure. Rebecca Solnit observes, rightly, that "the contemporary world is full of things that look beautiful and are produced through hideous means."[98] The presence of beauty, then, might also feel like a heaviness displacing the air, an enveloping darkness, or a ghostly matter.[99] It might determine that plentitude for some is poverty for others; it might even demand it, as an Israeli minister crowed during a bombing campaign that maimed and murdered tens of thousands of Palestinians, "North Gaza, more beautiful than ever. Blowing up and flattening everything is a delight for the eyes."[100] Or as the Palestinian poet Mourid Barghouti writes, "You are beautiful like a liberated homeland / And I am exhausted like an occupied one."[101]

The belief that beauty arouses in us a wish to share knowledge of its presence with others is also a human-unhuman divide. The we, the not-us. As Richard Wilk notes, "Judging beauty is an exercise that simultaneously divides people and brings them together."[102] It is not simply that the promise of beauty is concerned that another who might be a lover, a stranger, or a generation that follows after ours finds happiness or solace in the same flowers or faces that we do. It is that some promises claim to set right deviations or "errors" in judgment, with implications for the sensory perception of its arrangement. Beauty, like society, must be defended. In released videos, ISIS militants filmed themselves smashing ancient statues that many horrified observers argued represented a gift to humanity, which was now deprived of their presence for all time hereafter. Titled "The Promotion of Virtue and the Prevention of Vice #1—Nineveh Province" (2015), the video depicts men toppling limestone sculptures and modern replicas (identified remotely by archaeologists and historians scrutinizing the footage) from ancient Hatra, the capital of the first Arab kingdom in Iraq, pummeling them with sledgehammers and electric drills. These acts are presented on a continuum with videos of the same or fellow militants beheading hostages. *National Geographic* quoted an Iraqi archaeologist, now living in London, on the depth of loss through this destruction: "These things are part of the history of humanity. If you destroy them, you're destroying the history of everyone."[103] But this humanity, this "everyone," is not universal; a former US undersecretary of state for public diplomacy and public affairs stated that the "civilized peoples" value art, whereas "violent extremists" do not.[104] It is not just to be unbeautiful that presents an obstacle to aliveness. When Mary Mothersill asserts "that a description of a person who lacked that capacity [to foster beauty] would find its natural place, if anywhere, in the literature of psychopathology," we see unfolding knowledges about peoples with unsimilar capacities for beauty or aesthetic appreciation that are often epiphenomena of politics—temporal distance, moral distinction, or civilizational lapse.[105] In the mid-twentieth-century beauty manual *Mirror, Mirror on the Wall*, nutritionist Gayelord Hauser writes that his visit to Cold War Moscow inspired this tome: "You never realize the great importance of beauty until you are in a place where it does not exist." He continues, addressing himself in particular to "women of the Free World" who do not suffer so under communist regimes, "The thought that struck me so forcefully there was: 'Beauty is duty.'"[106] In this manner a demagogue's call for a *big beautiful wall* at the US-Mexico border molds a rigid aesthetic form whose presence (or promise of presence) commands the frenzied fortification of a paranoic order against an existential enemy.[107] To be unable to appreciate such beauty as a statue or a wall—to be insensible to it or, even worse, to want to destroy it—can become a racial divide, in the Foucauldian sense, between humanity ("the history of everyone") and those subraces that threaten beauty and thus life itself.

Here crisis as a historiographical concept announces the limits of a structure or a practice because such a structure or practice cannot or will not sustain a beautiful presence, which might also be democracy, art, harmony, love, or justice. Crisis as such might name the structures or practices necessary to secure that presence, but it might also predict its collapse. How have we lived in order to fail beauty in this way? How can we repair our broken promises to it, if at all? The title for a book review for Elizabeth Rush's *Rising: Dispatches from the New American Shore* asks, "Why Write Beautifully about Climate Crisis?" Martyn Smith argues that writing beautifully, rather than instrumentally, about a phenomenon we can do nothing to stop—the sea *will* rise, the shore *will* disappear—is not "about convincing people, but rather about preparing ourselves, emotionally and spiritually, for what is happening."[108] Beauty's presence is in being with others as we await an inevitability.

Here, or more specifically, not here—beauty might have no presence except as promise, or science fiction. Its otherwise achievement requires, as Asma Abbas observes about love (which is, after all, a sense or a feeling beauty often arouses), "shedding the aesthetic and sensual pathologies that are the gift of colonialism, liberalism, and capitalism."[109] Such pathologies are how a lethal weapon might be called beautiful (by some) because it is sensed as a totality (the circle of life, a beginning and an ending). As dozens of US Tomahawk cruise missiles destroyed a Syrian military airfield, illuminating the night sky above the Mediterranean Sea, a national news anchor praised "the beauty of our weapons" (misapplying Leonard Cohen's lyric about their terror while corroborating Walter Benjamin's warning about Fascism).[110] Here the knowledge of human-made destruction is marshalled as evidence of "our" capacity for human feeling, a genocidal aesthetic that "affirms" the humanity of the perpetrator in his melancholy. This swallowing shadow over beauty is not an exception, but the condition of the wretched of the earth, after Frantz Fanon. For them, for us, beauty is terribly vulnerable because it can be distorted or turned against itself—and against life. And yet Arundhati Roy insists, "There is beauty yet in this brutal, damaged world of ours. Hidden, fierce, immense." She continues, "We have to seek it out, nurture it, love it. Making bombs will only destroy us. It doesn't matter whether or not we use them. They will destroy us either way."[111]

Such brutal or alienating forms through which we experience presence might be upended yet. Here the promise of beauty puts a sharper point on the critique of whatever caused it to go missing, become ruinous, fraudulent, or fallow; of whatever narrows or hardens against beauty, or otherwise thrusts it into unpleasant or sickening purpose. The promise of beauty might name the longing for something other than capital or colony to organize our bonds to each other, or nurture a dream of self-presence, bringing forth the *I* or the *we* who would be free. After this manner, some call beautiful the infinite continuity between ourselves and the world, a harmony of unsimilar parts. The artist-activist Favianna Rodriguez manifests *migration is beautiful* in her much-reproduced print of a monarch butterfly, a transmutating form for "the right of all living beings to move freely."[112] A stray and secret beauty might slyly conjure what Saidiya Hartman calls "wayward," "experiment," through which a young Black woman might come to stand for herself, outside of sociological or criminological scrutiny—ungovernable.[113] In this way, beauty could promise what Derrida names *ipseity*, a "being properly oneself."[114] So might beauty gesture toward both what is to come, and how we bring that future into being—the repair of such wrongs that have withheld its presence from us, thus far. Invoking Black feminist theory as a commitment to beauty, marked by an ethics of risk and disclosure (rather than law and order), Jennifer Nash cites Ivone Gebara, who muses, "If justice is fundamentally about creating right relationships, beauty is in many ways the incarnation and measure of the integrity of those relationships. It is a kind of aesthetic love, an invitation to nurture the creativity and integrity of every created thing. It is an invitation to salvation."[115] When so much is missing or destroyed, this particular invitation to the *we* calls on beauty to speak to, and hear from, all those who are divided from it, and to grieve for those who are gone from it.

To think beauty as promise is to appraise how we have lived, and how we might build lives that make more sense, more beauty, than the ones we are living; but to think beauty as method is to appraise those arrangements that secure its presence (or claim to do so) for what these tell us about the human, history, and life. What is promised by a house with a door, or a wall, or a skin-care routine, or a crown, or a hand touching your hair, or an elegy for the sea and the air we breathe? It is possibility, or its foreclosure; it is a world held in common, or a species divided; it is the casualties of capital and colony, or their remedy. All are present, all are missing.

Promising Objects

If presence allows us to discover a principle, then the example is its means of transmission. This book's capacious collection is therefore part of the study. In this I follow the example of others, where treatises *on* beauty necessarily include lists of seemingly noninterchangeable objects *of* beauty, what Umberto Eco might call a *poetic list*. The poetic list is different from a practical one, such as a grocery list, or an inventory; what distinguishes one from another is its criterion of assembly. A poetic list, Eco argues, is made "because we cannot manage to enumerate something that eludes our capacity for control and denomination."[116] Indeed, it is the dizzying impossibility to name each beautiful thing in a comprehensive list that imparts to others a glimpse of beauty's significance. In *Speaking of Beauty*, Denis Donoghue offers these examples as each entirely singular but also universally recognizable, which suggests that some quality must nonetheless be replicable across them, though it is impossible to say what that might be: "And yet we continue to say without much hesitation that such-and-such and so-and-so are beautiful: tulips, roses, certain women, certain men, most children, a page of Chinese written characters, an African mask, a mathematical process, a piece of music, the view from Portofino, a certain sunset, a full moon, some animals (but not rhinoceroses), kingfishers, dragonflies, the air at Brighton, Alexander Kipnis's voice, the weather when noon's a purple glow."[117] In *On Beauty and Being Just*, Elaine Scarry names "Augustine's water, sky, cakes, and roses," and Umberto Eco's *History of Beauty* includes a series of art images organized loosely in well-established categories (including "nude

Venus" and "clothed Adonis," queens and kings), arranged in a chronological timeline.[118] Ivone Gebara starts her list with a list, "It is a place, a tree, a shore, a forest, a person that we love," while Henri Lefebvre's *The Missing Pieces* names the artworks, films, screenplays, photo negatives, poems, symphonies, buildings, letters, concepts, and lives that cannot be seen, heard, or known because they are missing, destroyed, buried, or otherwise left no trace.[119] In her 1963 documentary *The House Is Black*, filmed at an isolated leper colony, Iranian feminist poet Forough Farrokhzad presents a lyrical rumination on how we might care for one another and slow the progression of disease and inevitable darkness. In a classroom, the adult teacher points to a child and demands, "You, name a few beautiful things." The young boy answers, solemnly, "The moon, the sun, flowers, playtime." Ocean Vuong submits "a fresco, a peach-red mountain range, a boy, the mole on his jaw" among those things that please the soul, and Chloé Cooper Jones ends her memoir of disability, *Easy Beauty*, with a list that recalls her to her senses: "a morning song, a simple tune, the spatial rhythmic shuffle of Andrew in the kitchen in socks, the faucet singing, the tinkling melody of water running over the pots and dishes before striking the sink's metal basin, then a rinsing whisper, soap sloshing in the dirty coffeepot."[120]

Each list infers that beauty has no definitive form, and yet adopts certain structures and formalities of discourse to establish a logic or kinship among its collocation of things. In other words, a list is a scene setter. As it gathers those objects, persons, habits, and scenes that secure (even just for a moment) a principle, each list is particular and also propositional. If an example is the event of a statement, its entry in a list defines its enunciability. Both cohere at times into a formation or an institution—something like a case study, canon, or archive—that absorbs variations or adjustments while promising an encounter that can be foreseen, at least in part. And while a list does not wholly define the things that are included (whether roses, the mole on his jaw, or an African mask), it does designate an affective or interpretive range for any one thing bound through it to another. A list, then, is a dynamic arrangement of things that creates an event of knowledge in their closeness, and a politics of whatever underwrites it.

This book is a list that includes many things that appear to lash promise to beauty against the grain of terror, of what Berlant calls *crisis ordinariness*, which it turns out is quite a lot.[121] Each chapter describes how beauty operates as a reference for writing our sense of the human, of collectivity, of politics, ethics, and other forms of life; and each animates a concept of aesthetics in what Rancière calls the distribution of the sensible, as a historical situation.

From Plato to Adorno, Elaine Scarry to Saidiya Hartman, among others, I draw (sometimes unfaithfully) from these and other philosophical and aesthetic theories in order to observe them as objects of inquiry in and of themselves, as historical artifacts that do not precede but produce the infrastructure that renders beauty intelligible, perceptible, and sensible, conceived through concerns about how one ought to live and what conditions enable such a life. Circulating as abstractions as well as *things*, such theories organize events of knowledge and also induce ways of being and ordering the world. In among these theory-things I have a hundred memes saved onto my camera roll; a hundred songs or poems scattered across laptops; a hundred film or television plots noted in workbooks; a hundred stories collected from magazines, newspapers, and books, in which beauty smooths a passage to the other side of calamity. These might bring together realms of aesthetic experience once understood (if never truly so) as distinct, as in the slide made for circulation on an image-dependent digital platform that pull-quotes poet Rita Dove, "In the midst of horror we fed on beauty—and that, my love, is what sustained us." These sit alongside the philosophers and theorists in a history of ideas, a jumble of genres that are also *spaces of dissension*, throughout *The Promise of Beauty*.[122]

Specifically, where it is a response to the scarcities, acquittals, and crises of our time, the promise of beauty is a schema for conferring meaning and structure to events and phenomena, some of which are inaccessible, or transient, or unsettling, precisely because we are not yet sure what it would take to live, finally. (We know, but we don't know.) In the following, I do not uncover certain or sure knowledge of beauty through its copy (also known sometimes as heritage), or an education in it, or as an index of rights, ruin, or resilience, but the promises made on beauty's behalf can help us comprehend the arrangement of forms of life that cohere energies or administer capacities for living. Indeed, though beauty is undecidable, its promise demands that we engage in calculation even as transformation of a historical situation makes its plea beyond this moment—*a feeling of life being furthered*. In doing so, beauty carries multiple felt possibilities, whether an antagonism toward disorder and a push toward normalization, but also a capacity for alterity and becoming other. Toward this end, this book follows some beauty around, as it binds to or loosens forms and fantasies about sovereignty, freedom, and historical time, even as these forms and fantasies are stuttering, fragmenting, and congealing.

The distinct concern of this book are those things that are brought into being to replace, or repair, or ruin, or _____ through the aesthetic form of beauty's promise. First and foremost among these things is the copy. Elaine Scarry's opening salvo in *On Beauty and Being Just* is that "beauty brings copies of itself into being," as "a phenomenon of unceasing begetting."[123] Where the encounter with beauty arouses the desire for its longevity, how much more so where or when whatever is beautiful is also at risk? Crisis turns to copy to ensure that that which is loved but also vulnerable is not vanished, whether a book or a baby, a forest or a feeling. In other words, the promise of beauty solicits another such that a singular presence can be sensed or felt again. In taking up this consonance between crisis and copy, the first chapter posits beauty as a method for thinking about an *aesthetics of historicity* that saturates (or splinters) our perception of history "itself." And this is especially vital when we are made cognizant that, as Ocean Vuong put it in his novel about trauma and intimacy after wartime, *On earth we're briefly gorgeous*. This chapter turns to the most common figuration of beauty for a polity—the comely young woman in a beautiful dress. Edmund Burke declared, "To make us love our country, our country ought to be lovely," and almost two centuries later, Nguyen Cat Tuong, a Hanoi artist and intellectual who "modernized" the ao dai, opined, "We can determine if a country is civilized and holds a concept of beauty by looking at the citizens' clothing."[124] In other words, sometimes between woman and nation is beauty. *The comely young woman in a beautiful dress* is the promise of that beauty in a serial form, so much so that at times she might seem to have exhausted our critical attention. In order to reanimate her aesthetic register, this chapter takes *the comely young woman in a beautiful dress* not as a study of the principle it stands for—whether country, "heritage," or resilience—but as a study of the forms for normativity and narrativity that occasion and structure her presence. Through both crisis and beauty as genres of historical narrativization, the dress and the beloved body who wears it secures the promise of beauty against the ravages of time via her replica, or copy.

If aesthetic judgments are about social arrangements, as Sianne Ngai observes, they are also about interference in those arrangements.[125] The first chapter and the next consider seriously questions of those social arrangements presumed to be beautiful and life-affirming. In the first chapter, this is captured in the temporal understanding, *On earth we're briefly gorgeous*. In the second, the concern is posed in the familiar chant, *What does democracy look like?* How is democracy made aesthetically perceptible, including through acts of becoming one—or near enough, or not enough at all? That is, if one of the key dimensions of the concept of beauty is its radical singularity, another is its desirable replication in all directions, which presumably only certain ideological and institutional forms can secure. These chapters study beauty as a social form for the rescue of a besieged subject or subject-in-process, and of those other properties of liberal personhood that so often attach to beauty, like interiority, or dignity.

The second chapter turns to the transition to self-sovereignty promised by US empire to consider the aesthetic education that cultivates the identification with a liberal vision of humanity, including the interval before its accomplishment. Such an education raises the status of beauty as a promise for the elaboration and the judgment of history, including its postulates, crisis and continuity. In this iteration, the promise of beauty is a habitus that prepares one for democracy. The aesthetic forms for perceiving and recognizing the presence of democracy—the literary convention of the constitution that references a collectivity ("We the People"); the analogue of balance, proportion, and equality (one member, one vote) found in a representative body or popular assembly; and the lawful habits that conjure the desire and the discipline of beauty—are heralded as right arrangements. But right arrangements also imply the presence of wrong ones, and in the US war on terror, the wrong ones are at times condensed in hijab in general, and the burqa in particular, described as a premodern remnant, a metonym for barbaric Islam, or a crime against humanity. Established in 2003 by a small coterie of nongovernmental workers and industry professionals, the Kabul Beauty School operated under the name Beauty without Borders to instruct Afghan women in the art and commerce of beauty—a premise founded on beauty's erstwhile absence until liberal war bestowed its presence. Here I argue that beauty is not just an index of some other force but is itself an instrument and an objective for calculating and arranging the life of others; an education in beauty sustains a philosophical statement about a worldhistorical consciousness, which also comprises a political imperative for regime change. However, the inducement to copy a presumably perfectible form (democracy, beauty) announces the divide from itself that follows in the poor copy, the partial or failed presence, which then requires further repetitions through evaluation, regularization, and discipline.

Like the beauty school, the beauty pageant reminds us that being seen as human is not a condition of the flesh but its fabrication. My concern in the third chapter is with the aesthetics of liberal democratic forms of sovereignty, located in parliaments or congresses, constitutions, courts of law, including international ones, and the rule of rights and reason. To do so I examine the formulation of rights from which "the right to be beautiful" emerges and which it in turn secures. Staged just twice, first in Angola and later in Cambodia, the Miss Landmine pageant follows from a not uncommon faith that beauty is both a humanitarian problem and also its resolution. A short-lived pageant for women who had lost limbs from unexploded ordnance and who suffer the losses that follow, the spectacle sought to raise "awareness" and confer dignity. And what a spectacle it was! The photographs of the Cambodian contestants lounging at luxury hotels and among the temple friezes of *apsara* dancers, together comprise the aesthetic currency of Cambodia, still grappling with the compounding violences of US bombing campaigns, the Khmer Rouge, and the Hun Sen regime.

How to repair the humanity that has been severed from flesh? In this third chapter, I hold together the sprawling international complex that funds and conducts prosthetic manufacturing, rehabilitation and vocational training, infrastructural development, and cultural programming, with the aesthetic and moral discourses of rights, capacities, humanitarianism, and humanity at the postwar scene of this pageant heralding, "Everyone has the right to be beautiful." This slogan attests to the degree to which rights almost exclusively model claims to universality and the subject of freedom. The pageant copied democratic forms—rights, assemblies—to "uplift" the outcast, embrace the disenfranchised, and redress grievances. In the context of "show" trials and state abuses, it might be easy to dismiss the pageant as a poor (juridically adjacent) substitute for liberal government. But we need not dismiss *or* praise the spectacle to observe that the pageant might betray rights themselves as a poor presence. With a custom-fit prosthetic as prize, the pageant unwittingly corroborates the synthetic grounds for a "whole" humanity. What if the pageant being "unlike" the assembly, or the right to be beautiful being "unlike" the right to have rights, is not about the failure of the pageant, but about the failure of democratic forms to meaningfully secure what the pageant and beauty must summon through their semblance? Not as symptom but assessment, the right to be beautiful can tell us much about the collapse of normative horizons of justice.

But—the school disintegrates, the pageant cancels, and beauty fails us (we are told) because beauty can do nothing to stop catastrophe, or because it diverts us from what horrors lie outside its frame. The fourth chapter begins with the genre of ruin porn—what some commentators call the now-familiar art photographs and documentary images of decline in postindustrial cities in the Rust Belt, such as Detroit—to examine the accusation of aesthetic failure to accommodate political or ethical crisis. Here crisis is doubled; the ruin is the terrible consequence of a historical situation, and its representation is the unnerving collapse of the event of knowledge. The promise to diagnose what is missing or gone wrong, necessary for the naming and narration of crisis, is betrayed by a "purely" aesthetic beauty. I turn to a specific accusation of failure—the incapacity of these photographs to represent the violence of capital that wrecks the fortunes or peoples of the Motor City—in order to get at a broader proposition about the disturbance of the intelligibility of the world. Here, and in its other iterations as a complaint (poverty porn, humanitarian porn, etc.), the pornographic is a judgment in error, a deviation from truth, and the estrangement of the human from others, from history. But the complaint itself can help us to be more attentive to how we become attached to certain perceptual practices in the appraisal of beauty and its failures. Indeed, how the pornographic as a metaphor marks the alienation of the promise from the human might undo our presumptive prerequisites for knowledge and the entry of life into history. Inasmuch as these are hinged on those same properties underwriting what Annie McClanahan calls the dead pledge of capital that wrought a postapocalyptic world now, can we instead make the ruins we wish to see?[126]

If the fourth chapter concerns itself with the methodological impasse of a hermeneutics of suspicion that informs critique, and the accusation that what is aesthetic is pornographic, the fifth chapter lingers at the wreckage of vulnerability given a lovely form. I center a concept of *living beautifully* as an aesthetic style attenuating scenes of radical contingency to model how best to live on in catastrophic times. Living beautifully in this instance names the deliberate leaning toward freedom despite social or structural collapse, shaping our historical consciousness of time over (and sometimes against) an awareness of eventfulness. Weathering continuity and rupture, its promise serializes dispersed events (even if those events are interior ones) and scripts a biography of strength after brokenness, a desirable history of doggedness despite misfortune. With the disintegration of modernity's temporal order of progress and perfectibility, living beautifully is one response to irresolvable aporias in our experience of time. Here I follow the call to beauty to figure out what is collective and what is not about its promise toward and beyond survival, or our ending.

The Promise of Beauty is not the disclosure of beauty's scandal as philosophically messy, historically contingent, or empirically false. Nor is it a claim that without beauty, the humanities, or art, or justice has no usable future. Instead, the book names beauty as a method that attends to questions of aesthetics and politics from within a history (or histories) of the world. And where the promise of beauty precipitates crisis through critique of the conditions of existing possibility for a life that can be lived, what politics might follow? Here we see the promise of beauty take up politics in multiple senses. Rancière argues that what is called politics is actually the police, and that politics breaks from the police and its organization of powers and their legitimation through the aggregation of rules and populations. In doing so, "politics is aesthetic in that it makes visible what had been excluded from a perceptual field, and in that it makes audible what used to be inaudible."[127] We know beauty as the police, as the aesthetic arrangement of "right" forms for the achievement of norms or an order. But beauty is also a politics for reworlding the perceptual field and the theories we bring to it, for undoing the pressure of forms and the regularities of time and narrativity deployed through, as Kandice Chuh puts it, "the difference aesthetics makes."[128] In this spirit, beauty as method unfolds epistemologies, ontologies, and genealogies of the human and our activity—what Lisa Lowe calls the intimacies of four continents, and what Inderpal Grewal and Caren Kaplan name scattered hegemonies—and engages tensions and nonunities that erupt in narratives of crisis.[129] Beauty as method observes not just how beauty appears in arguments for certain arrangements or forms for and about its presence, but also how we *craft* those arguments for or against an arrangement or form; beauty as method underscores theory's relation to the practical, and the philosophical and political necessity of historical thought being *felt*. After all, where it implicates (and incriminates) certain structures for living on and not others, the promise of beauty plumbs the correspondences and contradictions between rule of law, private property, resource extraction, the antipersonnel landmine, the tribunal, and wealth consolidation, with and against small art, love, roses, prayer, a house with a door, a prosthetic limb, a broken vessel, or a police precinct on fire.

We live, or try to, in the ebb and flow of calamity. I at times struggled with the oblique engagement of this book with the urgencies of aspirational fascism, climate catastrophe, and fatal dispossession—all those things that suspend or end the life of so many. I remind myself that to dismiss beauty as trivial or superfluous is too often to sequester beauty (against all evidence of its powers) as an enthralling vision or numbing distraction that impedes our perception of the real, thus disallowing that the form of theory *does* matter. I turn again to Lauren Berlant and Kathleen Stewart, who assure me, "It matters that something was yellow, not red, that it passed in a blur, or something moaned. A bit of social debris, a scattering of material-aesthetic forms taken up or left to languish like litter are an archive of objects of attention."[130] And much might be lost in dispensing with (what is dismissed as) mere ornament, or second-order signification, because beauty might indeed weigh the gravity of a life, or provide a historical sensorium to focus our attention on those structures that call some persons and worlds into being, and not others. No wonder we often derive a method and a form for the narrativity of crisis from the promise of beauty. How else could we reckon with the heartbreaking TikTok videos of sixteen-year-old, round-faced Ma'Khia Bryant, demonstrating how she fashioned her voluminous black hair, circulated against the grim footage of her murder at the hands of Columbus, Ohio, police? Where politics obtains in forms for presence and absence, in the sensing of life being furthered or brutally cut short, beauty mediates the materiality of life and death found in these forms. And so a collectivity of *we* insists on beauty as a social form, a temporal loop, a psychic investment, an interpretive hermeneutic, and a relational presence, in order to demand the life she deserved. We take beauty's side, because we want it on ours.

Promise is an imperative cut like an invitation. This book is an invitation too, but I do not know quite what I want to promise you, because I do not know what is to come or if it is enough. Who would *not* want beauty to save us? Who would not wish a radical beauty that would free us from the failures of "actually existing" beauty, and provide redress, reparation, and redemption for all its erstwhile wrongs? Yet this study of beauty refuses to settle the issue for now, instead lingering on the contingencies and consequences of its claims for the reproduction of life, or the disruption of life as we know it. And before I turn to those things the promise of beauty pledges to make present in a given historical situation—what forms for a life that can be lived—I want to say, what does it mean for beauty to be an object or an ideal on which we hang our hopes? What do we really want from beauty?

chapter 1

The Beautiful, Finding Itself in Danger, Desires Its Copy

A is added to B.
A substitutes for B.
A is a superfluous addition to B.
A makes up for the absence of B.
A usurps the place of B.
A makes up for B's deficiency.
A corrupts the purity of B.
A is necessary so that B can be restored.
A is an accident alienating B from itself.
A is that without which B would be lost.
A is that through which B is lost.
A is a danger to B.
A is a remedy to B.
A's fallacious charm seduces one away from B.
A can never satisfy the desire for B.
A protects against direct encounter with B.

Barbara Johnson, "Writing"

I want to insist that our being alive is beautiful enough to be worthy of replication.

Ocean Vuong, *On Earth We're Briefly Gorgeous*

On Earth We're Briefly Gorgeous warns that beauty is finite, fading. In response to a professor who speculates (in the midst of a lecture on *Othello*) that gay men are inherently narcissistic, Ocean Vuong's narrator, Little Dog, is defiant. The professor's intimation is that to love another who is "alike" is autoaffection, which is vice or void. "But if so—why not? Maybe we look into mirrors not merely to seek beauty, regardless how illusive, but to make sure, despite the facts, that we are still here. That the hunted body we move in has not yet been annihilated, scraped out."[1] Little Dog continues (alluding to Elaine Scarry's *On Beauty and Being Just*), "I read that beauty has historically demanded replication. We make more of anything we find aesthetically pleasing, whether it's a vase, a painting, a chalice, a poem. We reproduce it in order to keep it, extend it through space and time. To gaze at what pleases—a fresco, a peach-red mountain range, a boy, the mole on his jaw—is, in itself, replication—the image prolonged in the eye, making more of it, making it last. Staring into the mirror, I replicated myself into a future where I might not exist."[2]

The promise of beauty is an entry into thinking about an *aesthetics of historicity* that makes or shapes our perception of "history" itself. By this I mean that history is often figured with or as an image, which could be a line, a diagram, an object, or a person, that substitutes for reality (because we cannot otherwise represent time and its passage) or renders it perceptible. And why shouldn't such an image be one of beauty? After all, its promise illuminates the structure of a relay between aesthetics and politics giving sense and significance to objects, events, and arrangements, and how we live with or without them over time. Through concepts such as origin, event, duration, crisis, mortality, or death, a beautiful image might secure (or attempt to secure) knowledge of aliveness and its presence, if only for a moment. In *Six Names of Beauty*, Crispin Sartwell muses that because we are losing things, and "in fact we are always in the process of losing everything we have," the longing that follows from such loss turns to the solace of beauty.[3] To this point, W. E. B. Du Bois sees both beauty and death striating Black life when he writes, "The boy clothed in his splendid youth stood before us and laughed in his own jolly way,—went and was gone."[4] (This boy could be Emmett Till, Trayvon Martin, Tamir Rice, or _____.) In other words, we call beautiful those objects, scenes, habits, persons, and worlds that might be capable of bearing the weight of history, or that measure the danger of its undoing. Such a weight and its measure bear on the life that can be lived and what can be wrung from it, which is to say that the promise of beauty shapes our sense of time as well as the quality of its precarity. It provides an aesthetics for grasping "a type of history—a form of dispersion in time, a mode of succession, of stability, and of reactivation, a speed of deployment or rotation," as well as their perturbation and upheaval.[5] To call a thing beautiful is not to say everything about it but to say something about how it feels, and how it begets knowledge about a world, about ourselves. And here, through its promise, we grasp how historical consciousness is distributed and made sensible, which Vuong's debut novel condenses as *On earth we're briefly gorgeous*.

If one of beauty's promises to us (and ours to beauty) is its dispersion in time, it is no wonder that the copy is often described as the first thing beauty solicits from us, or, as Scarry puts it in the very first paragraph of *On Beauty and Being Just*, "What is the felt experience of cognition at the moment one stands in the presence of a beautiful boy or flower or bird? It seems to incite, even to require, the act of replication."[6] We do so, she argues, so that others might have the benefit of its presence, or at least knowledge of its once having been in the world. Such a copy of *a beautiful boy or flower or bird* hopes to draw us toward certain forms and habits of feeling over and about time. But copy is also that which crisis sometimes names as its resolution, or at least its deferral. When and where something is in danger of disappearing—something beautiful, for instance—copy becomes a necessity, an image, or a turn of phrase that allows for or anchors the sensory perception of some anterior presence here and now. As such, the copy animates a sometimes comforting, sometimes discordant, consciousness of and relation between absence and presence, rupture and continuity, example and principle, exchange and substitution—without which writing and thinking would be impossible, and without which we would not be able to conceive of history, whether as a line or a circle, a palimpsest or a void. Without copy, we cannot account for the promise of beauty, let alone a history of the world.

Where copy names a form and a measure for persistence over time, I turn to one of its most banal guises in the comely young woman in a beautiful dress. When I write *the comely young woman in a beautiful dress*, I presume you have already encountered her a thousand times, as a goddess, a queen, a court dancer, a schoolgirl, a painting, a beauty contestant, a dream, or a commodity. She is a luminous surface onto which we might "see" crisis, change, or continuity, inasmuch as crisis, change, and continuity are categories of history, and history comes to us through the event of language or the emergence of image. *She* is so often that language, that image, especially in a crisis during which we might register (or mourn) her impending vanishing. And when defined as an example of a principle—a national or nostalgic femininity, the promise of loving her as well as the peril of losing her—such exemplarity infuses that principle with its power.

In this chapter, she dons the Vietnamese ao dai (long dress). The fulcrum of an intense historical sensorium of aesthetics and politics, this garment, like other garments, acts as both metaphor and medium for historical sense-making, population-breaking, and population-binding. Its signature silhouette emerged in colonial Indochina and the subsequent, turbulent decades as more or less (this *more or less* is not nothing) a tunic with a darted bodice, raglan sleeves, two front and back longer panels, split from above the natural waist and falling to the knee or below and worn with trousers. In the 1930s, Nguyen Cat Tuong, a Hanoi artist and a member of Tu Luc Van Doan (Self-Reliance Literary Group), an association of Vietnamese intelligentsia committed to anticolonial and nationalist activities, introduced brightly patterned ao dai featuring French-inspired alterations—darted bodices, ruffled collars, and lace cuffs.[7] In his columns for the magazine *Phong Hoa*, accompanied by his own illustrations, Nguyen, also known as Lemur, identified beauty as an allegory for national sovereignty, and a readiness for self-rule: "Frequently the moralists say that clothes are only to be used to protect the body against the cold and the heat. What matter that they are beautiful and magnificent! In my opinion, clothes, even if they are utilized to cover the body, are the mirror reflecting the intellectual maturity of a nation. We can determine if a country is civilized and holds a concept of beauty by looking at the citizens' clothing."[8] But though the young woman in a beautiful dress might stand for sovereignty, she might also cause a scandal. Echoing studies of social and political upheaval that followed after the New Girl, Martina Thucnhi Nguyen opens her sartorial history with a dramatic scene in 1935 set at a Saigon carnival, in which a middle-aged woman lunged at a group of young women in newfangled ao dai, "colorful, diaphanous tunics with puffed sleeves, worn over flowing white trousers, accented by daintily heeled shoes," slashing at their offending garments with a sharp blade.[9] Decades later, she is less a threat than a refuge. Ao dai pageants were conceived in the late 1970s in the United States as a rebuke to the socialist regime that apocryphally disavowed the ao dai as wasteful bourgeois extravagance. Where the pageant established a diasporic distinction from a corrupted "original," the ao dai became an armament.[10] This claim, however, was counteracted as *doi moi* reforms in the 1980s swept Vietnam into the global economy, and the prime minister's wife pronounced that "the task of carefully preserving the *ao dai* of our ethnic group . . . is an issue of the utmost importance."[11] But the end of the Cold War did not mean the end of antagonism. In the new millennium, the California State Senate easily passed SR 73, a resolution naming May 15 Ao Dai Day in perpetuity (at least in California). Sponsored by an anticommunist representative, the resolution read, in part, "WHEREAS, The Vietnamese traditional long gown, known as the Áo Dài, has long been recognized as the symbol of cultural aesthetics and pride of people of Vietnamese descent; and . . . now, therefore, be it / Resolved by the Senate of the State of California, That May 15, 2016, shall be recognized as Áo Dài Day."[12]

She appears in this chapter as a stage costume, a calendar girl, and a museum artifact—in other words, a work of approximation, a copy of an original, and a fragment of an archive. On one hand, I understand the comely young woman in a beautiful dress as a medium (as sign, as habit) for the bodily semiotics and sartorial performativity of a collectivity, at times (narrated as) riven by crises such as colonialism, war, and flight. But on the other, an image is not the same as a sequence, and the young woman in a beautiful dress can only be made sense of through her seriality, her inimitable reproducibility. What she means is just as much about the forms through which she labors. In Lauren Berlant's words, let us "think about being in history as a densely corporeal, experientially felt thing whose demands on survival skills map not the whole world in one moment but a way to think about the history of sensualized epistemologies in the atmosphere of a particular moment now (aesthetically) suspended in time."[13] For this reason, I stray from a reading of the image that might seem more accountable to history and ethnographic realism, one that would demonstrate structural determination or capture the complexity of human life. Instead, I take up the sensation of *feeling historical*, or the sensation of belonging to and extending into time, to elaborate further the promise of beauty.

In short, the promise of beauty does not simply appear in representations of history as the emplotment of continuity or change, whether as gender forms or indices of modernity. Beauty is one medium for constituting the objects with or around which "history" is made perceptible in the first place, and its copy is one idiom for surviving a situation and staying in the world. Intertwining the crisis demand, the structure of the copy, the pedagogical example, heterogeneous times, and the beloved body, this chapter elaborates on some of the promises of beauty for the rest of this book.

Crisis as the Event of Knowledge

It is a commonplace to say that Vietnam is more than a war, but also—there was a war, or wars, a decade or a century or five hundred years of wars. War could be said to be a part of our condition, inasmuch as it has come to live through us and with us and in us, and we are wrought by its wages and its debts. And yet we lived, or some of us did, and the lives we are living are bound to other circumstances and demands to remember, to avenge, to suffer, to love, to go on somehow, to imagine or to refuse futures in which we were not meant to exist. What does it mean then to say, as Vuong does, we are born not of war but of beauty, if our condition (as circumstance and stipulation) of becoming beautiful is crisis?

Crisis is a historiographical concept for the interpretation of causality; that is, what has gone wrong or will, and why. Crisis appears as a unified idea in all stories about the wars in Southeast Asia, though the conditions and consequences are not subject to the same agreement. It is crisis that settles in advance the justifications for the "hot wars" of the Cold War or the global war on terror, for targeting a racial, colonial other for extractions and other operations of knowledge and power, deemed necessary because the future of humanity, or "the world as we know it," is at stake.[14] It is crisis that demanded a US client to bulwark against Chinese communism, a staged incident at the Gulf of Tonkin, the encampment of peasants in "strategic hamlets," the CIA-backed assassination of Ngo Dinh Diem, the racial calculus of Hmong recruits as proxy soldiers, and so on. Crisis is also embedded in our prognoses of consequences, or failures. Thus the disastrousness of war in Southeast Asia is variously ascribed to South Vietnamese bungling, American atrocities, Soviet overreach, military underpreparedness, overzealous bombing, failing public support, loss of will, stubborn peasants, impossible quagmires, poor diplomacy, or native unsuitability to self-government. The whole range of crisis narratives overdetermining the significance of war-making—in Southeast Asia but also in Korea, Afghanistan, or Iraq—are structured in terms of origins and causes, bad turns and worse actors, errors in valuation and strategy, secret histories and distortions from a more correct historical progression that would reveal the "truth" of history itself. Such diagnoses ascertain and evaluate the structures and events that led to crisis, including those principles, suppositions, criteria, or causal relations gone awry. But no appraisal of crisis is value neutral. A military assessment of the United States' intensive bombing of Cambodia and its degree of responsibility for the rise of the Khmer Rouge might hinge on unexamined assumptions about the necessity of geopolitical strategies such as regime change or civilian strikes and their calculable outcomes. Such an assessment cannot (or will not) question the foundational premise of collateral damage, or imperial sovereignty, in the first place. Alternately, the Vietnam-era antiwar slogan "War is not good for children or other living things" and the Art Workers' Coalition poster featuring a photograph of corpses strewn across a dirt field after the 1968 My Lai massacre, asking, "Q: And babies? A: And babies," assert a moral crisis to counter claims for bombing or other atrocities as necessary statecraft.[15]

So does the withdrawal of the United States from its disastrous wars in Southeast Asia use the idiom of crisis as a turning point in the history of the world. Crisis is used to characterize the hasty evacuation of hundreds of thousands of Saigonese in cargo aircraft and freighters; the expedited legislation granting some refugees from South Vietnam unprecedented large-scale entry to, and residence in, the United States; the hundreds of thousands more refugees who sought escape on the high seas, with those who survived rescued or remaindered to camps throughout the Pacific. And just as the crisis concept diagnoses incommensurable or interrupted conditions, it also describes the potential for a new form of historical subject—the refugee, figured as the consequence of crisis and a crisis object in herself.

If crisis narratives are sometimes closures, they are also sometimes openings for new actions, new feelings, and new arrangements; the refugee is cited as one such closure, and one such opening. Ethnographic or sociological narratives about refugees posit the crisis of statelessness as a causal condition for pathology (figured variously as traumatic compulsion, criminal activity, or welfare dependency), centered on normative measures of self-possession as health; at other times these accounts locate crisis as a plot point to unfold stories about refugees navigating what is overwhelming, and sometimes building anew—families, enclaves, industries, selves.[16] That is, crisis is narrated as an *event of knowledge*, as an irruption that demands explanation, clarification, contemplation, or calculation. For instance, Vinh Nguyen theorizes *refugeetude* as an "enduring creative force" that is not "an irregularity or disruption of political personhood—a crisis to be resolved—but an experiential resource for developing significant and durable ways of being in and moving through the world"; Evyn Lê Espiritu Gandhi posits the "refugee settler condition" as "the vexed positionality of refugee subjects whose citizenship in a settler colonial state is predicated upon the unjust dispossession of an Indigenous population"; while Trung Phan Quoc Nguyen worries at the liberal reformist impulses that belong to the "op-ed form of the Vietnamese refugee" who analogizes their crisis to comment on contemporary states of emergency in Syria, Afghanistan, Ukraine, or Palestine.[17] In their work, and the work of others, refugee figurations come to stand for or to precipitate crises of the nation-state, citizenship, kinship, humanity, empire, temporal consciousness, sovereignty, and even beauty as the measure of the health and hale of these norms and forms of status-being. As a director of donor development for a nongovernmental aid organization said about another set of refugees, "In the media, refugees are portrayed deprived of their dignity, without any beauty left in them."[18] At the same time, Little Dog claims for himself, for his mother, the beauty of living through terror: "Let no one mistake us for the fruit of violence—but that violence, having passed through the fruit, failed to spoil it."[19]

And yet crisis is not a self-explanatory concept. Crisis purports to diagnose a decisive moment during which some imbalance or contradiction has derailed the course of historical certainty or, as Gayatri Chakravorty Spivak argues, the point at which the "presumptions of an entire enterprise are disproved by the enterprise itself."[20] This *moment of truth* is a familiar structure across narrativizations of history, including the survival or demise of a political entity or order, but also the personal revelation or conversion. In some, crisis establishes the conditions for a more perfectible form (also known as individual growth, social progress, or the moral arc of the universe) or more devastating ruin (such as trauma or civilizational collapse); in others, crisis is inherent in the structural contradictions of history (which also go by dialectics or antinomies).

However, the crisis concept is not an ontological description of historical time but an interpretation of its meaning. Reinhart Koselleck elaborates a conceptual history in which crisis is apprehended as history itself, or, as Janet Roitman puts it, "It is in that sense that crisis is the means to 'access' history and to qualify 'history' as such: crisis marks history and crisis generates history."[21] The narrativization of crisis organizes and supplies sense and significance, even and perhaps especially when that sense and significance break down or are perceived to be at their limit (the *now, more than ever*). Crisis is thus a cognate of critique, per Koselleck, because it is the judgment of history, and the determinations of the limits of reason and knowledge; Roitman tells us, "It equally serves expectations for world-immanent justice, or the faith that history is the ultimate form of judgment."[22] So while crisis could be anything we must survive or push against—a syndrome, a crime, a sudden illness, a bad situation, a sentence, or a war—it is also the condition of thinking ourselves as subjects who might, or must, act on history.[23]

Crisis is a being-toward-life as well as a being-toward-death; it solicits from us, as Thi Bui puts it in her refugee memoir, *the best we can do*. This is also an aesthetics, a sensorium through which our experiences of lifeworlds are made perceptible, which can include both knowledge of violence but also knowledge of its erstwhile others, such as beauty.

The promise of beauty is therefore an account of an event, the world in which it occurs, and our place within it. Where the status-being of beauty (or our narration of it) communicates to others a situation, a beautiful object (which at times is also a subject, which is not to say that in its objecthood it does not act) might easily come to organize knowledge about *crisis* in order to resolve its disturbance or reestablish a principle. This principle summons a specific quality—again, beauty—which cuts across time and space as a relay or structure for the human condition, as the desire to see an object endure longer in the world because we cannot bear to lose it, or for others to have never known it. *It* could be an empire or a colony, a museum or a painting; *it* could also be a person we love, or a house with a door. That is, where crisis is the event of knowledge, beauty is at times its precondition. Someone might murmur, passing a rotting house in the Ninth Ward in New Orleans, or a deforested habitat in Oregon, or a once-elegant neoclassical skyscraper in Detroit, "It was so beautiful before x happened...." Where beauty is vulnerable, or imperiled, the circumstances that led to its historical situation become clearer as a crisis story. And it is as a situation or a story that beauty also occasions the arrangement of time and space for life, death, and what lies between them—joy, mourning, renewal, ritual, or perseverance, for example. Christina Sharpe writes about her mother's Christmas ornaments, red felt hearts held together with straight pins, handmade even as she was dying, "What is beauty made of? Attentiveness whenever possible to a kind of aesthetic that escaped violence whenever possible—even if it is only the perfect arrangement of pins."[24]

And so beauty demands a reckoning with history, including histories of violence whose eclipse, correction, or transcendence conjures beauty as a promise to come together whether time marches on, or stops or stutters. To borrow an apt phrase from Roland Barthes, the promise of beauty is *a clock for seeing*, for making sense of a historical situation. Toward the end of the letter that is his novel for his mother, which she will never be able to read because she lacks English literacy, Little Dog ropes his stubborn sense of beauty to crisis, and to creation as stubborn persistence. "Yes, there was a war. Yes, we came from its epicenter. In that war, a woman gifted herself a new name—Lan—in that naming claimed herself beautiful, then made that beauty into something worth keeping. From that, a daughter was born, and from that daughter, a son. All this time I told myself we were born from war—but I was wrong, Ma. We were born from beauty."[25]

Violence, having passed through the fruit, failed to spoil it, grants an aesthetic or ethnographic detail its narrative importance. Or perhaps it is the other way around, and the detail grants crisis its significance. Fashioned from such details that compose her geometry (openings, closings, limbs, stitches, cuts), the comely young woman in a beautiful dress is no longer herself as she once was, and we are called on to be responsible to history through her image. To this end she is addressed to you, to me, to a "we" that is propositional, temporary, and precarious, gesturing toward another world—one in which we were once "whole," or another in which we are yet to become so. No wonder the young woman in the beautiful dress seems to overtly call forth certain methods for historical and ethnographic inquiry, or an elaboration of its subjective sensorium. In the usual manner, we might seek out her precedents in the archive (and perhaps find none, or only loose threads), adjudicate claims to originality or significance (whose hands first lay the bias seam, for instance), and write narrative histories or challenge extant ones. At times it is her individual inconsequentiality (because she is often anonymous, one of hundreds or more just like her) that is also the premise of her exemplarity. Her figuration, we might then argue, establishes intelligible patterns through which the pursuit of historical realism and ethnographic arguments unfold to make narrative or analytic claims about what she stands for, how she came to do so, and how in doing so she bears the burden of illustration for gender, nation, memory, history, and crisis. These concerns are known, despite their possible inversion, fragmentation, translation, citation, and destruction, because they are repeated so often. Just as the dress is always more than one—as a garment, a pattern—so is the one who wears it. Both solicit fidelity to a form, *her* form, that exists only through its copy.

To follow *the comely young woman in a beautiful dress* around, then, does not necessarily require reference to an interiority of intention or feeling, nor discovery of her origin. We could instead focus our attention on the specific forms of her accumulation, across which she might appear indistinguishable or discontinuous from an original or others as-like herself, and through which she might preserve essence or create rupture. Such palimpsestic forms are crucial where some figures—not just a body, or even an ideal body, but the amalgam of a body and its ornaments—especially "condens[e] and displac[e] the ecstasies and terrors of political life."[26] We can observe the significance of her copy to the perception of coherence for a collectivity, and more so in an emergency—or in the need to insist there is one.

In her work on the "veiled sister" of Iranian modernity, Minoo Moallem describes the commemoration of a specific body, what she calls a civic body, that "makes it possible for national and transnational forms of governmentality to contain the disruptive influences of history, class, race, gender, and sexuality by creating *sites of repetition*."[27] Such a figure mediates the structure of feeling of national or diasporic persistence, thematizing the conception of a "we" within a changing situation as an aesthetic and pedagogical problem. And indeed, as a refugee child sponsored to snow-white Minnesota, I forbore under the ubiquitous presence of the ao dai as a reminder of a serial femininity anchoring a scattered people. Daily I saw her as a performer on the bootleg VHS tapes my parents brought home, with the glitches and degraded resolution that testified to their being poor copies, or as a calendar girl hung in our laundry and storage room, as I dipped into our twenty-five-pound sack of jasmine rice.[28] Cheap advertisements for the local Vietnamese groceries and restaurants established along Nicollet Avenue, these ao dai calendars (more than irregular visits to temple or special occasions) measured refugee persistence via a continuity of form—one that sought to recruit me too into this series. While the promise of her beauty might seem banal or overly familiar, hers is also a story about *feeling historical*, and that is not simple at all.

Through both crisis and beauty as genres of narrativization, the dress and the beloved body who wears it not only connote contingency, vulnerability, and ephemerality but also furnish the grounds to then secure them against the ravages of time. In reflecting on *the comely young woman in a beautiful dress* as the most common and pervasive signifier of national love among a people, and as a manner of denoting "history" itself, I am not concerned to trace a precise history of *this* dress—its cut, its details.[29] Not that this would not be useful. Tracing a sartorial habit is a cultural history, which is a history of gender forms, which is a history of the human (and its others) in time and space. Such a contentious history is not beside the point, but it is also not *my* point.[30] Rather than simply repeat what I mean to unpack—that is, the reiteration of its ethnographic significance (to say that it stands for some quality of being Vietnamese is not quite an explanation, and it is certainly not a question)—what else can this accumulation tell us about *feeling historical*? How do we take the concept of the young woman in a beautiful dress and give it new life, animating her historical register to ask about the regularities and ruptures of time, and the narrativity her form deploys?

Doing so would become not a question of rediscovering what might bolster an assertion (she stands for this or that), but of following the conditions of emergence for such beautiful objects, the specific forms of their modes of being, and the principles according to which they shift or stay.

Cover Girl

As things fall apart, we make promises to protect, preserve, and make present what is at risk—all that we hold dear to us, and to others with whom we might share a historical consciousness. Copy is one form through which we might do so, loosely conceived as whatever seeks some likeness—whether through a child, a poem, a student, a sketch, a photograph, a pose, a commodity, or an analogy—to conjure some part of an irreducible presence that (narratively) precedes its copy.[31] Without copy, an object, person, scene, or world is at risk of disappearance, decay, or destruction. Each of these conditions, while not the same, nonetheless ends in void. When Vuong writes, "I want to insist that our being alive is beautiful enough to be worthy of replication," he gives shape to the style and the structure that might allow us to reencounter ourselves and our memories, fantasies, promises, grievances, and their tempos.

Take Dalena, a statuesque all-American blonde who is also a Vietnamese singing sensation. In the 1990s, Dalena became a worldwide star through the US-based diasporic entertainment industry, yielding over fifty albums and scores of VHS tapes and DVDs of her music videos, concert appearances, and performances at variety shows filmed before live audiences for wider distribution around the Vietnamese-speaking world.[32] Born in Muncie, Indiana, and "discovered" in a Chinese restaurant in Orlando, where she also worked part-time as a cast member at Walt Disney World, Dalena is the virtuoso performance of an apparently flawless imitation. Nguyen T. Tan-Hoang's video essay *Cover Girl: A Gift from God* (2000) is a meditation on this anachronistically wholesome vocalist, drawing promiscuously from a decade of videos and performances to consider the copy that herself becomes auratic. An economy of poor images, to gesture to Hito Steyerl, including substandard resolution and ghostly images, compressed, remixed, copied, pasted into other videos or sequences (such as those found in *Cover Girl*), follows after Dalena and informs her celebrity.[33] But copy here does not just refer to the medium of production, distribution, and redistribution (as much-pirated material, for instance), though I return to it later through other plural objects.[34] Instead, it points to her presence within a history that

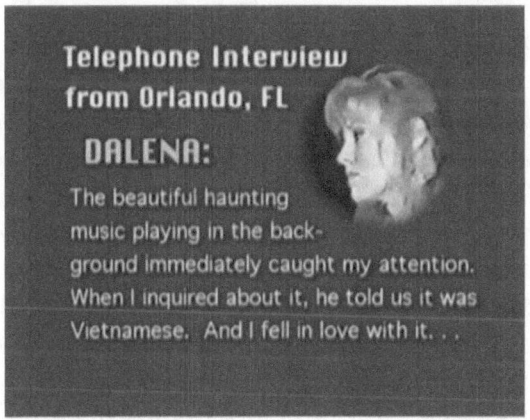

Figures 1.1–1.3. Still images from *Cover Girl: A Gift from God*, dir. Nguyen T. Tan-Hoang, 2000.

is not hers. In an uncanny palimpsest, *Cover Girl* features a layered rumination in which a quote from a *New York Times* profile titled "Miss Saigon, U.S.A.," crawls below a disembodied mouth framed by a black screen. A voice, out of sync with the movements of the smiling lips, demonstrates the Vietnamese tonal vowels as the words roll across: "Her long blond hair, blue eyes, and round, healthy face evoke the sunshine of Indiana, where she was born. Her full, melodious voice, with its mysterious minor undertones and subtle quaver, seems to flow directly from the mist-shrouded valleys of Vietnam, where she has never been."[35]

Does Dalena embody a stereotype, a misrepresentation, or a false mirror? Is this appropriation, or appreciation? Does it matter that she says she does it for love of the Vietnamese, and that "we" love her for it? What does it mean to propose these questions, and not others? What can we make of this sort of presence—nonidentical but nonsingular, elliptical, and partial? It is worth turning to Jacques Derrida, who turned to writing to propose a structure for the logic of the supplement. He describes a logocentrism in which speech is assigned a "truer," more immediate self-presence, and writing is a "dangerous supplement" that substitutes itself for that presence. The risk is that the supplement—found in the (written) image, the (substitute) copy—will be mistaken for that which makes the "world move."[36] According to this logic, the origin is constituted by that which threatens its presence and yet also prolongs it. As such Derrida suggests that the supplement is both accretion and substitution, which means that the supplement is "not more a signified than a signifier, a representer than a presence, a writing than a speech."[37] Or as Barbara Johnson writes, A is multiple things to B at once: A is substitute or "mere" ornament, compensation or usurper, restoration or alienation, seduction or failure; B is meaningful inasmuch as A cumulates or obviates its presence *as* presence. To this end, Little Dog is writing a letter to his illiterate mother in place of the words he cannot say. The passage through writing is a repair, "by a certain absence and by a sort of calculated effacement, of presence disappointed of itself in speech."[38]

It is as a supplement that copy incites a set of possible narrativizations of crisis. Copy might trigger a crisis (because the copy diminishes or displaces the aura of the original), or signal that a crisis is happening (because the original is threatened), or resolve a crisis (because the original is lost but through the copy some part of it can be found again). We could call these crisis-copies forgery, preservation, and restoration. The copy might also be the democratization of art, through which one might be given the right to copy a manuscript, a painting, or a film, or choose to violate intellectual property for others to have the benefit of it. (This is called piracy.) Another narrativization is the bad copy, which threatens to turn a principle into a parody, and what Hito Steyerl dubs *the poor image*. Poor in resolution and genealogy, it circulates as a compression of copy-events that leave no easily discernible forensic trace, the degraded debris of a global economy.[39] And because one must have knowledge of an original, its features and their interrelationships, to understand an object, person, or scene as a copy, a copy might also prompt an interruption of knowledge (as the confusion of categories) or its vindication (as a sign of expertise), as when the modernist avant-garde sought to undermine the myths of originality (while inventing new ones) with their circulation of mass-produced objects such as urinals and soup cans into the rarefied realm of Art, and as now Chinese copy villages generate thousands of handmade oil paintings for a global market in bootleg van Goghs and Matisses.[40] It might animate the uncanny too, as when a simulation, an image, or a puppet approaches too close to the threshold of a human original, or when the photograph discloses its funereal nature. "A shudder runs through the viewer of old photographs," Siegfried Kracauer warns, "for they make visible not the knowledge of the original but the spatial configuration of a moment; what appears in the photograph is not the person but the sum of what can be subtracted from him or her."[41] Whether the copy assumes the positivist form of appearing *as* or *like* or *in place of* something else that is its precedent, the judgment of a copy is never just about content or appearance but also about its promise.

When defined as a problem, the copy establishes the division between the original and the copy, measuring the accumulated density of one against the irreducible difference of the other. In doing so, it presents a methodological dilemma—how to make sense of resemblance or succession? To commence sense-making from an original might subordinate all that follows to a principle preestablished as its measure and its magnitude. But the promise of an original is often only secured by a spectrum of afterimages, whether literary descriptions, photographs, illustrations, cinematic scenes, or digital files. If I were to name a likely antecedent for the ubiquitous vision of "girls . . . seen riding along the streets of Saigon on motor bikes with the back of their ao dai flying loose, causing foreigners to comment that they look like butterflies, and beautiful ones at that," I would have to observe that this original is already a copy; she appears before us not as presence but already as beautiful image.[42] That is to say that this particular apocryphal original has already circulated in many forms, including its reproducible forms, and all those held as memory, knowledge, souvenir.

This same operation makes the copy a solution in other situations. Establishing that something is worthy of replication into the future, Dalena's commercial success points to how a copy of an original might itself become an exemplary figuration. Here the scene of citation, repetition, and interpretation carries with it a both temporal and affective dimension that lends weight to her performance. Most often clad in a modest ao dai (though for her iconic recital as Christine, she wore a long, white dressing gown to duet with the tuxedo-clad Phantom of the Opera), Dalena sings *only* covers, never original compositions. As Nguyen observes, "These songs are occasionally spiced up with whatever musical trend is in at the moment . . . but they're still the same old songs. This classic case of the compulsion to repeat reflects the desire of overseas Vietnamese to preserve the memory of home. That is to say, the uncorrupted precommunist Vietnam that they love, cherish, and left behind."[43] Her skillful mimicry of the Vietnamese tonal language and its intricate modulations in the standards of her song repertoire—popular sentimental ballads about love, lost or absent loves, the hope for love's return—bind Dalena to her audience and her audience to the performance's object of love, which is themselves. As Karen Tongson writes about reality television singing competitions, the cover song grants to an audience the chance to assess the "performance of a piece of an already existing repertoire [that] rings most true because it most sounds like a copy of *us*." She continues, clarifying that a *copy of us* "indicates a capacity to excel beyond our preordained station in life by expressing a passion and desire that can only be mediated by someone else's music and the experience of it."[44] Or as a voice-over from *Cover Girl* announces, "People appreciate Dalena because she appreciates them."[45]

A *copy of us* contains a multitude. Naming the relationship between the object at hand and its presumably indexical nature, the example allows us to discover a law or a principle, and is also its means of transmission. Or, as Jeffrey Nealon puts it, "Perhaps the example is a kind of promise: it promises further and more specific elaboration of the principle under discussion. The example is, in fact, a radically singular promise: I promise here and now to elaborate a point with an example."[46] By necessity, beauty lends itself to examples because it is immense, inexhaustible; as Steven Shaviro abridges Kant, "Each encounter with beauty is something entirely new; each aesthetic judgment responds to a contingency. This is why beauty is *incommunicable*; it cannot be copied and imitated. . . . Rather, Kant says, beauty is *exemplary*."[47] But the example is not singular, or alone. Elsewhere, Derrida outlines its nature: "An example always carries beyond itself: it thereby opens up a testamentary dimension. The example is first of all for others, and beyond the self."⁴⁸ In scaling from singular to general, object to principle, the example is instructive. Not only does the example organize a sensus communis to observe it, and thus to know it, but the example also solicits more like itself.⁴⁹ Establishing the possibility of another to come, the example cannot be an example unless it inspires reproducibility. In a circular manner, as is the way with these things, the copy is the precondition for the example. In other words, both copy *and* example present "a partial object, detached from a set . . . of which it would form part."⁵⁰ But repetition or replication is not (necessarily) petrification. Not only can the copy *not* be the same as the original for it to be evidence and example, but the original is only anything like an antecedent *once it is copied*—and in being copied, it becomes an example too.

Here I follow once again from Barbara Johnson, who, writing about writing, observes it as "an attempt to comprehend that which it is comprehended by."⁵¹ One of the most common forms of copy found in crisis is described as *heritage*, through which the copy that attests to the original becomes itself precious and dear. Heritage inscribes an iterative sense of genealogy through copies of aesthetic objects or formal conventions or habits, such as holidays, recipes, or garments, that organize time and history for our perception. Because heritage assumes sequence and succession, these objects, conventions, or habits are freighted with historical depth through their inimitable reproducibility. In *The Archaeology of Knowledge*, Michel Foucault offers, almost as a throwaway, "Take the notion of tradition: it is intended to give a special temporal status to a group of phenomena that are both successive and identical (or at least similar); it makes it possible to rethink the dispersion of history in the form of the same; it allows a reduction of the difference proper to every beginning, in order to pursue without discontinuity the endless search for the origin; tradition enables us to isolate the new against a background of permanence."⁵² In this way, copy is how we are kept in continuous contact with the principle's presence; repetition renders its radical nonsingularity recognizable as evidence of promises kept. To inhabit the serial body of the comely young woman in a beautiful dress, for instance, is to approximate ideal properties pre-scripted and rehearsed according to forms already given.

What does it mean to grasp an essence or a principle through the accumulation of its examples? Dalena, for one (who is not one), is exemplary because her copy is pure copy. Her flawless iteration of a serial femininity does not emanate from some original essence but instead through her spectacular labor of love. Not only is Dalena a blonde, blue-eyed Midwesterner, but she does not understand Vietnamese (or so the mythology goes). The particular pleasure of her performance lies in such wonder, felt on first hearing or seeing *her* in an ao dai emote in faultless Vietnamese, and subsequent anticipation, during which we await that wonder's echo (or its failure).[53] That the uncanny pronunciation of this "milk-and-honey American beauty" is matched by her reputed unfamiliarity with meaning (she sings "without understanding a word") is central to the sacred nature of her "gift from God."[54] This is what makes her copy original, because her precise capture of the referent requires no knowledge of it.[55] (She reportedly learned her songs phonetically, asking translators to transcribe the separate syllables as pronounced, and then to sing the lyrics so she could watch how they formed the sounds with their mouths.) If her seemingly perfect interpretation with no metaphysical origin appears at first discordant, that it then appears exemplary suggests that it is *because* she is unique in her particular emulation that she is *also* the instantiation of a general principle. So when Foucault adds that "things . . . are duplicated not only by copy or translation, but by exegesis, commentary, and the internal proliferation of meaning," we can make sense of the persistent rumor that Dalena must have some unknown Vietnamese ancestor (she is "actually" a genetic copy), or the sense of awe that is a testimonial to her labor of love ("we" are the original she cannot bear to see vanish from the world).[56] Still, that she is not Vietnamese after all is not a problem because already given forms, cohered under names including *tradition*, *heritage*, and *nature*, absorb such repetitions or supplements into historical categories.

In other words, Dalena's copy is how a collectivity knows we are still beautiful despite the ruptures of history. This copy evinces the heterogeneous relationship of the object to the past *and* the future, and though it is not the same as the original, it *is* a new original, or an original repetition. Famously, Walter Benjamin assumes that perfect reproduction, in which it is no longer possible to visually distinguish between an original and the copy, would not mean the end of all distinction. He argues that the original carries an aura that the copy does not, because of its *here and now*: "The here and now of the original constitutes the concept of its authenticity, and on the latter in turn is founded the idea of a tradition which has, to the present day, passed this object down as the same identical thing."[57] But Benjaminian aura is about the irreproducibility of a particular time and place; this does not mean that the original cannot be copied, or that the copy (which cannot occupy the same time and place as the original) cannot itself constitute another *here and now*. Indeed, the copy and its distinction from others in a chain might not be the disruption of a principle or presence, but their extension.

Calendar Girls

Our perception of time is an aesthetic sense-making. Dalena's flawless performance, as one example, is a particular experience of time through which the end of a world is not the end of a feeling of life being furthered. Her copy renders past events such as war and flight into a singular intelligible form, one so resilient that even a stranger to us might appreciate "our" beauty and wish to duplicate it. In other words, do we need an origin to perceive time or its passage as a duration, or will a copy do? In writing about minor gestures, of which the copy might be one, Erin Manning observes, "Persistence is never persistence of the same, but persistence of a cut that activates the conditions for a seriality in the making."[58] While at times an assignment of causality, intention, or eventfulness, at other times seriality carries its own temporal mass. Here the observation of surface or form is key to the historicity of the apocryphal image—not its actual history but the fantasy in there being an origin, essence, or principle. (And the origin of which part? The woman, the dress, or the genre in which she makes her presence known?)[59] A copy does not redeem the inviolability of an original but the possibility of a relationship to it. In other words, seriality makes the thing present at all.

Something like an ao dai calendar thus demands our attention to forms of auratic objecthood that stem not from originality but from inimitable reproducibility. Published since 1996 by the Minneapolis-based photographer Hoai Nam, the *Ao Trang* (white dress) calendar is not like the calendars of my refugee childhood, which featured colorful, glittering ao dai and studio backdrops (or heavily pixelated ones) of rice fields and willow trees. Instead, its painterly photographs lament the displacement of a people through a fascination with the surfaces and details of the most iconic image of the ao dai—a schoolgirl's white uniform. On the twelve-by-twelve cover photograph for the 2009 *Ao Trang* calendar, a young woman bends forward from her waist, her arms wrapped around her knees. Its shallow depth of field thrusts her toward the front of the picture plane, which is closely cropped around the triangle of empty space between breasts and arms and thighs. The photograph is suffused with a cool, pearly luminosity, merging background and foreground as a smooth, continuous envelope. We only know she is clothed at all because of the hallucinogenic detail of a slight stretch in the fabric under her arm, a wrinkle caressing the curve of her breast, the barely perceptible appearance of a seam running vertically down her side. These details arouse the eye to the sensuousness of silk on skin, and to the diminished contrast between them.[60] The ao dai is central to a diasporic erotic,

Figure 1.4. *Ao Trang*, 2009, Hoai Nam.

what I have elsewhere described as the consciousness of crisis-disturbance unfolding through allegories of love.[61] If, as Berlant describes, "love is a formal promise and an aspiration to try and try again to intend to be faithful to an enduring project of projection, mirroring, and repetition," then copy is sometimes a ritual of love.[62] Someone—it could be you or me—acts in response to a stimulus or an event in order for something beautiful to endure beyond that moment, a mixtape or a photograph of _____ (a song, a face, a feeling) experienced again for the first time.

The ao dai is an amalgam of arrested moments and details—the mandarin collar, the darted silhouette, the raglan sleeves—in its most recognizable form. But its copy also includes the transformation of the one who poses into another body, an image-body who shimmers into being before us as a column of light poured into a pristine envelope. Against portraiture, the subject of the *Ao Trang* photograph is not an individual in the humanist sense. It is instead a *collectivity* that is the unique being found in the photograph. Barthes explains, "Once I feel myself observed by the lens, everything changes: I constitute myself in the process of 'posing.' I instantaneously make another body for myself, I transform myself in advance into an image."[63] Contemplating this phenomenon of multiples, he continues, "In front of the lens, I am at the same time: the one I think I am, the one I want others to think I am, the one the photographer thinks I am, and the one he makes use of to exhibit his art."[64] To put it differently, the woman who slips into the pearl-pale sheath and coils her body into a sorrowful shape is in an important sense not the subject of the photograph. Posing in anticipation of becoming a nonsingular body in advance of the image's manufacture, she assumes the essence of a form predetermined by the principle she embodies or duplicates, and transposes its history (and its myth) into an image. Or, as the photographer assays, "I want the focus to be on the *ao dai*, the curves and the emotions of the photo, not the model."[65] This cognizance (which we can also call *feeling historical*) secures permanence through reproducibility, which is to say, the ao dai establishes a world, and how she is to inhabit it.

The body that poses also names for us certain media for ensuring that continued presence. For *Ao Trang*, the photograph is an apparatus for both return and anticipation, through which presence and absence, singularity and repetition, stasis and movement, first time and forever are tangled together. It is the medium for and is also itself a beautiful and beloved body, capturing in light and shadow a seemingly unambiguous presence even while bearing within it a great and terrible silence. In search of his mother, Barthes confessed that when he looks at a photograph he sees "only the referent, the desired object, the beloved body."[66] Through this medium, he suggested that love, "extreme love," enabled him to "erase the weight of the image" to see not the photograph but the object of his desire.[67] At the same time, Barthes could not dismiss the actual *thing* before him: "I am delighted (or depressed) to know that the thing of the past, by its immediate radiations (its luminances), has really touched the surface, which in its turn my gaze will touch."[68] Laura Marks, in her essay "Loving a Disappearing Image," describes how a viewer might identify with a decaying or disintegrating film or videotape. Such haptic or tactile visuality, she intuits, questions the consequences for dying images and images of death when the locus of identification and subjectivity shifts from the human figure to the surface of the image. Through a series of experimental films and videos—primarily erotic ones, ones that mourn love gone missing—she looks to these forms that concretize loss in an object, not just as a reference to an original but as itself a beloved object that dissolves and diminishes from view. The fullness of the image as presence is continuously crumbling, due both to film's (and our) fragile materiality as well as the passage of time; the promise lingers as residue or ruin. "We mourn the passing of the young lovers/actors because we are sure that they existed: the photograph is a sort of umbilical cord between the thing photographed 'then' and our gaze 'now.'"[69] But we need not be sure that these lovers existed *in reality* for us to mourn their passing; it is enough to know that they *might have*. If, as Marks argues, "disappearance restores aura to the work . . . as images decay they become unique again," then disappearance as an aesthetics generates aura for the copy-image of a beloved body.[70]

An aesthetics of *feeling historical* thus lies in an ambiguous pleasure in what one has missed, is missing. To feel this way, the *Ao Trang* photographs refer nostalgically to that property located in the shimmering celluloid images of the early twentieth century—glamour, or what Judith Brown calls a radiance of form. Glacial in their composition, these photographs partake in a modernist aesthetic she describes as "the draining of life into black-and-white images, stylized form, and a literature that so frequently—and lyrically—circulates around abstraction, loss, and a central, structuring emptiness."[71] Ao dai are lustrous sheaths or, to borrow from Brown, evocatively, "luminous envelope[s]"; in an ao trang, she appears to be sculpted from marble or porcelain, her incandescence a talisman against an encroaching dark.[72] Sleeves and collars merge almost invisibly into delicate wrists and elongated necks, while barely-there seams stretch taut to outline rounded shoulders and breasts.[73] Backgrounds are often empty of detail or setting; some are completely black or blank. At times she is sequestered within interior spaces whose proportions are registered through intimation rather than dimension. Claustrophobic dioramas show her in private reflection, bending close over an open book, an oil lamp, or a sheaf of wheat; her knees are pulled close to her chest, head tilted forward or laid on folded arms. Shadows accumulate and call attention to corporeal form, curves emerging from the page through subtle gradations of light. She is sinuously enfolded by large, curling leaves or floating sheers; or she is caught in an invisible undertow, her tresses and silks drifting like seaweed; or she wanders ethereal visions of nature, barefoot and alone. Her ao trang glows luminously against an unnaturally red-orange pillow of autumnal leaves or drags in the wavelets lapping at the bright edge of an endless shore. Folded in on herself or turned away, her head bowed and shoulders rounded with reverie, she is photographed in postures of quiescence or expectant waiting.

The *Ao Trang* calendar builds toward an idea of a disrupted but continuous history as an accumulation of copies that serves as evidence for an object's inimitable reproducibility, imbued with fantasies of love. As the camera lingers on every contour and surface of this *luminous envelope,* an intense absorption imbues the ao dai as a souvenir from another time and place. Originally a seventeenth-century medical term for pathological sadness among exiles, aroused by the desire to return home, nostalgia, as Bliss Cua Lim notes, eventually came to describe a more generalized condition of longing for a prior moment.[74] Or, as one year's English introduction to the calendar names its melancholic pleasures, "The images of *Ao Trang* (white dress) Calendar have been known for their poetic essence and romantic ambiance. They depict a moment of nostalgia, a remembrance of things past. Forever more, the purity of simplicity of *Ao Trang* remains a timeless inspiration." Nostalgia's appropriative incorporation of the past stages a temporal cohabitation with a reproducible detail, moment, or fragment whose time and place of *here and now* are insurmountable. The photographer Hoai Nam returned to Vietnam as a young man who then fell in love at first sight. "I was struck by the beauty of the schoolgirls in *ao dai trang* strolling down the street. I'd never seen anything so angelic and pure. . . . The image surpassed what I'd envisioned it would be."[75] Of this vision and his devotion, he muses in an interview, "I lost something I never had."[76] Derrida again: "Repetition *and* first time, but also repetition *and* last time, since the singularity of any *first time* makes of it also a *last time.*"[77] In the same moment he first sees her, he loses her; but he is always already losing her, because she first appeared to him as an *image*, which means that every sighting since is the ghost of a ghost.

The highly abstract composition of the *Ao Trang* photographs underpins this historical consciousness of loss and mortality. Its carefully staged tableaux are set outside of time while evincing, per Rey Chow (writing about the lush, sensuous films of Zhang Yimou featuring young women suffering beautifully), a "belated fascination with its own datedness, its own alterity."[78] She continues, "What are 'subjective' origins now include a memory of past *objecthood*—the experience of being looked at—which lives on in the subjective act of ethnographizing like an other, an optical unconscious."[79] In other words, these photographs can only reference themselves *as images*, as a history of images. Because photography allows us to apprehend time as duration precisely through making a cut in its flow, Benjamin's photoconductive analogy bears repeating here. "To articulate the past historically does not mean to recognize it 'the way it really was.' . . . It means to seize hold of a memory as it flashes up at a moment of danger."[80] Cast in repetitive scenarios that exemplify historical forms or forms that *feel* historical, the calendar girl cannot but reference her own interrupted passage through time. It is no coincidence that the photographs recall another event for wearing ao trang—rituals of mourning. It is precisely because of a historical consciousness of alienation—as a consequence of crisis, and as crisis itself—that these photographs resist foreclosure on the past and its innumerable losses through time's dilation. Danger lurks outside the frame, and the danger is history itself.

Historical orders are also aesthetic arrangements, inscribing knowledge and politics for the apprehension of time, through practices of legitimation that are indispensable to heritage preservation, imperial logistics, or speculative futures in the thing itself. Such aesthetic arrangements include the clock, the timeline, and the calendar. Henri Bergson, for instance, writes that the line traversing space "does not symbolize the time which is passing" but instead marks the historical consciousness of its passage.[81] Meryem-Bahia Arfaoui observes the compulsory time of the colony as "a bunch of notches on a timeline follow[ing] the march of progress demonstrated by an arrow moving from left to right which represents past, present, and future—implicitly suggesting that writing in the other direction would be like regressing, going against progress."[82] An instrument for time measurement and discipline, the calendar standardizes duration as a linear succession of uniform periods and intervals through its aesthetic formalization as a grid.[83] The graphic form of the grid renders and regularizes time though singularity and copy, each square a unique unit within a sequence that repeats over and over again, though as Rosalind Krauss warns, "The grid's mythic power is that it makes us able to think we are dealing with materialism (or sometimes science, or logic) while at the same time it provides us with a release into belief (or illusion, or fiction)."[84] Between ghosts and grids, in other words, the comely young woman in a beautiful dress is also herself a calendar.[85]

Through her, the feminine allegorizes time or times, teleological and linear on one hand, and recurring and looping on the other, in the order of the visible. Feminist scholars have long observed that between woman and nation is a necessary movement (or movements) that renders the feminine a performative register of national duration.[86] The significance of her garment, then, is a constitutive rather than exterior feature of this organization of time and space; the gendering of national time through the

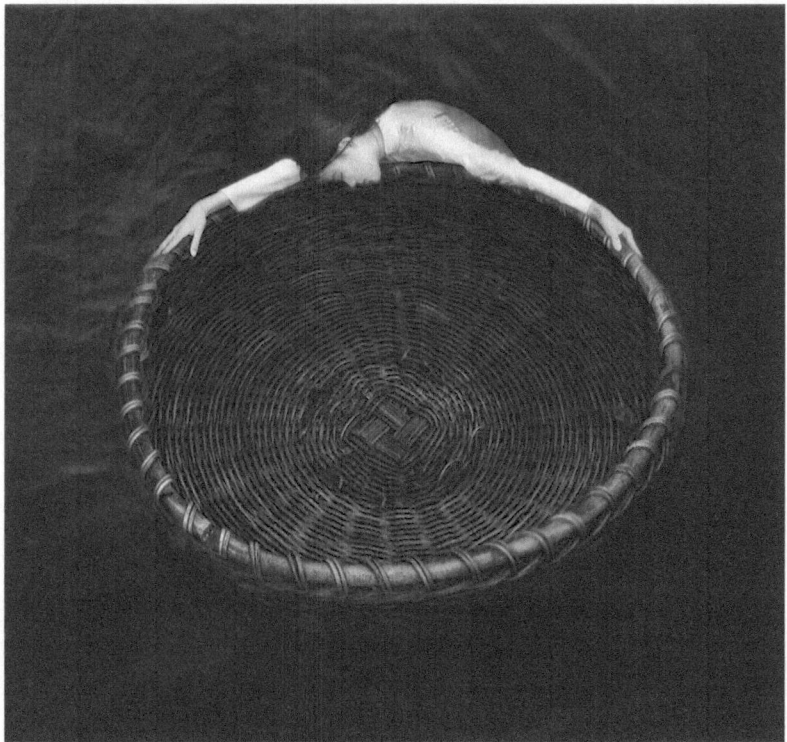

Figure 1.5. *Ao Trang*, 2008, Hoai Nam.

hem or the sleeve or the shoe is mobilized to resolve the familiar temporal paradox that lies between the recent invention of the nation as a political form and its felt quality of endurance. Between woman and nation is her garment (or *the* garment, whether ao dai, sari, terno, qi pao, chador, thobe, etc.), shaping how we perceive historical continuity or change. Such temporalization of the garment conjoins the concrete and empirical to the abstract and conceptual. In her study about the heeled shoe in 1930s China, Dorothy Ko astutely argues, "The demands placed on the modern woman are thus inherently contradictory: as a member of the nation she is to race time and march forward; as a woman she is to remain static, if not outside of temporality altogether—or at least give the illusion of stillness; herein lies the import of dress in altering the viewer's experience with time."[87]

This threshold is discernible in one *Ao Trang* series depicting the departure from a war-torn country. Restaging the scene of emergency, the calendar demonstrates how, as David L. Eng and David Kazanjian write, "apprehensions of and attachments to loss and its phantasms never simply dwell in the past, for the very process of narrativizing loss orients an impulse toward the future."[88] On its cover, a woman in an ao trang stretches out her arms to grasp the rim of what appears to be a large woven basket. This basket is also a boat—a small, round bamboo boat that is a small-scale replica of those still found among fishing villages along the Vietnamese coast. Her face in profile, her eyes closed, and her black hair unbound, this dark photograph is infused with a morbid mood. If freedom is found in this basket boat (literally so, as the cover image inscribes the word *freedom* in red script inside the boat), it is because it is the means of escape from an unseen terror. Inside, two women in ao trang huddle in a darkened room with barred windows (an evocation of wartime fear), their heads bent toward one another, their faces cast in shadow, and their limbs entwined (her hand on her thigh, her arm drawing her close), comforting one another in their loss or its anticipation. As each month passes, we see them enter the inky water, sometimes toward what appears to be their certain death. They crouch within woven baskets set adrift, the soft folds of the dress and their limbs tangling with the twisted geometries of twigs and branches. In one composition, she lists just beneath the surface of the water, her ao dai rippling in a lethal undertow.[89] In another, "SOS" is crudely painted across her chest as she twists in the ebb and flow of the tide, before she (or her companion) reaches shore under a glowering sky and folds her body in exhaustion.

Together, these photographs and their uncanny details—smooth silk catching against rough bark, a plea for help scrawled across her ao trang, her body washed ashore onto the sand—tell a story of refugee flight, the calendar girl as boat person. After the United States' intervention ended and thousands of Saigonese evacuated, tens of thousands more sought to flee the country in desperate hope of rescue in international waters. Boats were packed with hundreds, even thousands, of people, and many died by piracy, starvation, dehydration, or despair.[90] But the boats in these photographs are not the sort of vessels on which most sought escape on the open seas; nor do we get a sense of violence or struggle, even in the photographs that would seem to picture the ao trang unmoored, capsized, or drowned. This remembrance is not strictly historical, but *feelingly* so. In reference to its own dislocation and distance, the calendar's address, "Xin tuong nho tat ca nhung ai da phai bo minh tren duong tim tu do," asks us to remember everything and everyone already lost on the passage to freedom—but also that some are arrived at their destination. (Although such passage found thousands lingering in camps, repatriated, incarcerated, and deported—even decades later.) There are no jarring particularities, just absorbing details that establish a timetable toward the elimination of disruption, a horizon past crisis—in other words, a refugee resilience. Or, as Bliss Cua Lim observes so well of the ghosts of war and strife, "At the core of the allegorical mode, then, is an attempt to 'redeem for the present' a past whose relevance is in danger of vanishing by inscribing it anew."[91]

More than a double, the copy is the accessible fragment of a sometimes-elusive transaction or relation across thresholds of history and mortality. To look at a photograph, this series of photographs, this series of series, is to contemplate how the copy allows us to see or sense this scene again, in this fantastical manner, years after. For the refugee (or her child or grandchild or ____), it is both an encounter with a tumultuous history and its transcendence, because we are not ended. As Barthes explains, "I am the reference of every photograph, and this is what generates my astonishment in addressing myself to the fundamental question: why is it that I am alive *here and now*?"[92] This is so even with the photograph that is a copy of another body. To ask why I am not *there* or *then* in the photograph is to know that the time and place the photograph spirits into view are impossible, that I am already *here* and *now*, thousands of miles from ____. And yet copy is how we can be together at all, such that we might find ourselves *beside you in time*.[93]

Here I borrow a second cue from Marks, who suggests that identification is a bodily relationship with the image: "Thus when we witness a disappearing image we may respond with a sense of our own disappearance."[94] In the presence of the copy-image, one is aware that what is pictured there is disappeared, is disappearing, that it *must* disappear, not just because of the haunting nature of the photograph or the fragile materiality of the calendar—subject to wear and tear but also to individual scratches and scrawls that mark the concurrent passage of private time (which we may call evidence of "what's personal about love," after Berlant)—but because the calendar form itself necessitates this disappearance.[95] To baldly paraphrase Marks, the calendrical object is gradually transformed from what the image represents into the complex histories of its destruction.[96] Her reproducibility confirms that *on earth we're briefly gorgeous*. Or, as Eduardo Cadava mourns, "We need only know that we are mortal—the photograph tells us we will die, one day we will no longer be here, or rather, we will only be here the way we have always been here, as images."[97]

Staring into the mirror, I replicate myself into a future where I might not exist.

The Difference the Copy Makes

Memory and history belong to the possibility of repetition, citation, and inscription, but such a continuity of presence is not a pure becoming. At the same time that the copy comprises a field of precursive parts, constituting its own past and defining its fidelity (or lack thereof), it also jumbles and scatters such parts according to new compositions that emerge from its manufacture and our encounter. Because the copy does not have the same mode of existence, the same schemata of activity, the same relations within a world, as an original, the copy carries what Foucault describes as "a value that is not defined by their truth, that is not gauged by the presence of a secret content; but which characterizes their place, their capacity for circulation and exchange, their possibility of transformation."[98] Each copy is in a relation with an original—Johnson's A and B—but also ordains a presence (their place, their capacity, their possibility) that only copy can supply.[99]

Once, I wandered through an exhibition featuring dozens of ao dai from collectors, designers, and refugees.[100] In the accompanying catalog, curators herald the ao dai as a resilient form enduring a century of strife, and as a handsome metaphor for "the Vietnamese people themselves."[101] In one gallery, a low platform gathered a pyramid procession of headless mannequins, inviting the viewer to examine each garment and its distinctive details—exquisite embroidery, meticulous beading—from multiple angles. Traditional idioms from a wide range of inspired sources were combined in contemporary "art-to-wear" ao dai featuring tuxedo cuts, Persian-inspired fabrics, and adaptations of Victoriana such as padded bustles and beaded chenille lace. One would be hard-pressed (I thought to myself, as I leaned closer) to draw similarities between the gorgeous, cream-colored pleated garment draped with gold lace and velvet trim, featuring bell sleeves and a curved neckline adorned by large amber stones, and the equally lovely dress more conventionally cut with panels, mandarin collar, and raglan sleeves but tailored in a richly embroidered gold and russet silk inspired by Indian patchwork tapestries. A smaller, second gallery with glass vitrines and dim lighting displayed a late nineteenth-century "third-rank, first-class" mandarin's gown with the wide, rectangular sleeves in royal blue silk brocaded with aqua, gold, and fuchsia waves and four-toed dragons, and a loosely cut early twentieth-century empress mother's formal tunic in orange silk and a deep purple organza silk overlay brocaded with Chinese symbols. In a third room, projections on staggered scrims blurred private-familial and commodity-historical time; studio portraits and candid snapshots from family albums intermingled with stamps, postcards, cigarette cards, and fashion illustrations, encouraging contemplation of the emergence of something larger in the movement between each example and their accumulation. Mounted flat in glass cases on the walls or modeled on headless mannequins or captured as a digital copy of a time-ravaged photograph, this proliferation of examples and their aesthetic plentitude and categorical confusion was purposeful.[102] One of the curators hoped that the installation would challenge the viewer "to look really hard to even find what element you believe that's ao dai."[103]

What does it mean to have to *look really hard*? Years later, this collection makes another sort of sense if we understand each detail—idiosyncratic, singular, perhaps even personal—not as marginalia or surplus but instead as the promise of serial presence. That is, plural objects are intrinsic to the example but need not be selfsame or identical to uphold a singular principle; proliferation is close enough to permanence.[104] Seriality confers order on an incommensurate set of things, proposing not a continuity of pure becoming but an infinitude ontological to itself.

It is long established that gender is a copy without an original. Judith Butler's canonical argument about performativity, through which a series of potentially mutable referents appear to consolidate gender retroactively as a historical constant or "origin," serves as an obvious entry point. Because of this theoretical insight, we might now firmly grasp that the original does not exist as such except in its representation as reference. After all, the dress (every dress) has its openings, closings, and distinguishing features that establish a reliable map, or pattern. Repeatability as such is about the tenacity less of presence but more of form (whether as "heritage" or "femininity"); in this way, form is less a structure than an activity. After poststructuralism, such difference as might be found between copies is understood to be the origin of meaning. Copy thus names action (including self-rearticulation) derived from the capacity-bestowing discourses and institutions whose norms it variously mimics, betrays, transgresses, or affirms. Rey Chow elaborates on this sort of reading: "With the emphasis on material signifiers comes the determining function of difference—to be further differentiated as both differing and deferring—which would from now on take the place of sameness and identity as the condition for signification."[105] For this reason the analytic of repetition-with-a-difference has become a critical concept for figuring interiority and subjectivity as irreducible to preexisting conceptual properties. As Gilles Deleuze notes in *Difference and Repetition*, we are faced with at least two forms—one static, the other dynamic—of repetition: "The first repetition is repetition of the Same, explained by the identity of the concept or representation; the second includes difference, and includes itself in the alterity of the Idea, in the heterogeneity of an 'a-presentation.'"[106]

Distinct from earlier studies describing the demands of beauty as merely dupes, now familiar feminist readings proceed through slippage, heterogeneity, rupture, and difference. This adjustment shifts the objects (and arguments) of the study of the comely young woman in the beautiful dress, for instance, from nostalgic glances through which the anachronistic feminine figuration is denied singularity, to fine-grained slippages or excesses between an ideal and its others that gesture toward nonidentical interiority. In this way, the young woman in a beautiful dress interpellates a serial femininity that encourages contemplation of something larger in the movement between example and accumulation. I am reminded of Rosalind Krauss's observations about the avant-garde: "For originality becomes an organicist metaphor referring not so much to formal invention as sources of life."[107] In this way the copy is not necessarily alienated or alienating labor; nor is it a simple or selfsame activity. The self (of the performer, the pageant contestant, or the model before the camera) is the point of origin, rendering absolute the distinction between a past iteration and the present. Her own singularity guarantees the originality of what she performs or copies; the one who copies is also an author. It is its own paradox, that the copy serves as the grounds for the development of a sense of spontaneity and a sign of individuality. Or, put more simply, copy establishes a principle and transfigures the original into its supplement. Sianne Ngai argues in her account of serial femininity (as one woman attempts to enfold herself into another's life, as replica and then as replacement): "Yet insofar as emulation turns the thing emulated (whether this be a single characteristic or a whole person) into a thing that can be copied, and in doing so transforms that thing into something slightly other than what it was."[108] It is in these moments that theories of slippage, rupture, and difference might observe the ironies in failed copying, or imperfect mimicry, or regard them as disturbing, transgressive, or even resistant. Such misalignments are crucial to the optimism of improvisation. Through an idea of performativity, where repetition breaks the chain of signification via difference, presence might be destabilized (though this is at times a sanguine reading). Such moments are often called on to testify to the potentialities of disidentification against ontological privilege, of rupture perpetrated by individuals who resist enclosure, even just a bit.

In such readings, difference serves as a vantage to critique a structure or enterprise, where difference presumably precipitates a crisis of *partial presence*. Such a difference is often understood as a constitutive contradiction or as the failure of coherence or fullness, a reading that privileges difference as an entry point for understanding and unfolding the logics or rationalities of whatever appears to be continuous or true. And it is as crisis that difference from *what came before* is furthermore narrated as a condition of possibility for new historical subjects, aesthetic forms, and social arrangements. Consider the drag performer in the terno, the combat boot–clad lesbian artist in the sari, or the blonde chanteuse in the ao dai, each of which is a muddle of regularities.[109] Each announces herself as a copy, naming both her dissimilarity and her resemblance to an anterior presence, but only some are accused of being bad copies. When the ao dai pageant contestant whose indiscreet photographs bare more than deemed appropriate for a "good" example, she is cast out from the line of succession with apologies to "the community." When the country singer Kacey Musgraves wore a pale yellow ao dai with sparkling hot pants, revealing the long line of her bared legs, or when the Malaysian influencer Siew Pui Yi posted photographs of herself kneeling in a black ao dai, panels pulled aside to bare her round derriere in a sheer white thong, outrage thrummed at their "disrespect" for the ao dai's essential "elegance and modesty."[110] These infidelities or betrayals are not about the object—as we know, the dress might undergo multiple alterations without losing itself—but how it moves through a relational field, a field of histories, powers, signs, and feelings.

But there is no particular reason to assume that difference is always an aperture for anarchy; it does not and cannot deliver transgression at every turn. The more difference appears to disrupt, especially when it takes the form of a fragment or a detail, the more supple grows its power to decipher or even to determine the rules of its appearance. The regularization of difference as a resistant object forecloses other avenues of inquiry just as vital to the analytics of power, not least among them (though not the most significant either) how we construe our narrative or theoretical declarations, and diagnoses, of crisis. Though we might recruit difference to describe the limits of a structure or practice, difference might also manage or overcome those limits, especially as a serial example. It is through such inimitable reproducibility that an infinity of derivatives and deviations can be appropriated into a singular principle of a *nonhistorical continuity* over time. In other words, faithfulness need not be found in resemblance but in the promise to try and try again.

Against reading excess or slippage as outside of signification, it might instead be that difference produces a singularity that is itself a plentitude—a serial exemplarity. A breach or rupture because of crisis might retreat (aesthetically, feelingly) before a seemingly irreducible, inexhaustible, and infinite number of others *like enough* to follow. And so the beautiful, finding itself in danger, desires its copy. This is the lesson of the *Ao Trang* photographs that reincarnate as compressed images pasted into posters for Vietnamese Student Association pho night; or as photographs in a slide deck opening yet another six-hour Paris by Night / Thuy Nha variety show; or as hand-copied, oil-painted canvases hung alongside an incongruously life-size artificial tree (its leaves made up of tens of thousands of LED lights) at a Vietnamese restaurant in Philadelphia's Chinatown. Their presence testifies at the least to someone who cared enough to copy, convert, and circulate these images in new publics and novel translations. The aesthetic economy of the copy, then, is the origin of something other than originality or authenticity. This economy might include the condition or the production of the copy as itself uniquely new while nonetheless manifesting the principle of the original; it might also suggest that the act of replication or repetition is "new" or a "first time" within the experience of the one who copies, thus rendering all such acts in an unfolding progression of still more repetition as themselves a model, referent, or example. Even if a repetition is not a perfect copy of that which precedes it, slippage, heterogeneity, rupture, and difference, so often identified as those moments during which one might break free, could also be understood as precisely the chain's potency. What is actually being repeated is a situation for reproducibility, or a movement between and for consciousness of times, whether as a succession, a loop, or a sometimes-haunting cohabitation. Each example brings together formal contracts to repeat and return to an apocryphal encounter with this beloved body to tell a story about the experience of *feeling historical*. A "context of perpetual consumption," per Susan Stewart, shapes its promise of beauty.[111]

With and against History

This chapter sets the stage for my inquiry about how beauty is one name for how we know what we know about crisis and how to live through it, or with it. I have argued against reading copy (or diaspora) symptomatically, as a poor relation to an originary plentitude, or void; or ethnographically, with or against empirical truth or authenticity. Instead, where beauty is the reason and also the means for our endurance, it is its copy—rather than the original, which must stay behind—that brings presence into being in the present, and that plots those intensities that hold out a world worth living. Copy provides a sensory concreteness to abstractions of self and history, including the violence that might yet prevail, inasmuch as its promise protects you from *feeling* like disappearing, or dying. In this regard, copy is a condition of possibility, not "just" failure. A compressed, downloaded, defiled, retouched, and restored image of Barbara Johnson's multitudinous formulas, the copy might not be the origin of form, habit, or design, but it *is* the onset of activity. The copy is a turning point in its own right in the history of the world.

Throughout this book, the promise of beauty calls forth presence according to a principle that is also an arrangement; in doing so, its example solicits the consonant desire for other arrangements conceived as preserving or fostering the beautiful, though these will not always be fair. Beauty solicits from us habits of thought or formulas through which we recognize or describe it (*so beautiful it took my breath away, time stood still*), and through which we are known to ourselves and to others through our patterns and repetitions, the style and the structure of our attachments, but also our falling apart; we become intelligible through and within regimes of representation and normativity that train us to identify with some copies and not others. But where the promise of beauty found in an exemplary form and its copy might be a source of stability, it might also be the wellspring of terror.

Chapter 2

An Education in Beauty
(and the Necessity of Lawlessness)

The first haunting images transmitted from Taliban-occupied Afghanistan . . . showed us, if anything, that clothes and appearance are not trivial. Only now have we discovered the chilling extent of anticivilization. . . . Where vanity had been eradicated, so had women's voices, where reverence for beauty had been denied, so had education, and where vision-obscuring burkhas were forced upon women, there was no hope for a humane future.

Francesca Stanfill, "Fashion or Folly?"

When you save someone, you imply that you are saving her from something. You are also saving her *to* something. What violences are entailed in this transformation, and what presumptions are being made about the superiority of that to which you are saving her?

Lila Abu-Lughod, "Do Muslim Women Really Need Saving?"

In 2001, President George W. Bush sought to render US imperial violence commensurate with a rules-based international order through the invocation of an endangered humanity. The specter of such "terror" was made viscerally perceptible through the familiar mise-en-scène of the violated feminine body. In his remarks to the Warsaw conference on combating terrorism, President Bush included among the Taliban's offenses, "A girl of seven is beaten for wearing white shoes."[1] And the US State Department's

Report on the Taliban's War against Women, released on November 17, 2001, scolded, "Afghanistan under the Taliban had one of the worst human rights records in the world. The regime systematically repressed all sectors of the population and denied even the most basic individual rights. Yet the Taliban's war against women was particularly appalling." After condemning the denial of education and medical care, the report turned to "restrictions on movement" and other freedoms, condensed in the burqa, an ankle-length garment that covers the entirety of the body, with a narrow mesh screen for the eyes.[2] Decrying such illiberal misrule, the report further observed that "restrictions on clothing are matched with other limitations on personal adornment" and detailed harsh punishments for their violation. First Lady Laura Bush, in a national radio address released that same day, stated that "the fight against terrorism is also a fight for the rights and dignity of women," against those monsters that want to "pull out women's fingernails for wearing nail polish" and "impose their world on the rest of us."[3] Thus did white shoes and nail polish provide cover for war-making. As late as 2017, US national security adviser H. R. McMaster used a black-and-white photograph of Afghan college women in miniskirts strolling through 1972 Kabul to convince President Donald Trump that increased troop presence would encourage the return of lapsed "Western norms."[4]

In United Nations resolutions, US state reports, popular media, and news features, liberal-imperial warfare is strategically sutured to humanitarianism through the figuration of gender-based violence. For the global war on terror, waged by the United States with its Western European allies, she is the spectacle of the violated Muslim woman (at least, when violated by *others too much like her*). And yet the continuum from denial of medical care and education to a ban on nail polish might seem inane, or glib. One might ask, how are these at all comparable forms of suffering? Why would something as slight as nail polish be put on a list of prohibitions, and how did it become emblematic of an unreasoning absurdity, of the "chilling effect of anticivilization"?[5] "Can our bras, ties, pants, miniskirts, underwear, and bathing suits all be so easily arrayed on one or the other side of this divide?"[6] We might consider the compendium of such details to be a rhetorical flourish, underscoring how ornament, understood as feminine, trivial, and otherwise bearing no significance in the substance of righteous governance, is nonetheless subject to savage authority. Thus recruited, ornament performs a certain racial-religious knowledge about the enemy's overreach. Miniskirts and heels, nail polish and white shoes aim to focus our attention on those structures deemed lethal, antihuman, and antilife, because they would fold *even these* ornaments into the weft and warp of their cruel violence. Such an argument hinges on diminishing the ornamental as truly inconsequential; it is a barometer of the barbarically disproportionate and irrational terror of the racial, colonial other that he would assign to the ornamental so much gravity to want to banish it from sight. In this register, the abominable nature of terror is absolute, outside of politics and therefore the human.

But what is lost in diminishing the ornamental is a measure of those details—the body and how race or gender is manifest on its surfaces, among them—that actually tell us a lot about a life that can be lived?[7] As presumptive democracies cite humanitarian reason for their brutal incursions throughout the last century, the theater of war, as Judith Butler remarks, "seeks not only to produce an aesthetic dimension to war, but to exploit and instrumentalize visual aesthetics as part of a war strategy itself."[8] In this theater, the figure of humanitarian "rescue" is the covered Muslim woman, presumed to be especially vulnerable to patriarchal violence, and yet it is liberalism's own claim that the burqa's deficiency (because its near-continuous surface presents scopic impasse) *and* surplus (because its voluminous folds conflate things with persons) render her body, because of her ornaments, ineligible for full humanity. Beauty or its absence thus carries weight in being named in a chain of associations with other, seemingly more vital, freedoms.

As one chapter of forever war comes to a close, I linger with the imperial investment in the so-called "beauty of the arrangement"—after Adam Smith's account of good government—and the political effects of its imaginative capacity to build and also destroy lifeworlds.[9] Where it is an analogy for the fair and just, which are understood as commensurate to democracy, and an imitable model for human thought and activity (in other words, how to live), beauty limns a prerequisite or a path to just governance. Where beauty's absence appears as an empirical issue, perceived through anachronism, underdevelopment, or failure, the assessment of that absence may coincide or become complicit with the temporal logics of capital and colony. So *beauty* is no "mere" distraction. Through claims to act on behalf of humanity, liberalism's empire recruits a sensorium of beauty to mirror desirable forms for political economy, whether as health and wellness or as self-sovereignty. Michel Foucault, in the first volume of *The History of Sexuality*, writes of the nature of power that whatever intelligibility power possesses, it "is not because [force relations] are the effect of another instance that 'explains' them, but rather because they are imbued, through and through, with calculation."[10] When art critic Dave Hickey claims that "the vernacular of beauty, in its democratic appeal, remains a potent instrument for change in this civilization," he inadvertently posits *this civilization* as the enabling condition for beauty's accomplishment.[11]

Imbued, through and through, with calculation, beauty is not just an index of some other force but is itself an instrument and an objective for calculating and arranging the life of others. Here we might usefully align Claire Colebrook's observation that "what is beautiful is bound up with questions of how one ought to live and what interests one ought to have," with Didier Fassin's concept of humanitarianism as a politics of life, "in that [humanitarianism] takes as its object the saving of individuals" and "making a selection of which existences it is possible or legitimate to save."[12] In this chapter, I turn to a nongovernmental training program called the Kabul Beauty School to consider the promise of beauty not just as a mirror of democracy, or a justification for war, but as *itself* the calculation that thoroughly infuses the genres of being human. Established after the US invasion to teach Afghan women the "art and commerce of beauty," the school garnered widespread popular acclaim and industry support. Following from the premise that specific forms of social arrangement foster analogous or companion values, the politics of the Kabul Beauty School are that life is possible only when beauty aligns with law and order to triumph over chaos and misrule.[13]

Where law and order might recruit it to statecraft, the promise of beauty in turn illuminates how *law and order* is crafted as a message and a mode of governance. The determining foundation of liberalism is the necessity of law, where law is concomitant with legitimate violence, to establish a "peaceful" civic order. That law and order, in its associations with a properly clothed body, is also known as *civilization*, fashioning that body and its ungovernable other is an effect of a set of commonplace suppositions—among them, that an aesthetic education is central to liberal personhood, and specifically, that hijab condenses "backward" Islamic forms of gender. That is, beauty need not be conceived of as "mere" ornament, surface, or image that power then fastens to other calculations. Beauty is also a prime motor through which certain bodies, gestures, and desires come to identify and constitute rights-bearing individuals or sociolegal nonpersons. This onto-epistemological power might be most clearly manifest in a global order at the interventionary threshold of *becoming* beautiful where it corresponds to *becoming* human. Through beauty as method, claims about ontological being, forces of history, and habits for living unfold as an argument for freedom and also an archive of violence. Though the Kabul Beauty School is long defunct and the occupation ended (though of course, the United States continues to pursue military violence and counterterrorism operations across the globe), it offers a vantage from which to observe how the coupling of beauty with and against terror arranged a particular distribution of the sensible, including the configuration of just war and the democracy it promises.

The Interval

The promise of beauty and the war on terror might seem to have little to say to each other, but in their nearness we can observe a few ominous collusions. As a category for contemporary state action, *war* in the war on terror is expansively understood not just as a military conflict between sovereign powers (and sometimes against nonstate actors) with a beginning and an ending but as the strategic usage of this distinction, while terror is not a single, identifiable quality but a tactic, or an ideology, or a convenient name for that which must be annihilated. So too might *promise* in the promise of beauty be expansively understood, not just as a pledge succeeded by an action (put another way, the word calling forth a world) but as the strategic usage of this distinction, while beauty is not a single, identifiable property but a tactic, or an ideology, or a convenient name for that which must be defended. Perhaps I am making too much of this symmetry, though, especially given my suspicions about pleasing perceptual orders that grant sensory or narrative concreteness to otherwise abstract concepts. Perhaps the resemblance is just this, which is enough to go on—there is something vital that both war and beauty pledge to another, the power of which includes a beginning, an ending, and the interval between them.

Since the mid-twentieth century, US imperial ambition has sanctified its military violence as wars for humanity as a whole. The much-heralded gift of freedom, for instance, justifies the practice of liberal war as the political-military mechanism by which to overthrow enemy regimes.[14] Where freedom appears to be out of balance as an absolute value that is nonetheless calculable, its measure conceives and consolidates knowledge and power about those illiberal peoples and places for whom freedom's absence intensifies as *crisis*. As an observation that produces meaning, per Janet Roitman, the narrative use of crisis purports to describe a decisive moment during which an existential contradiction or a threat has derailed the course of historical certainty.[15] Where those peoples or places are construed as in "crisis," Neda Atanasoski argues that "humanitarian wars against terror, or atrocity, are regarded as a sacrifice necessary to humanize the world."[16] A world-desire for law and order is presumably paramount for the good of that humanity, and an obligation to actively make over other, deviant worlds in this image follows. According to this logic, nations that have adopted universal "human capabilities" must "commend this norm strongly to other nations," using, when required, "economic and other strategies to secure compliance."[17] Or, as Lisa Lowe puts it, "Control was not a counterprinciple to freedom; it was the condition from which it arises."[18] The gift of freedom thereby points to the internal difference that constitutes democracy as a form of self-government that can be brought by force to another. The claim to crisis, as well as assent to its narrative, is therefore a strategic observation that establishes a sometimes-radical course of action to forestall catastrophe; this is the story of regime change. *Transition* is as such key as event and process through which an occupying power attempts to re-create its institutions (and consolidate its interests) in illiberal elsewheres—in Vietnam, Afghanistan, or Iraq, for example, to which US military forces, proxy regimes, and private mercenaries promised freedom.[19]

If liberal war is the adjudication of powers to align a lapsed or "young" people with a civilizational imperative in the name of *global* life, or what Atanasoski describes as "fighting to bring inhuman geographies into the fold of historical progress," then the essential character of this interval before its achievement is that it is also impermanent.[20] As Mary Dudziak observes, "Once war has begun, time is thought to proceed on a different plane. There are two important consequences of this shift: first, we have entered a time that calls for the extraordinary action, and second, we share a belief that this moment will end decisively, so this shift is *temporary*. Because of this, built into the idea of wartime is a conception of the future."[21] Liberal war as an imperial discourse invariably refers to the near future and to a much-hastened tempo that anticipates, and labors for, the moment in which the racial, colonial other is "finally" capable of self-government. (Liberal war must do so in part to argue for its own efficiency, regularity, and rationality.) In this instance, the transition to democracy is the assurance that US-led forces will usurp illegitimate powers for a time, and that those forces will restore or build anew legitimate ones and soon enough bring an end to its own rule.[22] It is one name (occupation is another name, less cunning) for this suspension of sovereignty with the pledge that actions undertaken during such suspension will lead to civilizational achievement. The interval is thus an event at the level of history, and an event at the level of the *constitution* of that history—it is undertaken as the first to accomplish the second.

"After" the Cold War (a provisional post-), liberal democracy was alleged to be the only conceivable direction of political futures. In particular, US empire posited itself as an established endpoint for those elsewheres to which it is addressed as an example for inaugurating democracy. While each transition to democracy might be specific (because it arises from its historical conditions), it is met with recurring structural "solutions" because liberalism's order establishes that historical progress compels these analogous and already known modes for lawful governance. Thus, the founding of a new regime includes certain *political* norms—rights, constitutions, assemblies, and trials by jury among them—that are also *aesthetic* forms. Such aesthetic forms make it possible to perceive and recognize the presence of democracy (whether or not those forms actually do what they claim to do); the aesthetic form of the constitution, for instance, includes such literary conventions as references to a people ("We the People"), or the analogue of balance, proportion, and equality (one member, one vote) found in a representative body or popular assembly. Regime change to thereby establish rule of law requires the imaginative act of projecting an already-known image of a beautiful arrangement onto other times and places, and acts of interference and control to bring to pass what is *already known* must come.

One distinction between the Cold War and permanent war is the prognostication of war's end. The interval as the remnant promise of the Cold War produces the measures and the means by which the racial, colonial other is given to diminish, if never to close, the distance between anachronism and history proper, while allowing liberal powers to appear to be other than imperial in predicting the end of "crisis" and their rule—as long as conditions are met. If such conditions are never met—that is, if they do not come close enough to being *like us*—we are consigned to war forever. Encompassing genocidal violence, antidemocratic coups, extrajudicial massacres, and death squads, trained by the School of Americas, to commit assassinations and atrocities, dotted with occasional declarations of war and withdrawal and one decades-long, unfinished armistice, the Cold War established for the United States a global archipelago of military bases, black sites, weapons manufacturing, and surveillance. While not licensed as permanent exception, the Cold War inaugurated our liberal way of war now. In 2001, after the events condensed as "9/11," US lawmakers passed an "Authorization for Use of Military Force," which was not a formal declaration of war but a broad authorization of the use of force in the war on terror. With the 2001 invasion of Afghanistan, the 2003 invasion of Iraq, and the hundreds more incursions across the globe (drone strikes in Pakistan, war games in Niger, unconditional arms deals for Israel, and more still), the authorization is regularly renewed "to prevent any future acts of international terrorism against the United States by such nations, organizations or persons," and has been used to justify secret detentions and extrajudicial assassinations.[23] The war on terror then is more than a war. In distinguishing its violence as rational and lawful, the war becomes a globally comprehensive policing operation that presumes to act in the name of humanity against its others. Just as John Stuart Mill argued that justice is conditional and contextual on how far along states are on their path to civilization, the United States applies such reasoning to all its self-exceptions.[24]

The permanent war that identified this thing *terror* as the greatest threat since communism, and that (ironically) brought with it the singular horizon of occupation as a transitional time, is a useful situation to pass through liberalism's aporia. Where moral imperative and imperial violence are collapsed into the other, what can the promise of beauty and the related crises of governance it pronounces and also pledges to resolve tell us about lawfulness and truancy? Conscripted, beauty might bracket war's violence as accidental, the unfortunate consequence of democracy's unfolding in unfamiliar soil. But what if its promise is also the substance of liberal governance, especially as a duty to make live? Beauty's absence, characterized as a crisis in which a life cannot be lived without it, and beauty's presence, sanctioned as *the feeling of life being furthered* required to survive a dire situation, weaves in and out of the theater of war as an imperial good. But such attention to the conditions that beauty is called on to critique—here, condensed as Islamic fundamentalism, or terror personified—can eclipse the more elusive question of the grounds for positing beauty as a cognate of critique itself. What is going on here, where the object of beauty is both the event of knowledge about crisis (its allegory or metaphor) and also redemption after crisis, bearing witness to its overcoming, and thus providing meaning (of events, of suffering) for history?

Where an aesthetic education is understood as necessary to a democratic disposition, beauty names a structure for recognition and reciprocity proximate to its legal form—the rights-bearing person, the human being—within a rules-based order. Alongside constitutions, assemblies, and police, it is through the liberal sensorium of beauty that another might finally become free, or properly human. Thus standing in for an education in civilizational habits and implicating bodily knowledges, trivial details, and "minor" events in global governance, *Vogue* editor in chief Anna Wintour claimed that the Kabul Beauty School was crucial to the US-sponsored reconstruction effort.[25] We might call this, after Laleh Khalili, a tactic of counterinsurgency warfare.[26] The promise of beauty is here the means and the ends of a civilizing process, one that necessitates war on humanity's behalf.

Burqa Time

Beauty bears the weight of so much of what Minoo Moallem calls "civilizational thinking."[27] Such thinking conceives and at times codifies knowledge about distinctions of humanity, space, and time, as well as about the event of knowledge itself; it is not an ontological truth but claims its status as such to endorse or to denounce a particular moment or social arrangement. Sylvia Wynter calls those distinct categories that emerge from this divide "genres" of the human, each featuring its own aspirations and ways of relating which, taken together, make up what Wynter calls a culture's "descriptive statement." Wynter argues that the West, through imperial expansion and colonial violence, has imposed its genre-specific truths on the world; its descriptive statement is overrepresented in the history of humanity.[28] In this overrepresented statement, rational Man (who is a particular man) is in charge of his own destiny; as a rights-bearing being, he is the human being par excellence.

Central to this genre divide, the capacity for proper aesthetic judgment is fundamentally aligned with the enlightened modern subject against a racial, colonial other. According to Immanuel Kant, David Hume, Edmund Burke, and many, many others, human self-possession circumscribed as the consciousness to act, and to enter into covenant with others (to promise, in other words), is the property and precondition for the appreciation of beauty. Such criteria direct our attention to the symbolic plentitude and epistemic grounds of beauty subtending the legitimation of colony and capital, and the onto-epistemologies that secure their common sense. In his pre-*Critique* essay "On National Characteristics So Far as They Depend upon the Distinct Feeling of the Beautiful and the Sublime," Kant reasons that the beautiful and the sublime are qualities of the highest aesthetic and moral feelings, which the European alone has mastered in his cultivation of agreeable women. "In the land of the black, what better can one expect," Kant argues, than "the feminine sex in the deepest slavery."[29] The "inhabitant of the Orient" is also bankrupt, with "no concept of the morally beautiful." Perversely given to secrecy and opacity (which Kant abhors), "a woman [there] is always in a prison, whether she may be a maid, or have a barbaric good-for-nothing and always suspicious husband."[30] So when Edmund Burke reserves beauty for the aristocratic Englishwoman (as opposed to the African woman who, he said, could inspire only terror), or when Arthur Danto (speaking of aesthetic deprivation) muses "there would be no way—or no easy way—to transform Detroit or Pittsburgh into the Catskills or the Grand Canyon" (a quote to which I return in the fourth chapter), or when the *Los Angeles Times* reviewed the documentary about the Kabul Beauty School as "a profound reminder of the things that make us human," beauty is territorialized.[31]

These operations also create categories of nonpersons, who are *other* in their being and who oftentimes commit de facto status crimes, based on the interpretation of aesthetic or visible signs organized by descriptive statements as a rational mode of perception. A feature story published in the British daily *Independent* presents the war in Afghanistan as a contest between "beauty and the burqa," recalling a fairy-tale heroine and her triumph against a brute and primitive force.[32] In place of the beast is the *burqa*, a substitution functioning as a metonym for Oriental inhumanity.[33] This binary of beauty versus the beast, the animal, the monster, or the otherwise nonhuman is central to the effacement of Islamic political movements as constituted in, rather than outside or inimical to, colonial modernity. As Leila Ahmed observes, "Veiling—to *Western* eyes, the most visible marker of the differentness and inferiority of Islamic societies—became the symbol now of both the oppression of women ... and the backwardness of Islam."[34] Veiling as *a clock for seeing* (again, Barthes) maps onto the world as its division into zones and also *ages*. On such a clock, Afghan contemporaneity is inconceivable. Taliban rule cannot be the logical consequence of US support for the most reactionary mujahideen during the Afghan war with the Soviet Union, for instance, but of ancient tribalism and premodern regression.[35] According to such civilizational thinking, history proper belongs to humanity; the time of the burqa is a suspension, or a dead zone.

Humanity therefore is litigated through determinate norms that include aesthetic forms, or *styles*. Constructs of race, following after Frantz Fanon, teach us how to see flesh as an "epidermal schema" presumed to yield usable knowledge about the human and its others through a series of abstractions shaping subjectivization from surface. Such constructs that aim to render the monster, criminal, or terrorist visible or perceptible, educating the eye on how to see and otherwise interpret the signs of his lawlessness—which is also his availability for detaining and killing—are central to modern state powers of surveillance, reconnaissance, and prediction. The same ontoepistemologies that inform the descriptive statement also underwrite the sartorial-racial profile to codify predictive knowledge for how to use the body as an index for capacity and pathology.[36] Clothes and other ornaments transmute the body into a border zone and a contiguous surface as "an effect of how objects gather to clear a ground, how objects are arranged to create a background," to borrow from Sara Ahmed.[37] (Consider the visual shorthand of preoccupation Afghanistan—the burqa, the Soviet tank, the desert, the bearded warlord.) Through the abstraction of contiguous surfaces, the descriptive statement or profile teaches us to project onto racial, colonial others an *interior* truth of criminality, deviancy, or lawlessness. (Or as Pierre Bourdieu argued, "Aesthetic intolerance can be terribly violent.")[38] In doing so, clothes not only dramatize the materiality of bodies but also demonstrate that such materiality is itself animated by histories of abstraction.

The liberal disavowal of racism as the foundation for the rule of law thereby proliferates such abstractions as alibis that belong to a presumably rational system of profile and preemption. At the height of the forever war, the *New York Times* published "The War Is Fake, the Clothing Real," about a fashion-conscious costumer for a company that clothes playacting Afghan or Iraqi insurgents and civilians in war games staged for the US armed forces. "Though Mr. [David] Tabbert, 28, personally prefers G-star denim and concert tees, he was on the hunt for 150 dishdashas, the ankle-length garments worn by men in Iraq and elsewhere in the Arab world. In July, actors will wear them in a simulated Iraqi village, posing as townspeople, clerics and insurgents at a National Guard training ground in the Midwest."[39] As an effect of the racial-sartorial profile, costuming, whether for theater or war, presumes the stability of surfaces for visual recognition and reconnaissance. For example, "the exact embroidery on the epaulet of an opposition leader's military uniform" might instruct combatants to distinguish between "bad" and "good" Afghans or Iraqis. In the systemization of surfaces as indices, the profile divides the population into actionable categories. "It's teaching the people how to not kill people," as the costumer puts it, with the unspoken corollary of teaching them how to kill the *right* people, whom we might *know* from their ornaments.[40] In other words, the profile is a promise that an example might allow us to discover a rule or a principle (wrongfulness can be *seen* on the surface, for instance, as x or y) that attests to the de facto status crime.

Hijab is another racial onto-epistemological object that creates such categories, including the liberal humanitarian category for "making live." The now-familiar discourse of the veil as an anticivilizational other emerged in the nineteenth century, according to Leila Ahmed, from a social evolutionary sequence in which the colonial powers stood at the apex of historical progress. "The idea that Other men, men in colonized societies or societies beyond the borders of the civilized West, oppressed women was to be used, in the rhetoric of colonialism, to render morally justifiable its project of undermining or eradicating the cultures of colonized peoples."[41] In this way, the burqa condenses and organizes usable knowledge about Afghanistan, and not just about its forms of gender. The manufacture of her Muslim body is the manufacture of a highly visible racial distinction through the disappearance of that body into an effacing abstraction, according to which the burqa is a despised substitution for that which is presumably missing, whether beauty, education, freedom, sovereignty, or lawfulness. Again, what Moallem calls the *civic body* becomes the figuration of those material and semiotic practices—gestures, poses, and garments that shape them— concerned with the character of a people and their place on the clock of the world.[42] In the oppositions that order civilization thinking, the burqa is an agent of repression and invisibility, of religious and cultural subjugation, rendering the Afghan woman passive, unwhole, stuck.

Following Joseph Slaughter's study in which the human rights claim takes the aesthetic form of the bildungsroman, at least a dozen biographies and memoirs and reams of reportage in the aftermath of the US invasion narrate the interior life of Afghan women as an ongoing war for self-determination and expressivity against hostile forces.[43] Often these accounts narrate their similarity to an *us* through desiring the same things, those ordinary pleasures of *small art and love and beauty*, as we do. Media coverage in the months before and after the US invasion highlighted Afghan women's perseverance in the absence of a public culture of beauty. Journalists noted that mirrors were covered and hidden from view; beauty products and magazines featuring Bollywood stars smuggled from Pakistan were buried in the backyard. Saira Shah's documentary *Beneath the Veil*, aired in "seeming synchrony with U.S. military strategy" more than ten times on CNN during the lead-up to the American invasion, featured secret salons operating in private homes as rendezvous for women to commune together, away from the watchful eyes of others.[44] "If they are caught, these women will be imprisoned, but they still paint the faces that can never show in public. . . . Women trying to keep life normal in a world gone completely mad."[45] *Vogue* conjured the secret salon as a theater of conversation, in the model of French literary and philosophical circles: "For decades, beauty salons were refuges where Afghan women were able to speak freely."[46] This minor sensus communis, which the salon conjured as an intimate realm and liberalism enshrined as a political form, thus stood for all that the Taliban so adamantly opposed—beauty, freedom, democracy.

The statement and the profile render aesthetically perceptible the desire for beauty and also the denial of certain forms of interior life and social bond through hijab, or onto it. Specifically, the burqa is named an obstacle to personhood and to progress. Detractors describe it as fundamentally disabling—blinding, hobbling, and smothering. Nivedita Menon relates the story of a young Kashmiri woman compelled to wear the burqa, who tells a journalist that while she once went regularly to the beauty parlor, she no longer bothers with her face.[47] Julia Reed's *Vogue* profile named a litany of dismembering violences: "In addition to being hot, [burqas] are incredibly hard to maneuver in because the mesh eye holes do not allow you to look down. 'You have no eyes to see,' one student says when I ask her what she hated the most about wearing a burqa. Others talk of constantly tripping, of breaking the heels off their shoes."[48] The Bush administration reported, "One Anglo-Afghan journalist reported that the burqa's veil is so thick that the wearer finds it difficult to breathe; the small mesh panel permitted for seeing allows such limited vision that even crossing the street safely is difficult."[49] Condensing deprivation and deindividuation, a *Time* magazine article featuring photographs of unidentified women wearing the burqa, described the garment, "To Western eyes [it is] a kind of body bag for the living."[50] Latifa, the pseudonymous narrator of *My Forbidden Face*, accuses the burqa of choking her, confining her.[51] "I can feel the rustle of my own breath inside the garment. I'm hot. My feet get tangled up in the material. I'll never be able to wear this. I now understand the stiff robot-like walk of the 'bottle women,' their unflinching look directly in front of them. . . . These phantoms that now roam the streets of Kabul have a terrible time avoiding bicycles, buses and carts. It's even worse trying to run away from the Taliban. This is not a garment. It's a moving prison."[52] In her memoir about her "struggle for freedom," the pseudonymous Zoya mourns, "A woman in a burqa is more like a live body locked in a coffin."[53] In these accounts, the burqa is not an inert or passive garment but *a body bag, a cage, a prison*, or *a coffin* bearing great and terrible powers. Its unassimilable, illegible, phantasmatic, manifold *thingness* transmutes those who wear the burqa into specters, or the living dead, try as they might to resist such psychic death.[54]

The burqa is activated as an obstruction that erects the partition between the human and its other, while also blurring the line between the living and the living dead. In this schema, the burqa prevents one from seeing another, truly; she cannot see out from inside it, and we cannot see in from outside it. Clad in the burqa, the Afghan woman enters a series through which she is refused singularity as a person; this series, as a sensory experience of an abstract principle that is exhausting and even confounding (we know nothing from looking), is decried as an impasse. Gestures of disclosure are therefore crucial to the aesthetic genres of self-making and sociality. In 2001, the American playwright and performer V (formerly known as Eve Ensler) authored a "tribute" to the Afghan woman in *The Vagina Monologues*.[55] An adaptable series of disclosures of what (like the eponymous vagina) was once buried, hidden, or secret, each monologue models the process of a person "speaking out" or "breaking the silence." These monologues hew closely to the repressive hypothesis in defense of desire; such incitement to discourse, after Foucault, rests on the belief that "speaking out" in and of itself will refashion relations of power through its inscription of personhood.[56] In the late twentieth century, *The Vagina Monologues* had become central to this sort of aesthetic education, performed all over the world but especially at colleges and universities throughout the Global North to foster "empowerment," social bond, and civic responsibility. Such an education is also key to the premise behind V-Day, V's nonprofit organization raising funds and consciousness "to end violence against women and girls" through benefit performances. At New York City's Madison Square Garden for the sold-out 2001 V-Day gala, Oprah Winfrey performed V's audience-rousing monologue "Under the Burqa" as an Afghan woman (the pseudonymous Zoya) unveiled dramatically onstage. The Feminist Majority newswire noted that Zoya did so "as vocal sounds of pain and agony filled Madison Square Garden," an unsubtle captioning to cue the audience to feel horror at the wounds inflicted on the burqa-clad woman, and sorrow for her inexpressible interiority.[57]

Here the promise of beauty couples sexual autonomy with social liberation, coincidental with United States' war-making. As Vernadette Vicuña Gonzalez puts it, "The libidinal is woven into empire's design. But the American flavor of imperialism claimed righteousness as a pillar of its singular mission of uplift."[58] Indeed, the V-Day event also promoted the purchase of a "burqa swatch" to be pinned to the lapel as a fundraiser for the Feminist Majority. Such a purchase would evince solidarity—as other colored ribbons or badges might—with Afghan women in the deconstruction of this disabling garb. "This swatch of mesh represents the obstructed view of the world for an entire nation of women who were once free."[59] In this fantasy of substitution and subtraction, every remnant purchased *here* would lead to the decrease or diminution of the whole garment *there*. As Gonzalez might observe, this disrobing is a "particular colonial kink."[60]

Built into liberal-imperial governance is the promise that warfare would lead to peacetime, during which beauty might flourish (once uncovered). Early in the US-led occupations of both Afghanistan and Iraq, such optimism found bright signs in changing hemlines. In the immediate aftermath of US invasion, photographs circulated of Afghan women showing their faces, casting aside the burqa, as a happy consequence. Against the darkness and opacity of the veil, to go public, to be seen, and to be recognized were understood as a political achievement. Drawing on well-worn clichés, the *Christian Science Monitor* published an essay called "Lifting the Veil on Women's Subjugation," spinning a fantasy of sublime disclosure for readers. "Then imagine the unexpected pleasure, two weeks ago, of suddenly being able to take off that imprisoning garment and experience the world as you once did, unencumbered. Your oppressors have fallen from power, and you are free." This victory looks a particular way, of course. The essayist continues, "No wonder news photos coming out of Kabul in the past two weeks will rank among the most joyous journalistic images of 2001. They show the strong, proud faces of elated Afghan women, no longer under the cruel thumb of the Taliban, emancipated from the often-hated burqas."[61] So too did veteran war reporter Janine di Giovanni also deploy metaphors of visibility to describe a thrilling world of shining goods. "Within days of liberation, the country itself was coming out of hiding," writes di Giovanni. "There were new things for sale in the bazaar—strange, forbidden things: books, condoms, hair dryers. Now, packages of hair dye with scantily clad Swedish models adorn shop windows."[62] In such a description, a "fair" social order comes naturally from the attachment to beautiful things.

In occupied Afghanistan, the promise of beauty functioned as promise of normative time after its irruption or lapse, and as passage into the synchronous flow of the "civilized" world—through law, and through the market. This is also true with regard to our other terror-war incursion—Iraq. Following the US invasion in 2003, the *New York Times* published "What Not to Wear, Baghdad-Style: Fashion Rules Begin to Change," testifying that the woman in a Muslim country who desires beauty necessarily desires freedom, which only regime change can provide. During the worst of the violence, "'All my rouges and other makeup stuff expired, and my mother refused to accompany me to shops to buy more,'" one university student recounted. "She told me, 'This is not a time of makeup. This is a time of bombs.'" Here there is a clear temporal divide—wartime is the suspension of livable time during which beauty is luxury or scarcity. But fashion rules change with the regime: "Now that security has improved in Baghdad, the capital, some young women have begun shaking off their abayas and started dressing more like the women they see on satellite television channels beamed to the city from around the world." Indeed, we know things are returned to their rightful order as the story ends with a college student quipping, "'The militias did not succeed in preventing me from primping, but my final exams are.'"[63] A few months later, an optimistic NPR proclaimed, "In Baghdad, Hemlines Rise as Violence Falls."

This causal statement suggests that the higher the hemline, the greater the freedom. "The hot fashion items for this season? Short skirts, tight jeans with long boots, and short jackets for cold days. That may not sound exceptional, or even very trendy, but this is the fashion forecast from Baghdad, where the climate for more revealing women's wear has been steadily improving. Many Iraqi women say it is a sign of returning security and freedom after years of war and sectarian tensions."[64] Here such reportage recalls the breathless tempo of fashion, which divides and marks time into activities and events (both proliferating an increasing number of commodities), to also diagnose the state of the country. A shopkeeper duly repeats this correlation between fashion and freedom, beauty and democracy: "Ali Mohammed says the new trend is not really about fashion, but freedom. Iraqi women ought to be free to wear whatever they like. They should be free to choose *hijab* if they wish, or they ought to be able to express themselves with Western clothing. For the customers at Ali Mohammed's clothing store, the choice is clear: What to wear this season? Ali says it is absolutely not *hijab*."[65]

Again, transitional governance or occupation pledges a time and a place beyond war when exceptional measures end and "normal" life returns. It consists of the image (a timeline, "We the People," the assembly, the changing seasons found in the short skirt and jeans) and the intervention (military troops, governmental advisers, NGOs, and other service providers), or, in other words, liberal government as aesthetic form and liberal governing as disciplinary norm. Together, the image and the intervention produce a regime of control that provides *and* defers its substantiation for an indefinite time (an imperial iteration of Derrida's democracy to come). As Brad Evans and Julien Reid remind us, "Key here is the understanding that violence occurs at the interventionary threshold, where life ceases to become what it was and yet has not quite revealed its new formative conditioning."[66] Writing about "recent life narratives from Afghanistan," Gillian Whitlock (with ambivalence) describes just such a threshold as she narrates the violence she might wish to commit herself while regarding airport bookshelves—to unveil another, whether or not asked for. "And so you enter the bookstore and regard that mass display of veiled women. You wonder what extraordinary change of currents brought these lives into your habitat, which hitherto has paid so little regard to Afghanistan. You feel the unease produced by the crocheted faceplate of the *burqa*, and you feel the pull, the inexorable logic, of placing this as alien and other. You look at it, barefaced, and wish it stripped bare too."[67]

Democratic forms, forms that would otherwise presumably decry forced occupation or disclosure, call for their own suspension to achieve a desirable outcome. It is no wonder that Randall Williams calls human rights "the privileged epistemic form for political violence," legitimating forms of colonial and imperial governance to secure and defend the amalgam of humanity as a whole.[68] The occupying regime is one example of this calculation; or, as Lila Abu-Lughod asks so clearly, "What violences are entailed in this transformation, and what presumptions are being made about the superiority of that to which you are saving her?"[69] The statement and the profile render war apprehensible as the rational calculation of danger—*society must be defended*—and the promise of beauty plays its part to make this threshold violence seem worth it.

An Aesthetic Education

In between talking-head interviews and slice-of-life scenes from the 2007 documentary *The Beauty Academy of Kabul*, the camera lingers on smiling, laughing women as they maneuver between chairs, desks, and mirrors in a brightly lit room that serves as both salon and school.[70] They wield scissors, brow liners, and plastic spritz bottles on their mannequin heads and sometimes—teasingly, lovingly—on each other. Though some wear scarves over their hair, curls tumbling out from under, their faces are for the moment open and mirthful. The music of modern Afghan songwriter and composer Ahmad Zahir masks any discernible dialogue (and there are no translations or subtitles), underscoring at once the apparent ordinariness of this tableau as well as its extraordinary pleasure. Pictured thus, the Kabul Beauty School convened a therapeutic publicity as a realm of strangers (students and teachers, occupied and occupiers) who are bonded through a fantasy of intimacy, transcendence, and reciprocity.[71] *This could happen anywhere, but it is happening in Afghanistan.* But what else lies between these interstitial scenes that are *out* of time (the suspension in the presence of beauty) and also *of* their time (after invasion, during occupation, in transition)?

In the war on terror, civilian agencies—including NGOs, relief workers, development contractors, among them—are conscripted as counterinsurgency measures. Founded on the promise that beauty might inaugurate a new world order, in August 2003 the Kabul Beauty School opened under the management of the now-defunct NGO Beauty without Borders, administered by American and British fashion industry and nonprofit professionals.[72] Beauty without Borders references, of course, the transnational social movement organization Médicins sans frontières, the transnational social movement prototype for NGOs that, as Peter Redfield observes, "adopt a borderless sense of space and an ethos of direct intervention."73 Such direct intervention here involved the education of a naive subject, through which the curriculum sought to train Afghan women in "the art and commerce of beauty," including hairdressing, makeup application, manicures, and bookkeeping.74 But the beauty salon performs double, or even treble duty. "This isn't just about providing lipstick," repeated the project director, Patricia O'Connor, in interviews. "It's about restoring self-esteem and independence."75 Or, as the British *Sunday Times* told its readers, "As [the Kabul Beauty School students] learnt the unIslamic arts of bikini waxing, perming and colouring they grew in confidence and began to believe they could become independent providers and buy a bigger stake in their own lives," which are presumably unIslamic qualities too.76 In this way, the school is imagined to nurture not just a love of beauty but also a lateral community for its care or, in this wartime campaign, a democracy. The promise loops beauty, as a conduit for the power of life, to a future unity between the desire for it and its presence through reference to what is missing, incomplete, or at risk and what had to be given, secured, or made anew.

The promise of beauty rests in part, then, in the supposed correspondences (and noncorrespondences) between an aesthetic and its political effects. Within humanist formations, an aesthetic education projects into the world the promise of its beautiful arrangement as good governance. In Plato's *Symposium*, the seer and priestess Diotima encourages Socrates to ascend the beautiful shoulders of a boy as rungs of a ladder: "You start by loving one beautiful body and step up to two; from there you move on to physical beauty in general, from there to the beauty of people's activities [such as institutions or laws], from there to the beauty of intellectual endeavors, and from there you ascend to that final intellectual endeavor, so that you finally recognize true beauty," whose order is divine.77 Adam Smith argued that moral sentiments motivate the desire to perfect "a certain beautiful and orderly system," while Friedrich Schiller proposed the aesthetic of beauty as a means of joining "free" individuals, through an appeal to the common sense of a social arrangement, under a moral-political law.78 In his *Inaugural Address to the University of St. Andrews*, John Stuart Mill describes an aesthetic education (specifically, an institutional one), one that understands "a natural affinity between goodness and the cultivation of the Beautiful," as a resource and a disposition toward moral virtue. "He who has learnt what beauty is, if he be of a virtuous character, will desire to realize it in his own life—will keep before himself a type of perfect beauty in human character, to light his attempt at self-culture."79 A liberal education, an aesthetic education, is thereby heralded as promoting the social and political values of a democracy and transmitting the universal moral truths on which that democratic order is made. Salman Rushdie, in an essay about those who carried out the attacks on September 11, 2001, argued that the fundamentalist "believes that we believe in nothing." But this is not true, he says, before he catalogs a set of virtues critical to a liberal polity: "To prove him wrong, we must first know that he is wrong. We must agree on what matters: kissing in public places, bacon sandwiches, disagreement, cutting-edge fashion, literature, generosity, water, a more equitable distribution of the world's resources, movies, music, freedom of thought, beauty, love."[80] Schiller, Mill, Kant, and Rushdie, among others, marshal such principles as necessary lessons in moral living, as exercises in ethical judgment. Liberalism and the aesthetic education it nourishes, they say, *need* beauty as its moral compass. Beauty might convey knowledge about others living in a world apart or promote democratic values, but in this accounting, first and foremost beauty exists for itself as example, likeness, or model of the good.[81] But for it to do so, *we must agree on what matters.*

Originally presented as the Tanner Lectures on Human Values at Yale University, Elaine Scarry's *On Beauty and Being Just* declares that an innate sensitivity for beauty, through which certain arrangements of distribution or order are made available through perceptual means, is denied its legitimating force in contemporary debates about justice. Scarry argues that the love for beauty, and the openness to correct one's faulty feelings about what one finds less beautiful—such as palm trees, for her—is generative; it makes us want to reproduce it, to extend it, beyond a particular scene or moment. Such an attachment to beauty, she claims, induces a heightened attention, which is "voluntarily extended out to other persons or things.... Through its beauty, the world continually recommits us to a rigorous standard of perceptual care."[82] Such perceptual care that comes from attending to the beautiful objects among us directs our notice to the absence of like properties—symmetry, balance, proportion, and fairness, foremost—in other scenes or moments. This is how beauty exerts a "fair" distributional power, as "people seem to intuit that their own self-interest is served by distant peoples' having the benefit of beauty."[83] For Scarry, an education in beauty that alerts us to the aliveness of all persons is necessarily an education in justice.

But what of that which is deemed less than beautiful, or those who cannot experience it as such? "Being in error," Scarry writes, is one of beauty's "abiding structural features"; but the "mental event of conviction" is so "pleasurable" that "ever afterwards one is willing to labor, struggle, wrestle with the world to locate enduring sources of conviction—to locate what is true."[84] Optimistically, she counsels that the fear of *being in error* is so urgent that we wish to correct any such error, once we become aware of it.[85] But though opportunities for perceptual blunders proliferate (one might not understand the beauty of palm trees, as Scarry did not, until familiarity with them alerted her to it), yet there is also the seeming truth that some scenes, objects, or persons are less beautiful. As Rita Barnard writes in her own observations about *On Beauty*, Scarry "sh[ies] away from the very possibility that one person might find another's beautiful person or thing not simply 'lack[ing] the perfect features that obligate us to stare,' or 'less endowed with those qualities of perfection which arrest our attention,' but, quite simply, ugly."[86] In ignoring those aesthetic judgments that fuel disgust or even animus, for instance, which are not mere errors of supposedly imperfect vision, Scarry does not account for how to judge, let alone redress, what she calls aesthetic unevenness. Nor does she explain how to parse such judgments that act as alibis in racial, colonial encounters from somehow more impartial and fair assessments.

Instead, Scarry argues that beauty constitutes the grounds for regular and harmonious order, from which some have strayed. Acknowledging that "the surfaces of the world are aesthetically uneven," she suggests that in periods of "human community . . . too young to have yet had time to create justice, as well as in periods when justice has been taken away, beautiful things . . . hold steadily visible the manifest good of equality and balance."[87] This is a profoundly overfull statement that nonetheless outlines the promise of beauty as an agent of imperial governance. Perhaps most obviously, naming "a human community . . . too young to have yet had time to create justice," or lapsed in its aptitude for it, is the language of colonial and imperial incursion. It conforms to what Johannes Fabian calls a "denial of coevalness," which consigns the *young world*, the *lapsed world*, to a time other than the present of the observer (Scarry's ". . . to have yet had time . . .").[88] It is not just that other social arrangements produce error—erroneous value, faulty assessment, specious judgment—that presumably lead to a lapse of justice or historical progress. *Those social arrangements are themselves errors.* The status of beauty is thus called on to reflect, however slantwise, a rational order or its absence. Forms of human arrangement unmotivated by lawfulness or harmony seemingly correlate with hostility toward the beautiful. Such appraisals hew to the developmentalist story of the globe, in which certain peoples and places are civilizationally other, being infantile or juvenile, or having fallen behind or off the clock of the world. This is the temporal divide presented by a former

Afghan woman journalist who shows to Janine di Giovanni a picture from the era of the Soviet-backed Najibullah government. In the photograph, an Afghan woman wears a miniskirt, heels, and pale lipstick. "What I'm trying to show you . . . is that we were people before the burqa."[89]

For Scarry, beauty is discerned as true value found in the materiality of the world—in the symmetry of petals, for instance—not determined by constructivist valuations produced by systems and arrangements (i.e., beauty is idiosyncratic but not relative). Instead, the world itself comprises the sensorial ground for the rightful reorder of things. Beauty does not beget justice, she demurs, but nonetheless "beautiful things . . . hold steadily visible the manifest good of equality and balance."[90] Citing John Rawls's definition of fairness as "a symmetry of everyone's relations to each other," Scarry argues that beauty arouses the desire for symmetry, so crucial to fairness in both its aesthetic and legal senses.[91] "It is the very symmetry of beauty," she writes, "which leads us to . . . the symmetry that eventually comes into place in the realm of justice."[92] Beauty and justice are analogous but also counterparts each to the other; "when one term is absent, the other becomes an active conspirator for the exile's return."[93] Just institutions (according to this schema) are beautiful because they conform to those classic aesthetic principles of equality and balance; as beautiful objects demand that we copy them so that others might enjoy them, so too do institutions.

Scarry's concern for the training of persons (and populations) promised to the care of beauty as an analogue for justice follows from such watchwords as *stewardship, protection,* and *laws.* Justice, she insists, must be ordained within one or another normative legal or administrative apparatus for "democracy" to appear as a full presence. Here governance comprises an aesthetics, shaping our apprehension and experience of it and rendering its instruments perceptible, or legible. The political effects of a presumably fair system, according to philosophers from Smith to Scarry, are sensually compelling because of their aesthetic correspondences. Scarry names the second line of the US Declaration of Independence (admiring the cadence of its syllables, "We hold these truths to be self-evident . . .") and the assembly hall (with its "bowl of space" reminiscent of the equidistant proportions of a sphere) as lovely; she names the law, when "both written and applied with consistency across all persons," as beautiful.[94] Accordingly, we should want to preserve and replicate such forms for the benefit of others to share in such beauty. If the Declaration is beautiful, and therefore just, it follows that it is a model or example for others. In short, being beautiful and also just qualifies the example to solicit, perhaps even to demand, compulsion over others to repeat it. But this also is the historical promise-violence of colonial tutelage, which presumes to teach racial, colonial others how to copy their betters. "The indolent races of savages . . . needed only to be inspired by envy to desire his desires, imitate his wants, to be on the road to his progress and his civilization."[95] What is being copied is not just those "desires" and "wants" but the ordering of desires and wants that placed "progress" and "civilization" out of reach of some and not others in the first place. That an aesthetic education follows from copying *correct* and *already known* forms is the premise of the civilizational endeavor. What is empire to do when it encounters forms of human arrangement whose aesthetic sensibilities are judged defective or perverse?

Each of Scarry's arguments for love of beauty brings us to its distributive pressure. For her, distribution is a self-evident principle of justice, tending toward even shares and implicit fairness. The "live" perception of beauty is also its apportionable availability, where "the site of stewardship in which one acts to protect or perpetuate a fragment of beauty already in the world or instead to supplement it by bringing into being a new object" is mirrored in our regard for justice.[96] Thus she offers, in another of her lists, "The *Iliad* or the *Mona Lisa* or the idea of distribution arise out of the requirement beauty places on us to replicate."[97] But of course, distribution is very often *not* fair and is very often a force. Scarry calls for distribution as an effect of the encounter with the beautiful, but she already admits to aesthetic unevenness as an a priori statement. Unevenness implies a distribution has already happened, and it was unfair. Indeed, in the history of the world, distribution bears an insistent telos—not toward fairness or equivalence but toward the partition of territory, which inaugurates the dominion of property. Both territory and property (each implied through the other) lead to a partisan mapping that integrates a body of racial-civilizational knowledge about those people and places where beauty lives *and* lapses. Scarry presupposes fairness as a goal of distribution, but such distribution can only emerge from a social order that already disavows fairness as it exists; fairness both as an ideal and as a norm operates as a social distinction to divide those who "believe" in it and those who do not. Necessarily and continuously, partition is a relation of shared commons and their denial.

That beauty creates a disposition for democracy (including the wish for others to have the benefit of it) and another for fascism (including its often-lethal judgments about humanity and its others) converge under liberalism's empire. To understand how beauty obtains an empirical status as a measurable property, it helps to consider rule of law (the foundation of the rules-based international order) as a device for arranging and creating conditions (as circumstances and as stipulations) rather than as mere operations within them; in other words, it is the police. The same goes for beauty, especially as analogue or antecedent. As we know from feminist scholars, the proper reproduction of assigned gender forms is crucial to genres of being human, including those racial, colonial genres used to describe states of savagery and barbarism, civility and culture. The young woman in an *unbeautiful* dress is world-historically significant to such genres establishing young or lapsed worlds where justice has not yet been found, or regularized as right arrangements. In this order, only certain vestments produce a lawful, which is to say recognizably rights-bearing, body.[98] Precolonial, Indigenous, and other "native" sartorial forms (which are often "inappropriately" gendered) have been litigated as commensurate with an a priori being, a being commensurate with rightlessness, such that humanitarian violence (and, before it, civilizational rule, colonial paternalism, and benevolent assimilation) presumes to cover such vulnerability.

In this descriptive statement, we "know" the burqa as both an aid and an obstacle to recognition. It is an aid because it alerts us that the being it covers is rightless (even if by our own hand or law), and it is an obstacle because the covered being can be nothing else. If we cannot know if she is beautiful, we cannot experience her as a person at all. In this usual arrangement, Emmanuel Levinas proposed that the human face "orders and ordains" us, calling the subject into "giving and serving" an other.[99] Where the face is obscured, ethical communing with others is hard, if not impossible.[100] But the face is not all. Also necessary for the admission of another's "aliveness," per Scarry, is an aesthetic education—for the observer, but also for the *observed*. Here lies a cascading series of faulty assumptions, that the burqa actually encourages misrecognition, where misrecognition as nonrecognition or the withdrawal of recognition is a consequence of *the burqa as a visible obstacle* rather than the statement, profile, or schema that solicits that refusal, that withdrawal. The "solution," then, is more perfect recognition in order to restore personhood to rightful subjects—those who are not alien, or other—thereafter. This is again the premise of disclosure, a requirement in order to properly inscribe her into liberal structures of subjectivity, through which her interior life, assumed from the amalgam of her surfaces, can be understood to conform to a likeness with ourselves. In a 2002 issue of *Vogue*, in a feature called "Beneath the Burqa," the noncoincidence of the burqa and the beautiful face together create the political and epistemological background for the writer to consider the aliveness of others, against that which aims to smother it: "But the third, the bravest, the leader of the gang, rolled back the nylon to reveal a young girl in her twenties named Sahaila. Her hair was dyed blonde; she wore pink lipstick and blue eyeliner. She stared at me defiantly, a smile twitching at the corner of her lips, Ah you see, she said, I am a person after all." The setup ("the bravest, the leader of the gang") forecasts what follows—the revelation that this young woman is beautiful, like any other should be *by right*. Recognizably so with her lipstick and eyeliner, as Moallem wryly notes, only then does she achieve legible personhood.[101]

Coming together is presumed to follow once we share the same ideals, once we regard the same objects, scenes, or persons as harmonious, fair, proportionate—in sum, beautiful. To insist on seeing the Afghan woman's unveiled body is to insist that her covering impedes "our" perception of her beauty, and therefore her humanity. But the foreclosure routed through the burqa as obstacle instead evinces the refusal or inability to acknowledge that an erasure and denial have taken place, because that erasure and denial has been purged in turn. In other words, the insistence of the noncoincidence of the burqa with beauty locates the former as antihuman and anticivilizational, and the latter as a pathway to liberal, liberated personhood. The reporter's admiration, while purporting to accord to Sahaila an unguessed-at agency, appropriates what is assumed to be irreducibly foreign into existing schemata of civilizational thinking and "modern" femininity.[102] These genres of the human, of the civic body, tell us much about these properties and their distribution of the sensible, that themselves enact violence through "making live" as well as "making die." Here, the challenge to misrecognition inadvertently invites surveillance, where misrecognition presumes that there is a truth about a being behind an erroneous perception. It also invites the effort to make oneself *recognizable*. This is what the makeover promises to remedy.

The Makeover

The Kabul Beauty School documentary suggests that "After Decades of War and the Taliban the Women of Afghanistan Need a Makeover." Here the makeover allegorizes a new sensorium for *making live*, aligned with what Patricia Stuelke astutely observes as the ruse of repair. But the reparative commitment to "mak[e] room for pleasure and amelioration" and celebrate "survival strategies and coping mechanisms as beautiful seeds of that which might one day, in the future, save the world," she warns, "is entangled with the very history and practices of neoliberal empire and the settler colonial carceral state that advocates for such methods."[103] It is to this quandary, in which beauty is conscripted for counterinsurgency, that I turn.

For the Muslim woman (according to both the humanitarian and the warmonger), a desire for beauty, to become beautiful, is not enough; her aesthetic education is imperative, and it is also deeply logistical. Where the modern site of control came to be the population as a whole, per Foucault, the administrative rationale of the modern state is aimed at the government of all aspects of the life of the population. The project of governing is not reducible to "political structures or to the management of states" but rather encompasses any domain whereby "the conduct of individuals or groups might be directed—the government of children, of souls, of communities, of families, of the sick."[104] Norbert Elias describes the formation of good habits as "the civilization of the affects"; one acquires civility through the habituated "restraint of affect-charged impulses."[105] The assertion that certain forms of bodily comportment grant or ease access to a better life (as defined in this instance by liberalism's measures of the beautiful and the good) coincides with the sociological concept that Bourdieu called habitus, those specific techniques and knowledge formations that shape and occupy bodies to negotiate realms of sociality.[106]

Beauty is one such habitus that administers, in Foucault's words, "an intensification of the body, a problematization of health and its operational terms," on behalf of population life.[107] To these ends, Lisa Lowe observes, "Education was necessary for character formation, socialization, and the proper development of the moral and civic subjectivity of the 'competent agent' within deliberative participatory democracy."[108] Here the promise of beauty is a form of biopower, at the level of both anatomo-individual discipline and population health, recruited to liberalism's empire. Or as Emily Raymundo sums up so well, "regime as a system of government, and regimen as a regulated course of behavior designed to produce health" come together in the aesthetic education.[109] Spiraling out from the imperial core to *too young* or otherwise *lapsed* worlds, a long history of curricula seeks to transform, guide, and "improve" those racial, colonial others who must learn from those who hail from places where beauty holds sway.[110] Genevieve Clutario, for instance, traces the "benevolent assimilation" of the Philippines under the tutelage of the United States, which (among other things) sought to instill respectability and industry through an education in beauty.[111] Such a regime (or regimen) change claims to remake the natives' habits and customs in order to manage themselves properly (through gender forms, or civic norms) and in turn secure the social order. Like missionaries or industrialists from an earlier age, contemporary evangelists of beauty believe that the right commodities might manufacture new desires and disciplines, new forms of knowledge and society. This biopolitical totality is captured in the original name of Beauty without Borders, the Body and Soul Wellness Program. On the first day of class, filmed for the documentary, American volunteers used a chart outlining some basic rules for such a holistic disposition (blithely disregarding the war that brought them together): "Healthy Body and Mind, Rest and Relaxation, Enough Sleep 6–8 Hrs, Exercise: Look Good, Feel Good, Work Better." This and other scenes from the Kabul Beauty School draw attention to the way that presumably ornamental aesthetics involve intensive training to, pace Foucault, "establish rhythms, impose particular occupations, [and] regulate the cycles of repetition" of human activity.[112]

Establishing a commonsensical continuity between interior life and social order, the makeover therefore targets those whose aesthetic competencies are deemed untimely, inappropriate, or perverse, and redirects them toward specific objects or habits that are ascribed as beautiful, pleasing, and (personally and socially) hygienic. *Clean and modern* were watchwords for the beauty school's curriculum through which, as Paula Black might observe, "the salon is made use of to police the boundaries of an 'acceptable' bodily state."[113] Pointing to the dilapidated state of secret salons, hairstylist Terri Grauel told the *New York Times*: "'I was just appalled by the lack of sanitation. . . . They're using rusty scissors, they'll have one cheap comb for the whole salon and they don't sanitize it, there's no running water or Barbisol, and there's a real lice problem. . . . *They're doing it, but they really need the education. They don't have any technique whatsoever.*'"[114] The *Times* continues, pitying the absence of a proper education and its necessary ornaments: "They have no one to teach them [to look beautiful] and nowhere to lay their hands on a decent comb, let alone the panoply of gels, rinses, powders, liners and colors that spill from the shelves of the average American drugstore."[115] In *Vogue*, "Even those who have worked as hairdressers for years are working for the first time with scissors that don't look like pruning shears; they are mastering techniques they never knew exists ('Today we will learn the solid-form haircut')."[116] "Primitive" tools—for instance, a "crude, handcarved piece of wood with a rubber band attached" serving as a perming rod—are compared to the new gleaming instruments donated by industry giants such as Paul Mitchell and Frédéric Fekkai.[117] And Westerners in Kabul, according to Grauel, would go elsewhere for their needs if the school's apprentices failed to learn their lessons. "There will be NGOs, diplomats, people from all over the world going there to rebuild Afghanistan. Do you think that they would have their hair cut by someone who was not Western-trained?"[118]

The promise of beauty thus recruits the Afghan woman to the clock of the world, calling on her to *catch up, catch up*. *The Beauty Academy of Kabul* features scenes of instruction that double as scenes of shaming, in which the students are disciplined to first recognize, and second compensate for, their civilizational lack. In the documentary, Debbie Rodriguez, a volunteer from Michigan, scolds the initial cohort of women enrolled in the beauty school. In this encounter, the brassy, bossy Rodriguez demands, "All those who have makeup on, stand up! You know what? You're stuck in a rut, guys! You're stuck in a hole of the past that you can't get out of, and my God, before I leave here, you're getting out of the hole!" One of her students grimly counters, "In your country there's no fighting. You don't have to worry; you can talk back to your husbands. Women in Afghanistan aren't free like that."[119] The ways in which this moment sketches out the promise of beauty, defining the coordinates of freedom as well as the violence of ugliness, are multiple. On the one hand, we seem to witness the repudiation of the expert from the Global North and the considerable gaps in her knowledge. And yet both student and teacher appear to agree that making beautiful is making live, indivisible from a future tense. As a regime of expertise, beauty instruction circulates both techniques and dispositions that enable individuals to govern themselves and their fates, to learn to be *free like that*. Just as the US military and administrative occupation put into place continuous regulation and assessment to account for transition objectives, target strengths, and predictive estimates of return, the Kabul Beauty School set benchmarks for the achievement of civilizational criteria.[120] Or, as Rodriguez asserts loudly, "You can't have fuzzy perms, bad hair color, and bad haircuts. It's your jobs as the most progressive hairdressers, the most trained and educated hairdressers in Afghanistan, to set the new trends.... If you guys don't do it, how can Afghanistan change if you guys don't change?"[121]

Where the normative formations for recognizable sociolegal persons follow from the presence of Reason, those from young or lapsed worlds require guidance in the form of an ideal or principle. The example they are meant to copy is of course ours, *as the most progressive, the most trained and educated*—an empire of beauty. But to copy or to be a copy reiterates their preassigned subhumanity, as such presence as they might achieve does not mature from self-inaugurated intellectual or creative activity, or from an innate spirit striving toward freedom, but from an education in becoming human *enough*.[122] To be a "free" subject, as liberalism (and Rodriguez) exhorts, refers to a self-consciousness or enclosure that is a being-for-self; but such presence is withheld from those encouraged to become a being-after-another. Saba Mahmood is insightful here, helping us to observe the curriculum in its "efforts toward [Afghan women's] self-realization are aimed not so much at discovering one's 'true' desires and feelings ... but at honing one's rational and emotional capacities so as to *approximate the exemplary model of the [ideal] self.*"[123] Here the significance of copy is as a social act of establishing a principle and authorizing an example for the alleged benefit of others. *How else will you learn?* But when fathomed through the historico-ontological concept of a racial-civilizational order, the copy is belated, chronologically *after* in the history of the world. Thus, the aesthetic education coincides with "the ultimate aim of colonial mimicry," which, as Parama Roy notes, "is not simply to constitute natives as objects to be studied; it must also produce natives as self-reflective subjects, who know themselves as others (the colonizers) know them."[124]

Colonial mimicry thus powers the accusation of poor copy, poor because the presence it calls forth is partial, incomplete, and hopelessly estranged from the original. Shirley Jennifer Lim observes, "Beauty through the appropriate use of consumer culture signified the superiority of the Western democratic capitalist way of life," so what then to say about its *inappropriate* use?[125] Once pitied for their deprivation, Afghan women might instead be accused of deviancy. The school's instructors reported being "shocked at what these women did to their hair and faces."[126] Journalists catalogued with close detail Afghan women's preferences for saturated hues and dramatic lines for their eyes and lips and the school's students memorizing instructions on creating a "natural" face but declining to practice one.[127] In a classroom scene from *The Beauty Academy of Kabul*, the American volunteers chastise the students for the tight ringlet perms they and their clients favor, and advocate instead for "looser, more natural curls," to which no one much pays attention. The poverty of their copy is at times the accusation of the failure to absorb or affirm clearly the value of its precedent—the original, the example. The author of the *Vogue* feature is scandalized that "makeup is applied with heavy-handed enthusiasm by those denied access to it for so long ([one student] Hanifa, for example, though almost always in her shirt and tie, wears glitter on her cheekbones and eyelids and shiny purple on her lips)."[128] Such accounts assign to the students a developmental adolescence or artificial femininity, reporting bewilderment at both the heavy hand and lavish glitter reminiscent of the drag queen.[129]

Counter to the habits through which the school sought to establish the correct practice of freedom, the students are ungovernable. They are not yet oriented, as Sara Ahmed would put it, toward the objects or scenes they, or we, are told guarantee happiness.[130] The putative failure to adopt proper aesthetic judgment is the concomitant failure to achieve full self-consciousness. The paradox, then, is that a liberal political or social order that claims to foster an individual's capacities is precisely one in which deviation is a disciplinary problem. In other words, this regime cannot afford to nurture those freedoms that are presumably its highest value, such as self-sovereignty. This paradox is how the transition to democracy builds in the likelihood of the other's failure, in which the threshold of sovereignty is never quite crossed, and the conversion to full personhood is stunted. As Ava Kim notes about what she calls transition ideology, encompassing illiberal states and nonconforming bodies, "We know that for many vulnerable people, the violence they face has simply emerged in a different form."[131] Those who are promised an *afterward* find themselves accused of its miscarriage. And the poor copy that *remains poor* might become an existential threat to the original, threatening to degrade its value, becoming something worse—a parody, a cracked funhouse mirror, or a new enemy—leading to a never-ending interval of interference and control.

Rey Chow cautions against falling prey to the trap in which "it is the failure, the incompleteness or incompletability of the mimetic attempt... that makes the nonwhite subject theoretically interesting—indeed salvageable."[132] This too would have us yield to already known forms for the assessment of personhood, including liberal forms of political agency or theoretical value. Still, the ontological break between the original and the copy might usefully disturb the transfer of presence from one to another. That the contract of ultimate intelligibility and parallelism between the original and the copy cannot be fulfilled, according to this logic, is the point and its power. But also—the copy (of democracy, of the beautiful face) might obstruct the police powers of the original, which seeks to delimit the copy as a sphere of presence or possibility. Or the gap between the original and the copy might be contingent on what resources are available for replication, and the discrepancies that shadow it. Or finally, maybe, it might be a denial that understands the original is not so beautiful or fair after all.

Unfinishing School

In 2014, NATO formally ended combat operations by the International Security Assistance Force in Afghanistan, but US troop levels increased in 2017 (after H. R. McMaster showed Donald Trump the photographs of miniskirted Afghan women) before plummeting three years later, after the

Trump administration negotiated a withdrawal not with the Afghan government but with the Taliban. In 2010, President Barack Obama announced the American combat mission in Iraq had ended on September 1, but that the troops would remain "with a different mission." When, in January 2020, the Iraqi parliament voted against their continued military presence, the United States simply refused to comply. That same month, in the space of several days, President Trump pursued the extrajudicial assassination of a sovereign state's governmental official—the Iranian military commander Qasem Soleimani—without informing congressional leaders, required under the War Powers Act. Doubling down in response to global outrage, he threatened to destroy fifty-two cultural sites "important to Iran culture" (in belated retaliation, it seems, for "the 52 American hostages taken by Iran many years ago")—an act that is, according to international law, a war crime, and for which previous administrations had criticized the Taliban and ISIS (for destroying the Bamiyan Buddhas and the historic site of Palmyra, respectively). This second threat also drew swift and strong condemnation, less for the contravention of international law—which the US reserves the right to ignore—and more for its targets. Some critics protested that these sites inspire a necessary awe and sublime beauty that anchor us to a global humanity.[133] Others decried such a rash decision as evidence of the poor aesthetic education of a vulgar, boorish president who resists all such an education ostensibly provides. "Does the President know what would be lost? Probably not."[134]

Without rival after the Cold War (it crowed), the United States claimed world-historical ascension as the human rights regime par excellence, yet bedeviled by democracy-poor countries and even poorer copies. But in the war on terror, the sense of a right to global supremacy remains even after any claim to the protection and promotion of human rights or indeed *the regime that would do so* has long passed from political expediency to onerous burden. From black-site torture and mass incarceration, forced deportations and genocidal "self-defense," rights are now recalculated as a *deficit* for liberal governance.[135] Dispensing with all pretense of "civilizing mission" or international law (to which the United States and its proxies are unanswerable), democracy as an imperial polity is itself the catastrophe that threatens the world.

I first encountered the Kabul Beauty School while perusing an issue of *Vogue*, published just ahead of the 2003 US invasion of Iraq on the false pretense of "weapons of mass destruction," and for a while it seemed to be the war's signal humanitarian feat.[136] Decades later, I am struck by the *absence* of the Kabul Beauty School and all it stood for—it has gone missing.

The school under the financial and managerial auspices of Beauty without Borders closed after several years; the building and its materials passed to Debbie Rodriguez, who renamed the salon and school Oasis Rescue and successfully parlayed these into a controversial best-selling memoir (controversial because of its Islamophobic caricatures and sundry falsehoods). Of the Kabul Beauty School, a *Chicago Tribune* foreign correspondent declared, "The change was merely cosmetic," noting that the Afghan women Rodriguez had trained, and whose stories she liberally fabricated, "feel abandoned and used."[137] One of the women vented, "Debbie taught us, but left us with nothing." Indeed, what remains is ruin: "A pile of hair dryers now sits in the yard of the Kabul Beauty School. Old salon chairs line the courtyard walls. Everything is covered in the thick film of the Afghan dust that always threatens to swallow this country and turn everything beige."[138] (Beige, the color of the desert and decay.) Meanwhile, there are no copies anywhere of the school's curricula, including instructional manuals or training videos; despite its much-heralded institutional provenance (from the Wharton School of Business to Clairol to *Vogue*), we find no trace of its education in beauty.[139]

In his study of apocryphal time, David Scott observes that "the problem of time and the problem of history are thought of . . . as *irreducible* to each other; they are connected, undeniably, but not necessarily identical. A distinctive temporality is always embodied in—while not being the simple mirror of—each imaginary history."[140] Such is permanent war. The march of historical time as successive moments continues but diverges from political time, which goes nowhere—indeed, political time must go nowhere, because power lies in the interval, not the ending. The lesson here is not that an aesthetic education failed to matter much in the conduct of liberal war, but that the aesthetic education we got was *the war itself*. What is finally provocative, then, is this aspect (a useful synonym here for *face, form*, and *countenance*) of the Kabul Beauty School—the promise of beauty that never comes to fruition amid a war on terror that cannot end. The Beauty School as the promise of an aesthetic education and the good governance that would follow sought to narratively contain occupation as a discrete event, to herald a happy ending that would never come.

"I [am] not going to extend this forever war," Biden announced with the US withdrawal from Afghanistan, even as the CIA bolstered a secret base in the Sahara, from which it runs drone flights to Libya, Niger, and Mali, and the military's Africa Command resumed airstrikes in Somalia.[141] While an education in beauty once promised military violence and humanitarianism in the same operation, its collapse ushered in a liberal-imperial ethos through which law as *only* war is promised to another. As Lisa Bhungalia argues of "elastic empire," the "mechanics and manifold distributions of contemporary warfare ... work instead through securitized arrangements that persist in 'postwar' theaters, in sprawling surveillance and intellectual infrastructure developed over the last two decades, and in emergency laws now normalized and global in scope."[142] Almost every year since 2001, the US Congress has authorized a marked increase in funding to the Pentagon and the Department of Defense to conduct and continue counterinsurgency operations in Iraq, Pakistan, Somalia, Yemen, Haiti, and Iran, and to supply munitions for Israeli bombardment in occupied Palestine. Whether hospitals, schools, bakeries, universities, mosques, cemeteries, residences, or refugee encampments, there are no "red lines" for the United States (or its proxies) where the devastating "beauty of the arrangement" is reason enough.

And so, the promise of beauty in the war on terror illuminates the poverty of the promise of historical progress and perfectibility through reason, law, or a rules-based order (though there have been millions of such revelations since 1492). If one no longer believes in the contract (including the promise), between original and copy, word and the world, then there is no reason to believe that the contract is on the side of moral or ethical truth. The promise of beauty calls on us to honor the aliveness of others, but it also distributes its judgments unevenly, even unto injury and death. The absence of law is presumably catastrophic, but the law declares its absence in order to intensify its sphere of control and interference. Similarly, the transitional regime is not the end of empire, but its expansion. To believe that beauty gives us a mirror for justice, because it models fair and symmetrical decisions, is to believe that both beauty and justice exist before the law, outside the force of language and representation, and that the law is the transparent communication and codification of their shared normative values. But because after liberalism's empire we (we, the poor copies among us) know that this is not true—the law *is* itself violence—beauty and justice must exist elsewhere.

While beauty might be something we can each say we have experienced, justice is not—*not yet*, as long as the very notion of justice produces and requires the expulsion or death of others, understood as nonpersons, as normative and necessary. So, where lawfulness is promised as the consequence or copy of beauty, what is given by liberal governance in pursuit of forever war is the aesthetic form of the contract (which it contravenes continuously but imposes ruthlessly). The form of the contract is not nothing, because it delivers the violence of law, just as it is not nothing to break it—to become a poor copy because the original was never that beautiful, or fair. Here lies the path beyond often-repeated statements about the contradiction of democratic actuality, or the mirage of a beautiful untruth, to consider its built-in difference from itself. Against claims that beauty is mere ornament, or that it is analogous to the rule of law, democracy, or justice, beauty as method does no more or less than mediate our ethical engagement with life. That is to say, the capacity assigned to beauty as a being or becoming that enhances a feeling or even a model for *another world* might alternately lead us to observe the actual uselessness of our present order. If so, what might happen when beauty is understood as a right in the absence of a state, or a law, to guarantee it?

Chapter 3

The Right to Be Beautiful without Guarantee

This orientation to human rights as belonging to the world of aesthetic judgment might strike the reader as odd, for these rights are usually defined as juridical entitlements defended by political activists and defined by well-trained litigators.... But as Judith Butler has argued, an exclusively juridical orientation fails to do justice to the "passion and grief and rage, all of which tear us from ourselves, bind us to others, transport us, undo us, implicate us in lives that are not our own." Put differently, regarding human rights narrowly—as only relating to the administration of law—overlooks the emotional ties that comprise this social landscape, the affective appeals and deep-seated convictions that drive the grounds of this discourse.

Sharon Sliwinski, *Human Rights in Camera*

In Cambodia, my parents called bombs kro bike, which literally means broken seed.

Y-Dang Troeung, *Landbridge*

Cambodia remains one of the states most affected by landmines and other ordnance still undetonated from the wars of the last century. In the 1960s, the United States conducted secret programs with Special Forces personnel in Cambodia, whose primary activities (in nearly two thousand missions) included laying "sanitized self-destruct antipersonnel" mines well beyond the

Vietnamese border.¹ In another series of covert missions, the United States dropped half a million tons of murderous ordnance in Cambodia alone; at least half of these almost fifteen thousand sorties dropped their wayward payloads outside target zones. With their defeat of the US-sponsored Lon Nol regime, the Khmer Rouge commuted 1975 into Year Zero, schools into prisons, and the countryside into killing fields. Over three years, eight months, and twenty days of revolutionary violence (or what Cambodians call "Pol Pot time"), the Khmer Rouge was responsible for the deaths of almost two million Cambodians, due to starvation, execution, or torture. In 1979, Vietnamese troops entered Phnom Penh, ending the Khmer Rouge's turbulent reign. During the Vietnamese occupation, a barrier minefield was laid along the entire length of the Cambodia-Thailand border where the Khmer Rouge had retreated to its rural strongholds. In the following decade, Khmer Rouge and monarchist opposition forces used landmines to protect newly won ground or to contaminate the interior of abandoned Vietnamese defensive positions, until the 1991 Paris Accords ended these wars and established structures for managing the peace. And yet hundreds of thousands of bombs lie just beneath the earth's surface, still sleeping.

This chapter begins with the antipersonnel landmine that fulfills its purpose even after war as event—murdering or maiming an enemy, an indiscriminate category encompassing any and all living beings in a targeted lifeworld—and, in doing so, stages a complicated scene for multiple interventions.² In 2009, Norwegian theater director Morten Traavik, funded in part by the Norwegian Ministry of Foreign Affairs, convened the second Miss Landmine beauty pageant for women and girls who had lost limbs in landmine explosions in Cambodia.³ The first pageant was held the previous year in Angola, still heavily mined after a twenty-seven-year civil war, and featured the Angolan First Lady as one of the judges.⁴ The pageant would not go so well a second time. Drawing on its collaborations with humanitarian organizations and service providers, the Miss Landmine pageant promised to foster "female pride and empowerment" in pursuit of a politics of visibility, rendering cognizance of undetonated landmines through their violent inscription on amputees, and awarding a prize of a custom-fitted prosthetic limb.⁵ Partnering with the Cambodian Disabled People's Organization, Traavik selected twenty prospective queens, each hailing from one of Cambodia's provinces, among those already participating in NGO- or state-sponsored rehabilitation programs. With contestants made over in colorful, casual jersey dresses, Miss Landmine produced a documentary and a pictorial magazine, featuring the twenty amputee contestants posing at tumbled temples, beautiful beaches, and luxury hotels. But though the Cambodian government initially supported the pageant, officials from the Ministry of Social Affairs abruptly refused to allow the pageant to proceed, just days before the event, citing concerns about exploitation.[6] Instead, Miss Landmine continued online voting while staging a finale-in-exile in Norway where local Cambodian refugees also voted on life-size versions of contestants' photographs, carried down a red carpet runway strewn with roses. Afterward, Traavik traveled back to Cambodia in stealth—a trip also captured by a film crew—to award the pageant winner, nineteen-year-old Dos Sopheap from the province of Battambang, $1,000 for her education and fit her for a titanium prosthetic leg.[7]

The structures falling apart and coming together at the scene of the untimely detonation manifest total war as continuous presence, but also administrative peace as escalating governance. The latter unfolds through the human rights claim, the paradoxical possession of a right that nonetheless must be recognized by others with normative attachments to institutions such as the rule of law in order for that right to hold meaning (if not consequence), and the humanitarian mission, the campaign to ease suffering at the stratum of bare life where war persists as a suspended death sentence. The claim and the mission are not the same, but are increasingly yoked together to coconstitute normativity and vulnerability. From the sprawling international complex that funds and conducts prosthetic manufacturing, rehabilitation and vocational training, infrastructural development and cultural programming, to the aesthetic and moral discourses of rights, capacities, and humanity, all must be in place for the claim and the mission to promise, as the pageant does, beauty.

What is the promise of beauty for habituation in disastrous situations where *a life that can be lived* is hard to hold? Can beauty provide a place in the world for the vulnerable, violated self? Part intervention and part performance, the Miss Landmine pageant follows from a not uncommon faith that beauty is both a humanitarian problem and also its solution. That is to say, the humanitarian sensorium that once assigned undisputed value to forms of suffering as a conduit for empathy or "empowerment" might shift to beauty as a measure of that suffering and also its remedy.[8] The first part of this chapter addresses the pageant's maxim, *everyone has the right to be beautiful*, to consider the rights claim that unfolds tactically under a quasi-authoritarian regime, a constitutional monarchy inaugurated to close a violent history (one that includes genocide) and yet found to contravene rights (presumably the key to closure) continuously, through a humanitarian campaign for the social recognition of the war damaged. *The right to be beautiful* attests to the degree to which rights almost exclusively model claims to universality and the subject of freedom at the turn of the twenty-first century. Such claims follow from the constellation of modern powers that presume to adjudicate humanity, through which the human is the effect of rights, animated by the law, and those who have been abandoned or outcast through the law's lapse or suspension are rendered defenseless. Where their absence is dehumanization, and their presence redemption, rights are presumed to catalyze the transition from nonrecognition to recognition of another's humanity—and the capacity for beauty, the same. These frames of recognition require us to consider beauty with other rights, such as speech or assembly, in a series on whose behalf it is right to intervene against what terrors might follow in their absence.

That the right to be beautiful is not a political right in the juridical sense—it cannot be legally recognized—is obvious. This is often the first objection to its premise, that the right to be beautiful is meaningless because beauty, while often subject to judgment, is not a property that can be protected from or granted by a state. And yet because this claim adopts the aesthetic form of rights, it invites serious study. Through aesthetic forms that organize and render intelligible humanity, we perceive the absence or presence of rights as that which transforms bare life into a social world, as that which we presumably hold in common, over which we can argue or agree—or not. Instead of reading the right to be beautiful *against* other rights claims (for comparison, for failure), reading it *alongside* transcribes the forms of rightfulness and rightlessness through their aesthetic properties. Inasmuch as rightfulness is a utopian horizon of normativity, the right to be beautiful might unfold for us how its aesthetic produces forms for a life that can be, or ought to be. It fashions an argument for the right to be human as the a priori condition of the right to have rights (after Hannah Arendt) while disclosing—inadvertently, perhaps—the ambiguous purchase of rights *after rights* in the absence of a state or other institution (such as the United Nations) willing or able to secure them. The pageant thus surfaces two cuts into a life—the first through violence, and the second through beauty.

The second part of this chapter considers the rescue mission—in this example, designed as a pageant—as a normative ordering of sensibility and sociality. In this instance, the aesthetic strategies of the pageant attempt to render the "universal" properties of truth, beauty, and freedom perceptible. But (one might say) why not claim other rights for survivors, rather than beauty? Why the pageant and not a class action suit, for instance, pursued through a court of law? Because, as this chapter responds, what is *any* right after lawfulness (despite or because of universal declarations and constitutions and trials) proves to be the origin of violence? To desire to belong to the roster of those who hold rights is to desire belonging in a rules-based order, and a sense of continuity for oneself and with others who share a lifeworld. The absence of law is presumably catastrophic, but as we know from the previous chapter, the law declares its absence in order to intensify its sphere of control and interference.[9] So the world as it is—awful, ruinous, and devastating—requires that we consider *rights after rights*, by which I mean *the failure of the law to secure a livable life*.

Here the nonjuridical nature of the right to be beautiful can tell us much about the normative aesthetics of rights (as practices, fantasies, institutions) and the actual uselessness of the law (not "just" beauty) to secure justice. Even as the promise of beauty provides a surplus that imagines life beyond mere survival, it might also trace the absent center of the liberal rules-based order. As a structure for recognition and reciprocity within an affective economy proximate to, or as a substitute for, the law, the Miss Landmine pageant outlines an antipolitical aesthetic organized by fantasies of transcending, or revamping, the obstacles that shape survivors' life chances. The right to be beautiful both underlines *and* undermines the equation between law and the protection of the human. Because it cannot be juridically bestowed (despite the pageant form, which presumes to recognize what is already present), this right invites us to consider the possibilities for conceiving the human outside the law. In this instance, then, the right to be beautiful is not the precondition of claiming other rights, but the capacity for living on *without guarantee*.

Miss Landmine is an instructive scenario in which we can observe that claims about aesthetic capacities are also claims about political forces, and vice versa. Understanding such capacities and claims together alerts us to the problems of survival that violence poses to life, or some life, and the aesthetic forms named as solutions to its foreclosure. Inasmuch as rights constitute some of those aesthetic forms—the trial, the assembly, and the election—and beauty as a capacity for life despite crisis and catastrophe, what follows from deeming beauty as a right and rights themselves as beautiful? Where beauty is promised as a counter to political illiberalism, a protection against pain, deprivation, and suffering, what kind of subjects and political cultures does the right to be beautiful draw on, or bring into being, and what kinds does it preclude or aver? Here the attachment to beauty *as a right* articulates those normative practices, fantasies, institutions, and intuitions that organize people's worlds, in which the life that can be lived is balanced on the pinpoint of enduring in a particular fashion, through which one might become beautiful.

Ugly States and Ornamental Rights

The landmine is an instrument of total war, operating through what Mark Duffield calls *environmental terror* toward the devastation of an enemy's lifeworld.[10] Among its targets are critical infrastructure, social networks, and climate regimes, "together with the neurological and cellular processes that collectively support life and make it possible," such that earth, air, water, and biological life itself become carriers of latent deathliness. In the 1960s and 1970s throughout Laos, Cambodia, and Vietnam, the United States deployed chemical warfare with abandon, seeding silver iodide in cloud formations to prolong monsoon seasons, and dispersing twenty million gallons of herbicides to defoliate land and starve guerrillas (and civilians) of sustenance, coverage, and recruits, through the indiscriminate destruction of human and nonhuman life. Christine Hong describes such a "principle of indistinction" as "predicated on the lethal conflation of racialized humanity with suspect terrain that refused differentiation on the level of the individual."[11] Munitions buried below the earth, carcinogens and other toxins concentrated in the water and air—it is war without ending.[12]

It is not just war, though, that targets another. What Rey Chow calls the age of the world target names the structures that conceive the world simultaneously as an object of perfectible knowledge and a field of calculable interference. War and vision, violence and knowledge, share affinities, thus making it possible to bomb and to repair, at once or in succession. These insights render explicit the binds between interceding agencies—militaries and humanitarians, among them, which we know are close collaborators—and the objects they encounter in their simultaneous, converging fields of vision, dichotomized according to what Chow calls "the 'eye' and its 'target.'"[13] Writing about Haiti, for instance, Sibylle Fischer observes the "aesthetics of 'bare life'" "in the grotesque triangulation of a desecrated body of a victim, an intrepid photographer, and an awed metropolitan reader," along with the absent presence of the perpetrator who makes the photograph possible.[14] The humanitarian is therefore a partner (more or less reluctantly) to the warmonger in parsing the human and its others, and rendering judgments about wrong or hostile arrangements, arrangements that require incursion or cure. When and where the human has been diminished or destroyed through genocide, ethnic cleansing, or other violence, she is presumably reconstituted through the restoration or establishment of new institutions, including the rule of law. Both war and peace as such might interpolate an observer conscious of the vulnerability of *someone missing something—*

whether freedom, right, aid, beauty, or limb—and an operator capable of interceding to repair that absence.[15]

In this way, Cambodia has been a target for terror *and* repair, which are not distinct from each the other. The ending of civil war and occupation coincides with the ending of the Cold War and South African apartheid, leading some to name the 1990s the decade of human rights.[16] In this new world order, the rights regime combined democracy, free markets, and the rule of law.[17] The 1991 Paris Peace Accords established first, the United Nations Transitional Authority in Cambodia; second, election of a "constituent assembly" that would draft and approve a new constitution; and, third, "respect for and observance of human rights and fundamental freedoms." In declaring that the constitution would be consistent with the provisions of the Universal Declaration of Human Rights and other international agreements, the accords state, "Cambodia's tragic recent history requires special measures to assure protection of human rights. Therefore, the constitution will contain a declaration of fundamental rights, including the rights to life, personal liberty, security, freedom of movement, freedom of religion, assembly and association including political parties and trade unions, due process and equality before the law, protection from arbitrary deprivation of property or deprivation of private property without just compensation, and freedom from racial, ethnic, religious or sexual discrimination."[18] Rights and the instruments that guarantee them, such as elections and constitutions, are found absent, and then provided to Cambodia (or Vietnam or Afghanistan or Iraq) by those same parties or agencies that contravened its sovereignty in the first instance.

Histories of war in Southeast Asia are histories of bargains and breaches with devils with long reach. During the US war in Southeast Asia, Cambodia formally protested American violations of Cambodian sovereignty at the United Nations on more than one hundred occasions, to no avail. Under the Khmer Rouge, and while the United States looked away, life had become ungrounded as even the earth itself bled with mass graves, anonymous graves—the so-called killing fields. Millions were murdered or "disappeared," including bureaucrats, teachers, intellectuals, dancers, writers, Muslims, musicians, and monks, as the regime sought to transform Cambodia into an agrarian utopia. After their ouster, the United States rallied behind the Khmer Rouge against the Vietnamese occupation, refusing to condemn this strategic ally for its terrible abuses and pressuring other states to withhold humanitarian aid to Cambodia. Thus the 1991 Paris Peace Accords promised reconstruction but not recognition of genocide (the parties that would participate in free elections included the Khmer Rouge); instead, the accords described the atrocities in euphemisms, such as the agreement to the "non-return to the policies and practices of the recent past."[19] However, the Cambodian state, under the three-decade reign of Prime Minister Hun Sen, routinely relied on security force violence, including impunity for killings and torture, and politically motivated prosecutions, as well as forced evictions, illegal land acquisitions, restrictions on protest and information, and rampant corruption across political offices and legal courts.[20] Such contemporary Cambodian state violence is continuous with French colonialism, US-sponsored regimes, including the antidemocratic rule of Lon Nol following a CIA-supported coup, and the United States itself.[21] Even as the United States under the Obama administration claimed to be the "single largest financial support of humanitarian mine action," its Cold War–era bombing campaigns in Cambodia informed a 2011 Department of Justice white paper for the justification of targeted assassinations as "necessary and appropriate" force in areas outside of designated war zones, the very premise of contemporary surveillance infrastructure and drone warfare.[22] What is understood as peace, then, is a series of at times lethal norms dependent on a sovereign state, or international governance, to enforce them; neither is reliable as an arbiter of rights, let alone justice.[23]

When and where it appears or is called on, justice is, sometimes reluctantly, resolved in the trial. It is a common feature of transitional regimes pursuing international legitimacy to hold trials in response to political atrocities committed by their predecessors, though here (as elsewhere) a good number of successors are former Khmer Rouge officials, and thereby deliver closure to those who have lived too long in states of unfreedom. In this way, the trial might gesture toward liberal rule of law in the reconstruction of the social and political order, but it must also be limited in scope, lest the successor regime also be found deficient. While the 1991 Paris Peace Accords dictated that the new constitution must also "prohibit the retroactive application of criminal law," in 2006 the United Nations sponsored a hybrid tribunal composed of Cambodian and international judges prosecuting the Khmer Rouge's "crimes against humanity," which convicted just three men for the deaths of almost two million Cambodians, as well as the torture and displacement of millions more.[24] In 2018, the tribunal finally declared that two of these Khmer Rouge leaders committed genocide against the Muslim Cham minority and the Vietnamese. Over the course of more than a decade during which the tribunal struggled to deliver even those convictions, the Cambodian regime sought to limit the number of defendants to just "senior leaders" and those "most responsible," while denying access to possible witnesses who held influential positions, warning that more trials would result in chaos, even renewed civil war. These temporizing arguments manifest what Cathy J. Schlund-Vials calls the "Cambodian syndrome," or a "transnational set of amnesiac politics revealed through hegemonic modes of public policy and memory."[25] Such forgetting and remembering has aesthetic forms for the apprehension of political time, established not just after the Second World War (with the Nuremburg trials and the 1951 Genocide Convention) but following anticolonial and revolutionary upheavals. From the prime minister down to other former Khmer Rouge soldiers, a common refrain echoed: "They should only try the top leaders and stop there. Otherwise, it will be too fragile for society. Where will it end?"[26]

Claims to justice pursued through a rules-based order thus comprise a dim horizon. Whether as war crimes courtroom or truth and reconciliation commission (as two examples), the form of the trial is construed as a necessary instrument for securing the rule of law as the end of violence.[27] (This is not to say that the verdicts meant nothing to survivors.)[28] The trial is not simply the juridical norm for repair or justice under liberalism's regime, but an aesthetic form that coheres the attachment to its institutions. In other words, both the courtroom and the commission are aesthetic forms of transitional justice, and, with them, the confession (the truth to be told) and the conviction (not the sentence) establish the pastness of prior violence and manage the conditions and terms of its reentry in the present. Thus might the trial require *passing over* justice for a calculated production of historicity (or *feeling historical*). Its form gives violence a beginning and an end, rendering that violence a regretful aberration. Indeed, as Jolie Chea and Robert Eap have each observed, the trial isolated horrific violence to the four-year regime of the Khmer Rouge and, in doing so, precluded US culpability for its devastatingly indiscriminate bombing campaigns.[29] Through these erasures, the courtroom or commission attaches either malicious intent or unknowing complicity (and subsequent remorse) to persons, individuating and also dispersing responsibility for cruelty and crimes against humanity, for state-sanctioned violence and terror.[30] This post-Nuremburg definition of genocide as "singularly event-based per jurisprudential precedents," Zoe Samudzi observes, deflects responsibility from "entire nation-states and the logics that animate and sustain them."[31] The serial but stunted nature of such trials further establishes the recuperative intent of the transitional state (the violence is over), but also a timetable before justice becomes revenge (we cannot go too far). Where the past is no longer relevant, because too much time has passed in between the crime and the trial, the so-called cycle of violence names further trials (or convictions, let alone other more radical forms of accountability) as that which must be halted in order to march forward.[32] It is as such that the trial is the aesthetic form of closure; it narratively establishes and encloses violence as an event in the past, rather than a structure in the present.

Given all this, how are we to apprehend rights, where all manner of claims to freedom and justice are made in their name? Channeled through juridico-institutional structures and also stamped with moral certitude, the rights claim is conventionally understood as an instrument or technology for protecting the individual from a state, or a state of lawlessness. But while rights must be ordained within one or another normative legal apparatus for rights to manifest full presence, rights also frame an affective logic toward others (as Sharon Sliwinski notes, we cannot "overlook ... the emotional ties that comprise this social landscape"), whether those others are seen as deserving or undeserving of their protection. Rights therefore can be grasped as a conceptual frame, a social practice, a mode of governance, a form of conduct, an ontological truth, a coercive apparatus, or an amalgam of one or more of these cohering and coming apart. In other words, rights shape our aesthetic apprehension of the senses and structures of value making that license certain sensibilities as common sense, equilibrium, or enclosure, and preclude others as immiseration, barbarism, or deviancy. Consider how crucial the *appearance* of rights is to liberal democracy, administrative governance, law and order. "We the People" is a legal fiction (we know that it is a divide); the bountiful marketplace is one of its ciphers (we know that it is an engine of violence). The Civil Rights Memorial in Montgomery, Alabama, consists of a fountain in the form of an asymmetrical inverted cone with the dates of significant deaths and legal decisions and legislation inscribed in chronological order along the perimeter. This sculptural representation-image envisages rights as a linear succession, a timeline emplotted onto the curving "moral arc of the universe." On the other hand, the *disappearance* of rights—into the purported void of the burqa, for instance, if not the black site—is the measure of "not enough" freedom, which sets in motion the intervention. To understand the aesthetic dimensions here is to understand that such forms not only inscribe the rights we appreciate as inalienable to humanity, but also shape how we pursue such claims, and through them imagine a future for ourselves and for others.

As a juridical concept, *human rights* are commonly understood as ontologically prior to and separate from the institutions of power that comprise the political body in which one might find herself.[33] This precedence is especially crucial for this category of rights, or, as Ian Balfour and Eduardo Cadava argue, "We might even say that there could be no life without human rights, without, at the very least, the right to live."[34] In other words, human rights are the property of those who are "only" human, whose sole property is those rights that cannot be guaranteed. And yet the human is a *problem* for rights and not their ontological ground. We know too well the human is the subject of contentious inquiry, adjudicated and achieved through the law, its norms, and also its aesthetic forms.[35] Because racial, colonial rationalities are its foundation, what Samera Esmeir calls a juridical humanity and Angela Naimou dubs legal personhood, is always already the circumscription of human being, or dehumanization.[36] And because rights have become an instrument of increasing administration, A. Naomi Paik writes, "Rightlessness is therefore necessary, and endemic, to rights."[37] The paradox that follows after Arendt's *the right to have rights* is in its correspondences, when rightlessness coincides with becoming no one, "who seem[s] to exist nowhere."[38] This is to say that in the breach, those who are cast out from legal personhood are no longer recognized as human, at the same time that their vulnerability, especially in relation to their mortality, their flesh, renders them *only* human.[39] This state of being is represented in stark and graphic terms as nakedness before the law; for instance, as Giorgio Agamben's *nuda vita*, or bare life, or Emmanuel Levinas's ethics, found in the human face: "The face has turned to me—and this is its very nudity."[40]

The aesthetic tension between rightfulness and rightlessness is thus found in the gap between normativity and survivability, where rights are unusable without the preconditions necessary for their exercise, and survival as only human hangs in the balance. As Jacques Rancière posits, "So, either the Rights of Man are the rights of those who have no rights [and thus these rights amount to nothing] or they are the rights of those who have rights [where such rights are attached to the fact of being a citizen of a constitutional state]. Either void or tautology."[41] A study about landmine injuries in the medical journal *Lancet* puts this tension thus: "Still one of the poorest countries in the world with a painfully slow recovery after 30 years of conflict and civil war, [Cambodia's] huge numbers of disabled citizens are the legacy of landmines, poliomyelitis, and disease. The four core values of human rights law—dignity, autonomy, equality, and solidarity—might mean little to the rural farmer whose leg has been blown off by a landmine if he is unable to have a well-fitted and maintained prosthesis and basic primary and public-health care for himself, his family, and his community."[42]

This criticism echoes the well-worn charge that the contemporary human rights regime lacks the enforcement apparatuses that channel the force of law. However, it also perpetuates a rights aesthetic hinged on the autonomous, rational subjecthood that founds the modern political imaginary. Freedom has been defined through rights, and the expansion of rights equated with the expansion of freedom, but as Lisa Yoneyama puts it, "It unveils that the unevenness of the human rights regime may not stem from the differential *application* of human rights law, as often assumed, but its discursive logic and assumptions."[43] In this schema, the limits of humanity are commensurate with the limits of legal personhood; these limits bring into focus the lawful violence that constitutes the genre of the human, including the normative project of recognizing and granting to others standing as rightful, and through which disability is understood as incapacitation.[44] Such a descriptive analytics—the legless farmer for whom the law is meaningless—wears out disability as metaphor for the more *and* less human.[45] This criticism rests on the premise that a life that can be lived is one in which the rights-bearing human is an integral, "whole" person with an unfurling biography.[46] However, too often disability is inscribed as the suspension of a life—one is not whole, so one cannot move forward through time, in history. The mutilated body, the ruined flesh, is thereby refused full personhood.[47] Furthermore, the radical contingency of corporeal "integrity" is unevenly dispersed in the age of the world target because dismembering violence is conceived as "native" to some zones—Y-Dang Troeung observes that it was US bombing that produced Cambodian debility as endemic, bringing to bear, as Henry Kissinger called for, "anything that flys [sic] on anything that moves"—but distinct from the sovereign violence through which freedoms, rights, and constitutions arrive.[48] Or, as Keva X. Bui might say about the landmine as they do about napalm, it is "a political object . . . [that] coalesces the contradictory logics of a war fought on behalf of liberal humanity that enacted untold material violence on racialized peoples and ecologies in Southeast Asia."[49] The traction of the human is no ontological given, but instead a continual process of aesthetic (here, narratological) making and unmaking.

Some argue that it is just for these reasons that human rights, making "little practical difference," are merely "an *ornament* on a tragic world they do not transform."[50] Samuel Moyn proposes that human rights as we understand them now emerged with the death of utopian dreams of full communism. Haunted by failed revolutions, human rights cohere in the 1970s as a presumably nonideological form that is less about freedom from empire, and more about individual protection from the state. For Moyn and others, human rights thus enunciate a minimalist iteration of political life burdened with maximal significance, strategically feasible while disavowing a radical restructuring of the world.[51] Here the failure of grand narratives of human emancipation curls instead into a small fist—the rights claim, at once adjudicated through legal apparatuses and moral entreaties while also studiously heralded as apolitical, even antipolitical, because they belong to the whole of humanity.

I again linger with the accusation of *ornament* because of its suggestiveness for a rights aesthetics. In aesthetic-philosophical histories, the ornament, in its associations with the feminine, decorative, minute, and gestural, is often understood as the obfuscation of some core truth or its absence. Having no necessary relationship to the structure of a thing, ornament is accused of disguising the fundamental nature of the thing itself—such as a building, or a body.[52] Western modernisms worry at ornament as affectively excessive, improperly dramatic, and, as Austrian architect Adolf Loos infamously condemned, criminally degenerate and civilizationally ignoble. Such denunciations, as Anne Anlin Cheng notes, are deeply racialized (and often specifically orientalized).[53] And yet ornament, again, is not nothing. Consider again aesthetic metaphors of nakedness that account for the body that is "stripped" of rights or humanity. Nakedness, Elizabeth Grosz observes, "is a state of vulnerability" to the world, and "to the affect and the impact of the other."[54] For Agamben, nudity is the thing itself, a question of essence and also an event of ontological exposure; he names "the thing's knowability (its nudity)" as "nothing other than the giving of the thing over to knowledge, nothing other than the stripping off of clothes that cover it."[55] "Bare" or "naked" life is that which remains when human existence is stripped of all the ornaments of relationality, bereft of all the qualifications for properly political inclusion. Thus does the concept of bare life attain against all the historically specific and socially particular forms in which human life is qualified through a social order. More precisely, and also more expansively, Hortense Spillers reminds us that mere flesh is the "zero degree of social conceptualization." What is forcibly stripped in the process of becoming flesh is humanity. Such nakedness as a state of affectability is not an ontological truth but a process of *undoing* undertaken by genres of the human, such that what Agamben calls a donation (in "the giving of the thing" to knowledge) Spillers more aptly describes as a capture. Thus, "we lose any hint or suggestion of a dimension of ethics, of relatedness between human personality and its anatomical features, between one human personality and another, between human personality and cultural institutions."[56] Where nakedness is understood as commensurate with an a priori being also commensurate with rightlessness, the aesthetic of humanitarianism (and, before it, civilizational rule, colonial paternalism, and benevolent assimilation) presumes for itself the power to cover such vulnerability; so does the law vest bare life and naked flesh with personhood and social life *through its adornment.*

The right to be beautiful, I argue, allows us to recognize the ornamentality of rights under juridical schemata. While some might find that the increase to the stable of rights—beauty alongside speech, or assembly—is the diminishment of their influence or possibility, it might also be that the right to be beautiful is not so distinct from the others. The mine survivor who is presented with a new limb embodies this liberal principle, through which the prosthetic is the ornament that becomes fundamental to their humanity. To this end, beauty as a right has as much presence as any other right, given that the scene of the juridical is so often a ruin.

Salvage/Salvation

After (the failure of) the trial to deliver justice, the past must stay in the past unless it can be brought forward as *heritage*. As an organizing principle, heritage refers to the constitutive presuppositions that cohere and sustain objects, habits, essences, knowledges, and environments as a cultural world across generations. It is the (selective) identification and judgment of historical continuity, requiring a temporalizing consciousness capable of preservation, restoration, reenactment, or repatriation, each the retroactive iteration of a presence. Where culture binds in the faithful transmission of values and rituals, heritage signifies the marking out of time and status as property, especially foundational in postconflict states and diasporic cultures where gaps, crises, and divisions interrupt succession or continuity. (Here again is the auratic copy to ensure life after death.) Under dire circumstances, objects, habits, essences, knowledges, and environments are abandoned, destroyed, corrupted, looted, or otherwise wrested from their backgrounds, but such alienation from history and the revelation of true value and significance might thereafter be resolved through *heritage*.

The right to beauty as a concern for postconflict governance is most often manifest as the preservation of heritage, establishing provenance, authentication, and chain of custody. Where the transition from authoritarian to, well, otherwise authoritarian rule is located in the aesthetic education, as found in the previous chapter, it might also include a preservationist impulse; where the Khmer Rouge sought to destroy ancient temples, intellectual life, and the arts, the present regime understands these as precious resources for economic revitalization or national continuity. Beauty rescued from danger is a familiar story, sometimes named the spoils of war. James Clifford dubs this a "salvage paradigm," "reflecting the desire to rescue something 'authentic' out of destructive historical changes."[57] (Consider the imperial museum and its liberal-genocidal preservation of those targeted for extraction and death in the name of humanity.) In designating certain artifacts, structures, and forms as that which enhances the life of humanity but is menaced by politically volatile situations, preservation is a practice of modernity that is grounded in an acquisitive logic. Continuous with the French colonial sensibility for the "salvage" of Khmer culture, securing Khmer heritage undergirds the premise of state legitimacy as a historical principle.[58] The preservationist impulse is commended as proof of virtue apart and distinct from the predecessor regime, especially in the concern for the self-evident greater good of fostering beauty, and as proper "stewardship" of resources and profitability. Thus the historical and cultural specificity of such ornaments as carved columns, elaborate headdresses, and precise gestures order scenes of repair.

The "discovery" of Angkor Wat in the 1840s is a privileged reference for France in Indochina, as "a lieu de memoire, and a vision of an exotic utopia," salvaged by those who would inherit its grandeur (despite the contemporaneous presence of Buddhist monks, whose pagodas were later removed by archaeologists to "restore" the grounds and stone temples).[59] The French *mission civilisatrice* was staged on these vestiges of Khmer antiquity, subject to new techniques of mechanical reproduction and information retrieval. The chronicling of such discoveries cohered an imperial aesthetic, from French naturalist Henri Mouhot and naval officer Louis Delaporte's lithographs of the temple grounds (some as precise architectural plans, some as fanciful re-creations of royal life), to detailed archaeological records and "scientific" restoration campaigns by the École française d'Extrême-Orient. The culmination of the Palais d'Exposition of 1931 was the scale reproduction of Angkor Wat in minute detail, while the interior held exhibitions about colonial Indochina, including archaeological and ethnographic artifacts, samples of native resources, and evidence of the benefits of colonial rule, such as public instruction and French art.[60] This elaborate reconstruction was a showcase of Indigenous cultures but primarily a celebration of French modernity, establishing these ancient temples as a metonym for the rescue of the Indochinese peoples through their benevolent ministration. Amitav Ghosh wrote that in the Khmer empire, the French "discovered a mirror for themselves: of the Imperial State, l'Etat, in all its power and splendour."[61] This mirror is also a stage, orchestrating meaning-laden contradistinctions between the ornamental primitive and an imperial modern.[62]

Inseparable from this dream-image of Angkor Wat are Cambodian court dancers, lauded as the direct descendants of the highly decorated bas-reliefs of female figures (including the apsara, dancing spirits enacting Hindu-Buddhist mythologies) throughout its temple grounds. Or as the French colonial-era magazine *l'Illustration* put it, Cambodia was "a fallen country, which has preserved only two parts of its glorious past: its improbably grandiose ruins and its dancers, strange relics of a dead past."[63] Just as daguerreotypes, lithographs, and postcards sought to capture the sprawling complex of densely carved buildings—both as mythical spectacle and as denuded ruin—for a popular imaginary, so too were these dancers subject to both archaeological and also prurient display. The first French citizen born in Cambodia, and educated in Paris, George Groslier established the École de arts cambodgiens in Phnom Penh to rescue Khmer art from its perceived degeneration. In 1913, he published *Danseuses cambodgiennes anciennes et modernes*, a study of Khmer court dancers, in which he sketched bare-breasted women seeming to emerge from the bas-reliefs at Angkor Wat (a recurring motif in the decades to come).[64] Of them he enthused, "If *lokhon* [dance] in the modern aesthetic were suddenly turned to stone, we could precisely superimpose their gestures carved in the past."[65] In 1906, King Sisowath voyaged to France with a troupe of nearly a hundred dancers and musicians who together staged Cambodian classical dance, for the first time in Europe, at fabricated Angkor pavilions in Paris and Marseilles for the Exposition Coloniale. Their performances inspired ecstatic (and often erotic) odes describing the dancers as vanished antiquity metamorphosed into sublime flesh.[66] One witness, French naval officer and novelist Pierre Loti, rhapsodized, "One of the back doors opens; one small, adorable and almost chimerical creature rushes into the middle of the hall: an Apsara of the temple of Angkor!"[67] The French sculptor Auguste Rodin was also enraptured with these dancers, following their tour from Paris to Marseilles and rendering over 150 drawings in an uncharacteristically loose style.[68] Extolling their human perfection—"them and the Greeks"—Rodin wrote of his blissful encounter, "I am a man who has devoted all his life to the study of nature, and whose constant admiration has been for the works of antiquity: Imagine, then, my reaction to such a complete show that restored the antique by unveiling its mystery."[69]

After Cambodia won its independence in 1953, Princess Kossamak invented the apsara dance, drawing on Groslier's study to choreograph five apsaras emerging from the Angkor Wat temple walls and later, at the end of the performance, disappearing once again into the stone. This dance became the centerpiece of diplomatic ceremonies in Cambodia, featuring Norodom

Buppha Devi, the prima ballerina of the Royal Ballet and daughter of King Sihanouk.[70] In 1962 in the magazine *Cambodge Aujourd'hui*, Devi was photographed in costume, posed with her hands in formation, in front of a stone figure that appeared almost as if one of her supporting dancers; the photograph's caption drew between them a direct line, "Women in Angkorian history—Past and present."[71] It is this dance, comprising choreographic forms almost eliminated during Pol Pot time through the murder of its practitioners, that is later "recovered" as heritage. Under the Vietnamese-led regime, the Ministry of Culture searched for the scarce few dancers and teachers who escaped to refugee camps or to other countries.[72] Following the establishment of the United Nations Transitional Authority in Cambodia, UNESCO targeted both Angkor Wat and Cambodian classical dance for the rescue and resurrection of intact Khmerness.[73] As Toni Samantha Phim and Ashley Thomson observe, the apsara dance is "perceived as . . . essential to the perpetuation of Cambodia as a cultural and political entity."[74] And so, at hotels, casinos, and the Angkor Cultural Village, barefoot young women in form-fitting *sampot* and two-tiered crowns re-create the dances that nearly vanished.[75] Their carefully choreographed gestures and stylized movements are staged on temple grounds for diplomatic ceremonies, or at restaurants and theme parks as an ambivalent commodity, mustered as evidence of the resilience of the Khmer people, and an enduring connection to an ancient inheritance.

These associations between sensuous flesh and eternal stone have not abated in the decades since, proving immensely profitable. Images of the sprawling temple complex are everywhere as testimonials to Khmer continuity, arousing both the romance of ancient civilization and the glamour of a refitted modernity. In the postgenocide state, these ruins are scenes for modernization and investment, including new roads, water and sewage systems, internet services, golf courses, artisan workshops, and demining activities around Angkor, supervised by a loose collaboration of state and nonstate agencies.[76] Similarly, the Cambodian Royal Ballet travels around the world to perform what UNESCO calls a sacred form, even while NGOs train dancers in vocational programs to populate the tourism industry.[77] A brief 2008 video documentary (sponsored by UNESCO and the Ministry of Culture and Fine Arts) about the preservation of Khmer dance opens on a panoramic shot of the temple grounds of Angkor Wat; as the voice-over gives an account of the ancient stories told through these elaborate carvings, the camera pans across bas-reliefs and columns before coming to a standstill before a frieze of bare-breasted figures. From the sandstone emerges a smiling young (human) dancer in golden garb, an ancient statue come to life before our eyes.[78] And, in a collection on Cambodian dance, the American director and librettist Peter Sellars, who featured Cambodian performers in his 2012 restaging of Igor Stravinsky's opera *Persephone*, describes the temple and the dancer together in an echo of earlier, soaring prose: "The smiling, breathing stone *apsaras* clustered at the feet of the columns at Angkor Wat are there to remind us of the revivifying powers of pleasure and the spiritual bliss of discipline and freedom."[79]

It is as a beautiful vision of restoration and resilience that the court dancer, all her limbs intact and under her control, is the antecedent and the contemporary of the amputee pageant contestant. But the pageant contestant is not as easily recovered from ruin or the pastness of violence as the temple or the dancer. The right to be beautiful aims to repair her injury—however, as with other rights, the right to be beautiful becomes a right only when a body is at the edge of the perceptible distinction between the human and the nonhuman. Thus, despite the seeming discordance, rights and beauty are both provisional figurations of *a life that can be lived*. Both circumscribe an experience of wholeness and completion; both adjudicate who qualifies as a subject of recognition and through what norms of being or possible becoming, wherein the conferral of recognition, through rights or beauty, is understood to mend damage to a person, and to her bond to the wider world. The seemingly competing concepts of rights as order or as ornament are not incongruent; a rights aesthetic fashions justice as a presence even where it is not a practice. Both rightfulness and beauty provide cover to the naked body, the bare life, that requires interference. And where the apparatus of human rights is minimal or missing, something like the Miss Landmine beauty pageant aims to protect and project the authority of the rights claim. Given the contingencies of an idea of being human wrought through the premise of rights as a necessary condition, and a fraught history of beauty as an aesthetic form, dehumanized persons including those who are damaged through the zoning of the world as target become subjects of rightfulness—if only in parts.

Landmine Picturesque

Published in a bilingual pictorial magazine, the glossy photographs of the Cambodian pageant contestants are striking. Here the hallmarks of portraiture are used to both humanize and individualize, and are then coupled with the theatricalized tableaux of fashion photography.[80] Posing at Angkor Wat, pristine beaches, and resort hotels, the barefoot contestants are clothed in brightly colored sleeveless jersey dresses and satin pageant sashes (usually with the names of their provinces in Khmer script), and each is crowned with a rhinestone-encrusted tiara. In these photographs, the women expose bare limbs and their sudden absence (perched on a tree branch, one leg swinging, or propped against a gallery column), play with long loosened hair, and smile at the camera. One features a young woman (the eventual pageant winner) holding a silver plastic ray gun above her shoulder as she leans casually against a low white stucco wall. In others, contestants cradle a statuesque golden leg (topped with a high heel) in their arms, not quite an imitation or replication of the lost object but a totem for its promise.

Figured by this golden leg as trophy and the custom titanium limb as prize, such faith in the prosthetic device establishes that visible labors to redesign the body, to render it beautiful through its ornamentation, will also repair an individual's psychic life.[81] No wonder the golden leg is the center of the last photograph in the magazine, propped atop a red satin-swathed platform and draped with a Miss Landmine sash against a beautiful beach sunset. It is a somewhat jarring conclusion to the series of photographs featuring women missing limbs, not least because its auratic presence as a proximate object for a form of human being, a body with a claim, despite being amputated itself from willfulness, is both simplifying and enigmatic.

Consider also that the photographs of bombed beauty contestants that envision wartime damage, and the innovations that repair it, are contiguous with the regimes of munitions manufacture and reconnaissance that laid those mines in the first instance, but are mentioned only in passing in the materials for the Miss Landmine pageant. These geopolitical dimensions instead scale to the intimate, to the instrument—the landmine, alone. Some photographs of the contestants include basic information about the mines that cost them their limbs, identified by serial number, cost, release (detonation mechanism, commonly pressure, "9 kg or more"), explosive material ("300g TNT"), and manufacturer (Cuba, Hungary, People's Republic of China, "local"). However, these mines are not pictured with those who suffer their trespasses. In a separate photograph, disarmed mines are arranged in a diptych, shot from above to mirror the aerial perspective of the war planes that sometimes seeded them, with an image of rich strata of earth (dirt, pebbles, debris) under which such clandestine death once lay. The magazine credits include contributors from ground operations manager, styling and costumes, design and layout, photo locations, and also landmine manufacturers, though not the events or conditions under which the mines are sold and laid. Like the Paris Peace Accords, which name no parties responsible though they call for "all known minefields [to be] clearly marked," the pageant materials have little more to say.[82] The landmines are just there, under the dirt, dumb objects. These brief moments are the end point of the blunt encounter with unexploded ordnance—besides the bodies of the contestants themselves.

These photographs stage a sensorial narrative between ruin and repair. In doing so, they might appear startling, eccentric, or anomalous. But their significance, perhaps confounding at first glance (or second or third), resides in their contiguity with other images, other archives. A number of stories unfold from these photographs, not least among them the pageant portrait that lends to these women a glamour from its repertoire of gestures and emotions; the familiar feminization of humanitarian aesthetics that foregrounds vulnerability; and a curative therapeutics that aims to transfigure disability into the shape of a good life. But what Allan Sekula would call a *shadow archive* also haunts these images, here that most infamous photographic collection from Cambodia—the portraits of tens of thousands of doomed prisoners at Tuol Sleng, or S-21, the notorious torture and execution center.[83] These series are hardly commensurate—that is not the argument here at all—but they belong to a continuum of images of victims confronting the other with their vulnerability, their suffering. However, while the amputee might disrupt the pastness of violence—the detonation is untimely, after war—the pageant contestant foregrounds her suffering as anterior to every question. Therefore, to read the photographs of amputee contestants lounging on sandstone columns or tiled pools, and to grasp their semiotics of violence and recovery, I detour for a moment to mark the haunting presence of aesthetic idioms that inform such representations of racial, colonial others. The exposure of the body to multiple forces, to bomb and to image, comprises a palimpsest; the photograph is an inscription that conceals or repairs the damage preceding the camera's eye, without completely obliterating it.

Knowledge about Cambodia is often circulated as dream-images of premodern splendor and subsequent ruin. Among these dream images, which provide both the anterior references of these pageant photographs and some of their "on-location" sets, foremost are the ruins of Angkor Wat and Khmer dance. The mise-en-scène of grand colonnades and graceful dancers is, to borrow from Panivong Norindr, a colonial phantasmatic.[84] Whether capturing a contestant reclining on a pockmarked column covered in curling vines, or in front of a palm forest by a marble reflecting pool, the pageant portraits are haunted by ethnographic visions of native flesh. The contestants bare their remaining limbs and don tiaras in uncanny echoes or copies of bare-legged ballet dancers and crowned bas-relief figures. These meetings of human and environment, portraiture and landscape, abstraction and materiality cohere what I will call a landmine picturesque. As an aesthetic category introduced by the eighteenth-century British clergyman William Gilpin, the picturesque is an aesthetic and sensorial interlude between Edmund Burke's beautiful and sublime. Encompassing irregularity and roughness, the picturesque could be found in touring a natural landscape, including and sometimes especially its ruins. But while a pleasing roughness might be the consequence of natural erosion, inclement weather, or a long age of neglect, such an aesthetic property might also be the outcome of wanton or deliberate destruction—such as a bomb, or a mine. Gilpin proposed that while Palladian architecture is elegant, "Should we wish to give it a picturesque beauty, we must use the mallet instead of the chisel: we must beat down one half of it, deface the other, and throw the mutilated members around in heaps."[85] The Miss Landmine pageant photographs are not strictly landscapes, of course; they also borrow from the genre of portraiture. Nonetheless, these photographs refer to the picturesque an aesthetic feeling for brokenness, or a body in parts. With its evocative imagery of maiming and "sudden protuberance, and lines that cross each other in a sudden and broken manner," the picturesque as the pictorial composition of unlooked-for violence and its wake is apt.[86] To say, then, that these photographs inform a landmine picturesque is to describe them as an aesthetic enframing of *mutilated members in heaps*. It is no accident that the irregularity of the landmine survivor recalls or cites the crumbling temple statue, both damaged and yet persisting.

Of course, what is presented as ruin is not untouched. In the case of Angkor Wat, these are edifices and environs that are designed, built, "discovered," and reconstructed once again. Alongside what Krista Thompson might call their tropicalization, encompassing the aesthetics stage-managed for both tourist and heritage consumption and their implications for (representations of) arrangements of actual space and peoples, these pageant photographs visualize the convergence of design and a second life, postcrisis.[87] That is to say, these photographs are also about the conditions under which these temples, hotels, and bodies are the political and economic subjects of international and domestic management and rehabilitation. One way we can look at these photographs, then, focuses on what forms of damage control are shared between them. As earlier, at the 1931 Palais d'Exposition, these rough, rehabilitated bodies—the temples, the amputees—surface as signs of a modernizing sovereign state after decades of colonialism and conflict. Pictured at luxury hotels and oceanside resorts, posing within upscale interiors, sometimes appearing alongside postmodern replications of colonial architectural features, the contestants are, in a twist, also tourists of their own pleasing irregularity.

If these photographs draw on a sensual aesthetics of the manicured tropics, also here is an erotic materiality to the landmine picturesque that is in part *inorganic*. In one photograph a contestant might be reclined on top of a shattered Angkor column, her prosthetic propped on a fallen sandstone block, and in another she might be found on a poolside lounger, a shiny Apple laptop balanced on her thighs. These surfaces are charged scenes of sensorial aesthetics, modern materials, and spectacular histories of wear and repair at the boundaries of the body. In many of the photographs, the contestants wear what are presumably their prosthetic limbs, made from brown rubber or molded plastic polymer to look "realistic," puckered with the dents and marks of a life. Where plastics might have once heralded an avant-garde aesthetic, such materials are now more often a sign of poverty, cheapness, and disposability.[88] These injection-molded plastic prosthetics contrast with or complement other surfaces that appear within the photographs, including crumbling sandstone (its architectural analogue) but also the smooth extruded materials of laptops, loungers, golden totem legs, and, notably, the custom titanium prize limb. (These objects bear the aesthetic properties of a Burkesque beautiful—smooth and delicate, they lend their proportion and symmetry to others.) Generic and also custom prosthetics are available in Cambodia—again, prosthetics and orthotics being among the most widely supported humanitarian initiatives—which include rubber and thermoplastic but also 3D-printed limbs (available to those who can pay).[89] Yet despite the heterogenous presence of prosthetics in Cambodia, the Miss Landmine pageant presumes to offer an *inaccessible* futuristic prosthetic, designed and manufactured by distant Swedish engineers, as a prize. There is in these photographs not *just* the hope for repair that the prosthetic promises, replacing in most instances the lower limbs (the limbs most often lost to mines) so crucial to locomotion, but also the promise of surplus value as technological plenitude—signaled not by an aesthetically realistic prosthetic but by an architecturally modernist one. Such collocations of persons and things—prosthetics, yes, but a range of them, assigned differential value—tell us that *the life that can be lived* is not naked, or bare; it must necessarily be supplemented to grant to such life a depth. The laptop, the leg, and the tiara—these things are not just ornamental but are attached to promises of flourishing. Or as Anne Anlin Cheng writes, "Flesh that passes through objecthood needs ornament to get back to itself."[90]

These portraits thus picture radical vulnerability and also necessary repair. Writing about the damages of Agent Orange, Natalia Duong suggests, however, that "repair . . . becomes a much more complex process than attempts to 'cure' the effects of disability," where repair is as provisional (and political) as promise.[91] While violent disablement as a consequence of war is surely a radical alteration, we can nevertheless observe the aesthetic returns of a familiar mirroring between disablement and subjectivity; that the disablement of the body deforms also the mind. It is not just the missing limb that matters; this genre of plotting the maimed body's return to capacitation as a biographical resolution supplies, as Sharon Snyder and David Mitchell call it, a "narrative prosthesis."[92] Throughout the *Miss Landmine* documentary (dir. Stan Feingold, 2010), each contestant is portrayed as enduring multiple forms of capture and alienation that impede her life chances, most obviously the bomb blast, after which each contestant's body—boundaries, organs, limbs—is no longer her own.[93] Its violence is deeply corporeal and also profoundly psychic; it seizes them in this narration in the moment of the blast.[94] Furthermore, the same catastrophic event that desubjectifies also degenders, as coherent bodies become disaggregated flesh.[95] (Some confess to feeling like *less* of a woman.) The property of gender as well as the forms through which gender is lived are crucial to genres of being human; without it, without gender, she has no genealogy, which is to say, no history, nor biography, nor interiority.

Because not all pain can be understood as a sign of humanity, because some pain is ontologically "natural" to those pushed outside of the human, a longing for *something more than* must be present to signal a possessive interiority. The pageant's twofold "humanizing" strategy is therefore to presume that both pain and beauty are conduits of identification and transformation because freedom from pain and the promise of beauty are assumed to be universal. It is as a promise that the right to be beautiful presumes to counteract the deadening alienation of the landmine. Where radical vulnerability is represented through bare flesh, the pageant *vests* the maimed body with social life. While the pageant did not provide prosthetics for all the contestants, what it did grant (besides the small stipend to contestants, and the dresses) is that *something more than*, both more ephemeral and also more valuable—the promise of a biography. Each photograph of a Miss Landmine contestant is accompanied by a brief list of personal facts, including name, age, hometown, favorite color, and occupation, but also year of their mine accident and "future ambition." (These often belong to the neoliberal imaginary of the NGO-ization of Cambodia, including "running a small business," "advocating the rights of people with disabilities," and "accountant for an NGO.") These details, narrated through ordinary desires according to familiar plots (love, family, work), are rendered all the more precious for their precarity.[96] Here sentimental forms render scenes and stories of structural injustice in the details of lives as they are, and as they ought to be, through the promise of beauty.

As a narrative about normativity and vulnerability, Miss Landmine identifies the bomb blast as the defining crisis event (and not Pol Pot time, or the ongoing neglect of the Sen regime) that divides time before and time after, and the pageant as the recuperation of what had been lost in the meantime. The documentary (and the program) ends with the virtuosity of the prosthetic device and the impact on the user, winner Sopheap, who testifies that her participation has won her friends and happiness. Murderous structures of radical unmaking are superseded by an ideal concept of beauty as subjectivization, as the repair and revitalization of an interior life. Or, as a *National Geographic* essay on Cambodia's "healing fields" narrates this scene, "To the tearful clapping of her family, Sopheap is taking her new titanium prosthesis for a test run around their dirt front yard, scattering the ducks and chickens. As befits a beauty queen, she is wearing a flouncy, peach-colored dress lit up like a rose by the setting sun. Her twin sisters hang on to each arm as she walks stiffly in circles, and her mother weeps."[97] Her mother, it is noted, is grateful that Sopheap now can wear jeans like the other girls.[98] The sublime terror of total war becomes a landmine picturesque.

Beautiful Hells

Just days before the event was set to convene on December 3, World Disability Day, the Cambodian government abruptly reversed its approval of the Miss Landmine pageant.[99] Heng Ratana, director general of the government-run demining organization Cambodian Mine Action Centre, said of the pageant disparagingly, "When you look at the pictures, the purpose is not to highlight the beauty of the women, it's to display that the women have lost their legs."[100] These two conditions—beauty and lost legs—are named here as opposites, conceptually at odds, as if true beauty is impossible as long as *something is missing*.

This coupling (and decoupling) sets the Miss Landmine pageant against the postwar recovery and reconstruction of the Cambodian classical dancer (another comely young woman in a beautiful dress). If, as Anne McClintock put it, women figure as the boundary and limit of the national body politic, then recovery and reconstruction after terrible violence bear witness to this boundary and limit decisively.[101] *Some* bodies act as metaphors for ancient lineages, wartime damages, and therapeutic recoveries—but not others.[102] Like the French colonial administration a century earlier, postwar Cambodia promotes Khmer aesthetic forms associated with court culture and ancient regimes to support and establish its rule as continuous with the Angkor empire. Touring worldwide, as their predecessors once did, Cambodian Royal Ballet dancers "replace" those who perished alongside thousands and thousands of other arts practitioners under the Khmer Rouge. Rachmi Diyah Larasati, writing about postgenocide Indonesia and Cambodia, describes this historically cleansed dancer (and she counts herself among them, before she became a scholar) as a *replica* who recuperates the state that resurrects her *whole and intact* from the ancient past.[103] This replica dancer is the auratic copy of a mythic original (and the principle she stands for) once endangered in crisis, now resurrected in the aftermath. "In this context," Larasati argues, "the replica female dancing body plays its most important role, as an ever-present symbol of the 'pure' essence of the nation, and of the innocence and productivity of tradition, signaling the urgent need for its preservation."[104] Or as Toni Shapiro-Phim attests, "It was a way to try to put back together that which had been ruptured."[105]

Here lies the boundary and the limit—the replica dancer whose ethereal grace confirms that the horrific danger (the practitioner before her who lies quiet and still in the mass grave) is a mere interruption in an otherwise continuous lineage, apart from the amputee beauty contestant whose wounds bear witness to the awful past that persists in the not-yet redeemed present. The first, still intact, requires protection, protection that the state claims to provide, while the second, grievously injured, is beyond it, which the state cannot rectify. She is the victim who lives, whose history is not halted in a dreamtime before violence. Miss Landmine's contestants, though they might occupy those same grounds—the temples, the tourist hotels—as the dancers of a "recovered" court culture, are literally cut short from similar movements. (Of the Cambodian dancers he observed, Rodin wrote, "If they are beautiful, it is because they have a natural way of producing the right movements.")[106] As the state continues to insist that the past is past, unless it counts as *heritage*, the amputee is at odds with such wishful storytelling. So are state development projects invested in the feminine body, and the display of the feminine body—but not necessarily those whose damage is evidence of ongoing violence. Against the more commercial rescue of beauty in the apsara dancer, the amputee contestant disrupts the pastness of violence, highlighting all that which is *still* missing.

The Cambodian state is not alone in its concerns about Miss Landmine as prurient spectacle, though others might arrive at this criticism from other quarters. A fundamental axiom of humanitarianism in an age of publicity is the awareness campaign, in which the exposure of violence is a threat to its perpetrators, and the act of witnessing is the intervention. But the pageant, as a serial approximation of an ideal femininity, and as a fantasy of recognition, reciprocity, and subjectivity, is subject to suspicion as a form that can provide any of these seeming goods. Why, some have asked, is beauty the right through which the landmine survivor is made sense of here, and not a right to health care, or—? Is there something morally ugly in the appeal to beauty? Jacques Rancière observes that the "critique of the spectacle" is often the first and last resort of the "politics of art"; indeed, it is difficult for some observers to know how to *think* or *feel* the pageant besides or through the spectacle.[107] One newspaper poses the conundrum as a choice between exploitation and "bold publicity," while another journalist wonders about the scale of the altruistic gesture, querying, "And the do-gooders set out to address the greatest crisis in the life of, for instance, a maimed 19-year-old unemployed pregnant woman—that she doesn't feel beautiful?"[108]

Cohering what Claire Bishop calls a "critical queasiness," these and other objections argue the pageant is at worst an amoral and exploitative scheme, and at best a fumblingly inadequate reflection on war and injury.[109] In these objections, the promise of beauty is a feint or even a failure, an impoverished solution to an incommensurate problem. Acutely raised too are questions about *process* as well as *outcome*, especially about the nature of the women's involvement: "How did they get involved?" ("Through local NGOs") and "Were they compensated?" ("Yes, they were paid for their time"). Such concerns evidence Bishop's observation that participatory art is often judged by whether a work can be said to model a "good" or "bad" collaboration. (As though compensation negates exploitation, which it does not.) Indeed, though he describes the contestants as "fellow artists in a campaign," Traavik himself is readily available for criticism for his self-fashioned sense as savior.[110] (In a very confused but revealing reference, inadvertently cohering the shared vision of the world as target between militaries and humanitarians, Traavik said after the pageant's cancellation, "If I must, I will go to the border myself to deliver [the prize]. Rambo-style, in a cross-border raid, with a prosthesis instead of a gun.")[111] However, as susceptible as the pageant is to such criticisms, what else can we say? Not least because *all* pageants are spectacles, and so are many humanitarian campaigns.[112] How can we understand the pageant *as it describes itself*, both participatory art and public service?[113]

The portrait photographs are the most visible iteration of the Miss Landmine pageant, but what of the pageant itself as an *aesthetic* form? It is not that the pageant accomplishes more than what it does—crown a queen, award a prosthetic—but that the pageant illuminates more than it claims. Against the dismissal of the pageant as mere "packaging," its form is crucial for understanding the premise of this performance in situ. It is perhaps obvious to say first that the pageant is at once an event *in* the world, but also at a remove; it is a manifest desire for recognition and reciprocity, and also an aspirational fantasy of the glamorous life. But a familiar formula can still be made strange, within its specific circumstances—here, the decades of endemic poverty and political fraud and corruption alongside a massive humanitarian infrastructure at the scene of unexploded ordnance. We see in the *Miss Landmine* documentary the makeup artists and wardrobe specialists prepping the amputee contestants ahead of their photo shoots; the contestants smile and laugh delightedly, or perhaps nervously, at the sensual pleasures of being the center of such care. This is no small thing as the pageant produces drama from stories of personal tragedy, invoking conventional femininities as dream-images, becoming beautiful as feeling human.

In underscoring such tensions between its heterogeneous elements, Miss Landmine aims to disclose a truth, or elucidate a contrapuntal relationship between them. Its transfiguration of despair into beauty, damage into humanity, makes the pageant available, as Traavik himself claims, as "a good old theatre trick." Describing his practice, he continues, "Here the counterpoint is to put 'landmine' and 'miss' together. It's the counterpoint of the serious and tragic reality of landmines and the joyful celebration of life inherent in a beauty pageant."[114] Perhaps this trick seems crude or blunt, but Traavik is not alone; there are in fact hundreds of pageants that perform this counterpoint, this "joyful celebration of life," especially in situations wrought through law (as violence) and lawlessness (also as violence). Here lies the redemptive promise of naming someone or something once outcast or outlaw beautiful, in order to draw that person or object into another relation with others, with the world.[115] Such pageants stage the trauma of the contestant being judged less beautiful, and therefore less human, because of discrimination, illness, or injury, in order to break the cycle of violence ascribed to misrecognition; others hope that recognition will redeem contestants of their criminal or deviant ways.

In this familiar formula, racism, homophobia, cancer, incarceration, and extraction, among other things, wear out the body and soul, which require then something beautiful to ameliorate this wearing out. The National

Association for the Advancement of Colored People staged a "positive protest" against the whiteness of Miss America, organizing the first Miss Black America contest in Atlantic City, just blocks away from the 1968 Miss America pageant. Similarly, the queer Pinoy beauty pageant renders trans life conceivable, even against the specter of death, enacting what Robert Diaz (citing Martin Manalansan) calls "*biyuti* from below."[116] There are pageants for women with destructive diseases, such as the nonprofit Miss Pink Pageant, specifically for women with breast cancer.[117] There are pageants that promise glamour and communion outside of hard labor and punishing schedules, such as those organized by and for Filipina domestic workers in Hong Kong.[118] Pageants in prison, organized by state agencies, nonprofits, or commercial enterprises (which then might televise the proceedings), are oftentimes undertaken as rehabilitative measures for women incarcerated for illegal or illicit activities. Talavera Bruce, a maximum-security prison for women in Rio de Janeiro, Brazil (home of the world's fourth-largest prison population), has held a beauty pageant for its inmates for over a decade, organized by community and Christian church groups, "to restore the inmates' humanity and sense of self-worth—if only for one joyful afternoon."[119] Getty photographer Mario Tama documented the pageant in 2015 and, like Traavik, focuses on the purported contradiction of the pageant in prison—the contestants in their jewel-bright evening gowns and towering heels standing in line in the prison yard, before a canopied stage surrounded by high concrete walls, barbed wire, and guards in surveillance towers.[120] Other pageants aim to train imprisoned women in "proper" gendered and sexual forms, aligned with lawfulness and respectability.[121]

There are also pageants convened for survivors of war and genocide, or for those who may yet survive, each marrying beauty and lawfulness together as necessary conditions for the continued life of humanity. In this aesthetic arrangement, population life is tied to surviving beauty. In 1993, the first and last Miss Besieged Sarajevo, held in the former Yugoslavian capital during the brutal civil war, sought a global audience for its plea. The United Nations had sent observers and food packages, but little else to stem the death and destruction. As Serbian militias continued shelling outside the basement venue, the bathing-suit-clad contestants (some with shrapnel scars) unfurled a banner onstage, pleading, "Don't Let Them Kill Us." At the turn of the twentieth century, the German Reich waged a genocidal campaign against the Indigenous populations of German South West Africa, or in what is now Namibia; the commemorative centenary staged events to remember massacres, famines, and concentration camps, but also to honor resilience, including the Miss Genocide pageant. Again, commentary about the pageant follows the formula of heightened oppositions: "Hereros deliberately brought together two contradictory concepts: the notion of beauty and the notion of death. The live and vivid bodies of the beauty queens were proof that the genocide had been survived by its victims. Literally, they were embodiments of the Herero nation and the restoration of Herero culture."[122] The pageant might even be brought to bear on femicide, as the 2017 Miss Peru pageant did. Choreographed by Frecuencia Latina, the television network that broadcast the pageant, each contestant cited statistics about rape and gender-based violence instead of their measurements in a preplanned protest. Stepping up to the microphone before both live and televised audiences, dressed in a shimmering one-shoulder sheath, Camila Canicoba of Lima began the litany that others would follow. "My measurements are: 2,202 cases of murdered women reported in the last nine years in my country."[123] In each performance, the promise of beauty imbues the pageant with gravity through the specter of death, or at least vulnerability and attenuated life, that the pageant aims to defy, or forestall.

The pageant as an event might be at a remove from politics proper inasmuch as it makes no particular demands, but as an aesthetic form the pageant is thoroughly political, shaping itself as *prepolitical* when and where the experience prepares one for a *feeling* of order, or justice (which are, as I have said, not the same). In convention centers or concrete bunkers, the pageant is a placeholder that provides an affective imaginary in which a utopian ideal—everyone has the right to be beautiful—can be lived. The pageant thus offers a view into the aesthetics of democracy and conjures the body it imagines as a rightful being, if not necessarily a juridical one. The pageant is an analogue to the public assembly, itself a form for the recognition of individuals as abstract units come together as social body, and to the election, itself a form for the desire for the ideal representative or exemplar of a collective principle. In the hopes of capturing (even just for a moment) the public consciousness through the congruence of their aesthetics, the contest of beauty becomes the scene for persons to similarly demonstrate, to insist on, their humanity. But though the pageant copies such democratic forms (even as it crowns a queen), the pageant also keeps its distance, above and superior to the machinations of political antagonism. In this view, the Ministry of Social Affairs might denote such machinations as an exclusive realm of elites, interested more in "good" publicity than in the well-being of ordinary people. Despite the ministry's claims to care about their exploitation, the pageant's cancellation might be understood as an attempt to hide the pageant contestants because either survivors or unexploded ordnance are perceived as shameful, or geostrategically inconvenient. The usual returns on international pageants—showcasing capital investments and "native" assets while framing beautiful ruins as exotic destinations—are certainly repeated in the landmine pageant photographs, but its difference of *ruined limbs* is too much. The cancellation is thus a useful foil for the pageant itself, and for thinking about rights in the realm of the political—or proximate to it.

Through its distance from this realm, the pageant stages rich comparisons between humanitarian aesthetic forms (which mirror legalistic forms, including testimony, witnessing, and visual documentation) and their ethical claims. These forms aim to cultivate a capacious engagement with scenes of human suffering and vulnerability that often hinge on a social relation of compassion or pity.[124] Again, such a spectacle is the site of much critique. Among the most common complaints about the aestheticization of the horrors taking place throughout the world, or what some call beautiful suffering, is the edification of the observer without recompense for the observed.[125] Susan Sontag memorably called this "the pleasure of flinching," while Sherene Razack opines that those who witness evil come to know themselves as "compassionate people."[126] Of photographs of disability, Rosemarie Garland-Thomson argues that realist photographs in the service of political consciousness-raising invite false identification between the observer and the observed of the photograph.[127] Beautiful suffering is thus an uneasy encounter with surface, sensation, and subjectivity. Or, as even Traavik bluntly puts it, "I'm so fed up of social campaigns with black and white photos of Africans or Cambodians, in rags."[128]

As a humanitarian vision, the Miss Landmine pageant negotiates multiple histories of realist images and fantastical beauty. Bridging these aesthetic strategies that each authorize the observer to imagine that their regard might change the world, the portrait photograph must represent the body in parts (including the prosthetic) while also capturing the promise of beauty. The imprint of these histories is perceived in the *before* and *after* between the accident and the photograph, between the scene of her death-making and the scene of her life-saving. To this end, some critics argue that beauty might provide a powerful alternative to an aesthetics of injury. James Thompson, for instance, turns to participatory performance in disaster and war zones to submit that beauty can inform a politics of world-building pleasure. While pain, he argues, "reduces the person to the boundary of her or his body," beauty, in contrast, opens the body to an "intimate politics of sharing," as the sensual generosity of beauty provokes an "affective impulse towards engagement with others."[129] Since beauty (in this view) inspires an engagement with others in defining what is good, Thompson proposes that beauty *with* suffering is not a distraction from injustice but "can be part of its critique."[130] Or as Traavik, again, comments on these photographs, "What do I see when I look at the pictures of Miss Landmine contestants? I see true beauty. I see beautiful women who are proud, dignified, and comfortable with who they are. And that strong, feel-good factor is all the while undermined by the tragic and quite horrible back-stories of mutilation and war that inevitably stays with a landmine survivor. It is a picture of ambiguity, but where the forces of life prevail."[131] In these formulations, beauty catalyzes the consciousness that its loss harms us—so much so that it might even be world-ending—and renews in us a commitment to foster life.

Miss Landmine thus depends on the forms of the portrait and the pageant to stage scenes of recognition tied to its forms of rhetorical address—the photograph as humanist portraiture, the public assembly as democratic gathering, and the rights claim as juridical humanity. It is as an analogue to the public assembly that the pageant invokes the observer as a participant through their right to vote and stages the contestants' redemption as a representative of a shared principle to a collectivity. Some might argue that the pageant stages a "counterpublic," after Michael Warner, in which the display of nonconforming bodies might be celebrated as beautiful.[132] (More visibility for other forms of being or becoming beautiful is often assumed to be more fair distribution.) It is thus tempting to say that the pageant *is* a public assembly (rather than just its analogue), and that its cancellation is of a piece with the denial of public assembly for oppositional parties under the Hun Sen regime. In this reading, the pageant is an appeal to norms of gender (femininity) and governance (rights) that are found elsewhere than the place in which the pageant is not an event. (The show goes on—in exile, in Norway.) The pageant might then be read as a resistance to the conditions under which the contestants labor, including poverty and poor access to health care, but also as a social bond that has been denied to them. In this way, the pageant functions after what Lauren Berlant calls an intimate public, apart from the machinations of elites or institutions. Berlant elaborates, "A public is intimate when it foregrounds affective and emotional attachments located in fantasies of the common, the everyday, and a sense of ordinariness, a space where the social world is rich with anonymity and local recognitions, and where challenging and banal conditions of life take place in proximity to the attentions of power but also squarely in the radar of a recognition that can be provided by other humans."[133] In its aspiration to a more simple existence—to be merely human, which is more than enough—over and against a world that is complicated, messy, and unsatisfying, the intimate public of the pageant seeks emotional justice in something like happiness, or resilience. Consider again the glamorous photographs that solicit pity, perhaps, but also admiration for these contestants' capacities to overcome. A mine action program manager for Traavik's eventual partner in the pageant, Norwegian People's Aid, describes her own change of heart: "I think one of the reasons quite a few of us changed our initial reservations and are seeing it in a different light is very much linked to the fact that when you see the photographs, you see the women are profiled with dignity."[134] But what is the nature of dignity? Here I return to rights after rights via *the right to be beautiful*.

Just as the pageant borrows from the aesthetic forms of election and assembly to render an intimate public proximate to politics, the right to be beautiful also rehearses the aesthetic forms of legalistic norms, such as acts of petition, testimony, and witness. The right to have rights proposes that humanity is an inalienable feature, separate from and against the social negation that might accrue to particular exclusion. Ideally, such a right is not a measurable object ("more" or "less" freedom) but an ontological status, a *being*. But we know from racial, colonial histories that the subject of the right to have rights is the effect of power and as well the juridical enclosure of humanity. What is presumptively a *being* is a *doing*; and what is prepolitical does not precede the political. To complicate further, the failure of rights claims to mitigate state violence—and at times fashioning and fastening the subject tighter to them—returns us to the rights claim *after rights*, here made through the realm of art where a regime, or its foundation, is corrupt. When laws and institutions are not the guarantors of rights, rights are secured only by their own claims to universality. However, though contemporary human rights might grant that the mere fact of being human, and not the manifestation of a given feature or capacity (such as reason), qualifies one as a rights bearer, *the right to be beautiful* nonetheless accepts the premise that humanity is a matter of petition and declaration. The right to be beautiful proposes that beauty is an inalienable feature, separate from and against the social negation that accrues to her particular exclusion, and yet the pageant enacts speech acts that proclaim rightfulness in a performative mode—*I am human, I am beautiful*—as the foundation of normative personhood.

And yet, even as the juridical hoards the power to declare the presence of the human, the right to be beautiful inadvertently testifies to the law's uselessness as the absence of justice. Where rights are not commensurate with politics or justice, the aesthetic form of the rights claim *without politics or justice as a horizon* can be brought to bear with a nonjuridical humanity in mind. In the words of Cambodian Miss Landmine contestant Song Kosal: "The reason I take part in the contest is to seek out an equal right and call for an end to discrimination against disabled people. Though we are disabled women, we have our beauty to compete and to show people around the world. We have the rights to tell our own story to all people; and the beauty is not the physical appearance, but our pure heart."[135] The right to be beautiful testifies to the desire to be more than just "disabled women" but a purer vision of herself, and to have that desire and vision returned by a global intimate public. The pageant is thus prefigured as the instrument of their self-actualization, and beauty as an ethical reserve, rendering themselves recognizable to others. What is compelling (and troubling) about this statement and the pageant is that the rights claim makes no demands of her perpetrators, the law or other institutions (the United Nations, for instance, or the vast nongovernmental sector). Focused on the loss of social bond and its reconstruction, the pageant manifests a vision of aesthetics as a realm outside of politics proper, witnessing catastrophe while imagining another world is possible. In doing so, the pageant hails a humanity grounded in an attachment to beauty and a sensus communis. This could be radical, but it is very often antipolitical.

"Political *as ifs*," Diana Taylor observes, "create a desire and a demand for change; they leave traces that reanimate future scenarios."[136] That the pageant and its purpose take up democratic forms suggests an enduring faith in these forms even as these also rehearse their deferral. The *as if* of its performance depends on the affective common sense of traditional organization of political practices, here the assembly, the vote, and the right, *as if* these forms could adjudicate and deliver (as they presumably do, in other places) what they promise. Consider these statements from another study of the pageant:

> Even a cursory reading of such comments shows that the contestants know very well that the pageant is not so much about beauty per se, but about public recognition of their status as women and full human beings. They might enjoy the fashion and glamour aspects to which they [are] not accustomed (why should they be blamed for, or judged upon, such pleasure? Why should their poverty justify a purely utilitarian form of help and disqualify them from enjoying looking their best?). If one remembers their stigmatized status, one can fully appreciate this desire for public recognition as its just value. Instead of the habitual greeting by mockery, jeers and shunning, they

are applauded and rewarded, and they are listened to, their (modest) dreams are recognized, they have finally rights as persons.[137]

Recognition again registers as a humanitarian aesthetic, such that solicitations of feelings such as compassion are evidence that the world is changed, even if no social or political structures are. Charles Taylor and Axel Honneth, among others, argue that recognition of one's authentic self is a good in itself; it is a normative claim for what Lois McNay calls the "the universal structure of ethical life."[138] It might be that if one cannot be granted dignity by the principles of law, recognition in other compensatory realms will do. This is the distinction between recognizing a "legal personality" as opposed to one's "mere existence," in Arendt's words.[139] Through which recognition is construed as the truest confirmation of one's humanity, such art that choreographs its possibilities is understood to ennoble conscience, respect, inclusion, and consensual order—preceding or replacing struggle or justice, which cannot be guaranteed.[140]

Whether as humanitarian campaign or social practice performance, Miss Landmine aims to represent the duration and scale of the contestants' situation in recruiting the pageant form to envisage the decades-old fact of unexploded ordnance, which is just the most spectacular feature of the structural conditions of postwar governance, while also subsuming those conditions, which include tensions between biopolitical humanitarianism (consider that the NGO infrastructure is focused on rehabilitation and vocational training) and disciplinary quasi-authoritarianism. Simultaneously, Miss Landmine presents through the pageant the occasion for a valorous agency that is less about decisive action than it is about beautiful resilience. Such a promise of beauty is a defense against experiencing the wrecked world as it is—destabilizing, violent, and unpredictable. Inasmuch as the right to be beautiful provides a sense of place in the world in the absence of a structure that secures right or beauty, this claim, per Berlant, "converts the world to a space of moral action that seems juxtapolitical—proximate to, without being compromised by, the instrumentalities of power that govern social life."[141]

Perceived as an ontological truth that must be protected from and is itself protection against cruel machinations, beauty here becomes an *aesthetic* for antipolitics, where politics is a field of antagonism without guarantees. The pure heart and the body's dignity set the scene for this fantasy improvisation, where aspirational modes of building a life in the world without a horizon for justice are pursued because of structural hindrances that are understood as immovable features of the province of elites—whether NGOs or ministries. The ethical turn here suggests that we attend to the social bond and bear witness to catastrophe, and that these acts are in themselves forms of repair against the "merely structural." Soliciting the eye/I to enliven what the landmines (detached from the states that made them, laid them) tore asunder, the pageant form generates a *feeling* for democracy, where democracy is the recognition of others, rights are those attachments and capacities for true feelings, and compassion and conscience are that which binds strangers, for a moment. This iteration of democracy as a *feeling*—fleeting, transient—can do nothing to impede state or imperial violence which enact its sovereignty both through and outside of the law as it pleases. For this reason, *rights after rights* are less a resource for interceding in the world than a claim to happiness in spite of it.

Rights after Rights

As a solution to the destruction and atomization of bodies by terrible forces and sanctioned violence, *the right to be beautiful* requires the radical reorganization and administration of a life toward modes of habituation in extreme situations (landmines, chemical herbicides, authoritarian regimes, apartheid rule), without claim to the instrumentalities of power that govern them. But while the right to be beautiful might be a minimalist program for change (we could call it *barely structural*), this is not an argument to return to other forms of political speech. Tenderness and vulnerability do not inevitably sacrifice structural critique and other, alternate forms for collective being-together might yet emerge through practices such as the pageant or others like it, though these hopes hang on details (the hands that linger on another's cheek, the enigmatic glance that turns away) that act as our evidence for what we think might be happening, and what we think might happen after—and these are ultimately unpredictable. Through all this, we can still observe the right to be beautiful as an opportunity to understand how the aesthetics of rights are made and remade. Where demands to secure precarious life in the present are abandoned as a receding possibility, the right to be beautiful emerges as our compensation, naming as precious the capacity to accept and adapt to unavoidable vulnerability as the promise of the future. At the same time, the right to be beautiful as a horizon of ethical encounter, and as failure of imagination, is a directly political question about the need to create forms that do not depend on states or laws, but also that do not let them destroy life in the name of life. While it is true that the right to be beautiful is a nonjuridical form for democratic feeling, it is also true that justice cannot be established in the realm of a rules-based order.

The right to be beautiful puts on display law and order, as the presumed protection of the human, as both horizon and failure—in any case, foreclosing other possible conceptions for a life that can be lived.

I return here to the accusation that rights are becoming or have become ornaments, less ontological and more superficial, to ask—what if we understood *all* law as ornamental? Inasmuch as the bared body is perceived as rightless, rights are that which provides cover for flesh; such cover, however, is withheld for those who are "merely" flesh. To conjure a right to be beautiful thus does not erode some fundamental axiom of rightfulness; instead, it ungrounds as well as illuminates the ongoing contestability and vitality of rights as an aesthetic, or a practice. If what we are witnessing is the end of the human rights era, because these are no longer useful instruments for political claims, then what is happening with *the right to be beautiful* is not the degradation of rights, but the illumination of rights as already degraded, because no state cares to secure them, and how we continue despite their absence. Or to paraphrase Baedan, the right to be beautiful is not the suspension of rule, but the recognition of its nakedness.[142] To thereby consider the ornamentality of rights (or regimes, generally) is thus a matter of animating other ways of being in the world, other genres of the human, between normative personhood under the law, and an apocalyptic death-world of bare life. It is a provocation that we can and should consider other possible rights and another horizon of the human to come, more than what contemporary conceptions of rights or the human allow in the present.

Put another way, the right to be beautiful might not be a subjective disposition but a historical relation to a field of objects and forces that affect our capacities for life. Such a right establishes that the *merely human* bears no substance that preexists the forms of subjectivity resulting from those institutions—here the NGO, the portrait, and the pageant—claiming to simply recognize what was there all along. Even as rights are that which we cannot *not* want, the right to be beautiful gestures toward what else we might hope from justice when institutions and norms for law and order reach their threshold.[143] What *would* it mean to decouple juridical recognition from humanity? What if the right to be beautiful could be more than a feeling for life unmoored by political or legal definitions, but also the dismantling of their infrastructures? What would it mean to imagine politics as more than appeals to state sovereignty, *and also* more than mere survivability? Beauty's answers, though, will have to enter into political dispute, and not from the safety of distance or the moral certainty of a pure heart.

Chapter 4

Beauty's Ruin at the End of the World

In the US economy of the twenty-first century, the "dead pledge" of the capitalist system thus appears in all its horror, bringing us face-to-face with everything that is strange and violent about the most taken-for-granted aspects of our economic system: investments and liabilities, owing and ownership, repayment and default.

Annie McClanahan, *Dead Pledges*

I HOPE THIS EMAIL DOES NOT FIND YOU
I HOPE YOUR CHAIR HAS GROWN OVER WITH MOSS
I HOPE A PLEASANT BUT UNOBSERVED BEAM OF LIGHT HITS YOUR DESK PERFECTLY THROUGH THE COLLAPSED CEILING
I HOPE THE SILENCE IS DEAFENING

Not a Wolf, Twitter post

Human actions in service of colonial and corporate extraction are destabilizing the very conditions required to sustain life on earth. War and its aftermaths make mass graves and killing fields and desperate refugees, crowded onto buses or rafts cast adrift, or held indefinitely in semipermanent camps or detention centers at Christmas Island, Kakuma, Za'atari, Jenin, or Guantánamo Bay.[1] Racial and settler capital burns the Amazon rainforest, pumps toxins through pipelines, evicts dwellers from homes and underpasses, and abuses workers until they break, or are crushed in collapsed or burning buildings, whether garment factories in Rana Plaza in Bangladesh, an Amazon warehouse in Illinois, or a candle plant in Kentucky. Dire warnings about nuclear annihilation and climate catastrophe abound, from the Fukushima Daiichi disaster (in which an earthquake begat a tsunami that begat a nuclear meltdown) and Australia's and California's cataclysmic gigafires (one million acres on fire, no longer a rare designation), and aspirational and actual fascisms are on the rise around the world with, as Arundhati Roy put it, the depletion of democracy, now "used up, together with the other resources of our planet."[2]

Is it any wonder that we are every day met with spectacular images of untimely ruin in a radically unstable world, the scale of which dwarfs the human observer who wanders through its wreckage? From stark snapshots of grime-paned storefronts and cracked seas of big-box asphalt after bankruptcy and dispossession; to drone footage of desolate city streets during quarantine in the age of COVID-19; to phone videos of burning cars and barricades during protests against police violence and Black death; to aerial footage of collapsed bridges, carcinogenic clouds, and flooded lagoons of pig shit contaminating the water table in the wake of extreme weather or infrastructural failure; to forensic photographs of bombed-out blocks, bulldozed homes, and poisoned olive groves in occupied lands; the haunted bones of catastrophe are all around us. How should we respond to so much ruin?

Ruination is not exactly the subject of this chapter, though it is not *not* about it. Instead, I turn to the complaint that follows from representations of ruin that are perceived as aesthetically compelling and therefore politically suspect. Whether censuring war reportage, documentary photography, artworks, or scholarly inquiry, the complaint distinguishes between modes of responding to crisis and charges the perceptual disturbances of the beautiful, the ugly, and the pornographic with deforming our apprehension of it. Where crisis is described as an event of knowledge that demands from us clarity, reflection, and calculation, beauty is named an obstacle. What, this complaint demands, can beauty really do for our sense-making of crisis, terror? It is a question that haunts this book, where beauty is spurned as gratuitous, ornamental, or useless against the wreckage of history understood to circumscribe Vietnam, Afghanistan, Cambodia, or _____. *How does beauty alleviate suffering? Can beauty convey true knowledge about catastrophe?*[3] Because it can do nothing to alter these circumstances, beauty (some might say) at best is a diversion, at worst a crime.

Now-familiar photographs of contemporaneous ruins are often regarded as false witness to rot and decline. This perceptual inadequacy is commonly condensed as *ruin porn*, the colloquial accusation wielded by photographers and critics against images of urban desolation and disaster, and most often against scenes of large-scale abandonment and deindustrialization. In particular, Detroit is cited as the complaint's preeminent example of unseemly fascination, obscene pleasure, and memory's betrayal. John Patrick Leary calls it Detroitism, the aesthetic sensibility that blasphemously diminishes the city to "the Mecca of urban ruins."[4] Such "'pornographic' sensationalism" found in these photographs, these films, Leary writes, "aestheticizes poverty without inquiring of its origins, dramatizes spaces but never seeks out the people that inhabit or transform them, and romanticizes isolated acts of resistance without acknowledging the massive political and social forces aligned against the real transformation, and not just stubborn survival, of the city."[5] In this callous fashion, ruin porn stunts sociality and relays no useful knowledge of being alive or life-living. What is ruinous and pornographic in ruin porn is not simply the heap of rubble, the fallen archway, or the broken window, the complaint goes on, but what we fail to see about a crisis or catastrophe.

But just as the crisis concept is not an ontological description of historical time but an interpretation of its significance, the pornographic complaint is less an empirical statement than a judgment about an affective response to an aestheticized gesture. Echoing Leary, the archaeologist Krysta Ryzewski sums up the jumble of charges: "A Detroiter's definition of ruin porn would more likely read as: 'a superficial and one-eyed portrayal of urban decay that, with the snap of the camera's shutter button, creates something seductive and aesthetically pleasing that packages my life, my city, and my history into a narrative of social and material misery to be crafted and consumed by people who have limited connections to or understandings of this place.'"[6] What does it mean to accuse a beautiful image, *seductive and aesthetically pleasing*, with being pornographic? It bears noting that, as Carolyn Dean writes, "the vast referential powers of pornography have become indispensable to explaining, interpreting, and constructing the problem of moral habituation of suffering," but this is no simple substitution (in which pornography *is* suffering).[7] To say that something is pornographic performs a rhetorical labor that is assumed to be immediately accessible (as adverse consequences and ugly feelings) but is discursively mystifying. Where the pornographic is decried as insensitivity, titillation, or passivity, as anticathartic time, stunted vigor, or the theft of memory—a wildly oscillating set of possible crimes—the grievance against it presumes a particular distribution of the sensible.

Threatening what is possible to apprehend through the senses, including the "proper" configuration of time and space, what is aesthetically well-made or compelling might (according to the complaint) hasten our annihilation. The beautiful image fails so badly to perceive the truth of an object, including the crisis that is its condition, that it becomes pornographic, and in so doing impedes the perception of vitality, aliveness, or movement. Therefore, whether a category or a consequence of beauty's failure, the pornographic is understood to lead to moral atrophy or intellectual stultification, frustrating the sociological explanation or historicization that the crisis concept demands. Here and in its other iterations as a complaint (poverty porn, humanitarian porn, war porn, etc.), the pornographic is a judgment of error, a deviation from truth, and alienation of the human from others, and from history.

Tracing how an object or aesthetic such as ruin is named pornographic, we might untangle some of the presumptions of a causal relationship between aesthetics and politics, pleasure and action, sovereignty crisis. This chapter thus considers the complaint of specific failure—the capacity of aesthetically well-made photographs to represent the decline of an industrial city—that unfolds into a far-reaching claim about beauty's inadequacy. While the complaint is a minor key in considering those crises that litter our historical moment, it can help us to outline the aesthetics through which one can presumably *know* crisis in itself. That is, the pornographic does not just raise the dilemma of the very possibility of bearing witness to history; according to the complaint, it arouses only *feeling ahistorical*. In doing so, the pornographic presumably suspends the faculty for action as well. But is this truly all there is to the pornographic, and is the pornographic necessarily an obstacle to sense-making? Without pursuing another interpretation of these images of ruin (there are already urgent histories of Detroit, and discerning studies of the body of photographs themselves, that are alongside but also beyond my argument),[8] or an alternate schema for pornography (a genre that defies easy categorization),[9] I focus on how the pornographic complaint—collating failures of knowledge, sense, and agency—is a matter of how beauty and its others are sensed but also, through these acts and the cognitions, affects, and fantasies that imbue our perception, how beauty and its others are structured *prior* to their sensing. As a description of disorder, the complaint resorts to liberal schemata of epistemology (an epistemology that is historically transparent and emotionally proportionate) and aesthetics (an aesthetics that is contained, symmetrical, truthful) as ideal habits for sense-making. And yet beauty's ruin might give evidence to what property, credit, or mastery—all liberal schemata of epistemic and aesthetic value—

represses and disowns. In other words, how *ruin porn* achieves its status as a historico-philosophical concept, as a metaphor that marks the alienation of the promise—understood as the capacity to act on history—from the human, tells us much about what is demanded from beauty, about the crimes it is accused of committing, and about the crimes we might commit ourselves.

Ruination

Ruin is at once record and debris, dialectic and rubble. Relics such as the Elgin Marbles in the British Museum or the Temple of Dendur in the New York Metropolitan Museum solicit stories of imperial license to covet and preserve, or pillage and hoard. Other ruins in other places are seen as unambiguous landscapes of faded grandeur; the Roman Colosseum, for instance, is heralded as one of the enduring Seven Wonders of the World, while Machu Picchu and Angkor Wat obtain as the resplendent remains of ancient kingdoms.[10] Such lost civilizations whose greatness and beauty are foregone are object lessons about the fate of empires; or the ceaseless tension between culture and nature; or whose contemplation grants to an observer a sharp, or sometimes somnambulant, pleasure.[11] We might also call Elaine Scarry's argument that errors in judgment belong to *lapsed worlds* a theory of ruin, while Rose Macaulay, who coined the term *ruin lust*, submits, "It is pretty safe to suppose that the earliest ruin pleasure was inextricably mixed with triumph over enemies, with moral judgment and vengeance, and with the violent excitements of war."[12] Inevitably perhaps, death and ruin are close companions, from the concrete bunkers on the beaches of Normandy, France; to the former slave-trading fortresses on the Cape Coast, Ghana; to El Helicoide de la Roca Tarpeya, an unfinished, spiral-shaped futuristic mall turned semisecret prison from the mid-twentieth century in Caracas, Venezuela, which Celeste Olalquiaga calls "an extraordinary emblem of modernity's utopian dreams and their dystopian reality."[13] Not all rubble becomes ruin, however; ruin is the consequence of framing rubble as a signifier for memory or history, especially where the ruin contains clues to its own decline. Whether pleasure, triumph, melancholy, or disgust, our affective responses to waste and debris reanimate their substance with significance.[14] As Walter Benjamin put it, "Allegories are, in the realm of thoughts, what ruins are in the realm of things."[15]

Once called the Paris of the West for its monumental architecture, grand promenades, and electrified motorways, Detroit is an empire city. And like most empire cities, its onetime prosperity was built on extractivist violence brought to bear *on* Detroit, such as the dispossession and forced removal of the Anishinabeg tribes, including the Ojibwa (Chippewa), Ottawa, and Potawatomi, and anti-Black policies of redlining, racial covenant, and organized abandonment (after Ruth Wilson Gilmore), and *from* Detroit, including the murderous machinery brought to bear on more distant racial, colonial others. Detroit manufacturers became the chief supplier of war munitions to the US armed forces during the Second World War, assembling what Franklin D. Roosevelt dubbed the "arsenal of democracy." The federal government later tapped the Motor City's moguls for key appointments during the Cold War. As Dwight Eisenhower's secretary of defense, General Motors president Charlie Wilson managed the Pentagon as a business, reducing "manpower" and focusing on atomic weaponry. John F. Kennedy recruited Ford Motor Company president Robert McNamara to prepare Pentagon agencies for a "long twilight struggle, year in and year out."[16] As Greg Grandin observes, Secretary of Defense McNamara increased the US military presence in Southeast Asia and used a corporate, integrated "'systems management' approach to wage 'mechanized, dehumanizing slaughter,' as historian Gabriel Kolko put it," in Vietnam, Laos, and Cambodia.[17] McNamara would go on to become president of the World Bank until 1981, overseeing the turn toward structural adjustment programs that devastated postcolonial countries with wealth extraction and immense debt. And even as Ford, General Motors, and Chrysler moved their operations overseas to destroy domestic unions and evade regulations, Ford Motor Company plant property in dictator Juan Perón's Argentina hosted a brutal military interrogation center, torturing Ford's own workers, union activists, and "disappearing" thousands more into unmarked mass graves.

But Detroit is also a study of how empire ruins *itself*.[18] Fordlandia, an ambitious "jungle town" in the Brazilian Amazon built in the prefabricated, all-American image of Detroit, is long collapsed into ruins (Ford's complete disregard for Indigenous ways of knowledge eventually destroyed its rubber tree plantations and spawned worker revolts). Grandin writes about this abject fiasco, "And as we look back in the years to come, we may see the decline of the auto industry as a blow to American power comparable to the end of the Raj, Britain's loss of India."[19] Another critic hails Detroit as "the U.S. equivalent of a failed state."[20] Most recently, Detroit's ruination traces the shift in US economic power from manufacturing capital to finance capital, relocating surplus value from the extraction of labor to debt. In what David Harvey calls "accumulation by dispossession" (the return of so-called primitive accumulation) and Anna Lowenhaupt Tsing dubs "spectacular accumulation" (the premise of which rests on "a product that may or may not exist"), financial speculation generates a higher rate of return on investment than manufacturing, with money borrowed against a *hoped-for* future.[21] Predatory lending through mortgage-backed securities and collateralized debt obligations devastated holders of so-called subprime loans and precipitated the 2008 collapse of the housing market. In 2013, the Republican governor enacted a state emergency manager law; the largest municipality in the country to file for Chapter 9 bankruptcy, Detroit was no longer under democratic control. Under the declaration of emergency, the force of law exists without the law. The governor, the emergency manager, and bankruptcy judges, among others, raided the pensions of public workers, cut water to residences where bills were sixty or more days past due, and sought to auction the city-held art collection of the Detroit Institute of Arts for liquidity. In pursuit of ruin, "Everything is on the table," the emergency manager declared.[22]

Ruins are therefore politics in their historical essence. *Something*—whether an event, a structure, or both—led to all this wreckage. That same *something* cannot repair it. Under capital's long shadow, credit's history is one of predation, extraction, and dispossession—it destroys completely. As Nina Dubin writes, "Suspended . . . between plenitude and mere potentiality, between past value and future returns, credit exhibited precisely the condition that is the hallmark of the ruin."[23] As a signal indice of economic fluctuation, the concept of credit, or the extension of faith ahead of repayment or reciprocity, also known as investment, is haunted by the failure to remunerate that debt, also known as risk. The Atlantic slave trade in the seventeenth and eighteenth centuries required immense amounts of circulating capital and massive borrowing, leading to the establishment and regularization of banking firms, insurance houses, the stock exchange, and their financial instruments. The development of Europe and the Americas hinged on African slavery, which produced much of the funding for the establishment of institutions that would then finance further speculative, extractive enterprises around the world.[24] Zenia Kish and Justin Leroy write that the innovations spawned by the slave trade "could be applied to any kind of industry in a credit economy."[25] But it is because millions of Africans were made property that ownership as the principle of legitimacy, attachment, and credibility anchors liberal civil society; thereafter some are not to be extended enough credit, having once been property. To this end, "raciality," Paula Chakravartty and Denise Ferreira da Silva observe, "makes the colonial (African and Indigenous) other and their descendants as lacking the moral attributes (self-determination, self-transparency, and self-productivity) characteristic of persons and places (the ones they originate from) that truly embody the traits that distinguish the proper economic subject."[26] Credit underwrites the contract (as a cornerstone of law) and the obligation (as the imperative of morality) but is a promise that only some can reliably ensure. To be able to promise is a limit test in the achievement of liberal humanism; per Karl Marx, a person "without credit," then, "possesses no trust, no recognition."[27] What else is debt, if not an inscription or sign substituted for property, whether found in marks on a ledger or on a body dispossessed?

This racial, colonial history of capital depends on unpayable debt (including the debt of being "freed" in the wake) as a site of value extraction in perpetuity.[28] The "innovation" of debt securitization allows debt to function as a tradable financial instrument, as a commodity that has a secondary market for its sale, such that debt becomes an industry itself. This debt contributes value through, as Neferti Tadiar notes, a "racialized cleavage within society between the risk-takers, or risk-capable, and 'those unable to live by risk, [who] are considered 'at risk.'"[29] Labeling the 2008 financial crisis and its purported triggers as subprime thus reinforces "the racial subaltern as naturally (morally and intellectually) unable to thrive in the modern capitalist configurations."[30] In Detroit alone, subprime mortgage foreclosures claimed tens of thousands of homes, and tax foreclosures claimed at least a hundred thousand more, with homes in primarily Black neighborhoods ten times more likely to be beset for seizure.[31] Property desubjectifies these dwellers because of their debt. Such subprime subjects, as Ananya Roy put it, cannot promise to fulfill the future.[32] To them, the future is foreclosed even as their debt subsidizes it for others.

In other words, credit is a terminal crisis; it *ensures* ruin. But what does a credit crisis look like? It is not so odd to ask this, as Marc Shell observes in his literary history of money that "credit, or belief, involves the very ground of aesthetic experience."[33] Wrought through resource extraction, planned obsolescence, deliberate impoverishment, and interrupted logistics, it might very well look like photographs of dead malls, as shopping centers are emptied of goods and crowds, interrupted only by saplings and waist-high weeds, their wide, echoing corridors often interpreted as picturing the failure of limitless growth or its built-in consequence. Or like Nadav Kander's photographic series *Dust*, capturing the radioactive ruins of secret cities on the border between Kazakhstan and Russia, in which collapsed buildings shimmer through the pink-blue haze after decades of Cold War nuclear testing.[34] Or like aerial photographs of decommissioned runways, derelict big-box buildings, and the oceans of black, cracked asphalt surrounding them, composing what Alan Berger calls drosscapes, or waste landscapes of defunct economic and production systems.[35] Or like large-scale panoramic photographs of Chinese ghost cities, massive real estate and commercial developments financed through an unregulated economy of speculative lending, which are echoingly vacant.[36] Or like photographs of the crumbling facade of the Beaux Arts–inspired Michigan Central train station, once the centerpiece of the City Beautiful movement with its soaring ceilings modeled on ancient Roman baths, or the weather-beaten reading room in a former public library, "amid a dense matting of decayed and burned books, a grove of birch trees grows from richly rotting words."[37] These are places becoming no-places, where debt has a strong hold.

A landscape is full of information about the passage of time, or, in W. T. J. Mitchell's words, "It is almost as if there is something built into the grammar and logic of the landscape concept that requires the elaboration of a pseudohistory, complete with a prehistory, an originating moment that issues in progressive historical development, and (often) a *final* decline and fall."[38] Contemporary ruins, however, often picture for us unstable sites of temporal fluctuation tied to the ebbs and flows of capital—decline and growth, demolition and construction, erosion and accretion—that are not ended. Untimely and perturbing, such ruins manifest, as Celeste Olalquiaga puts it, "the paradox of a future that did not make it to the present."[39] In this way, Detroit stands for a futural aesthetic of civilizational decline as it might be found now. Since the 1990s, its picturesque dereliction is chronicled in coffee-table books such as Camilo José Vergara's *American Ruins*, Andrew Moore's *Detroit Disassembled*, Yves Marchand and Romain Meffre's *The Ruins of Detroit*, and Matthew Christopher's *Abandoned America* (to name a very few); in exhibitions and gallery shows like the Tate Modern's *Ruin Lust*; in publications such as the *New York Review of Books* and *Time*; and on urban explorers' media platforms (blogs, YouTube channels, Instagram, among them). Heidi Ewing and Rachel Grady in the *New York Times*, in an essay about their documentary *Detropia*, write, "We chose to focus our camera on Detroit out of a gut feeling that this city may well be a harbinger of things to come for the rest of the country."[40] And Vergara observes, of his own body of work, "[Detroit's ruins] are an essential part of understanding America."[41]

But the proliferate body of *ruin porn* is not aesthetically unvarying. Some are somber photographs framed at a middle distance, neither distant nor intimate in their cool, austere composition; in Vergara's photographs of the abandoned neoclassical Lafayette Building, rising like a V-shaped limestone headstone in a graveyard, we find his argument for an "American Acropolis."[42] Others revel in imposing proportions and lush, color-saturated details, such as Yves Marchand and Romain Meffre's high-definition photographs of the Renaissance revival–style United Artists Theater, the beautifully carved ceiling punctured by sunlight illuminating the decaying wooden stage below its proscenium arch. Some photographs allude to a cyclical return to nature—foliage sprouting from concrete, foxes running across asphalt, grasses growing over siding—the crumbling of civilization in some planetary reset, such as James Griffioen's series *Feral Houses*; critics like Joanna Zylinska posit that these images forecast the political fulfillment of the end of capitalism, after the human.[43] This warning is also found in the Detroitian geographies of postapocalyptic films such as Paul Verhoeven's *RoboCop*, a brutally prescient dystopian drama about the privatization and militarization of police forces in an urban hellscape; or in Jim Jarmusch's elegiac film *Only Lovers Left Alive*, starring Tom Hiddleston and Tilda Swinton as hundreds-years-old vampire aesthetes Adam and Eve, lingering in a ramshackle mansion filled with a hoarder's detritus of the city's musical history; or in *Red Dawn*, the Hollywood studio nostalgia-tinged remake about an ascendant empire (in this case North Korea) threatening to end this one.

These images' disparate aesthetic properties are consequential for readings of the flux of life and death pictured there, and I would not argue otherwise. But what holds these formally distinct objects together is "crisis" as an observation that produces their meaning, through which Detroit is the spectacular scene for reading past destruction and future devastation for either a specific entity (an empire, a people, an idea) or a general humanity (again, an empire, a people, an idea). We know something happened and worse, that something is still happening. Credit's violence is *there* on the surface of these at times forensic scenes of foreclosed homes, abandoned blocks, shuttered schools, dead malls, and deserted thoroughfares. As Annie McClanahan observes, "As metonyms of the twenty-first-century credit crisis, photographs of abandoned industrial and civic spaces in Detroit reveal the relationship between these two historical moments and these two forms of crisis: the crisis of deindustrialization and the crisis of finance that came in to repair it."[44]

But if the ruins of Detroit are exemplary of an aesthetic vision of the vicissitudes of capital—that is, racist violence and labor extraction, the seizure of property and the dispossession of life-living, and the financialization of terminal crisis—what does it mean to accuse these photographs of failure, if what is pictured there is commonly understood as *just those things*? What is the axiological structure of aesthetic failure to accommodate political crisis, to instead yield "wrong" pleasures?

Pornographic

While the possibility of error and deviation is understood to be inherent in its judgment, some argue beauty was abandoned altogether in the mid-twentieth century. How could there be beauty after the crises unfolding from the predations of capital and fascism, more devastating technologies of war-making, and challenges to the universal—or, in other words, empire? Theodor Adorno famously stated that composing poems after Auschwitz is "barbaric," though he later acknowledged that suffering nonetheless demands art, while Virginia Woolf worried at the abject failure of Clarissa's flowers to ameliorate the suffering of Armenians.[45] In his 1968 presidential address to the American Society for Aesthetics, amid wars, uprisings, and recessions, Monroe Beardsley mourns, "Even hardened aestheticians (an obvious oxymoron) may suffer from doubts that beauty or significant form is what the world needs most right now, when quite different goods—intelligence and charity, for instance—are more likely to restore our sense of community and stop us from creating a society whose answer to all problems—aesthetic and otherwise—will be violent repression."[46] Beardsley continues, "When so many of us in this troubled land do not seem to care very much even for one another—much less for the ravaged nature and crumbling cities our descendants will inherit—the aesthetic point of view becomes difficult to sustain. It may even seem absurd."[47] Or as Noor Hindi scoffs in the poem "Fuck Your Lecture on Craft, My People Are Dying": "Colonizers write about flowers. / I tell you about children throwing rocks at Israeli tanks / seconds before becoming daisies."[48] The absence of beauty is narrated both as evidence of devastation in our lives and as itself devastating, even as subsequent turns toward the sublime and other aesthetic qualities purport to more faithfully capture modernity's violence.

Habitual claims of fraud and frivolity haunt beauty, we know. But then how does such failure become (if not necessarily) pornographic? One definition, established under Lyndon Johnson's administration by the President's Commission on Obscenity and Pornography, identified pornography as "any form of sexual activity which is impersonal, which uses the body alone for pleasure, violates the integrity of the person and thereby reduces him to the level of an irrational and irresponsible animal."[49] But what if there are no bodies, no flesh at all? When something that does not depict sexual activity is said to be pornographic, one or several things might be meant by the complaint. The offending image or description might be understood as addictive, gratuitous, mindless, numbing, exploitative, illicit, and violent, yielding ill-gotten pleasure, cheap pleasure, found in others' misfortune or misery. Vigilant against uncritical creep, Fredric Jameson writes that "the visual is *essentially* pornographic; which is to say that it has its end in rapt, mindless fascination." He continues, proposing that the pornographic image is the "potentiation" of images in general, "which ask us to stare at the world as though it were a naked body."[50] In this tautological observation, the pornographic is an aspect of the visual, therefore the pornographic is everywhere. Worse still, the pornographic also contaminates the one who looks. Jacques Rancière proposes that the spectator has come to be regarded as a negative figure, first because of a belief that viewing is the opposite of knowing (the spectator is in thrall to an illusion and a state of ignorance about the process of image production and the reality it hides), and second because of the assumption that to be a spectator is to remain a passive voyeur and not a political actor.[51] According to such warnings, visual cognition and perception easily collapse into mindlessness and even harm.

In an important essay on the analogy, Carolyn Dean observes that references to pictures of atrocity—specifically, from the Holocaust—as pornographic operate as an accusation for a deficit of feeling. Dean traces the usage of the pornographic as accusation after the First World War to describe an objectifying, dehumanizing, and morally distorted perception of suffering, with the added dimension of commercialization further compounding the violation.[52] Where the display of human suffering appears to generate not empathic identification but instead an often eroticized objectification of pain, Dean notes, "The metaphor of pornography describes a general process by which bodily degradation and suffering—the indignity of the literal body and the metaphorical body of historical memory it is our responsibility to transmit—becomes a focus of fascination or pleasure for both erotic and aggressive drives."[53] But despite pornography's rhetorical and explanatory force, she cautions, "before employing the . . . presumption that pornography is synonymous with effaced dignity instead of with specific categories of material, we might begin by unpacking its apparently self-evident status, asking what cultural work this presumption now performs and what logical connections it assumes—and makes."[54]

What, then, can be known, and what cannot, in the pornographic? This is the problem to which the complaint is obliquely addressed—the difficulty of knowing what there is to know. George Steiner in his essay "On Difficulty" considers how *difficulty* intervenes in the "classic contract between word and world," the "contract of ultimate or preponderant intelligibility between poet and reader, between text and meaning."[55] But Steiner is also one of the first critics to denounce a postwar wave of historical novels about the Holocaust, which evince (he says) "diminishing reserves of feeling and imaginative reserve in our society," as pornographic.[56] The pornographic thus names a difficulty, or the arrangements through which something—a category, a person, an object—is understood as outside the promise of intelligibility. If "correct" aesthetic evaluation is supposed to inform and also issue from the capacity for judgment and moral reasoning, the pornographic (according to this) interferes with sensory perception and rational calculation. The complaint thus presumes to condense its wayward aesthetic properties into a coherent taxonomic order to point *not* to the something the pornographic is accused of missing or not knowing, but to the ruin of contract or credibility.

If the pornographic complaint alleges that something has gone wrong or is missing, what is the source of error and lapse in these beautiful photographs, in the heaps of rubble, debris, and wreckage, the crumbling masonry and gutted cross walls? What contract, or promise, is broken? Capturing the reflection of light across a surface (a silky-smooth dress, a pockmarked prothesis, a crumbling cinderblock), the photograph is a trace that establishes a direct association with the material world, evidence that the object it captures had, at one point, presence. But while we often approach the photograph as a reference or index, the pornographic is a warning not to do so. Indeed, the pornographic charges surface is not substance, such that we cannot know what else is there or *should* be there to see. Despite being closest to us, then, surface is decried as distancing. For instance, "The ruins are gazed upon for amusement, gratification and pleasure. While they may purport to show the city, they are incapable of contextualizing more than sixty years of capital extraction and de-facto apartheid."[57] Or, "The emotionally urgent but contextually shallow quality of ruin porn images performs a similar function of soothing viewers and preventing critical inquiry, prompting us to consider them as spaces of representation that rely on abstraction and nostalgia."[58] Or, "Photography that focuses only on the aesthetics of decay in architecture offers a narrative that distances and obscures the ongoing crisis of poverty and unemployment."[59] Because of these and similar complaints, beauty is often subject to what Paul Ricoeur calls "the hermeneutics of suspicion" and what Eve Sedgwick describes as a paranoid reading, one that assumes false consciousness and proposes methods for deciphering truth from noise.[60] If in looking we do not know much (the ruin photograph is accused of being a poor copy, a distorted likeness, and so on), the complaint also tells us quite a lot about how to see "properly." How is it decided, then, that what is aesthetically well-made or compelling is not an imitable model for human thought and activity—or that it might even be our downfall? Or, to put it another way, how does the beautiful become ugly?

As with beauty, ugliness is not simply an aesthetic concept but a perceptual problem. As the disturbance of the normative order, ugliness has a disordering relationship to presence and absence, inside and outside. Unlike beauty as ideal, associated with the boundedness of symmetry, harmony, and order, ugliness as error, allied with the disarray of ambiguity, abjection, and monstrosity, threatens to spread like a contagion. The cultural critic and architectural theorist Mark Cousins observed "the ugly" and its constitutive distinction from beauty as "an object which is experienced both as being there and as something that *should not be there*."[61] Cousins continues, and it is worth citing at length, "[The beautiful object] exhibits the proper relations to itself and to what is not itself, to its inside and to its outside. Its form is clear and distinct. Internally it exhibits coherence; externally it establishes a sharp boundary between itself and the world.... The perfect object is ... one which is finished, completed. Any addition or subtraction from the object would ruin its form. The idea of being finished relates, not to an aspect of the duration of the work, but to the expression of an indivisible totality."[62] In other words, ugliness is a perceptual disturbance of boundary (which is made the same as order), observing no propriety or property (which is hinged on boundary), sometimes as the wrongful copresence or clustering of things that *should not be there*. "From this it follows that an ugly representation, or an ugly object, is a negation not just of beauty, but of truth. The category of beauty plays an epistemological role; it represents the truth of an object. Ugliness belongs to whatever negates that truth. It belongs to a series of categories which similarly distort the truth of objects."[63] Such epistemic violence that is presumed to *distort the truth of objects* might be found in shallow knowledge, flat encounter, moral perversion, or thwarted interiority. We see this conceit (and its deconstruction) in Sianne Ngai's ugly feelings, such as compromised agency or anemic ambivalence, which are petty, trivial, or noncathartic, or in Elisabeth Anker's ugly freedoms "in which practices of freedom"—such as torture—"produce harm, brutality, and subjugation *as freedom*."[64] Ugliness is disorder, chaos, animal; lie, zero, void.

The pornographic complaint thus condemns the forms that makes such epistemic failure possible, where ugliness limits our field of perception. Beauty (according to the complaint) is ornamental, even as its ugliness is ontological. In this view, seeing is not sensing, and seeing is not knowing. Accounts of ruin porn are for this reason often interested in how the photographs are produced *as pictures*, balanced on the knife's edge that the photograph is an index (*it points to something . . .*) that is not yet evidence (*. . . but we know not what*). Kat Buckley observes of ruin photographs, "They are all expertly cropped: nothing from the shot exists to give the viewer a sense of place, being, or community. These pictures are devoid of people. They typically feature an abundance of natural light; these photographers know that their shots depend on their ability to show viewers the centuries-old dust particles as they linger in the air. Some authors have noted the 'frontality' of these images, which is the maximizing effect employed by photographers wherein they fill the image space with the site of decay."[65] Techniques such as high dynamic range (HDR) imaging can illuminate surfaces, colors, and details normally dulled, or cast deep in shadow, becoming an "index of refraction" rather than objects.[66] In doing so, some argue, "These images of ruins do not contest the conditions of their creation, but reassert them as picturesque."[67] And through their careful composition, these photographs further suggest the absent presence of human being. "A casual survey of the truly vast, virtual, visual archive of UrbEx [Urban Exploration photography] will reveal many, many relic chairs. The empty chair is an icon of abandoned sites around the world."[68] Photographs of an abandoned school might crop "the newer, successful school sitting right next to it."[69] Others deliberately stage what we expect to see from the dissolution of civilization, "like the French filmmaker who came to Detroit to shoot a documentary about all the deer and pheasants and other wildlife that have been returning to the city. After several days without seeing a wild one he had to be talked out of renting a trained fox to run through the streets for the camera."[70]

The chair, the tree, the school, and the fox are each evidence, according to the complaint, of the wrong thing in the wrong place. Here their closeness is not an event of knowledge but a source of distress, or a signal of wrongness. This situational arrangement of incongruous objects—inside things and outside things, for instance, that *should not be there together*—triggers the epithet *ruin porn* in their perverse intimacy.[71] Indeed, boundary is a tenuous effect of partition and its permanence; whatever ugliness is located in the anterior of the photograph (the ruination) pollutes also its surface (the photograph itself). These are the grounds of perceptual error. "It's almost as if the photos are too beautiful, and by extension the poverty and dilapidation is beautiful."[72] This unsettling spoilage can take the shape of a metaphor for privacy and property (both enclosures) being turned inside out and stripped of safety. Bill Brown writes, "It is all those spaces within—the inside of the chest, the inside of the wardrobe, the inside of the drawer—that . . . enable us to image and imagine human interiority."[73] (Bad boundaries, as we say to our friends, or as our therapists say to us, threaten to destroy our sovereign sense of self.) It is significant, then, that in his treatise on ugliness, Cousins, an architect, observes its disorderly nature through the derelict structure. Such a ruin has no actual interior that would in turn imply an exterior; one is always already inside it. As walls collapse, there is neither a steady surface from which to observe a structure at a distance nor the safety of enclosure. "In terms of building it appears as those spaces which can be thought of as a vacuum, negative constructions in which we experience a kind of horror. A missing stair is not simply dangerous; it needs us to lose our footing, indeed it needs our footing. We are always less by being here."[74] What depth lies therein threatens to engulf us; it is an abyss, a skeleton, a hole.

What we might sense from this structural metaphor is that the alienation of property, and property as alienating, is a function of a disordered relationship to interiority and exteriority. Consider the subgenre of ruin photographs that picture foreclosures and evictions. In the United States, the early twenty-first-century housing bubble burst as subprime loan policies resulted in unpayable mortgages, and despite temporary rental assistance programs and a nationwide eviction moratorium (given no teeth for enforcement), the COVID-19 pandemic worsened the vast gulf between property and debt. Freud's concept of the *unheimlich* or the uncanny, translated as the unhomely, captures the affective undoing of foreclosure and eviction, in which what is familiar or secure is turned inside out, undone by someone or something being *out of place*. To be *unheimlich* is to be within a structure that feels unsafe, in which we might lose our footing and fall through; indeed, the insecurity of private property as a structure is not just unsafe, it is violent. Annie McClanahan, elaborating on the etymology of the mortgage as a dead pledge, observes that ownership by another to whom one is in debt charges the domestic interior with a creeping uneasiness—an ontology as "neither living nor dead."[75] Karl Marx writes about the house that is not a home because someone else owns it, and because you can be thrown out of it, "The cellar dwelling of the poor man is a hostile element, 'a dwelling which remains an alien power and only gives itself up to him insofar as he gives up to it his own blood and sweat'—a dwelling which he cannot regard as his own hearth—where he might at last exclaim: 'Here I am at home'—but where instead he finds himself in *someone else's* house, in the house of a *stranger* who always watches him and throws him out if he does not pay his rent."[76] Thus, the dweller who is made to feel insecure in the house that is not his own becomes the object of suspicion and surveillance. Inside private property, the dweller is yet outside of it; they are its target of extraction and also the agent of its devaluation. McClanahan catalogs the multiple group photography shows and exhibitions about foreclosure, eviction, and housing debt (with names like *The Great Depression: Foreclosure USA*; *Foreclosed: Rehousing the American Dream*; *Foreclosed Dreams*; and *Scenes from Surrendered Homes*), centering "the image of the house as a precarious commodity, as a site of lived insecurity, as the stuff of both dream and nightmare."[77] The home thus contains within it, and is surrounded by, the potential for appalling violence. When Anthony Suau's photograph of a police-enforced home foreclosure won the World Press Photo award in 2008, the jury chair remarked, "Now war in its classic sense is coming into people's houses because they can't pay their mortgages."[78]

What is as uncanny as a ruin? It is the propertyless dweller, the unwelcome guest, the stranger, the spirit, or the debtor who malingers. This disorder is affective, aesthetic, and material all at once, and what is deemed disorderly is given as a reason for imposing, enforcing, and prosecuting. Writing about the anachronously named ugly laws, municipal statutes that criminalized public begging or loitering through outlawing the appearance in public of people who were, in the words of Chicago's law, "diseased, maimed, mutilated, or in any way deformed, so as to be an unsightly or disgusting object," Susan Schweik observes that this status offense "creates its 'ugly' through a process related to other city beautification efforts inscribed in class logics."[79] Like the house turned inside out, the pornographic is the disclosure of that which is rightfully private, according to bourgeois norms, which is an obscene operation.

Perhaps no situation exemplifies this aesthetics of suspicion more than the broken window, where being-in-error is also a crime. Cohering abandoned factories, foreclosed homes, and crumbling malls as forewarning, broken window policing is the commonplace criminological theory that *visible* signs of antisocial behavior and civil disorder creep, like a contagion, as an ontological ugliness. These are aesthetic arguments that naturalize political justifications for state-sanctioned violence, in which the gathering of some objects in a cluster (under the penumbra of "the destruction of private property") creates a ground for surveillance and control. Policing minor crimes, such as vandalism, loitering, public drinking, graffiti, and fare evasion—the proverbial broken windows—becomes necessary (according to the theory) to counter such depravity with an increase of order and lawfulness.[80] This distribution of the sensible—as reasonable, and as felt—helps us to grasp the virulent properties of the broken window to facilitate or impede the recognition, movement, or will and design of others, to transform and render a person into being-as or being-like the root of ruin—the criminal.

Such state violence is the necessary corollary for the capture of life through debt. Conceived as outside of ownership, having been property, and faulted for affectability—what Denise Ferreira da Silva defines as "the condition of being subjected to both natural (in the scientific and lay sense) conditions and to others' power," otherwise conceived as property in oneself—Black persons are policed in the name of accumulation by dispossession—they cannot but be in debt.[81] And if the cartography of debt is a "no-place," per Rocio Zambrana, then there is no place in which a debtor (a status-being) is not out of order.[82] As Jordan Camp and Christina Heatherton catalogue, "Akai Gurley was assassinated by officers patrolling public housing projects; twelve-year-old Tamir Rice was killed by police charged with securing a public park; and Eric Garner was strangled by police regulating a public street for the sale of untaxed cigarettes."[83] After Trayvon Martin's murder by a neighborhood vigilante who claimed to *recognize* him as an interloper, his hoodie became an index of paranoid reading, too weak a racial signifier and yet too powerful a racial threat.[84] All this death is justified through an aesthetics of perception based on profiling (reading surfaces for depths) and broken windows (reading ugliness as disturbance) in which police and vigilantes murder Black persons for minor or perceived infractions. Here, the debtor is herself a ruin, inciting the violence of law and order. This is the American horror story.[85]

The pornographic complaint contains an archive of the forms of social life understood as modernity's constitutive outside. It is as such that the sense-making of violence in a broken window through policing ("this window represents crime and thus demands more policing") and the sense-making of violence in a broken window through a critique of policing ("this window represents the criminalization of poverty and thus justifies more policing") both claim sociological insights into the violence that brought us before these windows, knowledge that comes from beyond the ruin, which can tell us nothing. In this predicament, the complaint marks historical conditions to qualify them as crisis and makes a judgment about what constitutes an appropriate affective response; what it deems pornographic is condemned as empty of "true" information or knowledge. But knowledge of this failure arrives through a prior and suspect history of how we credit such knowledge at all.

The Failure

So, the complaint is that the pornographic cannot us tell what went wrong. John Patrick Leary, formulating Detroitism in *Guernica*, observes, "Taken together, all the images of the ruined city become fragments of stories told so often about Detroit that they are at the same time instantly familiar and utterly vague, like a dimly remembered episode from childhood or a vivid dream whose storyline we can't quite remember in the morning. . . . A ruin photograph succeeds in providing the details of a familiar story whose major plot points we can't piece together."[86] While the prehistory of this photograph is inherent in the ruin, the pornographic disrupts this telos—no history, no progress can be read from its surfaces to observe another, more primary mover. Instead, the complaint goes, the historical consciousness figured through ruin porn is looping, repetitive, arrested. Stuck without a sense of progression, we lose the plot. We do not feel historical but instead *feel without history*.

The epithet *porn* thus names an obstacle or a hindrance to those calculative powers necessary for political critique and credible action, both of which are crucial to the narrativization of history; it can only produce aberrant or fallow forms of knowledge and modes of sense-making. Or, as Leary asks, "One often finds oneself asking of . . . all ruin photographs, first, 'What happened?' followed swiftly by, 'What's your point?'"[87] The accusation of failure mirrors the promise of beauty, inasmuch as ruin images are accused of failing first as a critique of structures or conditions, and second as a call to action to transform those structures or conditions *in time*. That is, the pornographic is the failure of the promise of beauty to be *credible*. It is a liberal regime of representation and meaning-making, of linking meaning to action, that makes the pornographic complaint stick.

Neither diagnosis nor cure, the pornographic is accused of being parasitic on beauty, luring us in and then away; it breaks both with what is there and what can be known from our perception. "Ruin photography's beauty is a reactionary one that invites pleasurable inspection but neither calls attention to its own circumstances of making nor does it invite viewer action."[88] But again—what *does* crisis look like, feel like? In crisis, it is often the scene without ornament—stripped down, rendered bare—that is perceived as truly capturing the reality of a historical situation. This scene is only sometimes a body, whether the AIDS-ravaged patient, the starving child, the lynching victim, the landmine amputee. Writing about film, Rey Chow observes that the aesthetic of Giorgio Agamben's bare life is generated in images through which "the historical weight of the catastrophe is shown or given to us through the muteness of the most ordinary of scenes, such as a lush green landscape or a decrepit empty building, even as the directors emphasize how difficult or impossible it is to represent the enormity of what happened."[89] The accusation of being pornographic thus follows after the supposition that one cannot adequately represent atrocity—and yet the pornographic still *tries*. In other words, the photograph of ruin is a bad copy of a historical situation. Its verisimilitude is a failure because the pornographic is awash in detail, all ornament—the distinct dust motes floating suspended in the beam of sunlight streaming through a broken window, the broken spine of a waterlogged book moldering in a pile of other library discards. These details in their sensory immediacy, paradoxically, are accused of abstraction.[90] Abstraction is central to the pornographic complaint as an *idea* of a real thing that is *not* that thing (the sex act that is rote, cheap, mediated, and "unreal"), or what Chow calls (writing about the agony of theory) the "morally degenerate dismissal of the real world out there."[91] The pornographic is the presumed failure to know history and the future that must follow; it is the discrepancy between promise and outcome. To misinterpret a crisis is to fail to understand what is going on and then to decide how best to correct it.

Most egregiously, genres of atrocity porn are charged with the abstraction of violence. Where persons, objects, or worlds are drained of liveliness (variously understood as agency, bond, or history), they become seemingly dumb and mute commodities, animated only by others' desires. (The British anarchist band Chumbawamba titled its 1986 album, as a sarcastic invective against the spectacle of Live Aid and other charity concerts, *Pictures of Starving Children Sell Records*.) But what is the pornographic if the human life it violates is not present, as in the photograph of rubble and ruin? Such photographs are perceived as the violent removal of humanity from their embeddedness in concrete histories for voyeuristic purposes. In that case it is *the absence* of humans rather than their exposure or display that renders the ruin photograph fetishistic. In this formula, absence is negation, blocking connection, empathy, and dignity. For instance, "'Ruin porn' is based purely on aesthetics and is *almost always devoid of people*. Employing the mismatched spoils of history, ruin porn ignores and overwrites the voices of those who still call Detroit home. When its ruins are fetishized as art, these injustices are, at best, ignored, and, at worst, mimicked. They ignore the humanity of residents' current struggles, while replicating the history that created them."[92] Or in another condemnation, "By largely 'disappearing' the victims of the city's decline, the discourse of ruination remains focused on architecture and the 'reclamation' of the city by nature."[93] Pivoting between imagined presence and projected absence in this reading, the photograph does not just depict depopulation; it *is* depopulation.

The pornographic exposes too much of the wrong thing (it is said) and not enough of the right thing. The ruin photograph is accused of evacuating the victim with whom we would otherwise empathize (though this is belied by the parallel accusation when victims *are* present), where the pornographic incriminates a pathological nonrelationality, as in, "Ruin porn allows viewers to feel a socio-historical distance, as if the devastation they view is safely ensconced in the past, or in a surreal post-apocalyptic city that nobody cares about anymore."[94] Because the complaint condenses a denunciation of betrayal and distance, to show no humans at all in these desolate landscapes is moral failure. What's worse, where vulnerability in crisis is often represented through nakedness—mere flesh or bare life—the ruin photograph refers to nakedness only to vest nonliving material with the social life of *being stripped*. Substructures are exposed, foundations are laid bare. In their introductory notes to *The Ruins of Detroit*, the photographers Yves Marchand and Romain Meffre refer to Detroit as a "contemporary Pompeii, with all the archetypal buildings of an American city in a state of mummification."[95] To them, the city is already dead, and these derelict structures are its bleached and broken bones. The ruin thus functions as an analogy for the body while accused of doing so poorly because it is *not* a body. Just as the inside turned out is a disordering operation, the willful confusion of persons and things is (in the complaint, at least) an ontological obscenity.

Thus accused, is ruin porn aestheticizing or anaestheticizing? The complaint answers *yes, the pornographic is all these things*. Where the pornographic renders the human inaccessible or alien through its aestheticization or absence, the complaint coheres, as Carolyn Dean puts it, an "allegory of the way in which we lose our feeling."[96] The pornographic stimulates too much involuntary sensation in a feeling observer as to border on the obscene, ironically resulting in numbness and stunted conviviality. A critic, describing *Only Lovers* as ruin porn (vampires Adam and Eve spend much of their time in a near-derelict house crammed full of Detroit's musical lore), defines it as "an infatuation with social breakdown that is indifferent to economic and political explanations or solutions."[97] The presumably illegitimate pleasures the pornographic solicits are self-negating because it suggests a failure to maintain an adequate or "correct" boundary with an outside stimulant, and world-negating because it is presumably antisocial and antihistorical. Ruin porn is thus personified by the undead vampire who collects things but drains people, who chases stimulation but feels numb. Such dissolute beauty as found in the monster's embrace becomes not the conduit for life but an obstacle—an interference that blocks the right sort of interference.

Crucial also to the narrativization of crisis is the tempo of urgency, wrought through the finitude of the conditions within which we encounter it. To refer improperly to crisis is to fail to communicate with clarity the obligation (and as well the calculation) to *do* something. That the photograph as a medium interrupts a teleological history is true of all photographs, but the ruin photograph stands accused of extending that interruption, sometimes indefinitely. Because nothing in it can be changed as *it will have been there*, the image disturbs the pastness of time and the certainty of death. Susan Sontag describes this untimeliness: "To take a picture is to have an interest in things as they are, in the status quo remaining unchanged . . . to be in complicity with whatever makes a subject interesting, worth photographing—including, when that is the interest, another person's pain or misfortune."[98] The pornographic complaint thus identifies an interlude that suspends correspondence with *real time*. Absent historical contextualization, one is left with *feeling ahistorical*. Consider this *New Republic* essay, "The Case against Economic Disaster Porn," in which the author accuses the ruin photograph of appallingly rendering Detroit a "still-life."[99] Though it by necessity references life in absentia (including the painter and the observer), the still life is indicted as a contained and composed tableau of objects (the rubble, the girder, the chair) without interruption from an outside world; it is an incision in the flow of time that arrests the possibility of change while also suggesting the inevitability of decay. Or, as another critic puts it, "Given Detroit's pressing need to move forward, photography that repeatedly echoes past moments might operate counter to this need."[100] The photograph's noncoincidence with the present of the ruin is thus seized on as tragedy. Its stillness disrupts the time-being of crisis.

To amend Dean, it might be that the pornographic complaint suggests an allegory of the way in which we lose *ourselves*. What does it mean to lose ourselves, or some vision of ourselves? Whereas Elaine Scarry heralds beauty as an unselving, a radical decentering that fosters attention to aliveness in the world, the pornographic is alleged to disarm a beholder wrongly, as a broken window might—as a crime against our sense of security, as the depletion of our will, or as a splintering of sense or knowledge. Such failures, according to this complaint, block us from recognizing the decisive moment for the entry of life into history. That is, aesthetic failure signals a miscarriage not only to act properly but also to act *in time*. In doing so, the photographs are not just not consciousness-raising; they are self-shattering. If, as liberalism claims, human consciousness bends toward possible action and probable consequence, and if agency is intrinsic to empathic imagination and to the promise as the foundation of sociality (and what follows from it, intersubjectivity), the object that disorders these capacities is pornographic. "They might serve to 'raise awareness' of the Rust Belt's blight, *but raising awareness is only useful if it provokes a next step, a move toward trying to fix a problem.* By presenting Detroit, and other hurting cities like it, as places beyond repair, they in fact quash any such instinct. Looked at as a piece of art, they're arresting, compelling, haunting . . . but not galvanizing."[101] The pornographic thus achieves a historico-epistemological status as a referent from which movement and change are apprehended as stalled, or still. And so, in a desultory series of essays called "Confessions of a Ruin Pornographer," Matthew Christopher accepts the terms of failure—in the photographs but also in himself. Their deficiency reflects his debt, their decrepitude his consciousness of suspended time. He did not act, his photographs rescued no one. Christopher frets, "I have not saved these places. I have not saved the people who lost their jobs from the unemployment lines, from poverty, or from any of the other problems the loss of these places caused. I am not perched somewhere safely above it all, impartially decreeing who was right and who was wrong. I live in a world that seems to me to be falling apart and I can't escape it."[102]

The pornographic, we are meant to understand, is depressing. To the extent that it refuses concreteness and chrononormativity, the pornographic stands in for a disturbing relationship between illicit pleasure and deliberate intent, moral perversion and political calculability. In other words, it is both a description and a process of ruination. This is what is finally at stake in the complaint—the withdrawal from normative time that makes signification and reference possible, and thus from our responsibility to it. If "a promise must . . . produce events, new effective forms of action, practice, organization, and so forth," the failure to produce *events, new effective forms of action, practice, organization, and so forth*, becomes a ruin.[103] Decrying the ruin photograph as the wrong order of visuality, obscuring otherwise obvious violence, the complaint both assumes that transparency is possible and that the pornographic renders it impossible. But what else can we observe from the coincidence between those properties deemed necessary for the proper consciousness capable of acting on history, and those properties that ordain the acquisition of credible personhood under capital? That is, what do the promise, the pornographic, and the subprime share in common?

Beautiful Demolition

Arthur Danto, on aesthetic deprivation, writes there is no easy way "to transform Detroit or Pittsburgh into the Catskills or the Grand Canyon."[104] This statement carries distinctive histories of violence, not least among them the extraction of labor and resources that erects the empire city, and the dispossession of Indigenous peoples that establishes the national park. Detroit and Pittsburgh, once bustling scenes of industrial growth before their gutting by the vicissitudes of predatory capital, are figured as ugly, blighted places of poverty and decline (that these are also Black cities is not incidental), as opposed to presumably timeless natural wonders (evacuated of Indigenous presence) worth preserving as "pristine" landscapes for contemplation. But Detroit and Pittsburgh and the Catskills and the Grand Canyon are not so distinct, as each requires the deprivation of another of her coveted property. Such are the aesthetics of scarcity subtending the production of the landscape as terra nullius. While some emptiness is sublime—the Grand Canyon, for instance—some emptiness is waste. And, as Tim Edensor observes of industrial ruins, "One of the lineaments of power is the authority to make waste, to decide what is no longer of use and disseminate common-sense ideas about what ought to be over and done with."[105] Such emptiness is, however, the necessary discursive precursor to beautification—transforming corner stores and abandoned factories into galleries and condos, sometimes called urban renewal or revitalization—which requires dispossession, displacement, and demolition to proceed.

Where speculation and racial capital previously sought to transform Detroit, ruin was a prerequisite for its renewal. The construction of Roosevelt Park and Michigan Central Station, centerpieces of the City Beautiful movement at the turn of the twentieth century (and the scene of so much contemporary ruin porn), demanded the eviction and erasure of entrenched immigrant and transient populations. Built to restore order and control of the city, a monumental landscape of neoclassical civic buildings and ornamental parks consigned whole neighborhoods and their architectural remnants (their rubble, in other words) to what Krysta Ryzewski calls the "sub-surface archaeological record."[106] In their campaigns, city planners described the residential district as a "sorry view of Detroit," blemished by "a row of rundown frame houses" each barely more than rubble; one member of the City Planning Commission claimed the park esplanade was necessary "to make people [coming through the train station] forget what they see along Michigan Avenue."[107] A bitter struggle ensued between residents and city planners; purchase offers were followed by condemnation suits and property seizures until, finally, an official promised he would "see to it that the buildings were taken away, even if he had to go and wreck them himself at night."[108] Finally, the mayor's office summoned a thirty-ton First World War British tank, on tour through Canada and the United States, to destroy the remaining homes as thousands stood by as witnesses. This is to say that blight is not a "natural" occurrence; it must be made before it can be cured. Emboldened by the Federal Highway Act of 1956, urban planners routed some construction directly, and sometimes deliberately, through Black and brown neighborhoods, including in Detroit, seizing homes in some cases through eminent domain. Urban renewal, as James Baldwin put it, has ever been "Negro removal."[109]

Since 2010, over a hundred thousand Detroiters have lost their homes to unconstitutional property assessments, and when these debts cannot be paid, Detroit turns them over to Wayne County for collection, which might charge homeowners with precipitously inflated interest (plus penalty fees) before confiscating and auctioning their properties, or just as often leaving them vacant and rotting. Something must be done, however; the impossibility of American ruins is that they cannot be allowed to exist *as is*. This is a long-standing apprehensiveness specific to contemporaneous ruins and their untimeliness, compared to the remnants of ancient civilizations. Of America, Nick Yablon observes, "The actual ruins forced by the great fires that periodically ravaged its cities, by the scorched-earth tactics of General Sherman's rapid advance through the South, or by the equally swift and destructive swings of the capitalist economy, were all instantaneous and largely unanticipated, and then radically different from those formed over time."[110] Case in point—in June 1805, the French settlement at Fort Detroit burned nearly to the ground. The city's official seal, adopted in 1926, reads, "We Hope for Better Things / We Shall Rise Again from the Ashes." As Whitney Moon writes, "Featuring two female figures—one representing Detroit's recent loss and the other its promising future—the seal reflects the city's dialectical relationship with renewal. In the background, the city is illustrated in flames; in the foreground, a new city is born. Thus, while symbolizing resilience, the seal likewise exposes the paradox of rebirth: loss is necessary for something new to be gained."[111] Chicago and San Francisco were reconstructed after the fires and the earthquake, respectively; the "hellish shards" of the World Trade Center after 9/11 could not stand as a reminder of American vulnerability. The ceremonial removal of the final steel column on May 30, 2002, was heralded as a communal recovery. As the *New York Times* put it: "But for the crews that have been at work on that unimaginable site—and at the holding areas where the debris has been sifted and analyzed—the one way to deal with the tragedy has been to dismantle it, fragment by fragment, until there was nothing left."[112] Now, the editorial board opined (echoing terra nullius), "The ground is open."

In place of ruins, then, are dreams of what might be built from the rubble. Of Detroit's recent trials, Rebecca Kinney notes, "Yet even as these awful events unfolded, they also provided fertile ground for yet another narrative. Detroit had fallen so hard, and so far, that it can now become a 'comeback city'; the poster city of economic crisis (and many other kinds of crisis) is now a space of possibility, or as I describe it—a *beautiful wasteland*."[113] This representation of Detroit as a beautiful wasteland positions it as a *frontier* in a settler colonial imaginary. In this way, "beauty operates as a modifier to suggest a productive possibility for new investment and new investors."[114] Beneath the rough and wild landscapes lies a sinister promise. Called "Destroying Detroit (in Order to Save It)," an essay in GQ about its present-day revitalization observes, "These days everyone in Detroit is talking like an urban planner." A demolitions contractor hired to tear down "the abandoned, godforsaken homes of Detroit—all 70,000 of them," explains, in an eerie echo of tanks rolling through the city, "'It's a process . . . but I see a future. I have to. The only other thing to do here would be to drop an A-bomb, but you can't do that. Demolition—there's the future. It paves the way to build.'"[115] "In short," Kinney posits, "there is promise in its peril."[116]

Who is "galvanized" by the ruin? The proverbial broken window does indeed incite further violence *but from capital and its proxies*. Demolition and all that it entails, including the expropriation of some life, is necessary for the reproduction of the life of others, of law and order. What Bernadette Atuahene calls predatory cities systemically dispossess residents of property—through eminent domain, tax foreclosure, or traffic and parking violations—and transfer these properties to developers, often in the form of subsidies and tax-exempt financing with the promise of *revitalization*.[117] At times, then, the pornographic complaint obscures the workings of the same structures that create ruin and then promise beauty—to rebuild, to secure, to foster life once again. These structures—capital, credit—depend on a properly bounded subject whose aesthetic capacities might repair and repopulate the ruins after those who once lived there are already dead, or close enough to it.

In the last decade, dozens of mixed-use developments have been proposed for Detroit with new units designed to attract "millennial urban dwellers," boasting high-end condos and apartments with waterfront views, as well as public access greenways and a new sand-filled beach. Like the "paper cities" of an earlier age, real estate developers are erecting new urban environs from proliferating documents of speculation, including land surveys, blueprints, and presentation drawings of proposed renovations and new structures featuring diverse crowds—multigenerational, multiracial (that is to say, decidedly not "just" Black)—repopulating empty buildings and commons with new life in a claim to de-extinction.[118] Other capital projects proliferate at the cost of hundreds of millions—the Detroit Pistons built a multiuse office, retail, and practice complex called the Henry Ford Performance Center; the Red Wings opened the new Little Caesars Arena in the new entertainment-focused District Detroit; the Henry Ford Cancer Institute broke ground on a new "destination" treatment center; and Quicken Loans bought the naming rights for the public-private rapid transit line servicing the city core. These capital projects are described as reparation, revelation, and repudiation; the *Detroit Free Press* trumpets, "This real estate rebound has been stripping the city of its unflattering reputation as a 'ruin porn' capital."[119] The complaint thus invites (from some) capital speculation as the reproduction of life even as austerity, precaritization, and expulsion rob others of life chances. Undeterred, an urban historian heralds, "[The] post-apocalyptic discourse . . . is challenged by the growing pockets of initiative and enterprise, evidenced in urban investment in buildings such as the Argonaut—now the Taubman Center for Design Education—and in the various brands and companies—for example, Shinola, Red Bull, and Twitter—that have attached themselves to the art and cultural movements that have emerged from the city."[120]

Both the Grand Canyon and Detroit are recapitalized as "empty land" or its surplus according to this racial, colonial order. Or as Cindi Katz argues, preservation and privatization are not distinct operations. "First, nature *qua* nature has become an 'investment' in the future. Second, to secure that investment nature has been commodified and privatized at all scales."[121] Extractivist capital turns to the "internal subdivisions" of nature to instrumentalize its possible profitability and usefulness.[122] In land-use planning, building urban green spaces is touted as revitalization—not just as ecological hygiene or social cure but also as supplemental value to nearby land and property. In 2009, John Hantz, a financial services entrepreneur, sought to acquire ten thousand acres of "vacant" and city-owned properties and convert this land into the largest private for-profit urban megafarm in the world. Such large-scale acquisition (which the city denied, selling to him instead two hundred acres of city-owned properties for the Hantz Woodlands) is the accumulation of private wealth on what was "public" land (multiply repossessed). Eric Holt-Gimenez tracks such land grabs as a global phenomenon, as neoliberal governments allow foreign investors to push aside subsistence farmers and pastoralists to establish megaplantations.[123] In 2013, the Detroit Future City plan sought to repurpose Detroit's highest-vacancy neighborhoods "with no market value" as blue and green infrastructure—installing retention ponds, carbon forests, urban farms, and greenways—while withdrawing, gradually, public services and the "gray" infrastructures that deliver them.[124] The architects and planners at Interboro Partners identified the practice of lot expansion, or "blots" ("from block and lot, i.e., a block of lots"), as an unspectacular but transformative "New Suburbanism." Identified as "the process through which entrepreneurial homeowners take, borrow, or buy adjacent vacant lots," lot expansion and its "cumulative effect will be a gradual rewriting of the City's genetic code."[125] The enclosure and appropriation of city-owned lots to one's private property, now remade into lawns, courtyards, and backyard gardens, figures beautification through a speculative settler logic of making the emptied land "productive" again through its privatization. Even Whole Foods opening a brick-and-mortar store is heralded as greening the ruins. As Terri Weissman describes it, despite the success of Detroit's community-based nonprofit urban farming movement, the store opening was much photographed as the dawning of new hope, presenting "Whole Foods as an oasis in an otherwise empty landscape; an oasis worthy of unadulterated celebration."[126]

For real estate brokers, land developers, hedge funds, and private equity firms, the ruins occasion investment opportunities. In a speculative economy, bankruptcy and the metastasization of debt are the preconditions for stockholder profit, and disruption a necessity for speculative potential (investment capital reorganizes to shed "human stock" and other liquid assets). Such logics condition us to an order of risk secured by credit, which in turn is secured by discriminating violence. Through credit and its blunt instruments, racial capital extends itself in growth and renews itself in crisis. As Stefano Harney and Fred Moten wryly note, "They say we have too much debt. We need better credit, more credit, less spending. They offer us credit repair, credit counseling, microcredit, personal financial planning. They promise to match credit and debt again, debt and credit. But our debt stays bad."[127] Between 2010 and 2016, Wayne County used ill-gotten tax revenue and subsequent foreclosures to balance the budget, profiting from the interest and penalties collected from "delinquent" property owners and transferring that surplus—upwards of $600 million, from mostly Black

Detroiters—to its general fund. One organizer for the United Community Housing Coalition said, "It was known that this wasn't done properly. It's a form of theft."[128] And although the city of Detroit admitted to illegal and inflated tax assessments causing devastating losses, while awarding multimillion-dollar tax abatements to developers and corporations, there is no plan to provide cash payments or tax credits to dispossessed residents.[129] Wherever blight or ruin provides cover, predatory cities extract revenue, property, and further debt by invoking civil forfeiture (which allows police to seize and then to sell any property they allege is involved in a crime), escalating parking and traffic citations, and imposing excessive court fines and bail fees.[130] Katharyne Mitchell observes that the future will be wrought through a racialized biopolitics in which "whiteness" is the capacity to control one's exposure to risk through preemptive action, and "Blackness" designates those who cannot shield themselves from inevitable risk.[131] The debtor, we might say after Friedrich Nietzsche, cannot "stand security for his own future."[132]

So do the police protect and serve capital over human (and other) life, including performing forced evictions for banks to expropriate assets from a "subprime" population. In Louisville, Kentucky, Breonna Taylor was murdered by plainclothes officers executing a no-knock warrant late at night. Alleging that the warrant (which police lied to obtain) was part of a broader effort to evict residents frustrating the city's redevelopment initiative, her family's lawyers accused the city of targeting an associate of Taylor's former boyfriend so it could repossess the house he rented; indeed, a few months after her death, the city and a land bank purchased the house for one dollar.[133] Although more than twenty properties on the two-block stretch were also purchased following foreclosures, Louisville officials in the economic development department claimed there was no conspiracy, though it noted, as if to justify one, "The community has told us they want to get criminal activity off this block, to get the properties torn down and returned to productive use."[134]

We are not meant to locate beauty in the destruction of life, or beauty in the destruction of property, where life and property are conflated on the side of order. But when that life and that property belong to those who are not credible—that is, subprime, untimely, savage, criminal, or remainder—the dead pledge leverages the ruin *and* the complaint on behalf of their dispossession. This dispossession is threefold. Within liberalism's social contract that determines that, in Asma Abbas's words, "property is an expression of life, as well as a means to it," the subprime being cannot hold property (having once been property, in some instances), and therefore they also cannot claim either rights or injury.[135] This broken promise—broken not by the one who shoulders the debt but by the one who burdens another with it—cannot be fulfilled in the present order of things. To this end, what if the broken window that so concisely condenses the pornographic as crime is that which allows us to see into the violence of property?

Complaints vs. Crimes

This chapter has not been about repudiating ruin photographs, appreciating ruin photographs, or otherwise contextualizing ruin photographs, but instead about questioning the assumptions that underline the accusation of their failure, of beauty's failure, to deliver to us a commensurate image of reality or truth. To call images of urban decay or terrible atrocity pornographic is an affectively saturated rhetorical strategy, one that conflates sensory distortion (surface without depth, depth without distance) with a disordered reading practice or method. The complaint positions the pornographic as oppositional, even obstructive, to fostering "correct" critique through deep engagement, at the same time it underlines the tension between the desire for truthful mimesis and the acknowledgment of its difficulty. Such difficulty is the premise of Martha Rosler's sequence of photographs and captions called *The Bowery in Two Inadequate Descriptive Systems*.[136] Twenty-one black-and-white photographs of mostly abandoned Bowery facades and stoops are brought together with twenty-four panels of words related to drunkenness, in which neither image nor word can quite grasp the nature of the phenomena it references.[137] Conceived in part as a meditation on economic recession in 1970s New York City, these carefully composed photographs of frontal shots of storefronts, doorways, and grates show traces of human presence—empty bottles, an abandoned shoe, and other urban detritus—but no humans.[138] Against documentary, these photographs and captions frustrate our capacities (and hopes) to capture "crisis" as an event of knowledge. So while the pornographic might not reveal the forms or contradictions of violence (but maybe it does), it turns out that our more sober descriptive systems might also be inadequate to the task.

The promise of beauty is one urge to give structure and form to events and phenomena that are somehow inaccessible, or unsettling, precisely because we are not yet sure what other forms of life are possible. In making a case here for beauty as a method, even in its guise as "pornography," I am grasping toward a number of lessons, among them that its crimes hold a lot of knowledge about how we envisage the world, and that alienation, agitation, and even apathy are occasions to forge other, more durable attachments. Where pragmatism, positivism, and historicism establish their truths through the authority to act on history "properly," the pornographic interferes with the forms of sovereignty these demand from us. That is to say, what might be most useful about the complaint is not the normative frame it offers as a corrective to the pornographic, but how it recommends the pornographic as an analytic itself. Against the complaint that in the pornographic something is unsaid, unseen, unknown, or untrue, perhaps looking at waste, debris, rubble, junk, dross, or ornament requires that we question not just what we expect from images but, crucially, how we "see" politics. Especially where and when human and other biological life is narrowing, continues to narrow, as environmental terror and total war, unpayable debt and captive labor, come to define the life of so many, the disordering of our habits of sense-making might require from us the rot and ruin of a society that should not be defended. (*We are always less by being here.*) And despite its seeming arrest of history—at least as linear, teleological—what is pornographic might also prefigure a future without foundations. In wishing for another "I HOPE THIS EMAIL DOES NOT FIND YOU" (from the second epigraph to this chapter), the familiar details of ruin porn—the chair covered in moss, the beam of light coming through the collapsed ceiling—compose a loving dream of unbothered absence from extractivist violence. Where the life that can be lived is awful, we might yet remove ourselves from the picture.

That is to say, if the pornographic is the disordering of a liberal sensorium that has not served us thus far, how might we live otherwise with disorder and decay? Could we spread such disorder as the devaluation of privacy, or the end of property? Can we remove commodities (including ourselves as units of debt) from their ceaseless circulation through credit and speculation? Could we transform property from individual asset or debt to social solidarity? Can what is condemned as pornographic nonetheless gesture toward a nonpermanent, noncontractual understanding of a relation to property? The first time I read this passage from *You Can't Shoot Us All*, a firsthand account of the riots in Oakland following the murder of Oscar Grant at the hands of transit police, I saw in its ruins a promise: "I wanted to break windows, to set fires, to strike fear into every cop on the streets that night. I wanted to show the powerful that they, too, would learn the meaning of violence, just as we have been forced to learn it time and time again. They needed to understand that we don't forget, we needed to feel that we were still alive."[139]

We needed to feel that we were still alive. And so, can we make the ruins we *want* to see? The destruction of property that prefigures the ruin might be a social bond of another magnitude. In his memoir of New York City during the early months of the COVID-19 pandemic, Jeremiah Moss finds a feral freedom in an emptied downtown, abandoned by developers and gentrifiers and reclaimed by queers, freaks, and people of color. "The ruin is a queer body, out of bounds and out of order. For the queer who finds few mirrors in the dominant culture, to arrive in the shattered, muddy, unsettling city is to arrive, at last, in oneself."[140] The end of the world is coming for us, but another end of the world is possible. And while we might well become numb or distracted at times because debt is crushing, catastrophe will not be diverted, and violence underwrites life as we know it, what happens next depends on the style in which we absorb the shocks and blows.

Chapter 5

Living Beautifully, or Resilience

A Klee painting named "Angelus Novus" shows an angel looking as though he is about to move away from something he is fixedly contemplating. His eyes are staring, his mouth is open, his wings are spread. This is how one pictures the angel of history. His face is turned toward the past. Where we perceive a chain of events, he sees one single catastrophe which keeps piling wreckage upon wreckage and hurls it in front of his feet. The angel would like to stay, awaken the dead, and make whole what has been smashed. But a storm is blowing from Paradise; it has got caught in his wings with such violence that the angel can no longer close them. This storm irresistibly propels him into the future to which his back his turned, while the pile of debris before him grows skyward. This storm is what we call progress.

Walter Benjamin, "Theses on the Philosophy of History"

Caught between war, ruin, and catastrophe, we might hunger for new stories to tell about ourselves after the grounds of progress and perfectibility, wherein paradise or a techno-utopia lies within reach or the moral arc of the universe bends toward justice, are gone, shattered, or withered. Because we do not know how to understand our present condition or craft our future from the wreckage, we grasp for anything that might help us, or at least capture something of how it feels to *be* in this historical *now*. This sense of impending disaster is why Walter Benjamin's angel of history remains a resonant and prescient figure. This backward-turning angel feels his own helplessness against the terrible press of time, unable to look away or beat his wings to slow his forward momentum away from the scene of unrelenting brutality. Against an irresistible progress, Benjamin refuses those laws of history that propose, as an article of faith, that liberation lies ahead on a path strewn with so many dead. Instead, the angel laments, our sense of time is ruptured from our expectations of history.

This chapter considers other figures among us besides angels—landmine survivors, rape victims, broken windows, fractured ceramics—to consider again how the story of our experience of time becomes a political problem and how beauty calls on us, or how we call on it, to respond. How might the promise of beauty engage such crushing harms and exhausted signifiers, whether through an ordinary wearing down or permanent war, slow violence or staggering terror? When our sense of time is disturbed, and there is no future on the horizon, how does the promise of beauty become a practical or philosophical concern? And what does it mean to call survival, in the face of catastrophe or damage, beautiful?

Just as certain politics and certain aesthetics unfolded from the moral and onto-epistemological foundations of modernity, liberalism, and freedom, other politics and other aesthetics surface from these structures in their crumbling forms. Their degradation affects our sense of possibility, how we live and imagine living, and our sense of what is just, fair, and beautiful. Indeed, our knowledge of crisis accelerates at such a rate and scale that we might not be able to conceive of a promise that will not be inevitably broken. This problem is what drew me to this project, in other words. A pageant for landmine survivors might be understood less as the instrument for their flourishing than as a prompt for recognizing that they have done so *despite* grievous injury. Or, as another scholar studying the Miss Landmine pageant writes, "[The contestants] had the beauty of resilience, of courage and enough spirit to make the most of what they have been dealt with. How could one not perceive their individual heroism, reaching beyond pain and social rejection, and fighting to make themselves a life as women?"[1] Or the chain of associations brought together following a reporter's observations about increasing depression, suicide, and disintegrating selfhood under the Taliban, "Those [women who] survived relied on the only things they had left, their self-respect and their ability to maintain what dignity they could by making themselves beautiful."[2] Where the promise of beauty is invoked to maintain hope and endurance in specific arrangements in which life has become acutely harder, she who survives (or has yet to survive but persists nevertheless) is imbued with radiance because of her particular *style* for living on.

Under the strain of registering the future as one disaster after another, what I call *living beautifully* is both a relief and a resource in awful or horrific situations; it names an aesthetic style attenuating such scenes of radical contingency to model how best to live in such circumstances. Whether posited as a purely ontological account of interiority such as inner beauty (which might be cataloged in turn as kindness, a loving nature, dignity, or purity of the heart) or perceived as an affectable capacity with which another might interfere such as well-being, *living beautifully* is an effect of power that maps uneasily onto foundational divides between the human and the subhuman. In what follows, a specific claim about living beautifully as an aesthetic for *a life that can be lived* despite violence or hardship coincides with the multitudinous concept of resilience to allay a politics of vulnerability to catastrophe as inevitable. This concept of resilience is often used to rehearse seemingly admirable capacities for adaptation in uncertain times, such as strength, tenacity, willfulness, or the stubborn refusal to die, but what gives resilience a structure to follow, to copy, especially when damage becomes habituated, and for what end? In answer, this chapter is concerned with how resilience as a capacity for *living dangerously*, through which continuous exposure to risk circumscribes life-living, encourages and coheres a style for *living beautifully*, or a deliberate leaning toward persistence despite social or structural collapse.

This chapter has no particular case study because I began it at the start of a global pandemic that, in the United States at least, cascades from one abysmal disaster to another. It wanders, because my own ability to focus was scattered while writing, especially as our neglected infrastructure proved vulnerable to collapse, and is still collapsing. As such, this chapter reflects that sense of *right now*, in which uncertainty stretches out indefinitely, there is no return to what was before, and the future of a life that can be lived feels achingly remote. It is a pile of wreckage, in other words, not unlike that which plagues Benjamin's angel. What interests me, then, is how living beautifully shapes our historical consciousness of time over and sometimes against an awareness of eventfulness—the provocation that because terrible events have happened, will happen, will have happened, what do we do, knowing that all is catastrophe and at best, or worst, slow fading? And if the repair of those conditions—ordinary, normal, or chronic, as well as catastrophic, critical, or sublime—that threaten beauty is neither the claim nor the mission, as the case may be, what is the significance of living beautifully when even the earth itself is a vector of despair? Here the promise of beauty solicits an attunement to inevitability, an appreciation of uncertainty, chance, and contingency, and a sensibility that enlivens despite—or because of—likely doom. With the collapse of a temporal order that fosters hope or longing for a future, living beautifully is an aesthetic response to irresolvable aporias in our experience of time. But here also reside other ghosts, those for whom the apocalypse has already come, is coming now.

An Elastic History of a Concept

In the last decades, resilience emerged as a common name for how to endure crisis, trauma, or disturbance. Following its origins in the nineteenth-century physical sciences as an ontological property of certain materials, understood as an elastic capacity to absorb energy and return to a prior state, the concept of resilience has since become a multidisciplinary one. Defined as "the capacity of a system to return to a previous state, to recover from a shock, or to bounce back after a crisis or trauma," resilience familiarly circulates through forms of planning and governance that forecast humanitarian, technical-logistical, financial, and environmental catastrophes, as well as ordinary disturbances, such as the death of a loved one, debt, or the police.[3] Spanning systems and selves, resilience interposes a theory of power but also an experience of time. It is framed as something we need to get by, to carry on, and to live further—as well as can be hoped for.

Resilience is willful, even as its genealogy wanders.[4] In engineering, resilience as the time (and effort) required to return to normal function after disruption is closely associated with theories about system complexity, self-organization, and adaptability. Beginning in the 1970s, resilience surfaced in national security circles to describe efforts to protect so-called vital infrastructure (such as oil derricks or pipelines) from sabotage and destruction in the midst of an ongoing state of emergency.[5] Benjamin Sims argues that this systems view of infrastructure is the basis of the all-hazards "critical infrastructure protection" paradigm that emerged in the 1990s to circumscribe homeland security activity (it is on these grounds that the United States deems anti-imperialist or abolitionist protests as both criminal *and* terrorist activity).[6] At the same time, an ecological concept of resilience also appeared as a critique of sustainable development, which aims for balance or equilibrium, to understand instead a dynamic of persistence despite destabilization.[7] Here its usage presumes that systems are found in nature and can survive disturbance—sometimes even thrive within it. In

The Mushroom at the End of the World, Anna Lowenhaupt Tsing follows the matsutake mushroom, which only grows in forests disturbed or damaged by human activity. Examining the possibilities of multispecies collaboration for continuing life on earth, Tsing ponders, "It's not easy to know how to make a life, much less avert planetary destruction. Luckily there is still company, human and not human. We can still explore the overgrown verges of our blasted landscapes.... We can still catch of the scent of the latent commons."[8] Resilience in this instance suggests the possibility for achieving another sort of equilibrium after what came before is gone.

In clinical literature, resilience once described a personality, but it has since come to name a *capacity* for living on or persisting despite hardship. As the start of one study begins, "Try as we might, we cannot prevent bad things from happening."[9] Resilience is variously put as "the ability to bounce back or cope successfully despite substantial adversity," "a stable pattern of low distress over time," and "the ability of adults in otherwise normal circumstances who are exposed to an isolated and potentially highly disruptive event ... to maintain relatively stable, healthy levels of psychological and physical functioning ... as well as the capacity for generative experiences and positive emotions."[10] Such literature maintains resilience is a *skill* that can be taught to or cultivated by all persons—whether "positive coping," "competent functioning," or "living well throughout the course of one's life."[11] Coping mechanisms that predict resilience, according to these studies, include humor and positivity in the face of crises and natural and other disasters.[12] Practices of self-discipline, subject to training or development, are central to programs for "empowerment" as an agency or a capacity of life (and *for* life) in the face of unavoidable vulnerability. Consider antibullying campaigns, or resilience training for queer youth ("It gets better"), or the uses of positive psychology, Buddhist meditation, and mindfulness in the US Army's Comprehensive Soldier and Family Fitness Program (what another scholar calls "the largest deliberate psychological intervention in history").[13] Former president of the American Psychological Association and the architect of the US Army's resilience training, Martin E. P. Seligman enthused, "What the military could do was move the entire distribution of the reaction to adversity in the direction of resilience and growth. This would not only help prevent PTSD but also increase the number of soldiers who bounce back readily from adversity."[14] As observed so well by Alison Howell, resilience in something like Comprehensive Soldier and Family Fitness adopts its most disturbing features, not least as an austerity measure reducing long-term health care costs attached to diagnoses of posttraumatic stress disorder, while conditioning soldiers for multiple tours, and ongoing violence, in our wars without end.

The elastic concept of resilience thus encompasses much as a capacity and a skill for *living dangerously*. In holding together without collapsing these phenomena, here I follow from Michel Foucault, who proposes this axiom for our age: "'Live dangerously,' that is to say, individuals are constantly exposed to danger, or rather, they are conditioned to experience their situation, their life, their present, and their future as containing danger.... In short, everywhere you see this stimulation of the fear of danger which is, as it were, the condition, the internal psychological and cultural correlative of liberalism. *There is no liberalism without a culture of danger*."[15] Such a capacity and skill for living dangerously, some argue, rise with the hegemony of neoliberal governmentality, which encourages individuals to regulate their own conduct according to the virtues of rational calculability and risk assessment.[16] Others point to the putative end of the Cold War, after establishing a sprawling infrastructure for permanent war, as another shift, in which the extant potentiality of terror becomes the rationale for increased surveillance and policing. Still others indict the sometimes slow, sometimes sudden violence of environmental disaster, from the 1986 Chernobyl explosion that spewed four hundred times more radioactive material into the air than was released by the bombing of Hiroshima and Nagasaki; to the ongoing Flint water crisis that saw governmental inaction exacerbate the lead poisoning of the water supply; and to the encroaching extinction horizon as the ice caps melt, the coral reefs die, and the birds and bees disappear from our skies. But whatever the crisis, for whatever the population, the capacity and skill are the same; the American Psychological Association launched the Road to Resilience campaign in 2002, with a free tool kit, a documentary video, and workshops for "kids and teens," journalists, soldiers, and survivors of 9/11, school shootings, and floods.

From ecology and engineering, resilience has spread to other fields to describe other structures as systems and their capacities for crisis, including urban planning, financial institutions, and population health—consider the language of the bubble, a container fraught with tension; or diversification, a practice for mitigating risk; and flexibility, a euphemism for our accommodation of precarity. It is the argument for the bank bailout after the 2008 subprime mortgage "crisis," through which the Obama administration sought to brace the responsible institutions, deemed "too big to fail," to maintain functioning of the financial system.[17] It is the argument for immunity debt, a conspiracy theory that mitigation measures such as lockdowns and mask mandates, established at the height of the COVID-19 pandemic, weakened population immunity; to repair such debt, its champions call for exposure to sometimes lethal viruses and repeat infections as necessary for species "survival" (or, more to the point, critical infrastructure survival even as hundreds of thousands might yet die). In its most mundane measure, resilience might be assessed by how soon emergency services arrive to a situation, or "normal operations" are recovered; but in a catholic sense, it is the condition of waiting for the emergency to occur, and the consciousness that it could happen at any time. (Its power lies in this interval.) To this end, resilience as a capacity for emergency—and planning for it, planning on it—is a planetary concern. In the last decades, the World Economic Forum, the World Bank, and the International Monetary Fund all established resilience as a means for "growing the wealth of the poor" and shoring up fragile states, climates, infrastructure, and human capital. Unsurprisingly, the United Nations is in the resiliency business, defining it as "the capacity of a system, community or society potentially exposed to hazards, to adapt by resisting or changing in order to reach and maintain an acceptable level of functioning and structure."[18] Where resilience takes up (and drops) seemingly distinct capacities—from persistence, to adaptation, to transformation, which are not the same—all at once, Sarah Bracke usefully observes that in the transposition of this concept, "from one level of analysis, and from one field of study, to another," "resilience as a keyword mobilizes all these meanings at once, and shifts between them, oftentimes unaccountably."[19]

No wonder resilience also informs such contemporary forms of governance that forecast catastrophe and inevitable vulnerability, and in doing so declare the impossibility of achievable security. Where securitization is those forms of police and regulation that permit and preside over "natural phenomena, economic processes and the intrinsic processes of population," realized as the indispensable reason for governmental action, resilience as a concept builds crisis into the administration of life, proposing that unforeseeable and likely inevitable disruptions are normal and survivable, and promising the intensification of capacities to adapt to systemic failure.[20] As a principle and a practice apart from, but nonetheless linked to, the law, sovereignty, and discipline, resilience as a complement or replacement for security combines these other principles and practices in new configurations addressed to the "ensemble of a population."[21] In the United States, the Department of Homeland Security asserts the need for resilience in "the system as a whole" and the "American spirit," with the overall aim to "disrupt the enemy's plans and diminish the impact of future disasters."[22] The 2009 National Infrastructure Protection Plan focused on "protection and resilience"; the 2014 *Quadrennial Homeland Security Review* listed "Strengthening National Preparedness and Resilience" as a core mission; and the 2017 National Security Strategy stated that an America First directive will best "reduc[e] risk and build[] more resilient communities."[23] Put another way, Mark Neocleous argues that resilience is central to the security state apparatus that no longer claims to protect against what threatens injury or harm (only to preempt or reciprocate).[24] He and other critics observe that resilience represents an adjustment in forms of governance as we confront the consequences of modernity that are (and have been) our destruction, again, whether climate catastrophe, settler capitalist violence, or extractivist capital.[25] Or, as the psychological literature defines it, resilience is about *maintaining functioning* despite whatever external stressor events might occur. One "resilient bereaved person" is quoted in a study as saying, after the untimely death of their spouse, "I'm terribly lonely, um, but I'm still doing the same thing, doing the same job, uh, making the same money, living in the same house, all that."[26] It is notable that the maintenance of structures or systems—not his well-being—is the measure of his resilience. Witness the triumphant crowing that the US economy "bounced back" from the COVID-19 pandemic (meaning corporations are making record profits), even as people are still dying or falling ill from the coronavirus, and the most vulnerable among us are no longer protected by any public health measures. This might also be called *damage control*.

In the embrace of vulnerability as inevitable, crisis is no longer an exceptional situation calling for decisive action. As Janet Roitman observes, "We now presume that crisis is a condition, a state of affairs, an experiential category. Today, crisis is posited as a protracted and potentially persistent state of ailment and demise."[27] Where crisis comes to name a contradictory temporal sense—eventfulness but also noneventfulness—resilience takes on the same recursive consciousness of time. In the global war on terror, for instance, the indeterminacy of *terror* fuels the preemptive exercise of power. Because security implies continuity and the extension of life, the primary direction of security is forward into time; security as *preemptive* constitutes a category of action that understands the threat to the future as a concrete possibility in the present. But where security is no longer achievable, because the threat is unavoidable (such as the inevitability of climate change, or economic devastation, or "they hate us because of our freedoms"), resilience is required to withstand the permanence of emergency. It is no wonder that living dangerously serves the premise of forever war so well, as it shapes a consciousness wrought from vigilance *and* normalization. Resilience conditioning, therefore, becomes a strategic practicum to address what risk management and disaster preparedness cannot, and to manage its costs—the consciousness that disaster is all around us now, and foreknowledge of the incalculability of what is yet to come. For instance, Secretary of Homeland Security Janet Napolitano, speaking to New York City first responders ahead of the ninth anniversary of 9/11, stated, "America is a strong nation. And we are a resilient nation. But . . . we can't guarantee there won't be another successful terrorist attack. . . . if that attack comes, our enemies will still not have succeeded, because our nation is too strong, and too resilient, to ever cower before a small group of violent extremists. We have always rebounded from hardships and challenges, and come together as a people to overcome disasters, attacks, and war. And we will do so again."[28]

Putting aside for a moment this triumphalism, the tempo of preemption and prediction is as follows—*it will have happened, and we will have overcome, because we are resilient.* In the immediate aftermath of 9/11, the image of the American flag on a shopping bag appeared at bus stops everywhere to encourage consumption, declaring, "America: Open for Business." Our freedoms, our first responders, our markets, our troops, our empire will endure. (Vandals repeatedly altered the American flag–shopping bag bus ad to appear as if the bag was holding missiles—our true trade.) It bears underscoring, then, that resilience encompasses those beings or forms who suffer violence but also *those who perpetrate it*. Consider again resilience training for the imperial soldier, or the weaponized vulnerability of critical infrastructure of pipelines and precincts. Resilience has no particular political claim, therefore—a viral mutation might be resilient, and so might be a single mother, a soldier, a refugee, a hedge fund.

Under such circumstances, the durative present of uncertainty or suffering might not cohere or coalesce into something that *feels* like an event, a tipping point, or a crisis, where an event, a tipping point, or a crisis functions (as a historiographical description) as the impetus for forward momentum. That is, the liberalist unfolding of historical time is organized around discrete but continuous change as a linear, diachronic succession of cumulative moments, a chain of displacements that sometimes cohere as events, tipping points, or crises. But this story of our temporal order, in which succession is progressive and change is improvement, no longer holds fast. The insecure moment has become a continuous state, a permanent and pervasive miasma saturating all aspects of life. Lauren Berlant describes this as "crisis ordinariness," where crisis "is not exceptional to history or consciousness but a process embedded in the ordinary that unfolds in stories about navigating what's overwhelming."[29] Where crisis becomes habitual routine, or when crisis narrates inevitable catastrophe, we are stranded in a present that extends endlessly, in which we are encouraged to stay (*be present, be here now*) in order to sustain life without a future. In his critique of postcolonial temporality, David Scott observes, "A distinctive temporality is always embodied in—while not being the simple mirror of—each imaginary of history."[30] But time and history, temporality and historicity, Scott argues, are diverging. Historical time continues without any sense of political time, without the promise of progress. As a faculty for both the embrace and the denial of vulnerability, especially championed when crisis is an ongoing historical situation, resilience attempts to resolve these aporias.

If living dangerously is our condition of being because crisis awaits us, the promise of beauty might provide a sense of personal-historical time *apart* from world-political time. Here lies the familiar convention of representing the encounter with beauty as an interruption, as a consciousness of life's minor key drumming on despite the failure to see a way forward through misery, abjection, despair, and even crushing boredom. Such an encounter often coheres as a singular event, introducing the unforeseen into an everyday existence and acting on an individual (or more) to believe or behave otherwise. Where the promise of beauty is a feeling of life being furthered, however incrementally, it works as a reminder of one's humanity otherwise rendered numb and dumb by the devastating forces of capital, war, or pandemic, or as the repair of the social bond under such wearying circumstances. Consider the TikTok videos of quarantined neighbors singing in unison from their balconies, or the sitcom pilot in which the floor manager of a superstore bitterly observes that her yesterday is indistinguishable from her today, or tomorrow, and so her coworker creates for her what he calls a moment of beauty.[31] He covers the vast ceiling of the store with glow-in-the-dark stars to form a luminous night sky when the lights are fortuitously, coincidentally, dimmed during a YouTube-inspired marriage proposal at the cash registers. As the floor manager experiences this brief but magical transformation (ignoring the plot hole of the well-timed power outage), this moment of beauty interrupts her sense of nonliving or living death that repetitive service labor otherwise demands. It renews her temporal consciousness, drawing a line before the encounter and after, and prompts a change in her sense of self or relation to time, to the world, to others. But this promise of beauty (and others like it) does not need to actualize into anything more than potentiality, because potentiality *is* the promise (there is nothing known on the other side of the moment).

Beauty's wonder works. Some inexorable but unpredictable danger, whether war or capital or virus, is the threat, but resilience is that which helps us to endure whatever it may be. Its promise soothes the temporal disjunctures involved in living on in the wreckage of past political time, but also in the wake of present political time pulling us out—like the storm that besets Benjamin's angel—toward future ruins. Is it any wonder that the certain inevitability of living dangerously, from within the storm of progress or its ending, champions a particular style for living beautifully?

A Minor Aesthetic

Living beautifully describes a program for enduring uncertainty and crisis as a *style*. Writing about an aesthetics of repair, and drawing on affect and action theories, Michael Dango theorizes *style* as action, as "the ways in which people improvise persistence."[32] Though resilience as elasticity suggests a capacity to return to a same state before disturbance, resilience in its contemporary iteration is not the same as repair or restoration to an original wholeness. It is instead how we live without such dreams when the present is struck through by ruin, and the future is no longer promising. As an aesthetic style, resilience reinterprets our experience of the world through a preoccupation or characterization of duration, reorganizing our felt relation between remembered pasts and impossible hopes, sovereign acts and certain catastrophes.

A historical consciousness for living dangerously might be usefully elaborated through the sublime, an aesthetic category understood to encompass that which is beyond calculation or measure. Briefly, the sublime is a feeling of awe brought on by the apprehension of overwhelming magnitude, an impasse in human powers of cognition or imagination, or the realization that a great malignance threatens to destroy us. In this way, the sublime is less about the properties of an object—though it is often associated with the vast, ill-defined, unbounded, or irregular in nature—than about the "subject who survives the experience of that object."[33] Kant provides the shell of this structure thus:

> Bold, overhanging and, as it were threatening, rocks; clouds piled up in the sky, moving with lightning flashes and thunder peals; volcanoes in all their violence of destruction; hurricanes with their

> tract of devastation; the boundless ocean in a state of tumult; the lofty waterfall of a mighty river, and such like; these exhibit our faculty of resistance as insignificantly small in comparison with their might. But the sight of them is the more attractive, the more fearful it is, provided only that we are in security; *and we readily call these objects sublime, because they raise the energies of the soil above their accustomed height, and discover in us a faculty of resistance of a quite different kind, which gives us courage to measure ourselves against the apparent almightiness of nature.*[34]

Described in *Critique of Judgment* as "merely in ourselves and in our attitude of thought," the sublime is a defiant posture rather than a supersensible object.[35] Where it resides in what imagination is unable to capture, another faculty, Reason, supplies that comprehension, being that which is "the bare capability of thinking this infinite without contradiction."[36] Reason provides a defense against the infinite; thus does Kant commend our power over formlessness, through which we gain a mental "dominion" over that which feels overwhelming to then furnish a sense of "humanity in our person."[37]

Accordingly, the sublime names a relation and a scene between an object and a subject, in which the awfulness of the object awakens in the subject a sense of endurance or survival. But where the sublime might be conceived through formlessness and beauty as its opposite (as it is often insisted), one might yet be transformed into the other. Whether through reason, imagination, or another faculty—such as empathy, or fellow feeling—the sublime might yet become beautiful. As Jacques Derrida remarks, "One cannot love a monument, a work of architecture, an institution as such except in an experience itself precarious in its fragility. It hasn't always been there, it will not always be there, it is finite. And for this very reason I love it as mortal, through its birth and its death, through the ghost or the silhouette of its ruin, of my own—which it already is or already prefigures."[38] Another's finite presence, in other words, sponsors a promise to oneself. Or as Dora Apel writes about an observer's communion with the much-photographed ruins of the World Trade Center, "The beauty of ruins helps us to cope with the terror of apocalyptic decline."[39] Or as the Kenyan artist Wangechi Mutu opines, "If something hurtful enters your body, you create something beautiful to protect yourself from it."[40] Such creation, which is also containment, is a practice for enduring what seems overwhelming. In the absence of guarantees for survival or living on—because of climate disaster, because of genocidal violence, because of speculative bubbles—living beautifully is the recognition of vulnerability before the monumentally incomprehensible, tempered through minor acts of self-sovereignty.

If Paul Klee's *Angelus Novus* (1920), an oil transfer drawing with watercolor of a strange, melancholy avian being, is the aesthetic figuration of a historicist consciousness of ruptured time, what then is ours? Benjamin's angel appears to him when it becomes clear that revolution is not coming; historical materialism had failed to bring forth a future for the end of capitalism, and the angel is instead witness to the march of progress into fascism. His wings spread in a gesture of surrender, such that he can no longer choose a direction, is the story of a despairing relation with the horror of history. He cannot intervene, or speak to a future, because all that he sees is catastrophe; meanwhile, the unrelenting passage of time prevents him from doing more. ("The storm irresistibly propels him toward the future to which his back is turned, while the pile of debris before him grows skyward.") But whereas Benjamin's angel looks on in horror, "would like to stay, awaken the dead, and make whole what has been smashed," would like to redeem the past in other words, *ours* might otherwise see in the "wreckage upon wreckage" some broken but beautiful thing that comprises a promise against the inexorable momentum of calamity. Beauty's presence is a suspension or a pinprick of intensity interrupting the linear experience of time—detail as punctum, in Barthes's words.

Between the sublime and the beautiful, we are left with the shattered bits of possibility and self-sovereignty we might eke out in an *ocean of uncertainty*.[41] In the effort to conceive or contain unbearable histories all at once, there is something necessarily minor about a resilient aesthetic. Elsewhere I describe a *minor object* as those marginal forms, persons, and worlds that are mobilized in narrative constructions to designate moments of crisis; its seeming inadequacy, its intermittent or fleeting manifestation, is part of its aesthetic power.[42] It could be an oppositional gesture or an ameliorative detail, but it is always a gesture or detail whose scale renders it that much more poignant or powerful against monumental threat, or inescapable terror.

The roses in Virginia Woolf's postwar novel *Mrs. Dalloway* might be one such minor object seeking to mitigate the infinite and incomprehensible. Taking place over the day of her party in the summer of 1923, nearly five years after the end of the war, Clarissa Dalloway's flowers preoccupy her, even as she wonders if they should. Pondering her husband's address to Parliament that same day, she muses, "Hunted out of existence, maimed, frozen, the victims of cruelty and injustice (she had heard Richard say so over and over again)—no, she could feel nothing for the Albanians, or was it the Armenians? but she loved her roses (didn't that help the Armenians?)."[43] Some critics fault Clarissa for insensitivity to the hundreds of thousands of Armenians, displaced and dying; indeed, this passage might be read as satirizing Clarissa's disavowal of her responsibility as an imperial beneficiary.[44] But Clarissa's roses might also draw attention to the crushing eclipse of our everyday capacity to absorb the proliferating horrors of war (after all, the novel is also about the shell-shocked soldier whose incapacity to feel *anything* becomes fatal), still unfolding (he said so *over and over again*), or how we give form (however politically inadequate or disproportionate) to our apprehension of terrible ruination. Lee R. Edwards writes, "The politics of *Mrs. Dalloway* are such that life is possible only when roses, parties, and joy triumph over war, authority, and death. Clarissa's celebrations—ephemeral and compromised though they may be—are a paradigm of sanity, a medium through which energy can flow into a world which is otherwise cruel, judgmental, and frozen."[45]

This passage haunts me as accusation and provocation as I regard the genre of commentaries contemplating our beauty routines under quarantine and political distress, or what feels like the overwhelming shadow of fascism, to render the dread manageable. These small acts of resilience in the aftermath of the 2016 election, of the sensual practice of self-care against the enormity of *wreckage upon wreckage* hurled before us, compose a minor aesthetic. In a *New Yorker* commentary called "The Year That Skin Care Became a Coping Mechanism," Jia Tolentino begins, "Over the summer, in one of many small, ridiculous attempts to affirm to myself that I will outlive the Trump Administration, I decided to incorporate both retinol and sunscreen into my daily skin-care routine."[46] Such a regimen becomes a predictive wish—or a will—for living on despite all that is ungraspably awful. She continues, "There's also something perversely, unexpectedly hopeful about skin care in today's political context. Traditionally, skin care represents an attempt to deny the inevitability of the future. For me, right now, it functions as part of a basic dream in which the future simply *exists*."[47] In another appraisal, a former professor and academic consultant reflects, "What I have found, for myself—and I emphatically make no claims with regard to anyone else—is that attending to my body through dance, clothes, skin care, and makeup has allowed me to better endure what would otherwise be debilitating political conditions."[48] Just a handful of years later, in the midst of the COVID-19 pandemic, Lesa Hannah testifies, "So even if our skin is dry from all our crying and we have dark under-eye circles from sleepless nights, the silver lining to all of this is that we'll all be skincare scholars by the time a vaccine arrives."[49] Sabbatical Beauty, a feminist skin care company, asserts in its manifesto the social nature of self-care: "We don't see beauty as a frivolous form of self-care, but a way of caring for ourselves, which allows us to better care for the people around us."[50]

The wish to fulfill a promise to ourselves, to put another way, summons resilience as the sponsor of a special form of beauty as a direction or a habit for being in a wretched world. In these reflections in times of crisis, we unsurprisingly find the frequent citation of Audre Lorde, who in 1988 writes, "Caring for myself is not an act of self-indulgence, it is self-preservation, and that is an act of political warfare."[51] Though Lorde penned these words about her harrowing experience with breast cancer, this paean has entered into the realm of resilience to help one to endure more terrible and overwhelming things that might otherwise be incomprehensible.[52] We might call this, after Berlant, "bargaining with what there is."[53] Here such bargaining becomes a habit for the care of the self in a crushing system that cannot provide it, will not. Such incommensurability is central to this minor aesthetic; the capacity to endure and to enjoy a reality (or a fragment of it) that contains the inevitable event of one's diminishing or dying, or others' diminishing or dying, becomes achingly beautiful.

This minor aesthetic connects one to the sensual experience of being alive despite alienation, vulnerability, or estrangement. That some irregular objects are also beautiful is a lesson in what might be gained with imperfection, being the result of a contingency unique to their histories, or having experienced the roughness of time as the sudden or gradual wearing out of their forms. Against overconsumption, disposability, and planned obsolescence, a more sustainable experience of the world might indeed foster interest and even pleasure in imperfect objects or objects of long duration. As analogues for living dangerously, broken objects might teach us how to live with scars and blemishes, transforming our relationships to time and its effects, including change, deterioration, and decline. Consider Leonard Koren's immensely popular *Wabi-Sabi for Artists, Designers, Poets, and Philosophers*, a manifesto of sorts for persons concerned with the human condition. For its practitioners, beauty is a relation, a state of mind, a container to hold the infinite or the inassimilable: "Wabi-sabi is ambivalent about separating beauty from non-beauty or ugliness. The beauty of wabi-sabi is, in one respect, the condition of coming to terms with what you consider ugly. Wabi-sabi suggests that beauty is a dynamic event that occurs between you and something else."[54] The multidisciplinary artist Cauleen Smith includes this tome among a series of gouache-and-graphite works made on letter-size black paper, lovingly re-creating the covers of thirty books dear to her, called, "BLK FMNNST Loaner Library, 1989–2019," alongside Octavia Butler's *Parable of the Sower*, Christina Sharpe's *In the Wake*, Toni Morrison's *Sula*, Trinh T. Minh-ha's *The Moon Waxes Red*, Saidiya Hartman's *Lose Your Mother*, and a guide to California desert wildflowers. These books, taken altogether as an animating force of personal influences, or as a reading list for others to follow (the Massachusetts Museum of Contemporary Art in 2019 facilitated a number of book club sessions with selections from this series), relay beauty's promise to help us endure political exhaustion and the historical weight of slavery, capital, genocide, and climate collapse.[55]

Through the idioms of vulnerability and perseverance, that which has been broken and forced apart, and put back together, becomes beautiful. Such a minor aesthetic might appear to us as *an image of the past as it flashes up in a moment of danger*, an image that we then do not let fade, or perish. As with wabi-sabi, the related concept of *kintsugi* too redefines aesthetic values when repair is required after injury or other violence. The hardcover book jacket for Chanel Miller's memoir *Know My Name* is a buttery-smooth, dark teal crisscrossed with uneven lines of gold. The publisher's note on the inside flap reads, "The gold veins on the cover represent the Japanese art of kintsugi, 'golden repair,' in which pieces of broken pottery are mended with powdered gold and lacquer, rather than treating the breaks as blemishes to conceal. The technique shows us that although an object cannot be returned to its original state, fragments can be made whole again." Similarly, Johanna Frueh draws on *kintsugi* to write of her cancer surgery, "Imagine creases and lines enhanced with a silver, gold, or platinum makeup, postmastectomy beauty marks similarly highlighted, flesh that has experienced trauma or undergone decades of age honored with the colors of precious metals."[56] Rather than disguise the act of repair, the conspicuous gold-filled fractures measure both care and durational time. As one curator puts it, "Instead of the altered physical appearance of the bowl diminishing its appeal, a new sense of vitality and resilience raised appreciation to even greater heights. Immaterial factors assumed a material presence through the lines of its mending and became an inextricable part of the bowl's appeal."[57] Contemplating such fractures and their mending, we could turn to Eve Sedgwick's argument for reparative reading and what she describes as the depressive position (after Melanie Klein), or "the position from which it is possible in turn to use one's own resources to assemble or 'repair' the murderous part-objects into something like a whole."[58] Such a minor aesthetic thus shapes an ethical regard toward the shattered, the worn out and down, the almost-dead, and the living dead. The saturation of brokenness with abstract and concrete forms of continuing presence, animating a feeling for life despite or through calamity, might indeed imbue an object, person, or scene with an immaterial quality of beauty.

These reparative qualities also saturate those craft objects with the labor of others who have endured much, where their labor transforms themselves and those objects into totems of living beautifully. Here resilience as a measure of persistence is a measure of productivity, transforming disposable people and material waste into resources for capital accumulation. In other words, resilience is value *extracted* from loss or injury. This is the premise of social business initiatives such as Covenant, ARTICLE22 (a reference to Article 22 in the Universal Declaration of Human Rights), and Brass Bombshell, minimalist jewelry lines that collaborate with NGOs and alternate trade retailers and engage local labor in Cambodia and Laos, converting unexploded ordnance into finely wrought jewelry.[59] Such are the excesses of war that whole industries emerge around the excavation and "recycling" of its material wastes, or, as Brass Bombshell states on its packaging, "from bombs to beauty." Like *kintsugi* ceramics, these bangles refer to their distressed histories as material objects. ARTICLE22 used the hashtag #buybackthebombs, and some bracelets are stamped with the words "DROPPED + MADE IN LAOS," highlighting the local deminers and artisans whose righteous labor create these lovely objects.[60] Such businesses include mini-profiles of their artisans, describing what goods ("books, school, fuel, and medicine") they are able to purchase with their earnings to enhance their well-being and that of their families. The demined land also is "recovered" (though recovery is too often understood as availability for the extraction of resources, labor, and capital); ARTICLE22 offers equations such as "The Peacebomb Story Ring clears 6 square meters of bomb littered land in Laos to make it safe for farmers to grow more pineapples." Since the 1970s, alternative trade organizations have made this means of production visible—handcrafted, artisanal—as part of the aura of the authentic commodity, imagined capable of creating bonds across time and space. Browse their inventory and one might find handmade dolls sold as "income generation and education project for poor and neglected children, adolescents, and poor women"; loosely tied bundles of Tibetan twisted rope incense valued at "$3.50, made by refugees"; drawstring pajama pants made from upcycled saris and sewn by former sex workers (some "rescued" by trafficking organizations, some organized among themselves as cooperatives); or teas wrapped in craft paper packaged by deaf or disabled persons.⁶¹ These objects accumulate value not because of any intrinsic use but because the labor-intensive conditions of production invest them with a surplus of meaning—the historical specificity of the object and its ties to a particular time or population, culture, or catastrophe are part of the aura of the bracelet, the charm, or the incense bundle.⁶²

Where resilience might transform the experience of being an object or a target of violence into a means of subjectivization, a fantasy of reparation consists of a *return* on suffering—resources or, more likely, recognition. In the latter instance, calling resilience beautiful renders those who are understood to be so as legible and legitimate subjects of life and living on. Photographs of landmine survivors as pageant contestants, for instance, solicit alternate or supplemental knowledge about living beautifully while dangerously to restore what is missing in the radical unmaking of a self. The familiar compulsion to then imagine for the contestant an inner life of dignity, to summon the frisson of willfulness in the subject of the pageant photograph, is the urge to render our recognition in aesthetic forms, such as the biography as narrative, that corroborate the promise of beauty.

The Subject of Living Beautifully

Resilience is one name for the conditioning of the self in anticipation of the crisis to come, the future anterior of misery that will have happened, while living beautifully is its aestheticization. It is a style that comes with its own comforts, including a story of self-continuity. In such a story, living beautifully is an agency where the meaning of history is (presumably) out of our power, and all we can control is our own passage through it. Reflecting on the literary fiction of an intelligible sense of time, Frank Kermode writes that the clock's *tick-tock* is "a model of what we call a plot, an organization that humanizes time by giving it form."⁶³ That is, "it is we who provide the fictional difference between the two sounds; *tick* is our word for a physical beginning, *tock* our word for an end. We say they differ. What enables them to be different is a special kind of middle."⁶⁴ The middle, or the duration that makes the difference between a beginning and an ending, becomes the plot that provides continuity. Clinical psychologists postulate that "one of the characteristics that seem to distinguish resilient individuals is that despite the sometimes convulsive changes that may accompany potentially traumatic events, they are able to experience an underlying continuity in the self and, armed with that continuity, to respond flexibly to the demands of a changed world."⁶⁵ In such biographical endeavors, where vulnerability becomes a capacity, a resource, and a condition of possibility, crisis is named an opening. One might of course "bounce back," but one might also become stronger once the fractures are filled with gold.[66] While it is sometimes a critique of the crises that circumscribe life as we know it, and will have known it, resilience also occasions the restructuring of one's capacities for living dangerously. In C. S. Holling's model of ecological resilience, "the time of greatest uncertainty yet high resilience" is also "a time for innovation and transformation; a time when crisis can be turned into an opportunity."[67] Put another way, "people might become resilient not in spite of adversities but because of them."[68] Or, as Ernest Hemingway writes in *A Farewell to Arms*, a sparse love story set against the First World War, "The world breaks everyone and afterward many are strong at the broken places."[69]

In the absence of another world to come, living beautifully might provide a sense of movement or progress; where no resolution to crisis or injustice can be expected, it emplots instead a story of oneself. In this familiar framing, potentially disturbing events are transfigured as occasions for personal growth or communal bonding (for those who suffer and for those who bear witness). Living beautifully thereby endows the duration or interval between the present and the uncertain future with significance. Those who endure injury, "accident," or disaster and *yet flourish* are imbued with an immaterial quality, or style, as the means and also the reward for their repair. Rebecca Fogg's memoir about her recovery, after a freak accident with an exploding toilet resulted in the partial amputation of her dominant hand, is titled *Beautiful Trauma*; more hard-fought loveliness might be found (per a quick internet search) in portrait photographs of breast cancer patients, trans women, and disabled animals, or in postearthquake Nepal and Haiti, microloan recipients, amputee pageant contestants, and more.[70] The accompanying music video for Christina Aguilera's single "Beautiful" features marginal characters (or characters who *feel* marginal), including a thin white woman scrutinizing her underwear-clad hips in a mirror, a drag queen carefully applying her makeup and wig, two young white gay lovers kissing on a bench despite hostile passersby, and a black-clad goth sitting down on a bus as others move away, whom we witness experiencing normative violence (that manifests as beating, as staring, as stigma, or as poor self-esteem), and whom Aguilera affirms, "You are beautiful." We could also turn to Gloria Gaynor's "I Will Survive," or Ariana Grande's "Thank U Next," or a thousand more; as Robin James writes about the tick-tock of the pop song, "Femininity is performed first as damage, second as resilience."[71] Such resilience describes a will to self-sovereignty despite suffering. In other words, living beautifully is an event both in the world (it is an enactment of a habit or capacity) and at a remove from it (it is a form or a passage for transcendence).

If this seems an odd and jumbled catalog, I am only mirroring the literature, which identifies resilience as a capacity that allows one to endure "such disparate experiences as direct exposure to the 9/11 terrorist attack, loss of a partner to acquired immunodeficiency disorder, an automobile accident, urban riots and violence, and physical assault."[72] Where violence is estranged from history into such abstraction, a landmine or a lost pension might be perceived as a political or structural fact or event (the Miss Landmine pageant magazine lists the mines' countries of manufacture), but recovery is most significant as an intimate and personal journey. While it sometimes condemns dangerous, disastrous conditions, resilience just as often accepts the *facticity* of violence through the "universal" truth of vulnerability. Living beautifully might reference an event or condition for its historical significance (the etiology of crisis), only to lend fulsomeness to imperfect if resolute vitality. In short, the source of anguish is less significant than the aesthetic of living through it, or with it. In *Living Beautifully with Uncertainty and Change*, American Buddhist nun Pema Chödrön argues that our habitual sense of who we are and our need for security are obstacles to overcome. "When we resist change, it's called suffering. But when we can completely let go and not struggle against it, when we can embrace the groundlessness of our situation and relax into its dynamic quality, that's called enlightenment, or awakening to our true nature, our fundamental goodness."[73] For those adaptive faculties of systems or beings to survive uncontrollable hardship or unending misery, it is all the same event of inevitability.

This story of ourselves, that pain is inevitable but suffering is avoidable, infuses a resilient aesthetic as a mode of subjectivization; it operates to make sense of suffering, to render perceptible, incorporable, and legible, pain as a story about ourselves and the world. The children's television host and friendly neighbor Fred Rogers advised, "There is no normal life that is free of pain. It's the very wrestling with our problems that can be the impetus for growth."[74] In this way, living beautifully is not dissimilar to Melanie Klein's concept of reparation, which David Eng describes as "an attempt to provide a new language for love and repair in order to rescue a besieged liberal human subject in the midst of utter destruction."[75] There is in such calls for living beautifully an imperative to work on oneself, to subject oneself to norms and rules for conduct in the name of well-being—ours, and that of others. Such work might entail self-mastery, the denial of vulnerability, the narrowing of focus to what we can control, or all this at once. If one does wish to repair or transmute hurt or suffering into a resource or an opportunity, there are thousands of tutorials, for instance, with directions to "build your resilience," "learn how to thrive in any situation," and "bounce back." To live beautifully is to accept the inevitability of risk and (commit) to recover from adversity. In this manner, "adjustment seems like an accomplishment."[76]

Such an aesthetic style creates an ethical imperative. Living beautifully is a normative judgment about virtue; it is also a call for a collectivity to esteem, copy, preserve, collect, and nurture it. To name someone who suffers beautiful because she is resilient renders her life instructive; she is an example for others to copy, under conditions that might encompass landmines, cancer, incarceration, or dying oceans. Against victimization and its perceived codification in the aesthetic appeal to compassion or pity, some have argued instead for *seeing otherwise* (literally and figuratively) victims as survivors, resourceful and resilient even or especially in the face of terrible disaster or slow death. And as Jeff Dolven writes in *Senses of Style*, "To respond to something in terms of style is to ask, always if not explicitly, *would I want to do something like that, make something like that, live that way?*"[77] Thus might *living beautifully* turn the wounded body into another order of spectacle to act as an example. The Miss Landmine pageant, portrait photographs of breast cancer survivors, and so on, celebrate those contestants or survivors who already have what they need—*their beauty*—to thrive after injury, despite harm. Such a style for living is sometimes "enough" to insulate the subject from the absence of protection from or prevention of more suffering.[78] The concept of living beautifully thus conveys rupture and continuity simultaneously, such that the experience of crisis and catastrophe need not be traumatic, or not traumatic for long, so long as one is resilient. But the lesson is a norm, and as Howell observes, "Woe unto the depressives among us, or anyone not considered fit for this future."[79] The crisis event is both before us and already behind us—and what will you do?

Inevitably, every articulation of resilience is haunted by the burial of those who were unsuccessful (and who were sometimes entombed by resilient soldiers, markets, and critical infrastructure). To call resilience beautiful might be profoundly confirming, at least for those who wish for their suffering to *mean* something, to be redeemed especially as a relation to violence, and for others to know them as free, pious, or good. (There are many familiar, even ancient, stories about beautiful or otherwise virtuous suffering.) But not all forms of endurance or failures to die are understood as beautiful. Endurance cannot be begrudging, it cannot be fatalistic, if it is to be beautiful; anger, resentment, and bitterness are correlated with captivity, anachronism, and discord. These would be ugly feelings, after Sianne Ngai, deficient or inadequate affects that do not rise to the occasion. Such feelings are perceived as unproductive and noncathartic, offering "no satisfactions of virtue, however oblique, nor any therapeutic or purifying release."[80] Berlant is another from whom we might again borrow, whose cruel optimism is counterposed to "what someone is doing when they are becoming dissipated, and not acting in a life-building way—the way that liberal subjects who are happy people are supposed to."[81] In the schematization of capacities according to liberal personhood, dysregulation where those internal structures that preside over the faculties of human consciousness are missing or maimed is cast as irresponsibility, incapacity, and nonlife. Such emotional disturbance generates other social and psychic negativity, and even aggressivity, through which ugly feelings or dissipation is consigned to an abstract or anachronistic category of suspicion. They do no one, we are told, any good.

The assumption that the subject against whom violence is committed (through deliberate harm, accidental injury, or inevitable calamity) has a responsibility to respond in an appropriate manner to that violence is central to the concept of living beautifully. Such an assumption, and naming such a responsibility lovely or desirable, underscores a long-standing tradition of moralizing opposition used to distinguish feelings or capacities that are politically adequate to their occasions, or efficacious to the continuation of life, and those that are not.[82] Because resilience presupposes the liberal capacity for an expressive interiority preceding the adaptive faculties to shape the formless infinity—Kant's Reason—those who are not resilient are not sovereign or free; they are instead affectable, a state of being that is historically infantilized, gendered, and racialized.[83] (Consider the familiar settler colonial story about Indigenous peoples who were not resilient enough and *died away*, and were subsequently replaced by those who were.) As Ngai observes, the state of being unusually susceptible to external control is an accusation of being too easily moved, of emotional excess and imperfect agency. Unsurprisingly, the resilient human is the same as the one who is able to promise; this individual exercises those faculties of reason, including diagnosis and prediction, to determine their own future (if no one else's). Or as Friedrich Nietzsche notes, "Man himself must first of all have become *calculable, regular, necessary*, even in his own image of himself, if he is able to stand in security for *his own future*, which is what one who promises does!"[84] In these terms, resilience as a *calculable* capacity to maintain *regular* functioning despite uncontrollable outside forces is *necessary* in a world without guarantees. Living beautifully is a habitus of hype, in order not to be that failed person who capitulates to adversity.

As it turns out, however, the segregation of populations and places as precarious life is also their segregation as hostile *to* life. The zones of the world as target (again, to cite Chow) perceived as unlawful, backward, violent, and ugly are also those who require more intervention—not just as regime change but also as resilience training, over and against other, more ungovernable forms for pursuing a life that can be lived. And too often those murderous structures that banish some beings from the human are rendered negligible (because they are *too big to fail*) for apprehending causality *or* casualty. Instead, the category of human failure or inevitability supersedes capital or colony through which some life is consigned to death. As Sara Ahmed notes, "Resilience is the requirement to take more pressure; such that pressure can be gradually increased."[85] That is to say, the relatively recent emergence of resilience as a category or a capacity for enduring what is unassimilable is itself too late, and not enough, for some of us. Tracie Washington, president of the Louisiana Justice Institute, requested that policymakers and the media cease calling Hurricane Katrina and BP oil spill victims "resilient." "Because every time you say, 'Oh, they're resilient, [it actually] means you can do something else, [something] new to [my community].... We were not born to be resilient; we are conditioned to be resilient. I don't want to be resilient.... [I want to] fix the things that [create the need for us to] be resilient [in the first place]."[86] Afterward, posters appeared throughout New Orleans, stapled and taped to power poles and streetlights. In a stark sans serif font, the posters read, "Stop calling me RESILIENT. Because every time you say, 'Oh, they're resilient,' that means you can do something else to me. I am not resilient."

Among the psychic consequences for political life when total transformation is abandoned, resilience or living beautifully smothers other forms of surviving—roughly, stubbornly, crookedly. Consider the crisis coverage of Black looting against white salvaging after Hurricane Katrina; the media panic about "retail theft" from billion-dollar corporations that compel infant formula and diapers to be locked in cabinets; or the Christian evangelicals who prowl the streets, handing out to sex workers (or anyone they assume is one) white roses with notes that read "You are beautiful," promising that beauty awaits them after spiritual rescue.[87] What may be called looting, larceny, or loose morals are not seen as acts of resourcefulness in the shadow of collapse. These are understood as criminal acts committed by those who require the interventions of others, to corral and discipline their faculties to better absorb the blows of racial or capital violence. This reasoning bolsters policies and programs that denounce and diminish so-called dependency (otherwise known as public goods or social welfare), turning to resilience as a principal rationalization of austerity. Simi Kang, for instance, argues that seeming praise for Vietnamese "refugee resilience" in New Orleans post-Katrina not only bolsters anti-Blackness, but also thereby defers (or even demurs) the provision of aid or support after "decision maker-produced disaster."[88] In doing so, such policies and programs disavow their responsibility for worsening precarious conditions because resilience is *enough*. (Mark Neocleous calls "beautiful"—in its deceitful sense, its symmetrical sense—this idea that "resilience is what the world's poor need . . . [which] turns out to be something that the world's poor already possess.")[89] The expansion of resilience as a capacity for living dangerously becomes an economic imperative in a biopolitical regime that ordains mechanisms of interference and control in the name of improving chances of survival, and quality of life. Calling it beautiful solicits an orientation to the world that feels less awful.

If rights became the dominant frame for political claims after the failure of utopian or revolutionary politics, then resilience is the dominant frame for political claims after the failure of rights. And if resilience is an affective discipline involving adjustments to the structural pressures of crisis, even or especially when uncertainty suffuses the everyday, such crisis ordinariness is experienced unevenly. While its call is promiscuous (everyone might at some time lose someone dear to them), resiliency's most programmatic target is the subject of the global South, who has endured settler colonialism, total war, extractive capital, and necropolitical austerity from those who first rendered them assailable and now hope to make them resilient—lest their vulnerability become resistance. Whereas minute or incremental "corrections" to the status quo and its structures circumscribe our horizon of the political, living beautifully is the management of vulnerability after the failure (or the anticipation of failure) to transform the conditions that unevenly distribute exposure and precarity.[90]

Furthermore, the seemingly inescapable conclusion that violence cannot be predicted or controlled also coheres as a political argument to adapt to infrastructural collapse. Our agency, we are told, is our resilience within decomposing or decimated lifeworlds. Citing the Intergovernmental Panel on Climate Change, Brad Evans and Julien Reid call attention to the blending of the terms *resilience* and *resistance* when speaking about environmental disaster or crisis. This panel defines resistance as "'the ability to avoid suffering significant adverse effects,'" which Evans and Reid describe as "a purely reactionary impulse premised upon some survivability instinct that deems the nature of the political itself to be already settled."[91] John Patrick

Leary reports that in the devastating onset of the COVID-19 pandemic, health care workers were given paltry personal protective equipment—reusing N95 masks or gloves over the course of days and days in the emergency room or intensive care unit—as well as resilience training. "Rather than address what she describes as chronic staffing shortages in her unit, Margaret says hospital management has recently offered resilience and mindfulness workshops to its overworked staff. Before the pandemic, Margaret says, she just rolled her eyes at this sort of break-room encouragement. 'I am more bitter about it post-COVID,' she explains, 'because the situation so catastrophically exceeds what any individual's resilience can do.'"[92] The capacity for resilience hinges on a willingness to embrace new forms of self-sovereignty even as claims to justice become impossible under conditions of unknowable but inevitable destabilization. The US response to the pandemic forced each of us to act as managers of our own well-being, collecting and sifting information about new variants and mitigation measures, and calculating risks for ordinary activities of life living in the midst of a mass-disabling event. In 2022, in response to CEO concerns about corporate profits, the Centers for Disease Control and Prevention changed the metrics for transmission maps and recommended we return to work even if we might still be infectious or unwell, because hundreds of thousands of deaths, repeat infections, and cascading organ failure are necessary to maintain *more* critical systems functioning. Fredric Jameson observes that we can more easily imagine the end of the world than the end of capitalism; so attuned to the apocalypse to come, resilience might foreclose other possible lifeworlds.[93]

Where present forms of governance depends on the omnipresence of risk and the inevitability of violence, resilience is a capacity of forbearance. But while resilience is easily contested as a policy—there are many critics of resilience as austerity, as preemption—as an aesthetic? Not as much. Who would not want to call our inevitable brokenness beautiful? To forge something anew from our grief and sorrow as a resource for a life that can be nonetheless lived? Against the failures of progress or revolution, historicist concepts that organize collective or shared time, resilience yields less confidence in a teleology of humanity and instead invests in a personal time. And yet calling certain forms of living on *beautiful* prevents us from seeing resilience as a symptom of our dispossession; instead, we become attached to *living beautifully* as a story of ourselves in an optimistic relation to that which prevents our actual flourishing. Or, as Stuelke observes, "Sometimes what feels like a relief, like hope, like change, like utopian possibility, actually signals a shifting orientation to existing violent infrastructures; sometimes, the will to repair helps instantiate something worse."[94] We are returned here to Berlant's cruel optimism, in which what we desire is in fact an obstacle, while our sense of time is unhinged from a less awful future.

So—two things are true at once. It is important to appreciate the sensual experiences through which those who are vulnerable (to one degree or another or more) abide unpredictable violence and neglect; the promise of beauty, as I have argued throughout, is not "merely" ornamental. It matters that Palestinians defiantly paint murals on the rubble after Israeli airstrikes flatten structures and destroy roadways in Gaza. It matters that the Nap Ministry, an ongoing performance installation and multimedia project, encourages Black liberation through the repair of bodies and minds against the grind of racial capital. "Y'all keep hollering about this New World that will emerge post-pandemic, yet you won't even rest or slow down enough to receive the innovative thinking necessary to build this World. You think you can create a new liberated world while being exhausted? It's not possible."[95] For these reasons, I have not argued resilience as a solely neoliberal phenomenon or as an ethos of entrepreneurial selfhood, though others have observed carefully how resilience is recruited for such ends as zombie labor and ecological dead zones. Care of the self or the desire for beauty might at times be a supplement to extractive capital, but such care or desire is not necessarily contained by it (though it might be contained by something else, commensurate or adjacent to other norms). This is not an argument that parties or roses are political alternatives to bread and "helping the Armenians," but to say that parties or roses might be that to which we turn when our approved avenues of political change—votes, rights, petitions, or protests—are shattered, shrunk, outlawed, or radically *useless*. Parties or roses highlight the failures thus far in securing the future.

The stories we might tell to honor living beautifully as a practice of self-continuity too often unfold in the absence of political claims about that which it is necessary to endure, including those also-resilient structures such as racial capital or settler colonialism, that inflict sanctioned violence. Such a concept of living dangerously accepts that precarity is borne by unfortunate peoples in target zones (which are increasingly spreading as viruses, wildfires, and rising sea levels care less about zoning laws or property values), who are subject to interventions (from war, to microcredit, to vocational training, to development, to self-esteem) to develop their capacities for continued life, but who at minimum require no more than a mindful turn toward adaptation and joy, however it can be found. If resilience is an agency of human freedom, the target of total war or racial capital is caught in a trap.

Where resilience—or whatever name is taken up next to circumscribe our survival—is an ethical obligation to live beautifully, and doing so is the precondition of a capacity for humanity, then the one who experiences violence *as* violence and not as a lesson, a resource, or an opportunity is banished to an outside of the human altogether.

Failing Resilience

In an essay asking how one might find pleasure during a pandemic, Collier Myerson worries about flowers, again:

> In the last couple of days on these walks, I've been listening to an old antiwar song by Pete Seeger called "Where Have All the Flowers Gone?" It's about the cycle of life under war and how the only constant, the only thing we will always have to rely on, are flowers. . . . The song goes: *"Where have all the flowers gone? / Young girls have picked them, every one / Where have all the young girls gone? / They've gone to husbands, every one / Where have all the husbands gone? / They've gone for soldiers, every one / Where have all the husbands gone? / They've gone to graveyards, every one / Where have all the graveyards gone? / They've gone to flowers, every one."*[96]

Living beautifully is a story about how we face an ending, or how we make sense of how we face *our* ending where there is no agreeable future. Grappling with attachments that emerge from, and can be masked as, iterations of resilience requires that we consider how we regard violence without hardening the scars or the fictions that produce (the need for) it. For while the subject of resilience is extralegal (resilience is often programmatic but not often legalistic), it is attached to philosophies of agency, sovereignty, and security in ways that push us to theorize this subject as one of empire, unrelenting. Between the centuries-long grind of colonial extractivism and racial capital, the acceleration of climate apocalypse, and the rise of far-right populisms that harry the old enemies (communism, foreigners, deviants) while dismantling the bulwark of democratic institutions, historical time is stricken with ruin and risk. Our sense of historical change is thus no longer teleological, imminent, or possible, and our frame of meaningful experiential reference is destroyed; it *feels like* there is only the style in which we live in the now. To put it another way, living beautifully is what we have when political justice is no longer on the horizon. And if there is only accommodation in the ever-extending present, the promise of beauty might turn inward to the minor adjustments required for such accommodation; it might become an embrace of the present *as it is*—broken, and made over as beautiful, through the necessities of living on while stranded within it.

Of course, there are more radical articulations of resilience. One might be captured in the phrase, adopted from a Greek poet and popularized by immigrant rights activists, *They tried to bury us, they didn't know we were seeds*.[97] Or found in the mantra, facing a future of radical uncertainty, *We already have everything we need*.[98] Here, persistence is explicitly resistance under conditions that wish some of us dead or disappeared, or that pursue policies and programs that ensure that our chances are at least diminished. Such an aesthetic might be at distinct odds with the regime it endures, or one name for that which hunted populations have always done. In its responses and judgments about the world, such a politics of necessity claims endurance through forms of collective care to ensure survival in sinister circumstances that are not changeable (not in the immediate sense, or only in increments). But another lesson to learn from such forms might be that the future has never been a public property; some have never had a stake in it. As Franny Choi titles her poem about cascading apocalypses from "boats of prisoners," "the bombed mosque," pipelines, dogs, coat hangers, and border fences, "The World Keeps Ending, and the World Goes On." Or as Thea Quiray Tagle points out, "For whom does the world feel like it is ending? And for whom has the world already ended and been reborn again, a thousand times over in cycles of alternating joy, madness, and grief?"[99]

While the promise of beauty is sometimes figured as a reprieve from the exhaustion of living through violence, can it also be a reserve to keep fighting? If resilience is continuity—for systems functioning, for self-sovereignty, despite the inevitability of our doom—what would its interruption bring forth? For whom is continuity, for living through this, desirable? What other orders of care and inhabitation can we conjure for this wrecked world out of joint? What other genres of historical consciousness and political action might be found through a promise of beauty that seeks, as Benjamin put it, to "make the continuum of history explode"?[100] And what if instead— crime is beauty?

epilogue

In Conclusion, Crime Is Beauty

The strong women told the faggots that there are two important things to remember about the coming revolutions. The first is that we will get our asses kicked. The second is that we will win.

Larry Mitchell, *The Faggots and Their Friends between Revolutions*

Beauty conceptually has been a tool used to stand out and individualize yourself, but it does not serve you or your community to be easily recognizable and thus tracked down. You can wear your lipstick, sure, fine, but wear a mask, too. Cover your face.

Arabelle Sicardi, "A Practical Beauty Guide to Fighting Fascism"

Jacques Derrida begins *Specters of Marx*, which is a "work of mourning" for all this debt and death around us: "Someone, you or me, comes forward and says: I would like to learn to live finally."[1] Concerned as he is with the haunting loss of revolution as the horizon of political emancipation, he observes that our sense of time is now ruptured from our expectations of history, citing Shakespeare's *Hamlet* that time is out of joint. To say *I would like to learn to live finally* is a wish, a plea, a line in the sand, a closed fist, and an open hand. Up until now, I have not lived, or I have half lived, or I have barely lived at all. To learn to live finally, what would I need to know and to do for this to be true?

In our assessments of the relation of events to structures or feelings, and how we might respond to and transform the scale and feel of terror, can the promise of beauty unmoor our planetary situation? The world can feel like one crisis after another, as we say their names, stockpile or ration medicines, share food and shelter, allocate funds to pay for strangers' debts or surgeries or pills, block highways and trains and boats carrying munitions, and check on our lovers and friends as we each witness the grievous harms of this death-world. Everything, we say, is *a lot*. Yet the promise of beauty is so often formed around threats to the image of the world that it aims to sustain or create, and that would in turn sustain or create beauty, and so the aesthetic category of beauty is not a property after all but a conjectural sociality, through which we invite each other to care about what we care about, to come together to appraise and then to admire a rose, a jawline, a house with a door, a rhinoceros, a forest, the noxious plume of an airstrike, a painting, or a police precinct on fire. In this, an aesthetic proposition is also a political proposition. A promise of beauty is a judgment about the world as it is and as it *should* be, and collectives, swarms, schools, or mobs form around those who do and do not hold its pleasures in common. *Every promise of beauty is therefore a partisan divide.* When she was scolded that "it did not behoove an agitator to dance," the anarchist Emma Goldman retorted, "I did not believe that a Cause which stood for a beautiful ideal, for anarchism, for release and freedom from conventions and prejudice, should demand the denial of life and joy. I insisted that our Cause could not expect me to become a nun and that the movement should not be turned into a cloister. If it meant that, I did not want it. 'I want freedom, the right to self-expression, everybody's right to beautiful, radiant things.'"[2]

This book is not exhaustive—how could it be?—but it comprises a catalog of meetings with beauty that unfold their promises as structure and method. In doing so, these chapters have sought to capture something of the dimensions of the political present to which the promise of beauty is addressed in the long wake of catastrophe. What can beauty promise us, those of us malingering in the shadow of all this? How do we live well within a world that circumscribes, forecloses, and metes out life-living for so many? In making my case, I perhaps run the risk in this book of turning beauty into too much, standing in for whatever marks the feeling of life-living. But how else should we measure the dispositional power of *beautiful, radiant things*, which might appear to us at once as a psychic investment, an interpretive hermeneutic, a relational presence, a political imperative, or a map of the soul? Beauty is not everything, but it is not nothing; it is ornamental, and it is world-making. W. E. B. Du Bois observed that nothing is more disgraceful than the Jim Crow laws of the American South, and nothing more beautiful than the light on Montego Bay in Jamaica. "And both things," he wrote, "are true and both belong to this our world, and neither can be denied."[3] And Arabelle Sicardi insists in the midst of encroaching fascisms, "There is still, absurdly, beauty here."[4]

I turned to the promise of beauty because it seemed to say so much about learning to live, finally. While beauty is often personal and intimate in the sense that our perception unfolds within the horizon established by our presence (what senses, what histories bring us to any *here and now*), it is political inasmuch as beauty is implicated in life-living. As I hope to have convinced you, beauty's promise organizes the measures by which we value a life and arranges those powers—or elaborates on them—that enrich some and dispose others to lives without it. And if politics is, as Judith Butler puts it, "minimally, a problem of living together," and beauty is nothing more than a feeling of life being furthered, then beauty is a problem of *feeling life being furthered together*.[5] We can sum up some of the questions this poses as, What is living, and what is a life worth living? What is our obligation to ensure that beauty is present in the lives of others, to demand that our lives, their lives, be furthered? What happens when we make injury or threat to beauty visible or perceptible in order to ask that others recognize it, to treasure it, for now or for a future? What happens when beauty stands in for the life that can be lived, and asks that we take responsibility for our capacity to harm such life, for the histories of violence that diminish life, in our name?

After all, the promise of beauty is something you might give to other people. Everyone I know is reading the 1977 utopian manifesto *The Faggots and Their Friends between Revolutions*, a trippy-hippy paean to transgression all the way down. Authored by Larry Mitchell and illustrated by Ned Asta with simple-seeming ink drawings of spiraling figures with elongated limbs and flowering extremities, *The Faggots and Their Friends* comprises a series of anecdotes, allegories, and allusions to another world far beyond this dull, damaged one, in which underground cells of chosen family plot revolution in an empire in decline (called Ramrod, and ruled by Warren-and-His-Fuckpole, to make its patriarchal authoritarianism clear). In this mythic cosmology for radical living and queer friendship, Mitchell boldly proclaims, "The faggots cultivate beauty and harmony and peace since these are states that the men do not know about." He continues, "Since the men are blind to beauty, they do not know that the lucky faggots live in the most beautiful places. And the lucky faggots do not tell them. Instead, they ask the unlucky faggots to come and join them."[6] Recalling Martin Manalansan's *biyuti*, clandestine beauty is one method for making a life *the men do not know about*. A refuge, a refusal. On her conversation with David Wojnarowicz about art and crisis, photographer and graphic artist Zoe Leonard muses, "You know, we were all just too busy for beauty. We were too angry for beauty. We were too heartbroken for beauty. I felt like an asshole with these picture[s] of clouds, but David was right. You go through all of the fighting not because you want to fight, but because you want to go somewhere as a people. You want to help create a world where you can sit around and think about clouds. That should be our right as human beings."[7] Saidiya Hartman writes, lovingly, about "the anarchy of colored girls assembled in a riotous manner":

> Esther Brown was wild and wayward. She longed for another way of living in the world. She was hungry for enough, for otherwise, for better. She was hungry for beauty. In her case, the aesthetic wasn't a realm separate and distinct from the daily challenges of survival, rather the aim was to make an art of subsistence, a lyric of being young, poor, gifted, and black. Yet, she did not try to create a poem or song or painting. What she created was Esther Brown. . . . She would make a beautiful life. What was beauty if not "the intense sensation of being pulled toward the animating force of life"?[8]

Or as the Palestinian civil defense volunteer answered a young girl, rescued from beneath the rubble after an Israeli airstrike demolished her home at the Al-Bureij refugee camp in Gaza, who tremblingly asked, "Are you taking me to the cemetery?": "No, my dearest, you are alive, and beautiful as the moon."[9]

What awaits in the gaps and spaces between what is present as beauty and what could be—in one's own life, in a life with others? Mere survival is not good enough; a life is not an intrinsic good because it is a life. A life without beauty, it is often said, or as Esther Brown knew, is not a life at all. Beauty is thus a measure of what is missing or lost and what must be given— and sometimes demanded. The words "Bread for all, and Roses too" first appeared in a magazine report by Helen Todd, a women's rights campaigner, before James Oppenheim composed his poem. Later, the Jewish labor militant Rose Schneiderman declared, "What the woman who labors wants is the right to live, not simply exist. . . . The worker must have bread, but she must have roses too."[10] That is, the promise of beauty informs a political vocabulary that can capture what it is to want another life that does not yet exist—while questioning whether under present conditions if this life is possible, and what conditions would make it so. (As British anarchists CRASS ask and answer, "Do they owe us a living? 'Course they fucking do!") At this threshold, the promise of beauty is an affirmation of life despite structural precarity, or overwhelming assault. It is here that some might vest their hopes that another politics of life-living can be found in our sensual and aesthetic relationships to the world and to each other. Beauty might allow us to touch that which we cannot apprehend directly, and maybe never will—not the grudging measure of sovereignty found (for some) in law and order, but the life we truly deserve. The faggots and their friends and Zoe Leonard and David Wojnarowicz and Esther Brown and Palestinian refugees pursue a practice of the self after Michel Foucault: "It was a question of knowing how to govern one's own life in order to give it the most beautiful possible form (in the eyes of others, of oneself, and of the future generations for which one might serve as an example). That is *what* I tried to reconstitute: the formation and development of a practice of self whose aim was to constitute oneself as the worker of the beauty of one's own life."[11]

In making the best of having to linger in this *between revolutions*, as we tell each other that we need to imagine otherwise, that another world is possible, more than ever, is *this* enough? Beauty might be found in a comforting thing, a thing that murmurs sweetly or ministers an immediate relief. But it is not enough, I would say; what promise can rest in comfort, empathy, or resilience, when state violence or racial capital ravages our prospects, or those of others, for whom there can be no comfort, empathy, or resilience? We cannot merely repair our capacities to endure more and continuous catastrophe. Indeed, the will to be human, to live as though human, under such conditions might feel like asking too much. Pushing against (or with) this "flourishing despite the facts," Cameron Awkward-Rich muses, "It's possible that I simply find joy exhausting work, but I also don't know how we will ever sustain ways of life outside of the logic of white supremacy unless we are first willing/able to suspend our attachments to the ideas of what it means to be a human that we've all inherited from it."[12]

This is how the promise of beauty acts as a measure of normative horizons for justice or their collapse. Already known "solutions" have not yet worked out for us. About Mrs. Dalloway's party preparations, and whether roses or parties help, Lee R. Edwards submits, "Suppose, however, we alter slightly the terms of Clarissa's interrogation, asking now not specifically about roses, but instead about what, in general, might help those like the Armenians 'hunted out of existence, maimed, frozen, the victims of cruelty and injustice.'"[13]

Clarissa's roses might be a provocation—if not beauty, because it is supposedly decorative, ornamental, and frivolous, then what? If what else has been tried has not helped, not petitions, or votes, or constitutions, or soldiers, or courts, or rights, then what? The promise of beauty is an argument that new forms, new actions, new arrangements have to be thought of as possible now, not just in the future, if we want a future at all. *Bread and roses* and *I HOPE THIS EMAIL DOES NOT FIND YOU* and *a world where you can sit around and think about clouds* allow us to evaluate the workings of what exists and its limits—and this should include the structure of our inquiries themselves. The question of how beauty is a method is a question of how the promise solicits radically distinct conceptions of the political. Does the promise of beauty lie in fortifications of the already known, in a parallel dimension within the wrecked world, or in the destruction of it altogether?

It is as a conception of history, or alternate history, that the promise of beauty could be a wish to *live through this*, but also to *live, finally*. Beset by so much slow violence and sanctioned death, the present cannot sustain such life-living; it cannot nurture beautiful, radiant things. We know, after Walter Benjamin, that "the tradition of the oppressed teaches us that the 'state of emergency' in which we live is not the exception but the rule. We must attain to a conception of history that is in keeping with this insight. Then we shall clearly realize that it is our task to bring about a real state of emergency, and this will improve our position in the struggle against Fascism."[14] Critique is therefore a cognate of beauty, as its promise requires that we fathom its presence (perhaps capacious, or as fragile as a bubble or a mood) but also its absence (perhaps thundering, or an emptiness quietly pooling around you or me or us or them) in the world as it is. In this frame, beauty cannot be found in harmony or order in the present, what Jacques Rancière calls the police (politics as we know it).[15] So too does Theodor Adorno argue that the promise is unfulfillable as things are: "Because all happiness found in the status quo is ersatz and false, art must break its promise in order to stay true to it."[16] Through its promise, we might yet come to understand those narrowing categories and hardened structures that withhold beautiful, radiant things, and then to secure them for all of us. Lorraine Hansberry avows, "There is simply no reason why dreams should dry up like raisins or prunes or anything else in America. If you will permit me to say so, I believe that we can *impose* beauty on our future."[17]

Here lies the distinction between a liberal sensorium that promises beauty as the object of its politics, and a more radical one that promises politics as the object of beauty—if politics is the end of the police. To fulfill a promise of beauty is to reorder the sensible, which might require breaking other social bonds, those contractual agreements with entities that have forfeited our trust and ravaged our world. These abandoned bonds might look like a temporary autonomous zone, a riot, an insurrection, an intifada, or a crime spree. Thus, in Leslie Kaplan's contemporary political fable called *Disorder*, ordinary people begin to murder their bosses, managers, politicians—nonchalantly, casually. A librarian of colonialism takes a champagne bottle to a representative from the Overseas Ministry; a literature student strangles her groping professor with his tie; a bank clerk drops a safe on his director's head; a machinist pushes a legislator under a bus after he proposes the recalculation of overtime pay, and says, "Stop the bullshit." It is, in other words, a history of the present that grapples with the limits of the already understood: "The question was asked, how much can any ordinary individual—the criminals were all just ordinary individuals—be driven by an idea, a concept, a representation, and then to what, to crime, is it really possible, it was possible since all this had taken place, but there had to be some other explanation, didn't there?"[18] The rational, sensible explanation (it might be a sociological case study, a historical inquiry, or a psychological profile) might be not enough to perceive the flux of life found in tumult and disorder. The social contract is demonstrably fucked—no one is protected by the state except for its institutions, its elites, that created all this—so what would it look like to acknowledge this, to fully know this deep inside our bones and blood to be true?

In writing about how to make art at the end of the world, Natalie Loveless argues that we will not change our historical situation with "more facts, differently figured, but by finding ways, through aesthetic encounters and events, to persuade us to care and to care *differently*."[19] This means, in part, that we will have to conceive of time askew. When the tempo of crisis is understood as inevitable, chronic, or flowing from a rational or teleological evaluation of history, how might the promise of beauty radically disrupt our *feeling historical*? On the state of emergency, Benjamin continues, "One reason why Fascism has a chance is that in the name of progress its opponents treat it as a historical norm. The current amazement that the things we are experiencing are 'still' possible in the twentieth century is *not* philosophical. This amazement is not the beginning of knowledge—unless it is the knowledge that the view of history which gives rise to it is untenable."[20] Indeed, it can be hard to hope under premises that make fascism appear certain and inescapable, and this is why abolitionist Mariame Kaba teaches us that hope is a discipline. But is it also a promise, a promise to make a difference in our habits of sense-making, to unmoor our bearings from the already known, from the foregone ending? Like hope, a promise is emergent, even as it shapes palpable energies and phenomenal forms for our passage through the world.

For this reason, beauty as a feeling for life being furthered is as good a name for what we might hope for as anything else, and beauty as a method unfolds and confronts what is claimed to make present the life that can be lived. Again, such promises as we might make to one another solicit our scrutiny of what cannot be supposed or conceived under a present regime, and beauty cannot appear to us in already known forms if it is to deny its rule. As Avery Gordon observes, "You have no other choice but to make things up in the interstices of the factual and the fabulous, the place where the shadow and the act converge."[21] Procedural rights or law and order or sovereignty will not be the same as justice—what is required for *living on* is not yet. In this regard, beauty *could* be an analogue for justice, but only if we follow from Derrida that justice enters a relation of alterity to law: "There is an avenir for justice and there is no justice except to the degree that some event is possible which, as an event, exceeds calculation, rules, programs, anticipations."[22] So, what will secure our beautiful, radiant things? What would it take to transform our distribution of the sensible, and the insensible?

Throughout this book, the specter of violence hovers over the promise of beauty, either as a threat to beauty or as beauty's consequence. Because it is about *what is* and *what ought to be*, the promise of beauty often describes a world that is deeply split even as it furnishes an intervention of one sort or another, even as a fantastical proposition about how we render our claims to a life worth living—through obstinance, through scarcity, through fire. Here at the end, I offer two more, seemingly impossible examples of the promise of beauty as a method, a direction, or a tendency. Because damage cannot be avoided, and death is coming for us, one example is a lesson, and the other is a warning.

The first comes from Argentinean fabulist Mariana Enriquez's gothic short story collection called *Things We Lost in the Fire*. Enriquez spent her childhood in Argentina during the Dirty War of the 1970s and 1980s, in which tens of thousands were tortured, killed, or "disappeared" through acts of state terror later nullified with blanket amnesty (though this amnesty was revoked over a decade later). Communists, students, trade unionists, writers, scientists, journalists, artists, guerrillas, and sympathizers—all the dead and disappeared still haunt, and their loved ones still mourn, stubbornly. In the eponymous short story, women who are survivors of patriarchal violence, including femicide, no longer bother to hide its consequences. In the midst of a wave of burnings as not-so isolated incidents—more and more men using fire to murder or attempt to murder sisters, mothers, wives, daughters, girlfriends, strangers—the narrator Silvina observes one such survivor on the subway, who strolls through the crowd with her burnt face and body, begging for money ("her method was audacious. . . . she greeted each [passenger] with a kiss on the cheek") while wearing "tight jeans, see-through blouses, even high-heeled sandals when it was hot out . . . bracelets on her wrists, and little gold necklaces hung around her neck."[23] Often commuters are repulsed, because the woman does not feel shame as she should, because she does not hide her burns as she should: "For her to flaunt a sensuous body seemed inexplicably offensive."[24] Yuliana M. Ramos Orta calls this a trashed beauty, as in "deliberately 'trashing' their beauty and becoming undefinable, i.e., abject."[25]

Silvina later sees the same girl at a protest outside the hospital after another two women—a mother and a daughter—are burned by their husband and father in an alcohol-fueled fire. The police, the doctors, the politicians, can and would do nothing. A group of unburned women are with her, nonetheless suffering with the others. "Then the subway girl said something dreadful, brutal: 'If they go on like this, men are going to have to get used to us. Soon most women are going to look like me, if they don't die. And wouldn't that be nice? A new kind of beauty.'"[26]

And so it begins, soon after the mother and daughter die from their injuries. Women burn themselves on ritual pyres in the company of other women, who whisk them out of the flames to secret hospitals and clinics to recover, in order to relieve one another of the burden of being alone, singular, exceptional. Is such burning any more violent than what has been done, is being done? Against the thinness of love in romance, or the lie of safety in the state, such burnings accuse patriarchy of being a catastrophe and the law, a crisis. So, they burn to make a decision, to create something beautiful from terror, including love for another. This promise of *a new kind of beauty* makes a noncoercive collectivity of Burning Women—a you, a me, an us, that do not exist prior to the pledge that performs this self-constitution. What emerges are clandestine webs of care that are called *crimes* by authorities seeking to stamp them out, and a refusal to disappear or to hide, to instead haunt the daylight—in the supermarkets, bar terraces, and buses. As one of the women declares, "Burnings are the work of men. They have always burned us. Now we are burning ourselves. But we are not going to die, we're going to flaunt our scars."[27] This new kind of beauty offers no relief from the political, but it does inaugurate another kind of relief in coming together. To truly live beautifully we might seek the end of the world *as it is* in favor for another. "When would the longed-for world of men and monsters come?" Silvina asks, and the Burning Women would seem to answer, *We can make that world now*.[28]

To live finally, for the promise of beauty to become a politics against the police, we might turn to a life of crime. Starring drag muse Divine as the miscreant Dawn Davenport, John Waters's camp classic *Female Trouble* is another argument for speculative disorder and radical uncertainty. Driven by her hunger for beauty—to have it, to possess it—Dawn cannot find satisfaction in compulsory heterosexuality, suburban domesticity, or regular occupation. And, so moved, Dawn breaks laws of all kinds in order to feel life being furthered, defiant to the end even as she is sentenced to death by electric chair. While this is not the ending we might want, or indeed the path we might follow, to observe the film's avowal that *crime is beauty* is to propose that beauty—so often perceived as symmetry, harmony, or loveliness—might best fulfill its promise to transform the world when it defies the norms of a society that should not be defended.

What, then, can we ascertain from burning women and their beauty as a method? It might be riot or ruin, care or crime, but whatever we need to live finally is not now nurtured by the present order in which we find ourselves. Instead, where it gestures toward a nonpermanent, noncontractual understanding of a relation to justice, *crime is beauty* prefigures a future without foundations. *Crime is beauty* might promise to destroy our deathworld, or it might just feel closer to freedom than the life circumscribed by the laws, norms, and rhythms of another. *Crime is beauty* claims that beauty is a requirement for surviving the world as it is, but it cannot tell us what comes next. *Crime is beauty* disturbs the intelligibility of the world, but it also intensifies our vulnerability to its structural violence. *Crime is beauty* does not cohere as a normative end in itself but is rather an ongoing struggle to open an inquiry about who we could be, the beauty we deserve, and the politics on which these depend.

Do they owe us a living, Esther Brown? Because I would like to learn to live, finally. I'm not afraid anymore. Cover your face. We will win. There is still, absurdly, beauty here.

NOTES

Introduction

1   Miller, *Know My Name*, 133.
2   Miller, *Know My Name*, 138.
3   Miller, *Know My Name*, 308.
4   Rancière and Panagia, "Dissenting Words," 115; Chuh, *The Difference Aesthetics Makes*, 22.
5   Wynter, "Rethinking 'Aesthetics,'" 245.
6   Tompkins, "Sweetness, Capacity, Energy," 852.
7   Berlant and Stewart, *Hundreds*, 63.
8   Loy, "Gertrude Stein (Continued)," 429–30.
9   For instance, David Hume writes, "Beauty is no quality in things themselves: It exists merely in the mind which contemplates them; and each mind perceives a different beauty." "Essay XXIII: Of the Standard of Taste," 136. George Santayana echoes him: "In less technical language, Beauty is pleasure regarded as the quality of a thing." *Sense of Beauty*, 49.
10 Panagia, *Poetics of Political Thinking*, 72.
11 Plato, *Symposium*, 210a–12b, in Plato, *Dialogues of Plato*, quoted in Russo, *Problem of God*, 138–39.
12 Kant, *Critique of Judgment*, 296.

13 Murdoch, "Idea of Perfection," 40.

14 "Before the Light."

15 Vanita Reddy, *Fashioning Diaspora*, 6, 17.

16 Taussig, *Beauty and the Beast*, 5.

17 Foucault defines freedom as "never anything other . . . than an actual relation between governors and governed." See my book *The Gift of Freedom*, 6, 9.

18 Soofiya Andry writes: "Beauty is a country, a fascist state with violent borders, in which I can, at best, only ever be a tourist. I visit that country for fleeting moments, during which it doesn't feel so malicious. It's a country in which I cannot and will not live." Andry, "Deviant Bodies," 228.

19 Scarry, *On Beauty and Being Just*.

20 Arthur C. Danto, *Abuse of Beauty*, 160; Gigante, *Life*, 36.

21 Arendt, *Human Condition*, 12–13.

22 Chuh, *The Difference Aesthetics Makes*, 22.

23 Sedgwick, "Paranoid Reading and Reparative Reading," 128, 150–51.

24 Quoted in Hillary Brown, "Holocaust, Art, Chicago, and Sickness."

25 Moten and Hartman, "The Black Outdoors," 35:39 min. Personal communication with scholar and curator Thea Quiray Tagle, after she attended a reading by Ocean Vuong, 2019.

26 Egbuonu, "Beauty of Becoming."

27 See my book *The Gift of Freedom*.

28 Kant, *Observations*, 111.

29 See Gilmore, *Golden Gulag*, 28; Cheng, *Ornamentalism*; Morrison, *Bluest Eye*; Walker, *A Subtlety*.

30 Cottom, *Thick, and Other Essays*, 65; Roelofs, *Cultural Promise of the Aesthetic*, 30.

31 Shakespeare, *Romeo and Juliet*, 2.5.73–74. Reference is to act, scene, and lines.

32 Mingus, "Moving toward the Ugly."

33 Solnit, *Orwell's Roses*, 202–3.

34 Shakespeare, *Romeo and Juliet*, 2.5.83–84.

35 Canuel, *Justice, Dissent, and the Sublime*.

36 Adorno, "Cultural Criticism and Society," 34.

37 Dabashi, "Gaza."

38 Ngai, *Our Aesthetic Categories*.

39 Adorno writes that "beauty establishes a sphere of untouchability." Adorno, *Aesthetic Theory*, 51.

40. I am referring to two different films that take place in camps—*Green Dragon* and *Schindler's List*. I have written about the former in my book *The Gift of Freedom*.
41. Semaan, "What Self-Care Looks Like in a Refugee Camp."
42. Quoted in Solnit, *Orwell's Roses*, 192.
43. Manalansan, "*Biyuti* in Everyday Life," 155.
44. Manalansan, "*Biyuti* in Everyday Life," 168.
45. Diaz, "*Biyuti* from Below," 417.
46. Du Bois, "Of Beauty and Death," 132.
47. See Rancière, *Dissensus*.
48. Piper Kerman writes: "By the time I left prison, this stubborn practice of feminine arts seemed like a natural resistance to a system that worked hard to reduce you to a sexless number. Those rituals were not just for visitors or vanity, but a way to say, 'I am not just a prisoner; I am many more things. And I am going to get out of here one day and never forget who I am when I look in the mirror.'" Kerman, "Beauty behind Bars."
49. Quoted in in Tolentino, "The Year That Skin Care Became a Coping Mechanism."
50. Chuh, *The Difference Aesthetics Makes*, 74–75.
51. Perri, "A Thousand Years."
52. Nuttall, "Introduction: Rethinking Beauty," 28; Zuo, *Vulgar Beauty*, 11.
53. Stendahl, *On Love*, 55.
54. Adorno, *Aesthetic Theory*, 82.
55. DeVeaux, "Conversation with June Jordan," 102.
56. Scarry, *On Beauty and Being Just*, 46.
57. Bedi, "'Beauty Day.'"
58. Morrison, *Bluest Eye*, xi.
59. Barnard, "Place of Beauty," 106.
60. Nietzsche, *On the Genealogy of Morals*, 63.
61. Sara Ahmed, *Promise of Happiness*.
62. Roitman, *Anti-crisis*, 49.
63. Foucault, *History of Sexuality*, 141.
64. Nietzsche, *On the Genealogy of Morals*, 57, my italics.
65. The full quotation from Nietzsche: "The man who has his own independent, protracted will and the *right to make promises*—and in him a proud consciousness, quivering in every muscle, of *what* has at length been achieved and become flesh in him, a consciousness of his own power and freedom, a sensation of mankind come to completion.

This emancipated individual, with the actual *right* to make promises, this master of a *free* will, this sovereign man—how should he not be aware of his superiority over all those who lack the right to make promises and stand as their own guarantors, of how much trust, how much fear, how much reverence he arouses—he '*deserves*' all three—and of how this mastery over himself also necessarily gives him mastery over circumstances, over nature, and over all more short-willed and unreliable creatures? The 'free' man, the possessor of a protracted and unbreakable will, also possesses his *measure of value*: looking out upon others from himself, he honors or he despises; and just as he is bound to honor his peers, the strong and reliable (those with the *right* to make promises)—that is, all those who promise like sovereigns, reluctantly, rarely, slowly, who are chary of trusting." Nietzsche, *On the Genealogy of Morals*, 59–60.

66 Or, as Lauren Berlant puts it: "It is often said therefore that the desiring subject is well served by the formalism of desire: although desire is anarchic and restless, the objects to which desire becomes attached stabilize the subject and enable her to assume a stable-enough identity." Berlant, *Desire/Love*, 76.

67 Arendt, *Human Condition*, 237.

68 See Lowe, *Intimacies of Four Continents*.

69 Derrida, *Specters of Marx*, 89–90.

70 Derrida, *Other Heading*, 78

71 Berlant, *Cruel Optimism*.

72 See Beauchamp, *Going Stealth*; Bettcher, "Evil Deceivers and Make-Believers"; Stanley, *Atmospheres of Violence*.

73 Derrida, *Negotiations*, 362.

74 Fleishmann, *Time Is the Thing a Body Moves Through*, 25.

75 Shaviro, *Without Criteria*, 3.

76 This phrasing for presence, a "body occupying space," is attributed to Hans Ulrich Gumbrecht by Mechtild Widrich in their introductory remarks. Berthold, Urspring, and Widrich, *Presence*, 11.

77 Berlant, *Cruel Optimism*, 52.

78 Foucault, *Archaeology of Knowledge*, 28.

79 Loy, "Gertrude Stein (Continued)," 429–30.

80 Butler, *Gender Trouble*; Sicardi, "Queer Person's Guide to Feeling Beautiful."

81 Scarry, *On Beauty and Being Just*, 90.

82 Quoted in Gagnier, *Insatiability of Human Wants*, 64.

83 Tippi Hedren received the 2013 Legacy of Style Award from the nonprofit foundation Beauty Changes Lives, established by the American Associa-

tion of Cosmetology Schools to provide scholarships for hopeful students in the beauty and wellness industries. Tam Nguyen, president of the Los Angeles–based Advance Beauty College, which graduates thousands of Vietnamese nail technicians from its bilingual and in-language courses, readily acknowledges, "She's the Godmother of the nail industry." Morris, "How Tippi Hedren Made Vietnamese Refugees into Nail Salon Magnates."

84 Paik, *Rightlessness*, 129.

85 See Tiffany M. Gill's chapter "'Among the Things That Used to Be': Beauticians, Health Activism, and the Politics of Dignity in the Post–Civil Rights Era," in *Beauty Shop Politics*, 121–36.

86 This project ran from 2002 to 2006. See John Mallory Rose, "Process Evaluation of the North Carolina BEAUTY and Health Project."

87 About risk-reduction initiatives, Vincanne Adams and Stacy Leigh Pigg mark that such scientific object-making establishes biopolitical forms of governance with a moral divide between deviance and norms. See Pigg and Adams, "Introduction: The Moral Object of Sex."

88 Joseph, *Against the Romance of Community*, 2.

89 See also Diola, "In Photos."

90 Gill, *Beauty Shop Politics*, 129.

91 "He then judges not just for himself, but for everyone, and speaks of beauty as if it were a property of things. That is why he says: The *thing* is beautiful, and does not count on other people to agree with him in his judgment of liking on the ground that he has repeatedly found them agreeing with him; rather he *demands* that they agree. He reproaches them if they judge differently, and denies that they have taste, which he nevertheless demands of them as something they ought to have. In view of this [*sofern*], we cannot say that everyone has his own particular taste." Kant, *Critique of Judgment*, 56.

92 Nehamas, *Only a Promise of Happiness*, 76–77.

93 Berlant, *Cruel Optimism*, 54.

94 James Thompson, *Performance Affects*, 154.

95 Quoted in Rich, "Spoils of War Coverage."

96 See Canuel, *Justice, Dissent, and the Sublime*.

97 Ferlinghetti, *Coney Island of the Mind*, 88.

98 Solnit, *Orwell's Roses*, 209.

99 Avery F. Gordon, *Ghostly Matters*.

100 Bruno Maçães (@MacaesBruno), 2023, "Another Israeli Minister calling for the complete destruction of Gaza, replacing it with beach condos. A current minister, Amichai Eliyahu." Twitter, November 2, 2023, 4:53 a.m. https://twitter.com/MacaesBruno/status/1720016201672278401.

A screenshot is attached of a Facebook post by Eliyahu with the translated text: "North of the Strip, beautiful as ever. Blow up and flatten everything. Simply a delight for the eyes. (A soldier in Gaza) We need to talk about the day after. In my spirit's eyes we give out plots to all those who have fought for Gaza over the years and to the evicted from Gush Katif—Inc. (Without dimension)." These words appear above a photograph of a bombed-out structure in occupied Gaza under a hazy blue sky.

101 Barghouti, "You and I." Thank you to Eman Ghanayem for introducing me to this poet.

102 Wilk, "Connections and Contradictions," 217.

103 Quoted in A. R. Williams, "ISIS Smashes Priceless, Ancient Statues."

104 US Department of State, "State Department Launches Global Cultural Initiative."

105 Mothersill, *Beauty Restored*, 277.

106 Hauser, *Mirror, Mirror on the Wall*, xii.

107 See Wendy Brown, *Walled States, Waning Sovereignty*.

108 Martyn Smith, "Why Write Beautifully about Climate Crisis?"

109 Abbas, "In Terror, in Love," 504.

110 Hawkins, "Brian Williams Is 'Guided by the Beauty of Our Weapons' in Syria Strikes." Walter Benjamin warns that Fascism renders a politics of self-alienation aesthetic, such that we might find pleasure in our own destruction. "The Work of Art in the Age of Mechanical Reproduction," 252.

111 Arundhati Roy, *End of Imagination*, 63.

112 Rodriguez, "Migration Is Beautiful Artist's Statement."

113 Hartman, *Wayward Lives, Beautiful Experiments*.

114 Derrida, *Rogues*, 11.

115 Quoted in Nash, "Writing Black Beauty," 111; the original is Gebara, "Yearning for Beauty."

116 Eco, *Infinity of Lists*, 117.

117 Donoghue, *Speaking of Beauty*, 25.

118 Scarry, *On Beauty and Being Just*, 103; Eco, *History of Beauty*.

119 Gebara, "Yearning for Beauty," 24–25; Lefebvre, *Missing Pieces*.

120 Vuong, *On Earth We're Briefly Gorgeous*, 137–38; Cooper Jones, *Easy Beauty*, 270.

121 Berlant, *Cruel Optimism*, 10.

122 "Spaces of dissension" is from Foucault, *Archaeology of Knowledge*, 152.

123 Scarry, *On Beauty and Being Just*, 3, 5.

124 Burke, *Reflections on the Revolution in France*, 172; Nguyen Cat Tuong quoted in Nguyễn Ngạc and Nguyễn Văn Luận, *Un siècle d'histoire de la robe des Vietnamiennes*, 52–53 (my translation and italics).

125 Ngai, *Our Aesthetic Categories*.

126 McClanahan, *Dead Pledges*.

127 Rancière, *Philosopher and His Poor*, 226.

128 Chuh, *The Difference Aesthetics Makes*.

129 Lowe, *Intimacies of Four Continents*; Grewal and Kaplan, *Scattered Hegemonies*.

130 Berlant and Stewart, *Hundreds*, 15.

Chapter 1. The Beautiful, Finding Itself in Danger, Desires Its Copy

1 Vuong, *On Earth We're Briefly Gorgeous*, 138.

2 Vuong, *On Earth We're Briefly Gorgeous*, 138–39.

3 Sartwell, *Six Names of Beauty*, 4.

4 Du Bois, "Of Beauty and Death," 130.

5 Foucault, *Archaeology of Knowledge*, 127.

6 Scarry, *On Beauty and Being Just*, 3.

7 Nguyen's introduction of the darted bodice to the once-loose ao dai (his most significant contribution to its silhouette, alongside flared trousers) required a particular body to go with the modern invention of a national dress (notably, he also suggested exercises for young Vietnamese women to become taller and bustier). These changes also required a brassiere or corset and were paired with high heels. This Vietnamese New Woman also sported some of the more iconic visual elements of this figuration across the globe, such as bobbed hair, painted lips, and an elongated body.

8 Nguyễn Ngạc and Nguyễn Văn Luận, *Un siecle d'histoire de la robe des Vietnamiennes*, 52–53 (my translation and italics). His defense was also subject to critique at the time, as some found his aesthetic sensibilities too French to be properly nationalist.

9 Martina Thucnhi Nguyen, "Wearing Modernity," 76. Nguyen's article provides a thorough English-language discussion of Lemur's designs.

10 Lieu, *American Dream in Vietnamese*, 61. Lieu cites the cohost of the Hoa Hau Ao Dai pageant in Long Beach, California, whose comments at the start of the 1996 pageant, on the occasion of the twenty-year anniversary of the war's ending, are a direct address to fellow refugees: "Much has changed as a result of the Vietnamese migration overseas, but the ao dai forever remains the same, like our love for freedom and democracy and our love for the homeland of Vietnam." Lieu, "Remembering 'The

10   Nation' through Pageantry," 127. See also Shirley Jennifer Lim, *Feeling of Belonging*, for more on Asian American beauty pageants in the Cold War–era United States.
11   Quoted in Leshkowich, "Fashioning the Field in Vietnam," 130.
12   Áo Dài Day, Senate Resolution No. 73.
13   Berlant, *Cruel Optimism*, 64.
14   See my book *The Gift of Freedom*, Jodi Kim's *Ends of Empire*, and Lisa Yoneyama's *Cold War Ruins*, as just some examples about this narrativization of the Cold War.
15   The Art Workers' Coalition was a group of New York artist-activists who designed this poster in 1970 after the atrocities committed by US soldiers in 1968 in the My Lai massacre came to public attention. Ron Haeberle, a US Army photographer, took the photograph, while the phrase "And babies" came from a news interview with Paul Meadlo, a soldier who had participated in the massacre.
16   See, for example, Long T. Bui, *Returns of War*; Espiritu, *Body Counts*; Phuong Tran Nguyen, *Becoming Refugee American*; Ong, *Buddha Is Hiding*; Um, *From the Land of Shadows*; Vang, *History on the Run*.
17   Vinh Nguyen, "Refugeetude," 110, 111; Gandhi, *Archipelago of Resettlement*, 2; Trung Phan Quoc Nguyen, "Labor of Absolution."
18   Semaan, "What Self-Care Looks Like in a Refugee Camp."
19   Vuong, *On Earth We're Briefly Gorgeous*, 231.
20   Spivak, *The Post-colonial Critic*, 138–39.
21   Koselleck, *The Practice of Conceptual History*; Roitman, *Anti-crisis*, 20.
22   Roitman, *Anti-crisis*, 8.
23   Roitman, *Anti-crisis*, 41.
24   Sharpe, "Beauty Is a Method."
25   Vuong, *On Earth We're Briefly Gorgeous*, 231.
26   Parker et al., *Nationalisms and Sexualities*, 13–14.
27   Moallem, *Between Warrior Brother and Veiled Sister*, 62 (my italics).
28   See Steyerl, "In Defense of the Poor Image."
29   See Duc and Bao, "Aesthetic Sense of the Vietnamese."
30   Ann Marie Leshkowich has written extensively about the ao dai as a national symbol. See, for instance, Leshkowich, "Ao Dai Goes Global."
31   In this I follow Scarry, who writes, "Beauty brings copies of itself into being. It makes us draw it, take photographs of it, or describe it to other people. Sometimes it gives rise to exact replication and other times to resemblances and still other times to things whose connection to the original sense of inspiration is unrecognizable." Scarry, *On Beauty and Being Just*, 3.

32 For an examination of the US-based Vietnamese diasporic entertainment industry, see Lieu, *American Dream in Vietnamese.*

33 Steyerl, "In Defense of the Poor Image."

34 See, for instance, Hilderbrand, *Inherent Vice.*

35 Mydans, "Miss Saigon, U.S.A."

36 Derrida, *Of Grammatology*, 144–45.

37 Derrida, *Of Grammatology*, 315.

38 Derrida, *Of Grammatology*, 142.

39 Steyerl, "In Defense of the Poor Image."

40 See Wong, *Van Gogh on Demand.*

41 Kracauer, *Mass Ornament*, 56–57.

42 For instance, Ann Caddell Crawford authored *Customs and Culture of Vietnam* while in the country with her husband, a US Army officer assigned to the Military Assistance Command. One of the first guides penned for readers among the thousands of troops and command and support workforce for the American intercession, Crawford opens her chapter titled "The People" with the image of the "smiling faces of countless children, and the lovely fragile-looking women in their flowing dresses reminiscent of butterflies." She continues, "Often, girls can be seen riding along the streets of Saigon on motor bikes with the back of their ao dai flying loose, causing foreigners to comment that they look like butterflies, and beautiful ones at that." Crawford, *Customs and Culture of Vietnam*, 51.

43 Nguyen T. Tan-Hoang, *Cover Girl.* Also, Nhi Lieu observes that live shows and video performances rarely feature "new" compositions, writing, "Songs are often recycled and sung by multiple artists on different recordings to display the talents of the artists rather than the artistry of the songs themselves." Lieu, *American Dream in Vietnamese*, 90.

44 Tongson, "Empty Orchestra," 98.

45 These and other lines spoken, and then repeated, come from Mydans's "Miss Saigon, U.S.A." This particular quote came from Yen Do, the editor of the Vietnamese-language newspaper *Nguoi Viet Daily News* in Westminster.

46 Nealon, *Alterity Politics*, 108.

47 Indeed, Kant argued that "clarification by examples" belongs to the "analytic of the beautiful." Shaviro, *Without Criteria*, 14.

48 Derrida, *Specters of Marx*, 34.

49 As Nealon usefully notes, "The example always inscribes or attests to an other at the heart of the same, always points to the 'one more' that can be grafted onto any seemingly static chain." Nealon, *Alterity Politics*, 94.

50   Deleuze, *Cinema 1*, 95.
51   Johnson, "Writing," 39.
52   Foucault, *Archaeology of Knowledge*, 21.
53   On the blog of Vietnamese American vocalist Thien Phu: "[Dalena's] performance of *Nguoi Yeu Co Don* was nothing short of flawless. She sounded completely like a native Vietnamese speaker when she sang that song. I couldn't get over it. I even had doubts that she was not Vietnamese, despite how she had blonde hair, looked all-American and sounded every bit like a native when she spoke in English." He continues, "The more famous she got, it seemed the more her Vietnamese fans would be buzzing about raising quite a bit of controversy which had everyone asking a certain question about Dalena: Is she or isn't she really Vietnamese? Even after an interview she had done on Little Saigon Television where Quynh Trang flat out asked her the question, 'Dalena, are you Amerasian?' and she answered with a no explaining how both her parents are Anglo-American, the general public was still not satisfied." Phu, "Thien Phu Sets Record Straight for Colleague."
54   My thanks to Christine Mok, who reminded me of Plato's *Ion*, a dialogue in which Socrates ponders whether a poet—a particular poet, but perhaps also any poet—performs from skill and knowledge, or by virtue of divine possession. Plato, *Statesman. Philebus. Ion.*, 534b–d.
55   Despite such mystical recourse, Dalena has described the multiple steps of her process to an interviewer, including translating lyrics from Vietnamese to English to better grasp their feeling.
56   Foucault, *Archaeology of Knowledge*, 120.
57   Benjamin, "Work of Art in the Age of Its Technological Reproducibility," 13.
58   Manning, *Minor Gesture*, 135.
59   In the essay on which this chapter is based, I pursue the pinup as the erotic figuration of the young woman in the beautiful dress. Mimi Thi Nguyen, "Diasporic Erotic."
60   As I write elsewhere, "The [*Ao Trang*] calendar sheds light on a shared dimension of diasporic works. In the spatialization and temporalization of love and loss, we find an erotic aesthetics of partial presence and ambiguous pleasure." Mimi Thi Nguyen, "Diasporic Erotic," 71.
61   For more, see Mimi Thi Nguyen, "Diasporic Erotic."
62   Berlant, *Female Complaint*, 14.
63   Barthes, *Camera Lucida*, 10.
64   Barthes, *Camera Lucida*, 13.
65   Schafer, "Romance Lives."

66 Barthes, *Camera Lucida*, 7.
67 Barthes, *Camera Lucida*, 12.
68 Barthes, *Camera Lucida*, 81.
69 Marks, "Loving a Disappearing Image," 98.
70 Marks, "Loving a Disappearing Image," 97.
71 Judith Brown, *Glamour in Six Dimensions*, 7.
72 Judith Brown, *Glamour in Six Dimensions*, 96.
73 The white ao dai is in these photographs an experience of surface, but in others it is an experience of transparency. While cruising ao dai on Pinterest, I found a genre of photographs featuring buxom Vietnamese women in white ao dai and colored panties, clearly visible through the thin silk. These photographs of nearly transparent ao dai tease the unimpeded view.
74 Nostalgia's formerly spatial dimension (a longing for a place) was gradually compounded by a temporal dimension (a desire to return to a lost time). Bliss Cua Lim, *Translating Time*, 159.
75 Quoted in Schafer, "Romance Lives."
76 Hoai Nam, phone interview with the author, January 2012.
77 Derrida, *Specters of Marx*, 10.
78 Chow, *Primitive Passions*, 145.
79 Chow, *Primitive Passions*, 180.
80 Benjamin, "Theses on the Philosophy of History," 255.
81 Bergson, *Time and Free Will*, 182.
82 Arfaoui, "Time and the Colonial State," 27.
83 The grid as the calendar form is no "natural" operation. Rosalind Krauss observes, "The grid's mythic power is that it makes us able to think we are dealing with materialism (or sometimes science, or logic) while at the same time it provides us with a release into belief (or illusion, or fiction)." Krauss, *Originality of the Avant-Garde*, 12.
84 Krauss, *Originality of the Avant-Garde*, 12.
85 See also Perkins, *Reform of Time*.
86 Here I refer to the 1999 collection *Between Woman and Nation*, coedited by Kaplan, Alarcón, and Moallem.
87 Ko, "Jazzing into Modernity," 142.
88 Eng and Kazanjian, "Introduction," 13.
89 These photographs are part of another associative chain that includes Shakespeare's Ophelia, a young beauty whose madness led to her drowning. I am reminded of Elisabeth Bronfen, who writes, "The death of a

beautiful woman emerges as the requirement for a preservation of existing cultural norms and values." Bronfen, *Over Her Dead Body*, 181.

90 Throughout the 1980s and early 1990s, some Asian states called for their border patrols to refuse to allow the Vietnamese onto land, lest they become responsible for the refugees, even as international humanitarian organizations sought them out for rescue. United Nations High Command for Refugees, "Flight from Indochina," 86. See also Lipman, *In Camps*. I look at other refugee images of this deadly passage in my book *The Gift of Freedom*.

91 Bliss Cua Lim, *Translating Time*, 156.

92 Barthes, *Camera Lucida*, 84.

93 Freeman, *Beside You in Time*.

94 Marks, "Loving a Disappearing Image," 95.

95 Berlant, "Love, a Queer Feeling," 434.

96 Marks, "Loving a Disappearing Image," 96.

97 Cadava, *Words of Light*, 8.

98 Foucault, *Archaeology of Knowledge*, 120.

99 This is, as observed in the third chapter, the premise of what Rachmi Diyah Larasati names the *replica dancer* in postgenocide Indonesia. See Larasati, *Dance That Makes You Vanish*.

100 Bui and Przybysz, preface to *Ao Dai*, 1.

101 Treen, introduction to *Ao Dai*, 3.

102 Jennifer A. González, citing the curator Susan Vogel: "Recognizing that the physical setting of an object is part of what makes it identifiable as art, the installation showed art objects and non-art objects in such a way as to raise the question in the viewer's mind and to make the trickery of the installation evident." González, *Subject to Display*, 66.

103 From BN Magazine, a defunct "Vietnamese lifestyle and business magazine" for Vietnamese Americans. Michelle Man, April 1, 2006, "Ao Dai: A Modern Design Coming of Age." Accessed July 15, 2006, http://bnmagazine.com/article_detail.php?art_id=197.

104 In *Beauty Regimes*, Genevieve Clutario notes that the terno too might "take on outside styles and influences while still retaining Filipino identity," 199.

105 Chow, *Age of the World Target*, 46.

106 Deleuze, *Difference and Repetition*, 24.

107 Krauss, *Originality of the Avant Garde*, 157.

108 Ngai, *Ugly Feelings*, 152.

109 See Diaz, *Confetti of Ordinary Dreams*; Gopinath, *Impossible Desires*.

110 Even without "bad" examples, the ao dai solicits a classic fetish through which the operation of eroticism suggests the unseen whole—regard the promised glimpse of flesh above the waistline, below the split seam. Armus, "'Put on Some Pants'"; Agrawal, "Meet Siew Pui Yi."

111 Stewart, *On Longing*, 135.

Chapter 2. An Education in Beauty (and the Necessity of Lawlessness)

1 George W. Bush, "Remarks to the Warsaw Conference."

2 US Department of State, Bureau of Democracy, Human Rights and Labor, *Report on the Taliban's War against Women*.

3 Laura Bush, "Radio Address by Mrs. Bush." Also cited in Abu-Lughod, "Do Muslim Women Really Need Saving?," 784–85.

4 Rucker and Costa, "'It's a Hard Problem.'"

5 Stanfill, "Fashion or Folly?"

6 Hirschkind and Mahmood, "Feminism, the Taliban, and Politics of Counter-insurgency," 353.

7 I argue this in my article "The Hoodie as Sign."

8 Butler, *Precarious Life*, 148. See also Fassin, *Humanitarian Reason*; Moyn, *Last Utopia*; Kramer, "Camera and the Burqa"; Ayotte and Husain, "Securing Afghan Women."

9 "The beauty of the arrangement" is from Adam Smith's *The Theory of Moral Sentiments*, quoted in Ryan, "'The Beauty of That Arrangement,'" 110.

10 Foucault, *History of Sexuality*, 94–95.

11 Hickey, *Invisible Dragon*, 24.

12 Colebrook, "Introduction," 134; Fassin, "Humanitarianism as a Politics of Life," 501.

13 As Charles Hirschkind and Saba Mahmood observe, "The rhetoric works something like this: a society in which women can't wear mini-skirts is also against adult suffrage; an equitable distribution of wealth demands kissing in public; eating bacon sandwiches (that is, pork) equips one to enjoy literature and movies. In other words, those who have increasingly come to see Islam as important to their lives, their politics, and their forms of public expression . . . are destined to live within authoritarian, intolerant, and misogynist societies." Hirschkind and Mahmood, "Feminism, the Taliban and the Politics of the Counter-insurgency," 350.

14 Mimi Thi Nguyen, *Gift of Freedom*.

15 Roitman, *Anti-crisis*.

16 Atanasoski, *Humanitarian Violence*, 14.

17 Nussbaum, *Women and Human Development*, 104.

18 Lowe, *Intimacies of Four Continents*, 112.
19 Mimi Thi Nguyen, *Gift of Freedom*.
20 Atanasoski, *Humanitarian Violence*, 14.
21 Dudziak, *War Time*, 22 (my italics).
22 Here I am writing sideways from transitional justice, a concept that I consider for a moment in the next chapter, which posits the necessary forms of justice—such as truth and reconciliation commissions, or trials—that are required in the aftermath of an authoritarian regime and the transition to another.
23 Authorization for Use of Military Force.
24 Scott, *Omens of Adversity*, 139.
25 Wintour, "Editor's Letter," 88.
26 Khalili, *Time in the Shadows*.
27 Moallem, *Between Warrior Brother and Veiled Sister*, 161.
28 Wynter, "Unsettling the Coloniality of Being/Power/Truth/Freedom."
29 Kant, *Observations*, 113.
30 Kant, *Observations*, 112–13.
31 See chapter 1 of *Home and Harem* for Inderpal Grewal's discussion of the aesthetics of empire and of Burke's *Philosophical Inquiry into the Origin of Our Ideas of the Sublime and the Beautiful* (1757). For Arthur Danto, see *Abuse of Beauty*, 33. For the *Los Angeles Times* article, see Chocano, "Joy in Good Hair Days."
32 Stuart, "Beauty and the Burqa."
33 Consider the repeated emphasis in the Western news media that the 9/11 hijackers believed they were to receive multiple virgins in heaven, and other related discourses linking Islam with gender and sexual nonnormativity. See Puar and Rai, "Monster, Terrorist, Fag."
34 Leila Ahmed, *Women and Gender in Islam*, 152.
35 See Hirschkind and Mahmood, "Feminism, the Taliban and the Politics of the Counterinsurgency."
36 See also my essay "The Hoodie as Sign."
37 Sara Ahmed, *Queer Phenomenology*, 87.
38 Bourdieu, *Distinction*, 56.
39 Nir, "The War Is Fake."
40 Nir, "The War Is Fake."
41 Leila Ahmed, *Women and Gender in Islam*, 151.
42 See Moallem, *Between Warrior Brother and Veiled Sister*.

43 Slaughter, *Human Rights, Inc.* Some of these biographies and memoirs include Sally Armstrong, *Veiled Threat: The Hidden Power of the Women of Afghanistan* (New York: Four Walls Eight Windows, 2002); Cheryl Benard in cooperation with Edit Schlaffer, *Veiled Courage: Inside the Afghan Women's Resistance* (New York: Broadway, 2002); Anne E. Brodsky, *With All Our Strength: The Revolutionary Association of the Women of Afghanistan* (New York: Routledge, 2003); Ergun Mehmet Caner, ed., *Voices behind the Veil: The World of Islam through the Eyes of Women* (Grand Rapids, MI: Kregel, 2003); Melody Ermachild Chavis, *Meena: Heroine of Afghanistan* (New York: St. Martin's, 2003); Jan Goodwin, *Price of Honor: Muslim Women Lift the Veil of Silence on the Islamic World*, rev. ed. (New York: Plume, 2003); Daphne Grace, *The Woman in the Muslin Mask: Veiling and Identity in Postcolonial Literature* (London: Pluto, 2004); Latifa, with Hachemi, *My Forbidden Face*; Harriet Logan, *Unveiled: Voices of Women in Afghanistan* (New York: HarperCollins, 2002); Azar Nafisi, *Reading Lolita in Tehran: A Memoir in Books* (New York: Random House, 2003); "Sulima" and "Hala" as told to Batya Swift Yasgur, *Behind the Burqa: Our Life in Afghanistan and How We Escaped to Freedom* (Hoboken, NJ: Wiley, 2002); Jean Sasson, *Mayada, Daughter of Iraq: One Woman's Survival under Saddam Hussein* (London: Doubleday, 2003); and Zoya, with Follain and Cristofari, *Zoya's Story*.

44 McLarney, "Burqa in Vogue," 3.

45 Harrison, "Beneath the Veil."

46 Reed, "Extreme Makeover," 465.

47 "In an interview with a journalist critical of the diktat, she said that she had never worn a burqa before, that it made her terribly unhappy, and that she felt restricted and bound. 'I used to go to the beauty parlour regularly,' she said plaintively, 'but now I don't have to bother about my face.' This statement is also put in a bold blurb across the article, so that it is what first strikes the reader—the poignancy of a young girl declaring sadly that she no longer has to bother about her face because she has been imprisoned inside a burqa." Menon, "Between the Burqa and the Beauty Parlor?," 209.

48 Reed, "Extreme Makeover," 469.

49 US Department of State, *Report on the Taliban's War against Women*.

50 Lacayo, "About Face," 36.

51 As Gillian Whitlock, writing about these "recent life narratives from Afghanistan," begins her essay, "What does one do but recoil at the sight of the *burqa* on the cover of Latifa's life narrative *My Forbidden Face*?" Whitlock, "Skin of the *Burqa*," 54.

52 Latifa with Hachemi, *My Forbidden Face*, 40–41.

53 Zoya, with Follain and Cristofari, *Zoya's Story*, 209.

54 It is worth observing Chandra Talpade Mohanty's caution, that "the mere proliferation of Third World women's texts, in the West at least, owes as much to the relations of the marketplace as to the conviction to 'testify' or 'bear witness.'" She goes on: "The existence of Third World women's narratives in itself is not evidence of decentering hegemonic histories and subjectivities. It is the way in which they are read, understood, located institutionally that is of paramount importance." Mohanty, *Feminism without Borders*, 77–78.

55 Feminist Majority Foundation Blog, "V-Day 2001."

56 Alcoff and Gray, "Survivor Discourse," 260.

57 Feminist Majority Foundation Blog, "V-Day 2001."

58 Gonzalez, *Empire's Mistress*, 55.

59 Feminist Majority Foundation Online Store, archived February 13, 2004, at the Internet Archive, https://web.archive.org/web/20040213034514/http://www.feminist.org/store/ProductGift.asp. This item, of course, is no longer available.

60 Gonzalez, *Empire's Mistress*, 55.

61 Gardner, "Lifting the Veil on Women's Subjugation."

62 Di Giovanni, "Beneath the Burqa," 254.

63 Timothy Williams and Mohammad, "What Not to Wear, Baghdad-Style."

64 Flintoff, "In Baghdad, Hemlines Rise as Violence Falls."

65 Flintoff, "In Baghdad, Hemlines Rise as Violence Falls."

66 Evans and Reid, *Resilient Life*, 109.

67 Whitlock, "Skin of the *Burqa*," 72.

68 Williams, *The Divided World*, xx.

69 Abu-Lughod, "Do Muslim Women Really Need Saving?"

70 Mermin, *The Beauty Academy of Kabul*.

71 The beauty school summons Lauren Berlant's intimate public, which "collaborates with a sentimental account of a social world as an affective space where people ought to be legitimated because they have feelings and there is an intelligence to what they feel that *knows* something about the world, that, if it were listened to, could make things better." Berlant, *Female Complaint*, 2.

72 The Kabul Beauty School emerged at the increasingly familiar convergence of fashion and philanthropy. See Mimi Thi Nguyen, "Biopower of Beauty."

73 Redfield, "Doctors, Borders, and Life in Crisis," 331.

74 From the now defunct Beauty without Borders website, accessed October 2003, http://www.heavenspa.com/clientmanager/Live/Sites/index.asp?CID=194.

75 As I have observed elsewhere, the Kabul Beauty School exemplifies the convergence of neoliberal rationality and global feminisms, through which new governmentalized regimes of welfare work are implemented to substitute for or to augment state powers. After the American invasion of Afghanistan, and with the Bush administration's adoption of women's rights as the humanitarian component of its military operations, Feminist Majority president Eleanor Smeal stated triumphantly, "We will never again think of ourselves as unable to affect foreign policy." With its Coalition to End Gender Apartheid in Afghanistan (supported by Mavis Leno, the late-night host's wife), Amy Farrell and Patrice McDermott remark, "the Feminist Majority positioned itself as the primary force behind the shift of U.S. policy toward the Taliban, pointing out the largely unrecognized work it had done since the late 1990s to alert the United States, particularly the president's office, to the plight of Afghan women and the horrors of the Taliban." Farrell and McDermott, "Claiming Afghan Women," 42–43.

76 Nelson, "A $1M Bad Hair Day in Kabul."

77 Plato, *Symposium*, 55.

78 Smith, *Theory of Moral Sentiments*, 216–17; Schiller, *On the Aesthetic Education of Man*.

79 Mill, *Inaugural Address*, 94–95.

80 Rushdie, "Fighting the Forces of Invisibility."

81 Where abandoning beauty is understood as a moral and ethical failure, the humanities—in other words, the core of an aesthetic education—is construed as heartless without a commitment to beauty, and without beauty the humanities has no usable future, only critique (including the dread "historical difference" or "cultural critique"), which is decried as repetitive, instrumentalist, paranoid, or ugly. For decades, right-wing critics have argued that "theory" and "identity" have corrupted literary and other aesthetic studies, displacing canons and masters in an uncivil disruption of our civilizational order. But from another flank comes a defense. Marxism and poststructuralism, as Alexander Dick and Christina Lupton condense from Elaine Scarry's characterization of their prohibitions, only see beauty as "a form of deflection from structural critique" or a "form of violence done to the object being viewed" (Dick and Lupton, "On Lecturing and Being Beautiful," 116). Thus beauty has been banished, much to the detriment of humanists. (In her 2005 academic satire called *On Beauty*, Zadie Smith associates the abuse of or inattentiveness to beauty with moral failure and intellectual poverty. See also Arthur C. Danto's *The Abuse of Beauty* for another defense against the "politicized" humanities.) These accusations denounce politics as too deterministic or oversystematized, and critique as too fracturing and disenchanting, to capture the promise of beauty as a moral disposition and ethical engagement with life.

82 Scarry, *On Beauty and Being Just*, 81.

83 Scarry, *On Beauty and Being Just*, 123.

84 Scarry, *On Beauty and Being Just*, 28, 31.

85 According to Elaine Scarry, the appreciation of a beautiful thing, especially the beautiful thing we did not at first grant the benefit of being beautiful, "ignites the desire for truth by giving us, with an electric brightness shared by almost no other uninvited, freely arriving perceptual event, the experience of conviction and the experience, as well, of error." Scarry, *On Beauty and Being Just*, 52.

86 Barnard, "Place of Beauty," 106.

87 Scarry, *On Beauty and Being Just*, 110, 97.

88 Fabian, *Time and the Other*, 31.

89 di Giovanni, "Beneath the Burqa," 254.

90 Scarry, *On Beauty and Being Just*, 97.

91 Scarry, *On Beauty and Being Just*, 93.

92 Scarry, *On Beauty and Being Just*, 97.

93 Scarry, *On Beauty and Being Just*, 100–101.

94 In an odd example, she also names the Greek trireme ships as beautiful, manned by the state's need for "a large navy of relatively poor but free citizens," whose arrangements as oarsmen in symmetrical lines is beautiful, which hardly sounds just. Scarry, *On Beauty and Being Just*, 102–3, 100, 104.

95 Gagnier, *Insatiability of Human Wants*, 4.

96 Scarry, *On Beauty and Being Just*, 114.

97 Scarry, *On Beauty and Being Just*, 5.

98 See, for instance, Emma Tarlo's *Clothing Matters* or Clare Sears's *Arresting Dress*.

99 Levinas, *Ethics and Infinity*, 97, 119.

100 While a 2010 French law banned "the concealment of the face in public," rather than directly prohibiting the wearing of the niqab, the law allowed leeway for motorcyclists, fencers, skiers, and carnivalgoers, among other non-Muslim exceptions. The irony of the French ban is that the niqab does not offer self-concealment at all; with the number of Muslim women who cover their faces hovering at less than a hundredth of a percent of the population, to be so covered in public is to stand out and draw attention. In public comments, President Nicolas Sarkozy clarified that the law is specific to Muslim veiling, with the presumption that veiling is religious coercion and therefore a rights violation. Even in the midst of the COVID-19 global pandemic, France (under another president)

mandated masks but did not unban Islamic face coverings. McAuley, "France Mandates Masks."

101 Moallem, *Between Warrior Brother and Veiled Sister*, 186. She is referring to di Giovanni, "Beneath the Burqa."

102 As Rey Chow suggests, "'Subjectivity' becomes a way to change the defiled image, the stripped image, the image-reduced-to-nakedness, by showing the truth behind/beneath/around it." Chow, *Writing Diaspora*, 29.

103 Stuelke, *Ruse of Repair*, 17.

104 Foucault, "Subject and Power," 221.

105 Elias, *Civilizing Process*, 202, 257.

106 Bourdieu, *Outline of a Theory of Practice*. Jennifer Craik elaborates on its prescription: "Body trainings create certain possibilities (such as special skills, knowledges, physical disciplines), impose constraints (such as not spitting, not slouching, not being naked) in the process of acquiring a range of body habits that are expected and taken for granted in a particular cultural milieu." Craik, *Face of Fashion*, 4.

107 Foucault, *History of Sexuality*, 123.

108 Lowe, *Intimacies of Four Continents*, 112.

109 Raymundo, "Beauty Regimens, Beauty Regimes," 104.

110 An aesthetic education, as Paul Bolin and Kaela Hoskings describe it, aims to guide its pupils to "develop a sense of appreciation and 'good taste,'" "increase vocational possibilities and contribute to the workforce," "grow in their independent and divergent thinking," "discover and develop their artistic talents," and "cultivate and express a sense of beauty." Bolin and Hoskings, "Reflecting on Our Beliefs and Actions," 41.

111 Clutario, *Beauty Regimes*.

112 Foucault, *Discipline and Punish*, 149.

113 Black, *Beauty Industry*, 74.

114 Halbfinger, "After the Veil, a Makeover Rush" (my italics).

115 Halbfinger, "After the Veil, a Makeover Rush."

116 Reed, "Extreme Makeover," 510.

117 Reed, "Extreme Makeover," 472. In interview after interview, the American volunteers speak about how the Afghan women need their skills and knowledge after a decade of Taliban rule; about their own "selfless service" and status as "pioneers" in the absence of a state, or any other entity, that can provide what is required.

118 Lei, "Rebuilding Afghanistan's Body and Soul."

119 Mermin, *The Beauty Academy of Kabul*.

120 In this model, PARSA, the organizational precursor to Beauty without Borders, recruited Afghan war widows into various cooperatives for textile and crafts export production. Progressive representations of such cooperatives, however, may reinforce the naturalization of craft labor to the position of the Third World native in late capitalism, and mystify the relations of production even as they are made visible as a part of the aura of the authentic commodity, which is rendered capable of creating social relationships across time and space.

121 Mermin, *The Beauty Academy of Kabul*.

122 Several of the school's teachers and organizers seem to imply that without their aid, their students would trade sex. Enrolling them in the school, Rodriguez further suggests, "gets them off the street so they can feed their families." Ghafour, "Afghans Flocking to Beauticians without Borders," 17.

123 Mahmood, *Politics of Piety*, 31 (my italics).

124 Roy, *Indian Traffic*, 39.

125 Shirley Jennifer Lim, *Feeling of Belonging*, 125.

126 Ghafour, "Afghans Flocking to Beauticians without Borders," 17.

127 Reed, "Extreme Makeover," 472.

128 Reed, "Extreme Makeover," 472.

129 Reed, "Extreme Makeover," 472.

130 Sara Ahmed, *Promise of Happiness*.

131 Ava Kim, "Trans Subterfuge."

132 Chow, *Entanglements*, 95.

133 The mosques, churches, and museums bombed and looted by the United States and Israel in Iraq and occupied Palestine, however, do not warrant condemnation from Western powers.

134 Steve Rose, "Here's What Could Be Lost."

135 See Paik, *Rightlessness*.

136 Mimi Thi Nguyen, "Biopower of Beauty."

137 Barker, "Change Was Merely Cosmetic."

138 Barker, "Change Was Merely Cosmetic."

139 Thanks are owed to the archivist Thera Webb, who sought to find any trace of these materials and found none.

140 Scott, *Omens of Adversity*, 7.

141 Landler, "20 Years On, the War on Terror Grinds Along, with No End in Sight."

142 Bhungalia, *Elastic Empire*, 164.

Chapter 3. The Right to Be Beautiful without Guarantee

1. For a comprehensive history of the wars in Cambodia, including the Pol Pot regime, see Kiernan, *Pol Pot Regime*.

2. As Rob Nixon observes, the personnel that mines are "anti" include the following: "An Afghan girl, late for school, who takes a short cut across a hill. A Vietnamese herder, dreaming of dinner, while rounding up his pigs. An Angolan peasant clambering down a riverbank to fill her water jug. A Laotian farmer, stooping to harvest his rice, who reaps blindness and amputation instead." Nixon, "Of Land Mines and Cluster Bombs," 164–65.

3. For those interested in the logistics of their participation, here are some details from the first Miss Landmine pageant. "The 18 contestants [in the Miss Landmine Angola pageant] were all willing participants, each representing their regions. Most were single with kids and were either unemployed or making do with 'survival jobs' such as street seller. Unlike contestants in a typical pageant, they were all sizes and shapes (one was even pregnant). They were paid for their time ($200 a day) as they worked with contest organizers to raise awareness of the global landmine threat, and many were offered employment by landmine aid organizations.... The winner also received $2500 and a variety of domestic appliances. The prizes were presented by Angola's First Lady, Ana Paula dos Santos." Bloul, "Ain't I a Woman?," 9.

4. A decade earlier, to show her support for demining operations, Princess Diana walked through an active Angolan minefield at a press event in 1997, months before her death in a car crash. Later, that year, 150 nations, excluding the United States and Iraq, signed the Ottawa Treaty, which banned the further manufacture, transfer, and use of mines—"weapons of indiscriminate effect."

5. Traavik, "Miss Landmine Angola."

6. The Ministry of Social Affairs ordered Traavik "to stop activity immediately in order to keep the honour and dignity of handicapped Cambodians, especially women." Bell, "Miss Landmine Beauty Pageant Banned in Cambodia." Since then, the Cambodian government has restricted the activities of international NGOs with barriers to assembly, restricting the right to Cambodian citizens only (though this right is highly curtailed as well, as protesters are often beaten and imprisoned with impunity). International Center for Not-for-Profit-Law, "Cambodia."

7. "This time, the winner (Dos Sopheap, 18) received a Norwegian custom-built prosthetic leg and $1000 cash to support her education. All candidates also received a cash prize of $300 each for their contributions to the Miss Landmine project, enabling them to invest in household goods or set up a small business in their home villages." Bloul, "Ain't I a Woman?," 10.

8   Sometimes this is practical; at Beddawi, one of the oldest and most densely populated refugee camps in Lebanon, a refugee aid organization testifies that beauty and cosmetology courses are its most popular job-training curriculum. Semaan, "What Self-Care Looks Like in a Refugee Camp."

9   See also Paik, *Rightlessness*.

10 Duffield, "Total War as Environmental Terror."

11 Hong, *Violent Peace*, 1.

12 Despite the International Convention on the Prohibition of Military or Any Other Hostile Use of Environmental Modification Techniques by the UN General Assembly, the United States continues to deploy such techniques, such as mountain blasting, fracking, and lead poisoning in pipelines, as forms of warfare, whether or not under the aegis of "military" actions. Consider, for example, the Dakota Access Pipeline or Flint, Michigan.

13 Chow, *Age of the World Target*, 36.

14 Fischer, "Haiti," 12, 1.

15 That so many of our technologies of repair follow from the uses of violence, with its accompanying cultivation of knowledge, is particularly relevant with regard to curative therapeutics and biomedical engineering, often sharing the same sets, experimental grounds, and scientific and other research vocabularies as war. See Terry, *Attachments to War*.

16 Schaffer and Smith, *Human Rights and Narrated Lives*, 1.

17 Or, more specifically, as Oliver P. Richmond and Jason Franks argue, "The *constitutional peace* rests upon the liberal Kantian argument that peace rests upon democracy, free trade and a set of cosmopolitan values that stem from the notion that individuals are ends in themselves, rather than means to an end." Richmond and Franks, "Liberal Hubris?," 29.

18 United Nations, Department of Public Information, *Agreements on a Comprehensive Political Settlement of the Cambodia Conflict*, 7–40, 46.

19 United Nations, Department of Public Information, *Agreements on a Comprehensive Political Settlement of the Cambodia Conflict*, 9.

20 Prime Minister Hun Sen, a former Khmer Rouge commander who escaped to Vietnam before the most fatal phase of the Pol Pot regime, has been in power since 1985. In 2023, he became president of the Senate after he resigned as prime minister and appointed his son as his successor. See, for instance, Human Rights Watch, "Cambodia"; or Karbaum, "Cambodia's Façade Democracy and European Assistance."

21 The United States has renewed calls for Cambodia to repay wartime debts incurred under the Lon Nol regime, now more than doubled to over $500 million with accrued interest. Even as US bombings devastated Cambodia's agricultural infrastructure, the United States made loans to

22. the regime to purchase agricultural commodities, "solving" the deficit the United States had imposed through punishing violence.
22. US Department of State, Bureau of Political-Military Affairs, "To Walk the Earth in Safety"; US Department of Justice, "Lawfulness of a Lethal Operation," sec. 1, par. 5.
23. The crimes committed by representatives of illiberal regimes are deemed to define the illiberal character of those regimes; not true for crimes committed by liberal ones. As well, we can observe that these wars in Southeast Asia were also "the start of a permanent war in U.S. culture that set into motion a range of military and economic activities across the Pacific including offshore procurement, the building of infrastructure, the training of armed forces, and the mobilization of civilian workers." Man, *Soldiering through Empire*, 8.
24. United Nations, Department of Public Information, *Agreements on a Comprehensive Political Settlement of the Cambodia Conflict*, 46. The remit for the tribunal has been criticized for being too narrowly conceived and cursorily pursued; some former commanders remain free despite warrants, and the tribunal has mismanaged (or possibly "disappeared") its operational funds, while rejecting hundreds of victim applications.
25. Schlund-Vials, *War, Genocide, and Justice*, 13.
26. Beech, "Khmer Rouge's Slaughter in Cambodia."
27. On redress culture and transitional justice, see, for instance, Yoneyama, *Cold War Ruins*.
28. Y-Dang Troeung writes in *Landbridge*, "I cannot cry enough tears for the closure that this trial does not bring. But what it does bring, the acknowledgement of our history, the evidence of our collective memories, I continue to carry" (183).
29. See Eap, "Contested Commemorations," and Chea, "This Is War."
30. My thanks to David Palumbo-Liu for this insight.
31. Samudzi, "Paradox of Recognition: Genocide and Colonialism."
32. See, for example, Meister, *After Evil*.
33. For instance, Lynn Hunt argues that the Universal Declaration of Human Rights is the necessary outcome of the American Declaration of Independence, the French Declaration of the Rights of Man and Citizen, and sentimental Victorian literature. Hunt, *Inventing Human Rights*.
34. Balfour and Cadava, "Claims of Human Rights," 277.
35. See, for instance, Barbara Harlow, who argues that the "thirty articles [of the Universal Declaration of Human Rights] translated the standard literary paradigm of individual versus society and the narrative conventions of emplotment and closure by mapping an identification of the individual

within a specifically international construction of rights and responsibilities. The Declaration, that is, can be read as recharting the trajectory and peripeties of the classic *bildungsroman*." Harlow, *Barred*, 252–53.

36   Angela Naimou writes, "The legal person—as a subject of certain rights and duties recognized before the law—is the originary legal fiction and the foundation of modern politics." Naimou, *Salvage Work*, 19. As Naimou points out, the language of rights creates the gap between the human and the person in order to disavow it. See also Esmeir, *Juridical Humanity*.

37   Paik, *Rightlessness*, 4.

38   Arendt, *Origins of Totalitarianism*, 291.

39   Arendt observes the collapse of the legal person with the human: "The destruction of man's rights, the killing of the juridical person in him, is a prerequisite for dominating him entirely." Arendt, *Origins of Totalitarianism*, 451.

40   I do not myself subscribe to Agamben's schema. See Sibylle Fischer: "There is, in the first instance, a striking geopolitical limitation to an argument that moves from the Greek polis to Hobbes, the French Revolution, to Auschwitz. Does colonialism belong to this story? What about slavery? On the face of it, there have never been more exclusionary strategies than slavery and colonialism, and both slavery and colonial administration could easily be regarded as instances of murderous biopolitics." Fischer, "Haiti," 5. See also Levinas, *Totality and Infinity*, 214.

41   Rancière, *Dissensus*, 67.

42   Mercer and MacDonald, "Disability and Human Rights," 549.

43   Yoneyama, *Cold War Ruins*, 10.

44   Esmeir, *Juridical Humanity*.

45   See also Vivian Sobchak on the limits of the disability metaphor. Sobchak, "A Leg to Stand On."

46   Joseph Slaughter argues the historical and ideological interdependencies between human rights and the literary form of the modern novel share a particular conception of the human as an individual, writing, "To become a subject within a particular sociopolitical formation is to be *capable* of fully exercising the rights enabled by that formation, which entails, at the same time, a 'free' submission to its norms." Slaughter, *Human Rights Inc.*, 9 (my italics).

47   Contemporary political theory, as Barbara Arneil observes, "conflate[s] physical and mental disabilities." "For if the *physically* disabled are systematically excluded from political theories ostensibly rooted in *rational* agency, it suggests there is *something* about disability itself (beyond a simple categorical antonym to 'reason,' as we have been suggesting thus far) that explains the long-standing exclusion and discrimination of the

physically disabled." If reason is the "constitutive meaning of both justice and citizenship in liberal democratic theory," then disability is configured as a loss or a disfigurement "that simply overwhelms the more obvious demarcation between mental and physical disabilities in relation to 'rationality' in liberal and democratic thought." Arneil, "Disability, Self Image, and Modern Political Theory," 226, 232.

48 See chapter 1 of Troeung's *Refugee Lifeworlds*. See also Erevelles, *Disability and Difference in Global Contexts*; Erevelles, "Color of Violence"; Meekosha on the "southern theory of disability" that "specifically incorporates the role of the global North in 'disabling' the global South," in "Decolonising Disability"; and Puar, *Right to Maim*.

49 Keva X. Bui, "Objects of Warfare," 300.

50 Moyn, *Human Rights and the Uses of History*, 143 (my italics).

51 Rights are variously marshaled for anti-imperialist and revolutionary, liberal, and universal claims. Golnar Nikpour, among others, observes the Eurocentrism of the revisionist understanding of human rights as merely an anti-ideological manifestation of postrevolutionary ennui. See Nikpour, "Claiming Human Rights"; Slaughter, "Hijacking Human Rights."

52 See Schor, *Reading in Detail*.

53 Cheng, *Ornamentalism*.

54 Grosz, "Naked," 125.

55 Agamben, "Nudity," 84.

56 Spillers, "Mama's Baby, Papa's Maybe," 68.

57 Clifford, "The Others," 73.

58 A 1993 conference in Tokyo established the International Coordination Committee for the Safeguarding and Development of the Historical Site of Angkor to guarantee the conservation and management of temple grounds and the surrounding townships of Siem Reap, absent state mechanisms in the new constitutional monarchy. See Peycam, "International Coordinating Committee for Angkor."

59 Norindr, *Phantasmatic Indochina*.

60 Norindr, *Phantasmatic Indochina*.

61 Ghosh, *Dancing in Cambodia*, 60.

62 For a fascinating account of French modernism and its vexed relationship to the so-called primitive, see Cheng, *Second Skin*.

63 Quoted in Penny Edwards, *Cambodge*, 14.

64 For more on the creation of this genre, see Falser, "From a Colonial Reinvention to Postcolonial Heritage," 708.

65 Groslier, *Cambodian Dancers*, 153.

66 Groslier, for instance, gushed, "Absolutely Beauty stands complete before me.... Of this absolute Beauty she is the sole pure expression.... Alone, she returns from the past to offer us her flower, while all else about her crumbles." Groslier, *Danseuses cambodgiennes*, 172–73; Groslier, *Cambodian Dancers*, 154–59.

67 Here is the rest of the quote: "Impossible to make a more perfect illusion of it; she has the same features because she is of the same pure race, she has the same enigmatic smile . . . the small Apsara from the old ages, slipped away from the holy bas-reliefs . . . these poses are the ancient tradition of this country, as the stone figures which inhabit the ruins. . . . May France, the protector of this country, understand that this royal ballet of the kings of Phnom Penh is a sacred legacy, an archaic marvel which should never be destroyed!" Loti, *Un pèlerin d'Angkor*, 204–13; quoted in Michael S. Falser, "From a Colonial Reinvention to Postcolonial Heritage," 702.

68 The popularity of ballet at this time as "the most highly articulated and aestheticized expression of idealized femininity" likely explains why these Cambodian dancers are later called ballet dancers. As Abigail Solomon-Godeau observes, "With the development of *pointe* in the second decade of the century, the ballerina became an etherealized vision of sublimity. Her airy weightlessness, embodied in the darting, floating movement of her body *en pointe*, is the emblem of a femininity purged of earthly dross and carnality. Like the fairy spirits, ghosts, and apparitions that populate the libretti of romantic ballet, the ballerina is a figure of another, more rarefied world." Solomon-Godeau, "Legs of the Countess," 85.

69 Quoted in Musée Rodin, "Rodin and the Cambodian Dancers."

70 In 1966, the Khmer Ballet performed a fantastical reenactment of a royal coronation ceremony (including hundreds of monks and extras in historical and religious costumes) for the French president Charles de Gaulle at Angkor Wat during his state visit—and then again two years later, for the socialist head of state of Yugoslavia.

71 "Women in Angkorian History," 46, quoted in Falser, "From a Colonial Reinvention to Postcolonial Heritage," 713.

72 Shapiro-Phim, "Mediating Cambodian History," 262–73.

73 Since then, multiple agencies have formed to cooperate (or not, as the case may be) with UNESCO's Phnom Penh coordinators, who commit "to protect the ancient city of the Khmer kings, an authentic symbol for the Cambodian people, from the corrosive fingers of time, the incursions of nature and the destruction by man." UNESCO, "Ankor."

74 Phim and Thompson, *Dance in Cambodia*, 2.

75 Heikkila and Peycam, "Economic Development in the Shadow of Angkor Wat"; Springer, *Cambodia's Neoliberal Order*.

76 Angkor Wat is the scene of contestation between the state and international agencies, not least with regard to corporate contracts privatizing the temple grounds or concessions management. "To survive in Cambodia, the ICC has thus been condemned to serve as an official legitimator for the power in place and its shadowy state practices." Peycam, "International Coordinating Committee for Angkor," 767.

77 For an exploration of NGOs that sponsor such dance training, see Tuchman-Rosta, "From Ritual Form to Tourist Attraction."

78 Wood, *Royal Ballet of Cambodia*.

79 Sellars, foreword to *Beyond the Apsara*, ix. Of their enduring nature, Sellars enthuses, "The breezes wafting through their garments suggest the invisible energies of their gentle movements which continue to subtly shift across the centuries as the sun moves across the sky and dynasties rise and crumble."

80 Traavik, *Miss Landmine*, 3–67.

81 See Smith and Morra, *Prosthetic Impulse*.

82 United Nations, Department of Public Information, *Agreements on a Comprehensive Political Settlement of the Cambodia Conflict*, 37.

83 Sekula, "Body and the Archive." The Cambodian Genocide Program at Yale University has obtained and scanned more than ten thousand photographic images pertaining to various aspects of gross human rights violations under the Khmer Rouge regime. More than five thousand photographs were taken of prisoners being processed at Tuol Sleng; many of the prisoners are still unidentified. These photographs can be searched in the "Tuol Sleng Image Database."

84 Norindr, *Phantasmatic Indochina*.

85 Gilpin, *Three Essays*, 7.

86 Price, *Essay on the Picturesque*, 44.

87 Krista A. Thompson, *An Eye for the Tropics*, 5.

88 Judith Brown, *Glamour in Six Dimensions*. See in particular her chapter on cellophane.

89 The UK-based Cambodia Trust was established in 1989 to provide cost-free prostheses to land mine survivors, while also operating the Cambodian School of Prosthetics and Orthotics (funded also by the Japan-based Nippon Foundation). Renamed Exceed, this model has since been replicated in the Philippines, Indonesia, Sri Lanka, and Myanmar. In 2016, two Cambodian American brothers opened up ARC Hub, a technology incubator in Phnom Penh, and created 3D-printed prosthetic limbs for survivors of unexploded ordnance in partnership with the Victoria Hand Project, a Canadian nonprofit, while the Cambodia Trust's for-profit

group Exceed opened a private clinic featuring higher-quality equipment and services, also including a 3D-printing prosthetics lab.

90 Cheng, *Ornamentalism*, 156.
91 Duong, "Agent Orange Bodies," 392.
92 Snyder and Mitchell, *Narrative Prosthesis*.
93 Feingold, *Miss Landmine*.
94 Such a concept of lost time because of disability or illness is captured baldly in the conceptual model behind the World Bank and World Health Organization's metric called the Disability-Adjusted Life Year, in which one DALY is one lost year of "healthy" life. The "product" of a five-year-long Global Burden of Disease Study, first commissioned in 1993, the DALY measures the "objective" burden of disease and injury to determine cost-effective resource allocation. See "Disability-Adjusted Life Years."
95 If a body is not a person, but is instead property, she cannot possess gender, understood as a property of her self. See Spillers, "Mama's Baby, Papa's Maybe."
96 The literary critic Wayne Booth proposed an interpretation of human right as protections of a person's "freedom to pursue a story line, a life plot." Booth, "Individualism," 89.
97 Jenkins, "Healing Fields," par. 22.
98 Jenkins, "Healing Fields," par. 25.
99 The Ministry of Social Affairs warned the organizers that the pageant would damage "the dignity and honour of our disabled, especially women." McCurry, "Miss Landmine Beauty Pageant Cancelled."
100 Duffet, "Cambodia's Miss Landmine Controversy."
101 McClintock, "Family Feuds," 62.
102 Cambodia held its first Miss Cambodia pageant in 2016, a private venture that crowned five winners—these contestants to represent Cambodia at international beauty pageants including Miss Universe, Miss Earth, Miss Tourism Queen of the Year, and Miss Tourism Metropolitan, with categories to showcase "heritage," making clear the linkages between development and recuperated "exotic" beauty.
103 Larasati, *Dance That Makes You Vanish*.
104 Larasati, *Dance That Makes You Vanish*, 117–18.
105 Shapiro-Phim, "Mediating Cambodian History," 270.
106 Quoted in Musée Rodin, "Cambodian Dancer."
107 Rancière, "Aesthetic Separation, Aesthetic Community," 7.
108 MacKinnon, "Miss Landmine"; Clark-Flory, "Miss Landmine 2008."
109 Bishop, *Artificial Hells*, 117.

110 Momaya, "Miss Landmine Cambodia Pageant."
111 Duffet, "Cambodia's Miss Landmine Controversy."
112 See Hesford, *Spectacular Rhetorics*.
113 Traavik, "Miss Landmine Beauty Pageant Helps Landmine Victims"; Momaya, "Miss Landmine Cambodia Pageant."
114 MacKinnon, "Miss Landmine."
115 Liberal disability rights frameworks, Jasbir Puar argues, are "invariably infused with certitude that disability should be reclaimed as a valuable difference—the difference of the Other—through rights, visibility, and empowerment discourses—rather than addressing how much debilitation is caused by global injustice and the war machines of colonialism, occupation, and U.S. imperialism." Puar, *Right to Maim*, xvii.
116 Diaz, "*Biyuti* from Below."
117 About "pink" initiatives, see King, *Pink Ribbons, Inc.*
118 The 2016 documentary directed by Baby Ruth Villarama, *Sunday Beauty Queen*, captures some of the workers who spend their days off preparing for it.
119 Women in the World Staff, "Maximum Security Prison in Brazil."
120 Tama, "Rio De Janeiro Prison."
121 For instance, Moran, Pallot, and Piacentini, "Lipstick, Lace, and Longing"; see also the 2007 documentary *Miss Gulag* directed by Maria Ibrahimova.
122 Förster, "From 'General Field Marshal' to 'Miss Genocide,'" 190.
123 Bryant, "Miss Perú Contestants Give Gender-Violence Statistics."
124 I have written elsewhere about the common claim that an observer is made vulnerable before the sight of another's suffering, and that this is the dynamic of the modern imperial subject. See "Grace, the Gift of the Girl in the Photograph," in *Gift of Freedom*, 83–132.
125 Reinhardt, Edwards, and Duganne, *Beautiful Suffering*.
126 Sontag, *Regarding the Pain of Others*, 41, 83, 85; Razack, *Dark Threats and White Knights*, 26.
127 Garland-Thomson, "Seeing the Disabled," 344.
128 Quoted in MacKinnon, "Miss Landmine."
129 James Thompson, *Performance Affects*, 155.
130 James Thompson, *Performance Affects*, 150.
131 Quoted in Bloul, "Ain't I a Woman?," 8.
132 Warner writes, "In a counterpublic setting, such display often has the aim of transformation. Styles of embodiment are learned and cultivated,

and the effects of shame and disgust that surround them can be tested, in some cases revalued." Warner, *Publics and Counterpublics*, 62; quoted in David and Cruz, "Big, *Bakla*, and Beautiful," 31.

133 Berlant, *Female Complaint*, 10.

134 Quoted in Saeed Ahmed, "Landmine Victims Star in Angola Pageant."

135 Song Kosal quoted in Bloul, "Ain't I a Woman?," 11.

136 Taylor, "Politics of Passion."

137 Bloul, "Ain't I a Woman?," 12.

138 McNay, "Trouble with Recognition," 275.

139 Arendt, *Origins of Totalitarianism*, 383.

140 Such socially engaged art, according to Bishop, supposedly "reduces isolation by helping people make friends, develops community networks and sociability, helps offenders and victims address issues of crime, contributes to people's employability, encourages people to accept risk positively, and helps transform the image of public bodies." Bishop, *Artificial Hells*, 14.

141 Berlant, *Cruel Optimism*, 224.

142 Baedan, "Musings on Nothingness," 156. The quote is, "The negation of rule is not its suspension, but the recognition of its nakedness."

143 Spivak, *Critique of Postcolonial Reason*, 172.

Chapter 4. Beauty's Ruin at the End of the World

1 Christmas Island is in Australia; Kakuma is in Kenya; Za'atari is in Jordan; Jenin is in the West Bank; and Guantánamo Bay in the United States.

2 Quoted in Zylinska, "Photography after the Human," 170; Arundhati Roy, "Is There Life after Democracy?"

3 These questions follow the work often: "Will learning to hairspray a bride's curls into place help heal the scars left by years of war and Taliban rule?" Or of ruin photographs of Detroit, "Where are the people?" The first question comes from Guest, "Extreme Makeover Freedom Edition," 12. The second question comes from Apel, *Beautiful Terrible Ruins*, 75.

4 Leary, "Detroitism."

5 Leary, "Detroitism."

6 Ryzewski, "Ruin Photography as Archaeological Method," 40.

7 Dean, *Fragility of Empathy after the Holocaust*, 41.

8 Dora Apel does both in *Beautiful Terrible Ruins*.

9 See Linda Williams's body of work, including *Hardcore* and the collection *Porn Studies*.

10   Shane McGowan writes, "The act of ruin gazing reaffirmed the Enlightenment's teleological narrative of progress, which depicted history as humanity's inevitable journey from Oriental despotism to Occidental rationality." Quoted in Apel, *Beautiful Terrible Ruins*, 14.

11   As observed previously, UNESCO identifies and boosts cultural heritage projects designed to "harvest the economic value" of some ruins through partial preservation and cultivated disrepair.

12   Macaulay, *Pleasure of Ruins*, 1.

13   Olalquiaga, "El Helicoide," 36.

14   As Michael Roth argues, "When we frame an object as a ruin, we reclaim that object from its fall into decay and oblivion and often for some kind of cultural attention and care that, in a sense, elevates its value" ("Irresistible Decay," 1). I am reminded how Kara Walker breathes an imitation of life (for a fleeting moment) into such abject materials in the echoing, hulking shell of a Domino Sugar compound in Williamsburg, Brooklyn; her summertime installation of a white-sugar, Black woman-sphinx called "A Subtlety, or the Marvelous Sugar Baby," monumentalizes the labor that built the American empire even as achingly sweet sugar sculptures puddle into viscous molasses.

15   Benjamin, *Origin of German Tragic Drama*, 178.

16   Quoted in Grandin, "Collapse of America's Imperial Car Industry."

17   Grandin, "Collapse of America's Imperial Car Industry."

18   Greg Grandin writes, "In Rome, the ruins came after the empire fell. In the United States, the destruction of Detroit happened even as the country was rising to new heights as a superpower." Grandin, "Collapse of America's Imperial Car Industry."

19   Grandin continues: "A marker of a world power as much as was the possession of a colony or the bomb, in the second half of the twentieth century, was the ability to make a precision V8 engine." Grandin, "Empire's Ruins," 117.

20   Luckerson, "Rise and Risk of the Mural Economy."

21   Harvey, "'New' Imperialism"; Tsing, *Friction*, 75.

22   Quoted in Isidore, "Detroit, in Financial Trouble." But not for the high-end golf clubs, the Red Wings' hockey arena, the Ford football stadium, and other commercial and industrial users who owed over $30 million.

23   Dubin, "Robert Des Ruines."

24   See, for instance, the bloodless account of Inikori, "Credit Needs of the African Trade."

25   Kish and Leroy, "Bonded Life," 643.

26   Chakravartty and Silva, "Accumulation, Dispossession, and Debt," 368.

27 Marx, "Comments on James Mill," 216.
28 See Zambrana, *Colonial Debts*.
29 Tadiar, "Life-Times of Disposability within Global Neoliberalism," 21.
30 Chakravartty and Silva, "Accumulation, Dispossession, and Debt," 365.
31 The number of mortgages issued in the city has yet to return to prerecession levels, and as *Vice* reports, "A majority of the 673,000 people in the city, once a bastion of black working-class homeownership, now rent instead of own." Betancourt, "Detroit's Housing Crisis."
32 Ananya Roy, *Poverty Capital*, 219.
33 Shell, *Money, Language, and Thought*, 7.
34 More than 450 tests were conducted there between 1949 and 1989, all of them well within range of the town's residents. Kander, *Dust*.
35 Berger, *Drosscape*.
36 Annie McClanahan discusses these foreclosure and ghost city photographs in *Dead Pledges*.
37 Moore, *Detroit Disassembled*, 119.
38 W. J. T. Mitchell, "Imperial Landscape," 12 (my italics).
39 Olalquiaga, "El Helicoide," 31.
40 Ewing and Grady, "Dismantling Detroit."
41 Quoted in Kinney, *Beautiful Wasteland*, 38.
42 Vergara, "American Acropolis."
43 By introducing the horizon of extinction, she argues that we might denaturalize the political and aesthetic frameworks through which humans see and understand themselves *as* life. Zylinska, "Photography after the Human," 167.
44 McClanahan, *Dead Pledges*, 132.
45 Adorno, "Cultural Criticism and Society," 34; Woolf, *Mrs. Dalloway*, 182.
46 Beardsley, "Aesthetic Experience Regained," 3.
47 Beardsley, "Aesthetic Experience Regained," 3.
48 Hindi, "Fuck Your Lecture on Craft," 223.
49 US Commission on Obscenity and Pornography, *Report of the Commission on Obscenity and Pornography*, 516.
50 Jameson, *Signatures of the Visible*, 1.
51 Rancière, *Emancipated Spectator*, 7.
52 Dean elaborates, "Above all, 'pornography' shapes and defines a problem in a disarmingly clear moral language whose meaning on closer inspection turns out to be pretty opaque: designating something 'pornographic,' among its other functions, passes for an argument about the

relation between moral and political perversion where there is really no argument and attributes responsibility for Nazism and fascism implicitly to particular sorts of illicit, sexual emotions." Dean, *Fragility of Empathy after the Holocaust*, 45.

53 Dean, *Fragility of Empathy after the Holocaust*, 31.
54 Dean, "Empathy, Pornography, and Suffering," 92.
55 Steiner, "On Difficulty," 273.
56 Steiner, "Night Words," 17.
57 Doucet and Philp, "In Detroit 'Ruin Porn' Ignores the Voices."
58 Wells, "Detroit Was Always Made of Wheels," 18.
59 Apel, *Beautiful Terrible Ruins*, 75.
60 Sedgwick, "Paranoid Reading and Reparative Reading."
61 Cousins, "The Ugly [Part 1]," 63 (my italics).
62 Cousins, "The Ugly [Part 1]," 61.
63 Cousins, "The Ugly [Part 1]," 61.
64 Ngai, *Ugly Feelings*; Anker, *Ugly Freedoms*, 9.
65 Buckley, "It Will Arise from the Ashes."
66 Vasseleu, "Material-Character Animation"; quoted in Kushinski, "Light and the Aesthetics of Abandonment."
67 Kushinski, "Light and the Aesthetics of Abandonment."
68 Crane, "'Take Nothing but Photos, Leave Nothing but Footprints,'" 96–97.
69 Arnold, "Urban Decay Photography and Film," 328.
70 Morton, "Something, Something, Something, Detroit."
71 Tim Edensor conjectures, "Monstrous forces have inverted the order of things." Edensor, *Industrial Ruins*, 116.
72 Klein, "Poverty Is So Photogenic."
73 Bill Brown, *Sense of Things*, 7.
74 Cousins, "The Ugly [Part 2]," 5.
75 McClanahan, *Dead Pledges*, 127.
76 Marx, *Economic and Philosophic Manuscripts*, 54 (italics in original).
77 McClanahan, *Dead Pledges*, 102.
78 Reuters Staff, "U.S. Foreclosure Image Is 2008 World Press Photo."
79 Schweik, *Ugly Laws*, 293, 286.
80 As Clare Sears demonstrates in *Arresting Dress*, cross-dressing law and ugly laws both are techniques of "spatial regulation" focused on what can appear in public.

81   Silva, *Toward a Global Idea of Race*, xv.
82   Zambrana, *Colonial Debts*, 44.
83   Camp and Heatherton, "Introduction: Policing the Planet."
84   Mimi Thi Nguyen, "Hoodie as Sign."
85   For instance, Annie McClanahan discusses horror films and the uncanny home in *Dead Pledges*.
86   Leary, "Detroitism."
87   Leary, "Detroitism."
88   Piccini, "Profane Archaeologies," 32.
89   Chow, *Entanglements*, 88.
90   Susan Buck-Morss's assertion that "the simultaneity of overstimulation and numbness is characteristic of the new synaesthetic organization as *anaesthetics*." Buck-Morss, "Aesthetics and Anaesthetics," 18.
91   Chow, "Resistance of Theory," 97.
92   Doucet and Philp, "In Detriot 'Ruin Porn' Ignores the Voices" (my italics).
93   Apel, *Beautiful Terrible Ruins*, 76.
94   Wells, "Detroit Was Always Made of Wheels," 22.
95   They also call it "the volatile result of a change of era and the fall of empires" and a "natural and sublime demonstration of our human destinies and of their paradoxes," which would seem to contradict each other—unless empires are understood to simply give way to an inexorable force. Marchand and Meffre, introduction to *The Ruins of Detroit*, 16.
96   Dean, *Fragility of Empathy after the Holocaust*, 18.
97   White, "Grand Detroit Hotel."
98   Sontag, *On Photography*, 12.
99   Malone, "Case against Economic Disaster Porn."
100 Arnold, "Urban Decay Photography and Film," 332.
101 Malone, "Case against Economic Disaster Porn" (my italics).
102 Christopher, "Confessions of a Ruin Pornographer."
103 Derrida, *Specters of Marx*, 89.
104 Danto, *Abuse of Beauty*, 33.
105 Edensor, *Industrial Ruins*, 105.
106 Ryzewski, "No Home for the 'Ordinary Gamut,'" 409.
107 Quoted in Ryzewski, "No Home for the 'Ordinary Gamut,'" 413–14.
108 Quoted in Ryzewski, "No Home for the 'Ordinary Gamut,'" 425.
109 Quoted in Moore, *Take This Hammer (the Director's Cut)*.
110 Yablon, *Untimely Ruins*, 10.

111 Moon, "Reclaiming the Ruin," 37.
112 *New York Times* Editorial Board, "Last Steel Column."
113 Kinney, *Beautiful Wasteland*, xi.
114 Kinney, *Beautiful Wasteland*, xvi.
115 The full quote is: "These days everyone in Detroit is talking like an urban planner. You can't spend even a day driving through the city and not think in terms of land use, redevelopment, and urban identity. Entire neighborhoods, people gone and houses razed, are on their way to becoming prairies. The neo-Gothic shell of Cass Tech High School, fifteen emptied Art Deco floors of the Lee Plaza Hotel, the four remaining towers of the vacant Brewster Projects, hulked up identically off the interstate like broken soldiers locked in a standoff—they're all coming down. The question becomes: *What do we do with all this space?*" Kahn, "Destroying Detroit."
116 Kinney, *Beautiful Wasteland*, xvi.
117 Atuahene, "Predatory Cities," 121.
118 See Yablon on paper cities in *Untimely Ruins*, chap. 2.
119 Reindl, "How Detroit Lost Its Title as 'Ruin Porn' Capital."
120 Arnold, "Urban Decay Photography and Film," 331.
121 Katz, "Whose Nature, Whose Culture?," 48.
122 Katz, "Whose Nature, Whose Culture?," 46–48.
123 Holt-Gimenez writes, "Once acquired, the easiest and most effective, low-cost way for big financial dogs to quickly mark their newly-acquired territory has been to plant trees—trees require little maintenance and if global carbon markets ever really kick in, could pay dividends." Holt-Gimenez, "Detroit."
124 Safransky, "Greening the Urban Frontier," 238.
125 In their essay "Improve Your Lot!," Interboro outlines four distinct examples of blots: "The Garden Blot," "The Billboard Blot," "The Courtyard Blot," and "Blot for Two Sisters." Quoted in Moon, "Reclaiming the Ruin," 37, 41.
126 Weismann, "Bankrupt, but There's a Whole Foods."
127 Harney and Moten, *Undercommons*, 61.
128 Quoted in Betancourt, "Detroit's Housing Crisis."
129 Neavling, "Detroit Illegally Overtaxed Homeowners $600M."
130 Again from Atuahene: "For instance, operating a vehicle while intoxicated now carried a two-year fine of $1000 a year, while driving with a suspended license resulted in a two-year fine for $500 per year. With the new fines, the state raised between $99 million and $115 million a year." Atuahene, "Predatory Cities," 135.

131 Katharyne Mitchell, "Pre-Black Futures," 243–44.
132 Nietzsche, *On the Genealogy of Morals*, 58.
133 Beck, "Role of Police in Gentrification."
134 Loosemore, "'A False Narrative.'"
135 Abbas, *Liberalism and Human Suffering*, 25.
136 Rosler, *Bowery in Two Inadequate Descriptive Systems*.
137 This series is not dissimilar from a new approach to landscape photography called *new topographics*, emerging in the 1970s, preceding contemporary ruin photography. This aesthetic embraced a photojournalistic aesthetic, after anonymous commercial photographers commissioned to record everyday industrial and civic projects. These archives inspired the German photographers Bernd Becher and Hilla Becher, who created typologies of such structures as water towers, coal bunkers, breakers, grain elevators, blast furnaces, steel mills, and factory facades, arranged in grids or suites of black-and-white photographs. At the start of deindustrialization, their work was conceived as an "industrial archaeology," which meant a documentation of future ruins. As Collins writes, "The photographs are portraits of our history." Collins, "Long Look."
138 Rosler, "In, Around, and Afterthoughts," 86.
139 *You Can't Shoot Us All*.
140 Moss, *Feral City*, 116.

Chapter 5. Living Beautifully, or Resilience

1 Bloul, "Ain't I a Woman?," 15.
2 Reed, "Extreme Makeover," 469.
3 Neocleous, "Resisting Resilience," 3.
4 Claudia Aradau and Rens van Munster observe that resilience "smoothly combines meanings derived from physics (the capacity of material to return to a previous state), psychology (the capacity of an individual to return to normal after a traumatic event), ecology (the capacity of systems to continue functioning and renew themselves after a disruptive event), and infomatics (the capacity of a system to keep on functioning despite anomalies and design flaws)." Aradau and van Munster, *Politics of Catastrophe*, 46–47.
5 See, for instance, Collier and Lakoff, "Vulnerability of Vital Systems."
6 Sims, "Resilience and Homeland Security."
7 LeMenager and Foote, "Editor's Column."
8 Tsing, *Mushroom at the End of the World*, 282.
9 Bonanno et al., "What Predicts Psychological Resilience after Disaster?," 671.

10 Earvolino-Ramirez, "Resilience," 73; Mancini and Bonanno, "Resilience in the Face of Potential Trauma," 973; Bonanno, "Loss, Trauma, and Human Resilience," 20–21.

11 Shing, Jayawickreme, and Waugh, "Contextual Positive Coping"; Schulenberg, "Disaster Mental Health," 1226.

12 For instance, "among survivors of the 1999 earthquake in Turkey, individuals with greater self-esteem, optimism, and perceived control over earthquake-related stress were able to manifest greater feelings of being able to cope with subsequent stress (coping self-efficacy)." Shing, Jayawickreme, and Waugh, "Contextual Positive Coping," 1290.

13 See, for instance, Asakura and Craig, "'It Gets Better' . . . but How?"; Lester et al., "Bringing Science to Bear," 77. Over the last century, the pressing psychological queries for military readiness shifted, from the Second World War court-martial offense of malingering, or feigning an incapacity or illness to evade service, to the Southeast Asian diagnosis of posttraumatic stress disorder, or the medico-legal defense for perpetrating atrocities on civilian others. See also O'Malley, "Resilient Subjects"; Howell, "Resilience, War, and Austerity."

14 Seligman, *Flourish*, 128.

15 Foucault, *Birth of Biopolitics*, 66–67 (my italics).

16 For instance, see Neocleous, *War Power, Police Power*.

17 See Roitman's *Anti-crisis*, with particular attention to the 2008 financial "crisis."

18 United Nations Office for Disaster Risk Reduction (UN/ISDR), *Living with Risk*, chap. 1, sec. 1, pp. 16–17.

19 Bracke, "Bouncing Back," 55, 56.

20 Foucault quoted in Colin Gordon, "Governmental Rationality," 19.

21 Foucault quoted in Colin Gordon, "Governmental Rationality," 20.

22 US Homeland Security Council, *National Strategy for Homeland Security*, i.

23 US Department of Homeland Security, Cybersecurity and Infrastructure Security Agency, *National Infrastructure Protection Plan*; US Department of Homeland Security, *2014 Quadrennial Homeland Security Review*, 83; US Trump Administration, *National Security Strategy of the United States of America*, 14.

24 Neocleous, "Resisting Resilience."

25 A "risk society" coheres in the historical wake of disasters that threaten the life of the planet, such as the explosion in the Chernobyl nuclear power plant in the Ukrainian Soviet Socialist Republic in 1986.

26 Mancini and Bonanno, "Resilience in the Face of Potential Trauma," 979.

27   Roitman, *Anti-crisis*, 16.
28   Napolitano, "Remarks as Prepared by Secretary Napolitano."
29   Berlant, *Cruel Optimism*, 10.
30   Scott, *Omens of Adversity*, 7.
31   This is the plot from the pilot episode of *Superstore*, which first aired on November 30, 2015.
32   Dango, *Crisis Style*, 26–27.
33   Cousins, "The Ugly [Part 1]," 62.
34   Kant, *Critique of Judgment*, 125 (my italics).
35   Kant, *Critique of Judgment*, 104.
36   Kant, *Critique of Judgment*, 115.
37   Kant, *Critique of Judgment*, 126.
38   Derrida, "Force of Law," 44.
39   She also writes, "We must recognize that the implicit warning against imperial hubris and the burden of grief imparted by the images are in conflict with the impulse to find beauty in the ruins. Yet these contradictory narratives coexist—the beautiful and the terrible—indeed, one mediates the other, beauty making the terrible bearable." Apel, *Beautiful Terrible Ruins*, 5, 2.
40   Cited without source by Rose Musyoki, "ANA Spotlight: Wangechi Mutu Sets the Tone for African Art Fairs in June," July 4, 2023, https://artnewsafrica.com/ana-spotlight-wangechi-mutu-sets-the-tone-for-african-art-fairs-in-june/.
41   Arendt, *Human Condition*, 237.
42   Mimi Thi Nguyen, "Minor Threats."
43   Woolf, *Mrs. Dalloway*, 182.
44   See, for example, Tate, "*Mrs Dalloway* and the Armenian Question," 471.
45   Lee R. Edwards, "War and Roses," 162.
46   Tolentino, "The Year That Skin Care Became a Coping Mechanism."
47   Tolentino, "The Year That Skin Care Became a Coping Mechanism."
48   Kelsky, "#MakeupMonday."
49   Hannah, "Pandemic Has Changed Our Relationship with Skincare."
50   Sabbatical Beauty, "About Us."
51   Lorde, *A Burst of Light and Other Essays*, 131.
52   We can see this convergence in the aforementioned British officer's diary about a shipment of lipstick that arrives to a concentration camp along with other Red Cross supplies, and returns to the Jewish internees a sense of individuality (not unlike the compact for the prisoner), decades later

cited on recent educational materials on "self-esteem" produced by the British trade association Cosmetic Toiletry and Perfumery Association. See UK Cosmetic Toiletry and Perfumery Association, "Faces of Science."

53 Berlant, *Female Complaint*, 31.

54 Koren, *Wabi-Sabi for Artists*, 51.

55 Cate McQuaid's *Boston Globe* review of Smith's 2019 exhibition, *We Already Have What We Need*, at the Massachusetts Museum of Contemporary Art, is titled, "At Mass MoCA, Artist Cauleen Smith Offers Visions of Black Resilience."

56 Frueh, *Unapologetic Beauty*, 89.

57 Bartlett, "Tearoom View of Mended Ceramics," 9.

58 Sedgwick, "Paranoid Reading and Reparative Reading," 128.

59 For more on the afterlife of military waste, see Sisavath, "US Secret War in Laos."

60 The structure of this statement is also provocative, inasmuch as it pairs the absence of a culprit for the bombing with the presence of its survivors.

61 On the "rehabilitation" of sex workers through craft labor, see Shih, *Manufacturing Freedom*.

62 As James Clifford argues, "I do not argue, as some critics have, that non-Western objects are properly understood only with reference to their original milieus. Ethnographic contextualizations are as problematic as aesthetic ones, as susceptible to purified, ahistorical treatment." Clifford, *Predicament of Culture*, 12.

63 Kermode, *Sense of an Ending*, 45.

64 Kermode, *Sense of an Ending*, 44–45.

65 Mancini and Bonanno, "Resilience in the Face of Potential Trauma," 979.

66 Davoudi, "Resilience," 299.

67 Quoted in Davoudi, "Resilience," 303.

68 Davoudi, "Resilience," 304.

69 Hemingway, *Farewell to Arms*, 264.

70 See Fogg, *Beautiful Trauma*. Consider entries in the genre such as Bust .com's post "12 Stunning Photographs of Breast Cancer Survivors Show the Beauty of Resilience," featuring the photo series "Grace" by Charise Isis, who creates "portraits of survivors of mastectomies with the majesty and beauty of the ancient Greek goddesses" (by Brenda Pitt, April 1, 2014, https://bust.com/arts/11884-12-stunning-photographs-of-breast -cancer-survivors-show-the-beauty-of-resilience.html); the discussion of an award-winning photograph in Lane Santy's Buzzfeed article "This Beautiful Image of a Transgender Woman Shows Strength and Resilience"

(May 3, 2015, http://www.buzzfeed.com/lanesainty/this-beautiful-image-of-a-transgender-woman-shows-strength#.abPzLdPD0); an Australian photographer featured in a DesignTaxi article titled "Heartfelt Photo Series of Disabled Animals Reveals Their Beauty and Resilience" (http://designtaxi.com/news/379860/Heartfelt-Photo-Series-Of-Disabled-Animals-Reveals-Their-Beauty-And-Resilience/); a Santa Barbara–based radio show on "the beauty and resilience of Nepal in the wake of destruction" (by Elizabeth Barrett, May 22, 2015, http://kcbx.org/post/beauty-and-resilience-nepal-wake-destruction); a faith-based "custom-designed" travel organization that offers a fellowship trip called "Haiti: Hope, Beauty, and Resilience Tour" ("When we think of Haiti, most of us picture poverty, corruption, and devastation following the massive 2010 earthquake. Yet it's also a country of hope, beauty, and resilience") (https://www.tourmagination.com/tours/481-haiti-hope-beauty-a-resilience-tour haiti-hope-beauty-a-resilience-tour); a travel recommendation in the DC-based publication *Washington Diplomat* noting that among the Baltic states' "many charms" are their "resilience and beauty," as yet intact after the region's emergence from Soviet control as these states seek to lure tourists (by Anna Gawel, March 28, 2011, http://www.washdiplomat.com/index.php?option=com_content&view=article&id=7288:among-baltic-regions-many-charms-its-resilience-and-beauty&catid=1089:april-2011&Itemid=470); an Oakland-based group called Outdoor Afro that describes its hikes as opportunities to "reflect on beauty and resilience" in nature as well as "black America" (http://www.meetup.com/Outdoor-Afro/events/223816507/); and World Vision Australia presenting a series called "Strength in Adversity: Portraits of Resilience and Beauty," featuring portraits taken by so-called ambassadors of the agentive subjects of the organization's aid.

71 James, *Resilience and Melancholy*, 82.
72 Mancini and Bonanno, "Resilience in the Face of Potential Trauma," 972.
73 Chödrön, *Living Beautifully with Uncertainty and Change*, 6.
74 Quoted in Godlewski, "Mr. Rogers Quotes."
75 Eng, "Colonial Object Relations," 5.
76 Berlant, *Cruel Optimism*, 3.
77 Dolven, *Senses of Style*, 118.
78 Phan Thi Kim Phuc, the so-called napalm girl from Nick Ut's award-winning photograph of the US war in Vietnam, for instance, imparts lessons about living beautifully with those scars. See Mimi Thi Nguyen, "Grace, the Gift of the Girl in the Photograph," in *Gift of Freedom*.
79 Howell, "Resilience, War, and Austerity," 15.
80 Ngai, *Ugly Feelings*, 6.

81 Berlant, *Cruel Optimism*, 100.
82 I am greatly influenced here by Sianne Ngai and her brilliant book *Ugly Feelings*.
83 On affectability, or impressionability, see Kyla Schuller, Sianne Ngai, or Claudia Castañeda, among others.
84 Nietzsche, *On the Genealogy of Morals*, 58 (italics in the original).
85 Ahmed, *Living a Feminist Life*, 189.
86 Feldman, "MSNBC Guest: Stop Using the Word 'Resilient.'"
87 See Cacho, *Social Death*, and Fleetwood, "Failing Narratives, Initiating Technologies," among others; see Pendleton, "Captivated."
88 Kang, "What Is Refugee Resilience?" 50–51.
89 Neocleous, "Resisting Resilience," 4.
90 Thank you to the audience at the conference Prisons, Borders, Pipelines: Toward a Queer Abolitionist Movement for the conversation that led to this insight. University of North Carolina Asheville, April 6, 2018.
91 Evans and Reid, *Resilient Life*, 6.
92 Leary, "Resilience in the Goal of Governments and Employers."
93 Jameson, "Future City," 76; Bracke, "Bouncing Back," 63.
94 Stuelke, *Ruse of Repair*, 217.
95 The Nap Ministry (@thenapministry), "Y'all keep hollering about this New World."
96 Myerson, "Where Have All the Flowers Gone?"
97 Alexandra Boutopoulou, who is a doctoral researcher of visual social media and digital culture at the University of Sheffield, identifies the origins of this phrase in a 1978 couplet composed by the Greek poet Dinos Christianopoulos. Included in the collection *The Body and the Wormwood* (1960–93) and translated into English by Nicholas Kostis (1995). The couplet reads: "what didn't you do to bury me / but you forgot that I was a seed." Boutopoulou, "On the Origins of 'They Tried to Bury Us.'"
98 Words spoken by General Leia in the *Star Wars* film *The Last Jedi* (dir. Rian Johnson, 2017), and the old crone Razz in the *She-Ra: Princess of Power* series on Netflix (season 4, episode 9), to young women (Rey and Adora, respectively) struggling against seemingly insurmountable odds to save their worlds.
99 Choi, *World Keeps Ending*, 1; Quiray Tagle, "After the Apocalypse," 11.
100 Benjamin, "Theses on the Philosophy of History," 261.

Epilogue

1. Derrida, *Specters of Marx*, xvii.
2. Goldman, *Living My Life*, 56.
3. Du Bois, "Of Beauty and Death," 135.
4. Sicardi, "The Year in Ugliness."
5. Butler, "Finishing, Starting," 295.
6. Mitchell, *Faggots and Their Friends between Revolutions*, 11.
7. Quoted in Solnit, *Orwell's Roses*, 192.
8. Hartman, "Anarchy of Colored Girls," 469.
9. Jorts (and Jean) (@JortsTheCat), "'No my dearest,' he says to her. 'You are alive, and beautiful as the moon,'" Twitter, November 2, 2023, 6:52 p.m., https://twitter.com/JortsTheCat/status/1720227414008312311.
10. This speech was published under the heading "Votes for Women," in *Life and Labor*, 288.
11. Foucault, "Concern for Truth," 259.
12. Awkward-Rich, "Feeling Strange."
13. Lee R. Edwards, "War and Roses," 175.
14. Benjamin, "Theses on the Philosophy of History," 257.
15. Rancière writes: "This distribution is precisely the presupposition of what I call the police: the configuration of the political community as a collective body with its places and functions allotted according to the competences specific to groups and individuals." Rancière, "Thinking of Dissensus," 3.
16. Adorno, *Aesthetic Theory*, 311.
17. Hansberry, *To Be Young, Gifted, and Black*, 130.
18. Leslie Kaplan, *Disorder*, 27–28.
19. Loveless, *How to Make Art at the End of the World*, 107 (italics in the original).
20. Benjamin, "Theses on the Philosophy of History," 257.
21. Avery Gordon, *Ghostly Matters*, 196–97.
22. Derrida, "Force of Law," 27.
23. Enriquez, *Things We Lost in the Fire*, 186–87.
24. Enriquez, *Things We Lost in the Fire*, 187.
25. Ramos Orta, "Trashed Beauty," 134.
26. Enriquez, *Things We Lost in the Fire*, 191.
27. Enriquez, *Things We Lost in the Fire*, 193.
28. Enriquez, *Things We Lost in the Fire*, 197.

BIBLIOGRAPHY

Abbas, Asma. "In Terror, in Love, Out of Time." In *At the Limits of Justice: Women of Colour on Terror*, edited by Suvendrini Perera and Sherene H. Razack, 503–25. Toronto: University of Toronto Press, 2014.
Abbas, Asma. *Liberalism and Human Suffering: Materialist Reflections on Politics, Ethics, and Aesthetics*. New York: Palgrave Macmillan, 2010.
Abu-Lughod, Leila. "Do Muslim Women Really Need Saving? Anthropological Questions on Cultural Relativism and Its Others." *American Anthropologist* 104, no. 3 (September 2002): 783–90.
Adorno, Theodor. *Aesthetic Theory*. 1970. Edited by Gretel Adorno and Rolf Tiedemann. Translated by Robert Hullot-Kentor. London: Continuum, 2002.
Adorno, Theodor. "Cultural Criticism and Society." 1951. In *Prisms*, translated by Samuel Weber and Shierry Weber, 17–34. Cambridge, MA: MIT Press, 1983.
Agamben, Giorgio. "Nudity." In *Nudities*, translated by David Kishik and Stefan Pedatella, 55–90. Stanford, CA: Stanford University Press, 2011.
Agrawal, Vandita. "Meet Siew Pui Yi, the Controversial Malaysian Influencer Whose Ao Dai Photo in Vietnam Sparked a Social Media Storm." *South China Morning Post*, April 20, 2022. https://www.scmp.com/magazines/style/celebrity/article/3174852/meet-siew-pui-yi-controversial-malaysian-influencer-whose.
Ahmed, Leila. *Women and Gender in Islam: Historical Roots of a Modern Debate*. New Haven, CT: Yale University Press, 1992.
Ahmed, Saeed. "Landmine Victims Star in Angola Pageant." CNN, April 1, 2008. http://edition.cnn.com/2008/WORLD/africa/04/01/angola.landmine/index.html.

Ahmed, Sara. *Living a Feminist Life*. Durham, NC: Duke University Press, 2017.

Ahmed, Sara. *The Promise of Happiness*. Durham, NC: Duke University Press, 2010.

Ahmed, Sara. *Queer Phenomenology: Orientations, Objects, Others*. Durham, NC: Duke University Press, 2006.

Aizura, Aren. "A Mask and a Target Cart: Minneapolis Riots." *New Inquiry*, May 30, 2020. https://thenewinquiry.com/a-mask-and-a-target-cart-minneapolis-riots/.

Alcoff, Linda, and Laura Gray. "Survivor Discourse: Transgression or Recuperation?" *Signs* 18, no. 21 (Winter 1993): 260–90.

Andry, Soofiya. "Deviant Bodies." In *Can We All Be Feminists? New Writing from Brit Bennett, Nicole-Dennis-Benn, and 15 Others on Intersectionality, Identity, and the Way Forward for Feminism*, edited by June Eric-Udorie, 225–38. New York: Penguin, 2018.

Anker, Elisabeth S. *Ugly Freedoms*. Durham, NC: Duke University Press, 2022.

Áo Dài Day. Senate Resolution no. 73. California Senate 2015–2016 regular session. 2016. Accessed February 4, 2017, https://leginfo.legislature.ca.gov/faces/billTextClient.xhtml?bill_id=201520160SR73.

Apel, Dora. *Beautiful Terrible Ruins: Detroit and the Anxiety of Decline*. New Brunswick, NJ: Rutgers University Press, 2015.

Aradau, Claudia, and Rens van Munster. *Politics of Catastrophe: Genealogies of the Unknown*. London: Routledge, 2011.

Arendt, Hannah. *The Human Condition*. 1958. 2nd ed. Chicago: University of Chicago Press, 1998.

Arendt, Hannah. *On Violence*. San Diego: Harcourt Brace Jovanovich, 1969.

Arendt, Hannah. *The Origins of Totalitarianism*. 1951. New York: Harcourt Brace, 1973.

Arfaoui, Meryem-Bahia. "Time and the Colonial State." Translated by Chanelle Adams. *Funambulist* 36 (June–August 2021): 26–29. https://thefunambulist.net/magazine/they-have-clocks-we-have-time/time-and-the-colonial-state.

Armus, Teo. "'Put on Some Pants': Critics Accuse Kasey Musgraves of Degrading a Traditional Vietnamese Garment." *Washington Post*, October 16, 2019. https://www.washingtonpost.com/nation/2019/10/16/kacey-musgraves-slammed-online-allegedly-degrading-vietnamese-garment/.

Arneil, Barbara. "Disability, Self Image, and Modern Political Theory." *Political Theory* 37, no. 2 (April 2009): 218–42.

Arnold, Sarah. "Urban Decay Photography and Film: Fetishism and the Apocalyptic Imagination." *Journal of Urban History* 41, no. 2 (2015): 326–39. doi: 10.1177/0096144214563499.

Asakura, Kenta, and Shelley L. Craig. "'It Gets Better' . . . but How? Exploring Resilience Development in the Accounts of LGBTQ Adults." *Journal of Human Behavior in the Social Environment* 24, no. 3 (2014): 253–66. doi: 10.1080/10911359.2013.808971.

Atuahene, Bernadette. "Predatory Cities." *California Law Review* 108, no. 1 (2020): 107–82. doi: 10.15779/Z38NS0KZ30.

Authorization for Use of Military Force. S.J. Res. 23. 107th Cong. (2001).

Awkward-Rich, Cameron. "Feeling Strange." Special issue edited by Evie Shockley. *Evening Will Come: A Monthly Journal of Poetics* 65 (April 2017). https://thevolta.org/ewc65-eshockley-p13.html.

Ayotte, Kevin J., and Mary E. Husain. "Securing Afghan Women: Neocolonialism, Epistemic Violence, and the Rhetoric of the Veil." *NWSA Journal* 17, no. 3 (Autumn 2005): 112–33.

Baedan. "Musings on Nothingness and Some of Its Varieties." *Baedan Journal of Queer Nihilism*, no. 1 (August 2012): 147–77.

Balfour, Ian, and Eduardo Cadava. "The Claims of Human Rights: An Introduction." *South Atlantic Quarterly* 103, no. 2–3 (Spring/Summer 2004): 277–96. doi: 10.1215/00382876-103-2-3-277.

Banet-Weiser, Sarah. *The Most Beautiful Girl in the World: Beauty Pageants and National Identity*. Berkeley: University of California Press, 1999.

Barghouti, Mourid. "You and I." 1983. In "You and I: A Poem about a Timeless Love Story." *Women of Egypt Mag*. Translated and republished by Dina Al Mahdy, February 7, 2019. https://womenofegyptmag.com/2019/02/08/you-and-i-a-poem-about-a-timeless-love-story/.

Barker, Kim. "The Change Was Merely Cosmetic." *Chicago Tribune*, June 1, 2008.

Barnard, Rita. "The Place of Beauty: Reflections on Elaine Scarry and Zakes Mda." In *Beautiful/Ugly: African and Diaspora Aesthetics*, edited by Sarah Nuttall, 102–21. Durham, NC: Duke University Press, 2006.

Barthes, Roland. *Camera Lucida: Reflections on Photography*. Translated by Richard Howard. New York: Hill and Wang, 1981.

Barthes, Roland. *The Pleasure of the Text*. Translated by Richard Miller. New York: Hill and Wang, 1975.

Bartlett, Christy. "A Tearoom View of Mended Ceramics." In *Flickwerk: The Aesthetics of Mended Japanese Ceramics*, 8–13. Ithaca, NY: Cornell University, Herbert F. Johnson Museum of Art, 2008.

Beardsley, Monroe C. "Aesthetic Experience Regained." *Journal of Aesthetics and Art Criticism* 28, no. 1 (Autumn 1969): 3–11.

Beauchamp, Toby. *Going Stealth: Transgender Politics and U.S. Surveillance Practices*. Durham, NC: Duke University Press, 2019.

Beck, Brendon. "The Role of Police in Gentrification." *Appeal*, August 4, 2020. https://theappeal.org/the-role-of-police-igentrification-breonna-taylor/.

Bedi, Nikki. "'Beauty Day' Gives Respite to Women in Calais 'Jungle.'" Produced by Kristy Starkey. *BBC Radio 4: Women's Hour*, August 2, 2016. Podcast. https://www.bbc.co.uk/programmes/b07m4cvy.

Beech, Hannah. "Khmer Rouge's Slaughter in Cambodia Is Ruled a Genocide." *New York Times*, November 15, 2018. https://www.nytimes.com/2018/11/15/world/asia/khmer-rouge-cambodia-genocide.html.

"Before the Light." Featuring Toni Morrison, Molly Ringwald, Mary Terrier, and Alex Dimitrov. In *Paris Review Podcast*, season 2, episode 13. Morrison recordings from 1992. Published online October 22, 2019. Podcast. https://www.theparisreview.org/podcast/6047/before-the-light.

Bell, Thomas. "Miss Landmine Beauty Pageant Banned in Cambodia." *Telegraph*, August 3, 2009. https://www.telegraph.co.uk/news/worldnews/asia/cambodia/5965720/Miss-Landmine-beauty-pageant-banned-in-Cambodia.html.

Benjamin, Walter. *The Origin of German Tragic Drama*. 1928. Translated by John Osborne. London: Verso, 1998.

Benjamin, Walter. "Theses on the Philosophy of History." In *Illuminations: Essays and Reflections*, edited by Hannah Arendt, translated by Harry Zohn, 253–64. New York: Schocken, 1968.

Benjamin, Walter. "The Work of Art in the Age of Its Technological Reproducibility [First Version]." Translated by Michael W. Jennings. *Grey Room* 39 (Spring 2010): 11–38.

Benjamin, Walter. "The Work of Art in the Age of Mechanical Reproduction." In *Illuminations: Essays and Reflections*, edited by Hannah Arendt, translated by Harry Zohn, 217–52. New York: Schocken, 1968.

Berger, Alan. *Drosscape: Wasting Land in Urban America*. New York: Princeton Architectural Press, 2006.

Bergson, Henri. *Time and Free Will: An Essay on the Immediate Data of Consciousness*. 1889. Translated by F. L. Pogson. London: Swan Sonnenschein, 1910.

Berlant, Lauren. "The Commons: Infrastructures for Troubling Times." *Environment and Planning D: Society and Space* 34, no. 3 (2016): 393–419. doi:10.1177/0263775816645989.

Berlant, Lauren. *Cruel Optimism*. Durham, NC: Duke University Press, 2011.

Berlant, Lauren. *Desire/Love*. Brooklyn, NY: Punctum, 2012.

Berlant, Lauren. *The Female Complaint: The Unfinished Business of Sentimentality in American Culture*. Durham, NC: Duke University Press, 2008.

Berlant, Lauren. "Love, a Queer Feeling." In *Homosexuality and Psychoanalysis*, edited by Tim Dean and Christopher Lane, 432–52. Chicago: University of Chicago Press, 2001.

Berlant, Lauren. *On the Inconvenience of Other People*. Durham, NC: Duke University Press, 2022.

Berlant, Lauren, and Kathleen Stewart. *The Hundreds*. Durham, NC: Duke University Press, 2019.

Berthold, Jürg, Philip Ursprung, and Mechtild Widrich, eds. *Presence: A Conversation at Cabaret Voltaire, Zurich*. Berlin, Sternberg, 2016.

Betancourt, Mark. "Detroit's Housing Crisis Is the Work of Its Own Government." *Vice*, December 29, 2017. https://www.vice.com/en/article/kznzky/detroits-housing-crisis-is-the-work-of-its-own-government.

Bettcher, Talia Mae. "Evil Deceivers and Make-Believers: On Transphobic Violence and the Politics of Illusion." *Hypatia* 22, no. 3 (Summer 2007): 43–65.

Bhungalia, Lisa. *Elastic Empire: Refashioning War through Aid in Palestine*. Stanford, CA: Stanford University Press, 2024.

Bishop, Claire. *Artificial Hells: Participatory Art and the Politics of Spectatorship*. London: Verso, 2012.

Black, Paula. *The Beauty Industry: Gender, Culture, Pleasure*. London: Routledge, 2004.

Bloul, Rachel A. D. "Ain't I a Woman? Female Landmine Survivors' Beauty Pageants and the Ethics of Staring." *Social Identities: Journal for the Study of Race, Nation, and Culture* 18, no. 1 (January 2012): 3–18. doi: 10.1080/13504630.2012.629507.

Bolin, Paul, and Kaela Hoskings. "Reflecting on Our Beliefs and Actions: Purposeful Practice in Art Education." *Art Education* 68, no. 4 (July 2015): 40–47.

Bonanno, George A. "Loss, Trauma, and Human Resilience: Have We Underestimated the Human Capacity to Thrive after Extremely Averse Events?" *American Psychologist* 59, no. 1 (2004): 20–28. doi: 10.1037/0003-066X.59.1.20.

Bonanno, George A., Sandro Galea, Angela Bucciarelli, and David Vlahov. "What Predicts Psychological Resilience after Disaster? The Role of Demographics, Resources, and Life Stress." *Journal of Consulting and Clinical Psychology* 75, no. 5 (2007): 671–82. doi: 10.1037/0022-006X.75.5.671.

Booth, Wayne. "Individualism and the Mystery of the Social Self; or, Does Amnesty Have a Leg to Stand On?" In *Freedom and Interpretation: The Oxford Amnesty Lectures, 1992*, edited by Barbara Johnson, 69–102. New York: Basic Books, 1993.

Bourdieu, Pierre. *Distinction: A Social Critique of the Judgement of Taste*. Translated by Richard Nice. Cambridge, MA: Harvard University Press, 1984.

Bourdieu, Pierre. *Outline of a Theory of Practice*. Translated by Richard Nice. Cambridge: Cambridge University Press, 1977.

Boutopoulou, Alexandra. "On the Origins of 'They Tried to Bury Us, They Didn't Know We Were Seeds.'" Interview by An Xiao Mina. *Hyperallergic*, July 3, 2018. https://hyperallergic.com/449930/on-the-origins-of-they-tried-to-bury-us-they-didnt-know-we-were-seeds/.

Bracke, Sarah. "Bouncing Back: Vulnerability and Resistance in Times of Resilience." In *Vulnerability in Resistance*, edited by Judith Butler, Zeynep Gambetti, and Leticia Sabsay, 52–75. Durham, NC: Duke University Press, 2016.

British Museum Press Office. "British Museum to Work with Experts from Iraq to Set Up Emergency Heritage Management Programme." 2015. Accessed July 2019. https://www.britishmuseum.org/about_us/news_and_press/press_releases/2015/emergency_heritage_management.aspx.

Bronfen, Elisabeth. *Over Her Dead Body: Death, Femininity and the Aesthetic*. Manchester: Manchester University Press, 1992.

Brown, Bill. *A Sense of Things: The Object Matter of American Literature*. Chicago: University of Chicago Press, 2003.

Brown, Hillary. "The Holocaust, Art, Chicago & Sickness: A 3,500-Word Interview with *My Favorite Thing Is Monsters* Mastermind Emil Ferris." *Paste Magazine*, February 23, 2017. https://www.pastemagazine.com/comics/emil-ferris/the-holocaust-art-chicago-sickness-a-3500-word-int/.

Brown, Judith. *Glamour in Six Dimensions: Modernism and the Radiance of Form*. Ithaca, NY: Cornell University Press, 2009.

Brown, Wendy. *Politics Out of History*. Princeton, NJ: Princeton University Press, 2001.

Brown, Wendy. *Walled States, Waning Sovereignty*. New York: Zone, 2010.

Bryant, Kenzie. "Miss Perú Contestants Give Gender-Violence Statistics Instead of Their Body Measurements." *Vanity Fair*, November 1, 2017. https://www.vanityfair.com/style/2017/11/miss-peru-my-measurements-are-protest-femicide-2017.

Buckley, Kat. "It Will Arise from the Ashes, or Exploring the Aesthetics of Postmodern Ruin Photography in Detroit." *Kritikos: An International and Interdisciplinary Journal of Postmodern Cultural Sound, Text and Image* 13 (Winter 2016/2017). https://intertheory.org/buckley.htm#_ednref10.

Buck-Morss, Susan. "Aesthetics and Anaesthetics: Walter Benjamin's Artwork Essay Reconsidered." *October* 62 (Autumn 1992): 3–41.

Bui, Keva X. "Objects of Warfare: Infrastructures of Race and Napalm in the Vietnam War." *Amerasia Journal* 47, no. 2 (2021): 299–313. doi: 10.1080/00447471.2021.2021775.

Bui, Long T. *Returns of War: South Vietnam and the Price of Refugee Memory*. New York: New York University Press, 2018.

Bui, Mai, and Jane Przybysz. Preface to *Ao Dai: A Modern Design Coming of Age*, 1. San Jose, CA: San Jose Museum of Quilts and Textiles, 2006. Exhibition catalog.

Bui, Thi. *The Best We Could Do: An Illustrated Memoir*. New York: Abrams ComicArts, 2017.

Burke, Edmund. *Reflections on the Revolution in France*. 1790. Edited by Conor Cruise O'Brien. Harmondsworth, UK: Penguin, 1968.

Bush, George W. "Remarks to the Warsaw Conference on Combatting Terrorism." George W. Bush White House Archives. November 6, 2001. https://georgewbush-whitehouse.archives.gov/news/releases/2001/11/20011106-2.html.

Bush, Laura. "Radio Address by Mrs. Bush." George W. Bush White House Archives. November 17, 2001. https://georgewbush-whitehouse.archives.gov/news/releases/2001/11/20011117.html.

Butler, Judith. "Finishing, Starting." In *Derrida and the Time of the Political*, edited by Pheng Cheah and Suzanne Guerlac, 291–306. Durham, NC: Duke University Press, 2009.

Butler, Judith. *Gender Trouble: Feminism and the Subversion of Identity*. New York: Routledge, 1990.

Butler, Judith. *Precarious Life: The Powers of Mourning and Violence*. London: Verso, 2004.

Cacho, Lisa Marie. *Social Death: Racialized Rightlessness and the Criminalization of the Unprotected*. New York: New York University Press, 2012.

Cadava, Eduardo. *Words of Light: Theses on the Photography of History*. Princeton, NJ: Princeton University Press, 1997.

Camp, Jordan T., and Christina Heatherton. "Introduction: Policing the Planet." In *Policing the Planet: Why the Policing Crisis Led to Black Lives Matter*, edited by Camp and Heatherton. London: Verso, 2016. E-book.

Canuel, Mark. *Justice, Dissent, and the Sublime*. Baltimore: Johns Hopkins University Press, 2012.

Castañeda, Claudia. *Figurations: Child, Bodies, Worlds*. Durham, NC: Duke University Press, 2002.

Chakravartty, Paula, and Denise Ferreira da Silva. "Accumulation, Dispossession, and Debt: The Racial Logic of Global Capitalism—An Introduction." *American Quarterly* 64, no. 3 (September 2012): 361–85. doi: 10.1353/aq.2012.0033.

Chea, Jolie. "This Is War: Cambodian American Exceptionalism and the Settler Colonial Logic of Incorporation." Unpublished manuscript.

Cheng, Anne Anlin. *Ornamentalism*. New York: Oxford University Press, 2019.

Cheng, Anne Anlin. *Second Skin: Josephine Baker and the Modern Surface*. New York: Oxford University Press, 2011.

Chocano, Carina. "Joy in Good Hair Days." *Los Angeles Times*, April 28, 2006. https://www.latimes.com/archives/la-xpm-2006-apr-28-et-beauty28-story.html.

Chödrön, Pema. *Living Beautifully with Uncertainty and Change*. Boston: Shambhala, 2012.

Choi, Franny. *The World Keeps Ending, and the World Goes On*. New York: Ecco, 2022.

Chow, Rey. *The Age of the World Target: Self-Referentiality in War, Theory, and Comparative Work*. Durham, NC: Duke University Press, 2006.

Chow, Rey. *Entanglements, or Transmedial Thinking about Capture*. Durham, NC: Duke University Press, 2012.

Chow, Rey. *Primitive Passions: Visuality, Sexuality, Ethnography, and Contemporary Chinese Cinema*. New York: Columbia University Press, 1995.

Chow, Rey. "The Resistance of Theory; or, the Worth of Agony." In *Just Being Difficult? Academic Writing in the Public Arena*, edited by Jonathan Culler and Kevin Lamb, 95–105. Stanford, CA: Stanford University Press, 2003.

Chow, Rey. *Writing Diaspora: Tactics of Intervention in Contemporary Cultural Studies*. Bloomington: Indiana University Press, 1993.

Christopher, Matthew. "Confessions of a Ruin Pornographer Part II: A Chronicle of Failure." *Abandoned America*, January 24 2012. https://www.abandonedamerica.us/ruin-pornographer-part-ii.

Chuh, Kandice. *The Difference Aesthetics Makes: On the Humanities "After Man."* Durham, NC: Duke University Press, 2019.

Clark-Flory, Tracy. "Miss Landmine 2008." *Salon*, November 19, 2007. https://www.salon.com/2007/11/19/angola/.

Clifford, James. "The Others: Beyond the 'Salvage' Paradigm." *Third Text* 3, no. 6 (1989): 73–78. doi: 10.1080/09528828908576217.

Clifford, James. *The Predicament of Culture: Twentieth-Century Ethnography, Literature, and Art*. Cambridge, MA: Harvard University Press, 1988.

Clutario, Genevieve. *Beauty Regimes: A History of Power and Modern Empire in the Philippines, 1898–1941*. Durham, NC: Duke University Press, 2023.

Cohen, Colleen Ballerino, Richard Wilk, and Beverly Stoeltje, eds. *Beauty Queens on the Global Stage: Gender, Contests, and Power*. New York: Routledge, 1996.

Colebrook, Claire. "Introduction." *Feminist Theory* 7, no. 2 (2006): 131–42. doi: 10.1177/1464700106064404.

Coleman, Rebecca, and Mónica Moreno Figueroa. "Past and Future Perfect? Beauty, Affect and Hope." *Journal for Cultural Research* 14, no. 4 (October 2010): 357–73. doi: 10.1080/14797581003765317.

Collier, Stephen J., and Andrew Lakoff. "The Vulnerability of Vital Systems: How 'Critical Infrastructure' Became a Security Problem." In *Securing "the Homeland": Critical Infrastructure, Risk, and (In)Security*, edited by Myriam Dunn Cavelty and Kristian Søby Kristensen, 17–39. London: Routledge, 2008.

Collins, Michael. "The Long Look." Tate Research Publication, 2002. Accessed November 20, 2020. https://www.tate.org.uk/art/artists/bernd-becher-and-hilla-becher-718/long-look.

Cook, Barry, and Tony Bancroft, dirs. *Mulan*. Walt Disney Pictures, 1998.

Cooper Jones, Chloé. *Easy Beauty: A Memoir*. New York City: Simon and Schuster, 2022.

Cottom, Tressie McMillan. *Thick, and Other Essays*. New York: New Press, 2019.

Cousins, Mark. "The Ugly [Part 1]." *AA Files* 28 (Autumn 1994): 61–64.

Cousins, Mark. "The Ugly [Part 2]." *AA Files* 29 (Summer 1995): 3–6.

Craik, Jennifer. *The Face of Fashion: Cultural Studies in Fashion*. London: Routledge, 1994.

Crane, Susan A. "'Take Nothing but Photos, Leave Nothing but Footprints': How-To Guides for Ruin Photography." In *Ruin Porn and the Obsession with Decay*, edited by Siobhan Lyons, 83–102. New York: Palgrave Macmillan, 2018.

Crawford, Ann Caddell. *Customs and Culture of Vietnam*. Rutland, VT: C. E. Tuttle, 1966.

Cruikshank, Barbara. *The Will to Empower: Democratic Citizens and Other Subjects*. Ithaca, NY: Cornell University Press, 1999.

Dabashi, Hamid. "Gaza: Poetry after Auschwitz." *Al Jazeera*, August 8, 2014. https://www.aljazeera.com/opinions/2014/8/8/gaza-poetry-after-auschwitz.

Dango, Michael. *Crisis Style: The Aesthetics of Repair*. Stanford, CA: Stanford University Press, 2022.

Danto, Arthur C. *The Abuse of Beauty: Aesthetics and the Concept of Art*. Chicago: Open Court, 2003.

David, Emmanuel, and Christian Joy P. Cruz. "Big, *Bakla*, and Beautiful: Transformations on a Manila Pageant Stage." *WSQ: Women's Studies Quarterly* 46, no. 1–2 (Spring/Summer 2018): 29–45.

Davoudi, Simin. "Resilience: A Bridging Concept or a Dead End?" *Planning Theory and Practice* 13, no. 2 (June 2012): 299–333. doi: 10.1080/14649357.2012.677124.

Dean, Carolyn J. "Empathy, Pornography, and Suffering." *differences: A Journal of Feminist Cultural Studies* 14, no. 1 (2003): 88–124.

Dean, Carolyn J. *The Fragility of Empathy after the Holocaust*. Ithaca, NY: Cornell University Press, 2004.

Deleuze, Gilles. *Cinema 1: The Movement-Image*. Translated by Hugh Tomlinson and Barbara Habberjam. Minneapolis: University of Minnesota Press, 1986.

Deleuze, Gilles. *Difference and Repetition*. 1968. Translated by Paul Patton. New York: Columbia University Press, 1994.

Derrida, Jacques. "Force of Law: The 'Mystical Foundation of Authority.'" In *Deconstruction and the Possibility of Justice*, edited by Drucilla Cornell, Michel Rosenfeld, and David Gray Carlson, 3–67. New York: Routledge, 1992.

Derrida, Jacques. *Negotiations: Interventions and Interviews, 1971–2001*. Edited, translated, and with an introduction by Elizabeth Rottenberg. Stanford, CA: Stanford University Press, 2002.

Derrida, Jacques. *Of Grammatology*. 1967. Translated by Gayatri Chakravorty Spivak. Baltimore: Johns Hopkins University Press, 1974.

Derrida, Jacques. *The Other Heading: Reflections on Today's Europe*. Translated by Pascale-Anne Brault and Michael B. Naas. Bloomington: Indiana University Press, 1992.

Derrida, Jacques. *Rogues: Two Essays on Reason*. Translated by Pascale-Anne Brault and Michael Naas. Stanford, CA: Stanford University Press, 2005.

Derrida, Jacques. *Specters of Marx: The State of the Debt, the Work of Mourning, and the New International*. Translated by Peggy Kamuf. New York: Routledge, 1993.

DeSilvey, Caitlin, and Tim Edensor. "Reckoning with Ruins." *Progress in Human Geography* 37, no. 4 (2012): 465–85.

DeVeaux, Alexis. "A Conversation with June Jordan." *Essence*, September 2000, 101–2.

Diaz, Robert. "*Biyuti* from Below: Contemporary Philippine Cinema and the Transing of *Kabaklaan*." *TSQ: Transgender Studies Quarterly* 5, no. 3 (2018): 404–24. doi: 10.1215/23289252-6900781.

Diaz, Robert. *A Confetti of Ordinary Dreams: Queer Filipinos and Reparative Acts*. Durham, NC: Duke University Press, forthcoming.

Dick, Alexander, and Christina Lupton. "On Lecturing and Being Beautiful: Zadie Smith, Elaine Scarry, and the Liberal Aesthetic." *ESC: English Studies in Canada* 39, no. 2–3 (June/September 2013): 115–37.

di Giovanni, Janine. "Beneath the Burqa." *Vogue*, May 2002, 254–62. https://archive.vogue.com/article/2002/05/01/beneath-the-burqa.

Diola, Camille. "In Photos: Filipino Who Cuts Hair of New York's Homeless." *Philippine Star*, August 18, 2014. https://www.philstar.com/news-commentary/2014/08/18/1358960/photos-filipino-who-cuts-hair-new-yorks-homeless.

"Disability-Adjusted Life Years (DALYs)." World Health Organization. Accessed August 19, 2020. https://www.who.int/data/gho/indicator-metadata-registry/imr-details/158.

Dolven, Jeff. *Senses of Style: Poetry before Interpretation*. Chicago: University of Chicago Press, 2018.

Donoghue, Denis. *Speaking of Beauty*. New Haven, CT: Yale University Press, 2003.

Doucet, Brian, and Drew Philp. "In Detroit 'Ruin Porn' Ignores the Voices of Those Who Still Call the City Home." *Guardian*, February 15, 2016. https://www.theguardian.com/housing-network/2016/feb/15/ruin-porn-detroit-photography-city-homes.

Dubin, Nina. "Robert Des Ruines: Speculating in the Market for Ruins." *Cabinet* 20 (Winter 2005–6). https://www.cabinetmagazine.org/issues/20/dubin.php.

Du Bois, W. E. B. "Of Beauty and Death." In *Darkwater: Voices from within the Veil*, 130–44. New York: Verso, 2016.

Duc, Duong Thi Kim, and Mingxin Bao. "Aesthetic Sense of the Vietnamese through Three Renovations of the Women's Ao Dai in the 20th Century." *Asian Culture and History* 4, no. 2 (July 2012): 99–108. doi: 10.5539/ach.v4n2p99.

Dudziak, Mary L. *War Time: An Idea, Its History, Its Consequences*. Oxford: Oxford University Press, 2012.

Duffett, Claire. "Cambodia's Miss Landmine Controversy." *World*, August 8, 2009. https://theworld.org/stories/2009-08-08/cambodias-miss-landmine-controversy.

Duffield, Mark. "Total War as Environmental Terror: Linking Liberalism, Resilience, and the Bunker." *South Atlantic Quarterly* 110, no. 3 (2001): 757–69. doi: 10.1215/00382876-1275779.

Duong, Natalia. "Agent Orange Bodies: Việt, Đức, and Transnational Narratives of Repair." *Canadian Review of American Studies* 48, no. 3 (2018): 387–414.

Eap, Robert. "Contested Commemorations: Violence and Memory in Cambodia," PhD diss., University of Southern California, 2014.

Earvolino-Ramirez, Marie. "Resilience: A Concept Analysis." *Nursing Forum: An Independent Voice for Nursing* 42, no. 2 (April–June 2007): 73–82.

Eco, Umberto. *History of Beauty*. New York: Rizzoli, 2004.

Eco, Umberto. *The Infinity of Lists*. New York: Rizzoli, 2009.

Edensor, Tim. *Industrial Ruins: Space, Aesthetics and Materiality*. Oxford: Berg, 2005.

Edwards, Lee R. "War and Roses: The Politics of *Mrs. Dalloway*." In *The Authority of Experience: Essays in Feminist Criticism*, edited by Arlyn Diamond and Lee R. Edwards, 160–77. Amherst: University of Massachusetts Press, 1977.

Edwards, Penny. *Cambodge: The Cultivation of a Nation, 1860–1945*. Honolulu: University of Hawaii Press, 2007.

Egbuonu, Oge, dir. "Beauty of Becoming: Fashion a New World Forward." Featuring Naomi Osaka, Willow Smith, Jaden Smith, Leyna Bloom, Dolores Huerta, and others. Launched January 2021, on Levi's website, Instagram, and YouTube. Levi-Strauss & Co. 2021. https://www.levi.com/US/en_US/blog/article/beauty-of-becoming.

Elias, Norbert. *The Civilizing Process: The Development of Manners*. 1939. Translated by Edmund Jephcott. New York: Urizen, 1978.

Eng, David L. "Colonial Object Relations." *Social Text* 34, no. 1 (2016): 1–19.

Eng, David L., and David Kazanjian. "Introduction: Mourning Remains." In *Loss: The Politics of Mourning*, edited by David L. Eng and David Kazanjian, 1–25. Berkeley: University of California Press, 2003.

Enriquez, Mariana. *Things We Lost in the Fire*. Translated by Megan McDowell. New York: Hogarth, 2017.

Erevelles, Nirmala. "The Color of Violence: Reflecting on Gender, Race, and Disability in Wartime." In *Feminist Disability Studies*, edited by Kim Q. Hall, 117–35. Bloomington: Indiana University Press, 2011.

Erevelles, Nirmala. *Disability and Difference in Global Contexts: Enabling a Transformative Body Politic*. New York: Palgrave Macmillan, 2011.

Esmeir, Samera. *Juridical Humanity: A Colonial History*. Stanford, CA: Stanford University Press, 2012.

Espiritu, Yến Lê. *Body Counts: The Vietnam War and Militarized Refuge(es)*. Oakland: University of California Press, 2014.

Evans, Brad, and Julian Reid. *Resilient Life: The Art of Living Dangerously*. Cambridge, UK: Polity, 2014.

Ewing, Heidi, and Rachel Grady. "Dismantling Detroit." *New York Times*, January 18, 2012. https://www.nytimes.com/2012/01/19/opinion/dismantling-detroit.html.

Fabian, Johannes. *Time and the Other: How Anthropology Makes Its Object*. New York: Columbia University Press, 1983.

Falser, Michel S. "From a Colonial Reinvention to Postcolonial Heritage and a Global Commodity: Performing and Re-enacting Angkor Wat and the Royal Khmer Ballet." *International Journal of Heritage Studies* 20, no. 7–8 (2014): 702–23. doi: 10.1080/13527258.2013.794746.

Farrell, Amy, and Patrice McDermott. "Claiming Afghan Women: The Challenge of Human Rights, and the Politics of Global Crisis." In *Just Advocacy?*

Women's Human Rights, Transnational Feminisms, and the Politics of Representation, edited by Wendy S. Hesford and Wendy Kozol, 33–55. New Brunswick, NJ: Rutgers University Press, 2005.

Fassin, Didier. "Humanitarianism as a Politics of Life." *Public Culture* 19, no. 3 (Fall 2007): 499–520.

Fassin, Didier. *Humanitarian Reason: A Moral History of the Present.* Translated by Rachel Gomme. Berkeley: University of California Press, 2012.

Feingold, Stan, dir. *Miss Landmine.* The Eyes, 2010.

Feldman, Josh. "MSNBC Guest: Stop Using the Word 'Resilient' to Describe Katrina Victims." *Mediaite*, August, 29, 2015.

Feminist Majority Foundation Blog. "V-Day 2001: To End Violence against Women." Feminist Majority Foundation, March 30, 2001. https://feminist.org/news/v-day-2001-to-end-violence-against-women/.

Ferlinghetti, Lawrence. *A Coney Island of the Mind.* New York: New Directions, 1958.

Ferreira da Silva, Denise. *Toward a Global Idea of Race.* Minneapolis: University of Minnesota Press, 2007.

Fischer, Sibylle. "Haiti: Fantasies of Bare Life." *Small Axe* 11, no. 2 (June 2007): 1–15.

Fleetwood, Nicole R. "Failing Narratives, Initiating Technologies: Hurricane Katrina and the Production of a Weather Media Event." *American Quarterly* 58, no. 3 (September 2006): 767–89.

Fleischmann, T. *Time Is the Thing a Body Moves Through.* Minneapolis: Coffee House, 2019.

Flintoff, Corey. "In Baghdad, Hemlines Rise as Violence Falls." NPR, December 16, 2009. https://www.npr.org/templates/story/story.php?storyId=120822831.

Fogg, Rebecca. *Beautiful Trauma: An Explosion, an Obsession, and a New Lease on Life.* New York: Avery, 2023.

Förster, Larissa. "From 'General Field Marshal' to 'Miss Genocide': The Reworking of Traumatic Experiences among Herero-Speaking Namibians." *Journal of Material Culture* 13, no. 2 (July 2008): 175–94.

Foucault, Michel. *The Archaeology of Knowledge and the Discourse on Language.* 1969. Translated by A. M. Sheridan Smith. New York: Pantheon, 1972.

Foucault, Michel. *The Birth of Biopolitics: Lectures at the Collège de France, 1978–79.* Edited by Michel Senellart. Translated by Graham Burchell. New York: Palgrave Macmillan, 2008.

Foucault, Michel. "The Concern for Truth." 1984. In *Politics, Philosophy, Culture: Interviews and Other Writings 1977–1984*, edited by Lawrence D. Kritzman, translated by Alan Sheridan, 255–67. New York: Routledge, 1988.

Foucault, Michel. *Discipline and Punish: The Birth of the Prison.* 1975. Translated by Alan Sheridan. New York: Vintage, 1995.

Foucault, Michel. *The History of Sexuality, Volume 1: An Introduction.* 1978. Translated by Robert Hurley. New York: Vintage, 1990.

Foucault, Michel. "The Subject and Power." Afterword to *Michel Foucault: Beyond Structuralism and Hermeneutics*, by Hubert L. Dreyfus and Paul Rabinow, 208–26. 2nd ed. Chicago: University of Chicago Press, 1983.

Freeman, Elizabeth. *Beside You in Time: Sense Methods and Queer Sociabilities in the American 19th Century*. Durham, NC: Duke University Press, 2019.

Freeman, Elizabeth. *Time Binds: Queer Temporalities, Queer Histories*. Durham, NC: Duke University Press, 2010.

Frueh, Joanna, with photography by Frances Murray. *Unapologetic Beauty*. Minneapolis: University of Minnesota Press, 2019.

Gagnier, Regenia. *The Insatiability of Human Wants: Economics and Aesthetics in Market Society*. Chicago: University of Chicago Press, 2000.

Gandhi, Evyn Lê Espiritu. *Archipelago of Resettlement: Vietnamese Refugee Settlers and Decolonization across Guam and Israel-Palestine*. Oakland: University of California Press, 2022.

Garafola, Lynn. "The Travesty Dancer in Nineteenth-Century Ballet." *Dance Research Journal* 17, no. 2 (Autumn 1985); 18, no. 1 (Spring 1986): 35–40.

Gardner, Marilyn. "Lifting the Veil on Women's Subjugation." *Christian Science Monitor*, November 28, 2001. http://www.csmonitor.com/2001/1128/p15s1-lihc.html.

Garland-Thomson, Rosemarie. "Seeing the Disabled: Visual Rhetorics of Disability in Popular Photography." In *The New Disability History: American Perspectives*, edited by Paul K. Longmore and Lauri Umansky, 335–74. New York: New York University Press, 2001.

Gebara, Ivone. "Yearning for Beauty: What Do Beauty and Justice Have to Do with Our Salvation?" *Other Side: Strength for the Journey* 39, no. 4 (2003): 24–25.

Ghafour, Hamida. "Afghans Flocking to Beauticians without Borders." *Telegraph*, February 21, 2004. https://www.telegraph.co.uk/news/worldnews/asia/afghanistan/1455025/Afghans-flocking-to-Beauticians-Without-Borders.html.

Ghosh, Amitav. *Dancing in Cambodia, at Large in Burma*. Delhi: Ravi Dayal, 1998.

Gigante, Denise. *Life: Organic Form and Romanticism*. New Haven, CT: Yale University Press, 2009.

Gill, Tiffany M. *Beauty Shop Politics: African American Women's Activism in the Beauty Industry*. Urbana: University of Illinois Press, 2010.

Gilmore, Ruth Wilson. *Golden Gulag: Prisons, Surplus, Crisis, and Opposition in Globalizing California*. Berkeley: University of California Press, 2007.

Gilpin, William. *Three Essays: On Picturesque Beauty; On Picturesque Travel; and On Sketching Landscape*. London: R. Blamire, 1792.

Godlewski, Nina. "Mr. Rogers Quotes: Wisdom from the Children's Television Host on His Birthday." *Newsweek*, March 20, 2018. https://www.newsweek.com/fred-rogers-birthday-quotes-wont-you-be-my-neighbor-movie-854013.

Goldman, Emma. *Living My Life*. 1931. New York: Cosimo Classics, 2011.

González, Jennifer A. *Subject to Display: Reframing Race in Contemporary Installation Art*. Cambridge, MA: MIT Press, 2008.

Gonzalez, Vernadette Vicuña. *Empire's Mistress, Starring Isabel Rosario Cooper*. Durham, NC: Duke University Press, 2021.

Gopinath, Gayatri. *Impossible Desires: Queer Diasporas and South Asian Public Cultures*. Durham, NC: Duke University Press, 2005.

Gordon, Avery F. *Ghostly Matters: Haunting and the Sociological Imagination*. Minneapolis: University of Minnesota Press, 1997.

Gordon, Colin. "Governmental Rationality: An Introduction." In *The Foucault Effect: Studies in Governmentality*, edited by Graham Burchell, Colin Gordon, and Peter Miller, 1–54. Chicago: University of Chicago Press, 1991.

Grandin, Greg. "The Collapse of America's Imperial Car Industry." *Mother Jones*, June 23, 2009. https://www.motherjones.com/politics/2009/06/collapse-americas-imperial-car-industry/.

Grandin, Greg. "Empire's Ruins: Detroit to the Amazon." In *Imperial Debris: On Ruins and Ruination*, edited by Ann Laura Stoler, 115–28. Durham, NC: Duke University Press, 2013.

Grewal, Inderpal. *Home and Harem: Nation, Gender, Empire, and the Cultures of Travel*. Durham, NC: Duke University Press, 1996.

Grewal, Inderpal, and Caren Kaplan, eds. *Scattered Hegemonies: Postmodernity and Transnational Feminist Practices*. Minneapolis: University of Minnesota Press, 1994.

Groslier, George. *Cambodian Dancers: Ancient and Modern*. 1913. Edited by Kent Davis. Translated by Pedro Rodríguez. Holmes Beach, FL: DatAsia, 2011.

Groslier, George. *Danseuses cambodgiennes: Anciennes et modernes*. Paris: A. Challamel, 1913.

Grosz, Elizabeth. "Naked." In *Encounters with Alphonso Lingis*, edited by Alexander E. Hooke and Wolfgang W. Fuchs, 119–32. Landham, MD: Lexington, 2003.

Guest, Jocelyn. "Extreme Makeover Freedom Edition: An American Beauty School Sets Up Shop in Afghanistan." *Iris: A Journal about Women* 50 (Spring 2005): 12.

Halbfinger, David. "After the Veil, a Makeover Rush." *New York Times*, September 1, 2002. https://www.nytimes.com/2002/09/01/style/after-the-veil-a-makeover-rush.html.

Hannah, Lesa. "The Pandemic Has Changed Our Relationship with Skincare." *Elle*, October 13, 2020. https://www.ellecanada.com/beauty/skincare/pandemic-skincare.

Hansberry, Lorraine. *To Be Young, Gifted, and Black*. New York: Penguin, 1970.

Harlow, Barbara. *Barred: Women, Writing, and Political Detention*. Hanover, NH: University Press of New England, 1992.

Harney, Stefano, and Fred Moten. *The Undercommons: Fugitive Planning and Black Study*. Wivenhoe, UK: Minor Compositions, 2013.

Harrison, Cassian, dir. "Beneath the Veil: The Taliban's Harsh Rule of Afghanistan." Season 15, episode 5, of *Dispatches*, hosted by Saira Shah.

First broadcast June 26, 2001, on Channel 4 (UK) and subsequently on *CNN Presents* (US).

Hartman, Saidiya. "The Anarchy of Colored Girls Assembled in a Riotous Manner." *South Atlantic Quarterly* 117, no. 3 (July 2018): 465–90. doi: 10.1215/00382876-6942093.

Hartman, Saidiya. *Lose Your Mother: A Journey along the Atlantic Slave Route.* New York: Farrar, Straus and Giroux, 2007.

Hartman, Saidiya. *Wayward Lives, Beautiful Experiments: Intimate Histories of Social Upheaval.* New York: W. W. Norton, 2019.

Harvey, David. "From Space to Place and Back Again: Reflections on the Condition of Postmodernity." In *Mapping the Futures: Local Cultures, Global Change*, edited by Jon Bird, Barry Curtis, Tim Putnam, George Robertson, and Lisa Tickner, 2–29. London: Routledge, 1993.

Harvey, David. "The 'New' Imperialism: Accumulation by Dispossession." *Socialist Register* 40 (2004): 63–87. https://socialistregister.com/index.php/srv/article/view/5811/2707.

Hauser, Gayelord. *Mirror, Mirror on the Wall: Invitation to Beauty.* 2nd ed. New York: Farrar, Straus and Cudahy, 1961.

Hawkins, Derek. "Brian Williams Is 'Guided by the Beauty of Our Weapons' in Syria Strikes." *Washington Post*, April 7, 2017. https://www.washingtonpost.com/news/morning-mix/wp/2017/04/07/beautiful-brian-williams-says-of-syria-missile-strike-proceeds-to-quote-leonard-cohen/.

Heikkila, Eric J., and Philippe Peycam. "Economic Development in the Shadow of Angkor Wat: Meaning, Legitimation, and Myth." *Journal of Planning Education and Research* 29, no. 3 (2010): 294–309. doi: 10.1177/0739456X09359167.

Hemingway, Ernest. *A Farewell to Arms.* London: Jonathan Cape, 1929.

Herron, Jerry. *AfterCulture: Detroit and the Humiliation of History.* Detroit: Wayne State University Press, 1993.

Herron, Jerry. "The Forgetting Machine: Notes toward a History of Detroit." *Places Journal*, January 2012. doi: 10.22269/120109.

Hesford, Wendy S. *Spectacular Rhetorics: Human Rights Visions, Recognitions, Feminisms.* Durham, NC: Duke University Press, 2011.

Hickey, Dave. *The Invisible Dragon: Four Essays on Beauty.* Los Angeles: Art Issues, 1993.

Hilderbrand, Lucas. *Inherent Vice: Bootleg Histories of Videotape and Copyright.* Durham, NC: Duke University Press, 2009.

Hindi, Noor. "Fuck Your Lecture on Craft, My People Are Dying." *Poetry* 217, no. 3 (December 2020): 223. https://www.poetryfoundation.org/poetrymagazine/poems/154658/fuck-your-lecture-on-craft-my-people-are-dying.

Hirschkind, Charles, and Saba Mahmood. "Feminism, the Taliban, and Politics of Counter-insurgency." *Anthropological Quarterly* 75, no. 2 (Spring 2002): 339–54.

Holt-Gimenez, Eric. "Detroit: A Tale of Two . . . Farms?" *Huffington Post*, July 10, 2012. https://www.huffpost.com/entry/a-tale-of-two-farms_b_1660019.

Hong, Christine. *A Violent Peace: Race, U.S. Militarism, and Cultures of Democratization in Cold War Asia and the Pacific*. Stanford, CA: Stanford University Press, 2020.

Howell, Alison. "Resilience, War, and Austerity: The Ethics of Military Human Enhancement and the Politics of Data." *Security Dialogue* 46, no. 1 (2015): 15–31.

Human Rights Watch. "Cambodia: New Waves of Repression." January 27, 2016. https://www.hrw.org/news/2016/01/27/cambodia-new-waves-repression.

Hunt, Lynn. *Inventing Human Rights: A History*. New York: W. W. Norton, 2007.

Ibrahimova, Maria, dir. *Miss Gulag*. Neihausen-Yatskova and Vodar Films, 2007.

Inikori, Joseph E. "The Credit Needs of the African Trade and the Development of the Credit Economy in England." *Explorations in Economic History* 27, no. 2 (April 1990): 197–231.

International Center for Not-for-Profit Law. "Cambodia." July 13, 2022. https://www.icnl.org/resources/civic-freedom-monitor/cambodia.

Isidore, Chris. "Detroit, in Financial Trouble, Gets Emergency Manager." CNN, March 14, 2013. https://money.cnn.com/2013/03/14/news/economy/detroit-emergency-manager/index.html.

James, Robin. *Resilience and Melancholy: Pop Music, Feminism, Neoliberalism*. Winchester, UK: Zero, 2015.

Jameson, Fredric. "Future City." *New Left Review* 21 (May/June 2003): 65–79. https://newleftreview.org/issues/ii21/articles/fredric-jameson-future-city.pdf.

Jameson, Fredric. *Signatures of the Visible*. New York: Routledge, 1992.

Jenkins, Mark. "The Healing Fields." *National Geographic*, January 2012.

Johnson, Barbara. "Writing." In *Critical Terms for Literary Study*, edited by Frank Lentricchia and Thomas McLaughlin, 39–49. Chicago: University of Chicago Press, 1990.

Joseph, Miranda. *Against the Romance of Community*. Minneapolis: University of Minnesota Press, 2002.

Kahn, Howie. "Destroying Detroit (in Order to Save It)." GQ, June 2, 2011. https://www.gq.com/story/detroit-renovation.

Kander, Nadav. *Dust*. Nadav Kander, 2012. Accessed August 2, 2022. https://www.nadavkander.com/works-in-series/dust/single.

Kant, Immanuel. *Critique of Judgment*. 1790. Translated by J. H. Bernard. Rev. 2nd ed. London: Macmillan, 1914.

Kant, Immanuel. *Observations on the Feeling of the Beautiful and Sublime*. 1764. Translated by John T. Goldthwait. Berkeley: University of California Press, 1991.

Kaplan, Caren. "Desert Wars: Virilio and the Limits of 'Genuine Knowledge.'" In *Virilio and Visual Culture*, edited by John Armitage and Ryan Bishop, 69–85. Edinburgh: Edinburgh University Press, 2013.

Kaplan, Caren, Norma Alarcón, and Minoo Moallem, eds. *Between Woman and Nation: Nationalisms, Transnational Feminisms, and the State*. Durham, NC: Duke University Press, 1999.

Kaplan, Leslie. *Disorder: A Political Fable*. Translated by Jennifer Pap. Chico, CA: AK, 2020.

Karbaum, Markus. "Cambodia's Façade Democracy and European Assistance." *Journal of Current Southeast Asian Affairs* 30, no. 4 (2011): 111–43. doi: 10.1177/186810341103000405.

Katz, Cindi. "Whose Nature, Whose Culture? Private Productions of Space and the 'Preservation' of Nature." In *Remaking Reality: Nature at the Millennium*, edited by Bruce Braun and Noel Castree, 45–62. New York: Routledge, 1998.

Kee, Joan. "Visual Reconnaissance." In *Alien Encounters: Popular Culture in Asian America*, edited by Mimi Thi Nguyen and Thuy Linh Nguyen Tu, 130–49. Durham, NC: Duke University Press, 2007.

Kelsky, Karen. "#MakeupMonday: Skin Care as Coping Mechanism and Catalyst." *Professor Is In*, January 15, 2018. https://theprofessorisin.com/2018/01/15/makeupmonday-skin-care-as-coping-mechanism-and-catalyst/.

Kerman, Piper. "Beauty behind Bars." *Allure*, June 2, 2014. https://www.allure.com/story/piper-kerman-beauty-behind-bars.

Kermode, Frank. *The Sense of an Ending: Studies in the Theory of Fiction*. New York: Oxford University Press, 1968.

Khalili, Laleh. *Time in the Shadows: Confinement in Counterinsurgencies*. Stanford, CA: Stanford University Press, 2012.

Kiernan, Ben. *The Pol Pot Regime: Race, Power, and Genocide in Cambodia under the Khmer Rouge, 1975-79*. 2nd ed. New Haven, CT: Yale University Press, 2002.

Kim, Ava. "Trans Subterfuge: Toward an Antinational History of the Philippines." Chancellor's Postdoctoral Research Associate in Trans Studies Annual Lecture, Department of Gender and Women's Studies, University of Illinois, Urbana-Champaign, March 23, 2023.

Kim, Jodi. *Ends of Empire: Asian American Critique and the Cold War*. Minneapolis: University of Minnesota Press, 2010.

King, Samantha. *Pink Ribbons, Inc.: Breast Cancer and the Politics of Philanthropy*. Minneapolis: University of Minnesota Press, 2006.

Kinney, Rebecca J. *Beautiful Wasteland: The Rise of Detroit as America's Postindustrial Frontier*. Minneapolis: University of Minnesota Press, 2016.

Kish, Zenia, and Justin Leroy. "Bonded Life: Technologies of Racial Finance from Slave Insurance to Philanthrocapital." *Cultural Studies* 29, no. 5-6 (2015): 630–51. doi: 10.1080/09502386.2015.1017137.

Klein, Andrew Sargus. "Poverty Is So Photogenic." *Splice Today*, January 3, 2011. https://www.splicetoday.com/pop-culture/poverty-is-so-photogenic.

Ko, Dorothy. "Jazzing into Modernity: High Heels, Platforms, and Lotus Shoes." In *China Chic: East Meets West*, edited by Valerie Steele and John S. Major, 141–54. New Haven, CT: Yale University Press, 1999.

Koren, Leonard. *Wabi-Sabi for Artists, Designers, Poets and Philosophers*. Berkeley, CA: Stone Bridge, 1994.

Koselleck, Reinhart. *The Practice of Conceptual History: Timing History, Spacing Concepts*. Translated by Todd Samuel Presner, Kerstin Behnke, and Jobst Welge. Stanford, CA: Stanford University Press, 2002.

Kracauer, Siegfried. *The Mass Ornament: Weimar Essays*. 1963. Translated and edited by Thomas Y. Levin. Cambridge, MA: Harvard University Press, 1995.

Kramer, Martin. "The Camera and the Burqa." *Middle East Quarterly* 9, no. 2 (Spring 2002): 69–76. https://www.meforum.org/177/the-camera-and-the-burqa.

Krauss, Rosalind. *The Originality of the Avant-Garde and Other Modernist Myths*. Cambridge, MA: MIT Press, 1985.

Kushinski, Alysse. "Light and the Aesthetics of Abandonment: HDR Imaging and the Illumination of Ruins." *Transformations: Journal of Media and Culture* 28 (2016). http://www.transformationsjournal.org/issue-28/.

Lacayo, Richard. "About Face: An Inside Look at How Women Fared under Taliban Oppression and What the future Holds for Them Now." *Time*, December 3, 2001, 34–49.

Landler, Mark. "20 Years On, the War on Terror Grinds Along, with No End in Sight." *New York Times*, September 10, 2021. https://www.nytimes.com/2021/09/10/world/europe/war-on-terror-bush-biden-qaeda.html.

Larasati, Rachmi Diyah. *The Dance That Makes You Vanish: Cultural Reconstruction in Post-genocide Indonesia*. Minneapolis: University of Minnesota Press, 2013.

Latifa, with the collaboration of Chékéha Hachemi. *My Forbidden Face*. Translated by Lisa Appignanesi. London: Virago, 2002.

Leary, John Patrick. "Detroitism: What Does 'Ruin Porn' Tell Us about the Motor City?" *Guernica*, January 15, 2011. https://www.guernicamag.com/leary_1_15_11/.

Leary, John Patrick. "Resilience Is the Goal of Governments and Employers Who Expect People to Endure Crisis." *Teen Vogue*, July 1, 2020. https://www.teenvogue.com/story/whats-wrong-with-focus-on-resilience.

Lefebvre, Henri. *The Missing Pieces*. Translated by David L. Sweet. Pasadena, CA: Semiotexte(e), 2014.

Lei, Serena. "Rebuilding Afghanistan's Body and Soul: Program Provides Beauty School Education to Widows in Kabul." *Washington Diplomat*, August 2002.

LeMenager, Stephanie, and Stephanie Foote. "Editors' Column." *Resilience: A Journal of the Environmental Humanities* 1, no. 1 (Winter 2013). http://www.resiliencejournal.org/past-issues/1-1-1-3/issue-1-1/.

Leshkowich, Ann Marie. "The Ao Dai Goes Global: How International Influences and Female Entrepreneurs Have Shaped Vietnam's 'National Costume.'" In *Re-Orienting Fashion: The Globalization of Asian Dress*, edited by Sandra Niessen, Ann Marie Leshkowich, and Carla Jones, 79–116. London: Berg, 2003.

Leshkowich, Ann Marie. "Fashioning the Field in Vietnam: An Intersectional Tale of Clothing, Femininities, and the Pedagogy of Appropriateness." In *Fashion and Beauty in the Time of Asia*, edited by S. Heijin Lee, Christina H. Moon, and Thuy Linh Nguyen Tu. Durham, NC: Duke University Press, 2019, 127–53.

Lester, Paul B., Sharon McBride, Paul D. Bliese, and Amy B. Adler. "Bringing Science to Bear: An Empirical Assessment of the Comprehensive Soldier Fitness Program." *American Psychologist* 66, no. 1 (January 2011): 77–81. doi: 10.1037/a0022083.

Levinas, Emmanuel. *Ethics and Infinity: Conversations with Philippe Nemo*. Translated by Richard A. Cohen. Pittsburgh: Duquesne University Press, 1985.

Levinas, Emmanuel. *Totality and Infinity: An Essay on Exteriority*. 1961. Translated by Alphonso Lingis. Pittsburgh: Duquesne University Press, 1969.

Lieu, Nhi T. *The American Dream in Vietnamese*. Minneapolis: University of Minnesota Press, 2011.

Lieu, Nhi T. "Remembering 'The Nation' through Pageantry: Femininity and the Politics of Vietnamese Womanhood in the 'Hoa Hau Ao Dai' Contest." *Frontiers: A Journal of Women Studies* 21, no. 1–2 (2000): 127–51.

Lim, Bliss Cua. *Translating Time: Cinema, the Fantastic, and Temporal Critique*. Durham, NC: Duke University Press, 2009.

Lim, Shirley Jennifer. *A Feeling of Belonging: Asian American Women's Public Culture, 1930–1960*. New York: New York University Press, 2006.

Lipman, Jana K. *In Camps: Vietnamese Refugees, Asylum Seekers, and Repatriates*. Oakland: University of California Press, 2020.

Loosemore, Bailey. "'A False Narrative': Louisville Leaders Scoff at Gentrification Claims in Breonna Taylor Suit." *Louisville Courier Journal*, July 6, 2020. https://www.courier-journal.com/story/news/local/2020/07/06/louisville-leaders-rebut-gentrification-claims-breonna-taylor-police-shooting-case/5382558002/.

Lorde, Audre. *A Burst of Light and Other Essays*. Ithaca, NY: Firebrand, 1988.

Loti, Pierre. *Un pèlerin d'Angkor* [A pilgrim of Angkor]. Paris: Grevin, 1912.

Loveless, Natalie. *How to Make Art at the End of the World: A Manifesto for Research-Creation*. Durham, NC: Duke University Press, 2019.

Lowe, Lisa. *The Intimacies of Four Continents*. Durham, NC: Duke University Press, 2015.

Loy, Mina. "Gertrude Stein (Continued)." *transatlantic review* 2, no. 3–4 (November 1924): 427–30.

Luckerson, Victor. "The Rise and Risk of the Mural Economy." *Ringer*, October 18, 2018. https://www.theringer.com/2018/10/18/17989192/mural-economy-street-art-detroit-graffiti.

Lyons, Siobhan. "Introduction: Ruin Porn, Capitalism, and the Anthropocene." In *Ruin Porn and the Obsession with Decay*, edited by Siobhan Lyons, 1–10. New York: Palgrave Macmillan, 2018.

Macaulay, Rose. *Pleasure of Ruins*. 1953. New York: Walker, 1966.

MacKinnon, Ian. "Miss Landmine: Exploitation or Bold Publicity for the Victims?" *Guardian*, April 21, 2008. https://www.theguardian.com/world/2008/apr/22/cambodia.internationalaidanddevelopment.

Mahmood, Saba. *The Politics of Piety: The Islamic Revival and the Feminist Subject*. Princeton, NJ: Princeton University Press, 2005.

Malkki, Liisa. "Citizens of Humanity: Internationalism and the Imagined Community of Nations." *Diaspora: A Journal of Transnational Studies* 3, no. 1 (Spring 1994): 41–68.

Malone, Noreen. "The Case against Economic Disaster Porn." *New Republic*, January 21, 2011. https://newrepublic.com/article/81954/detroit-economic-disaster-porn.

Man, Simeon. *Soldiering through Empire: Race and the Making of the Decolonizing Pacific*. Oakland: University of California Press, 2018.

Manalansan, Martin F., IV. "*Biyuti* in Everyday Life: Performance, Citizenship, and Survival among Filipinos in the United States." In *Orientations: Mapping Studies in the Asian Diaspora*, edited by Kandice Chuh and Karen Shimakawa, 153–71. Durham, NC: Duke University Press, 2001.

Mancini, Anthony D., and George A. Bonanno. "Resilience in the Face of Potential Trauma: Clinical Practices and Illustrations." *Journal of Clinical Psychology* 62, no. 8 (2006): 971–85. doi: 10.1002/jclp.20283.

Manning, Erin. *The Minor Gesture*. Durham, NC: Duke University Press, 2016.

Marchand, Yves, and Romain Meffre. Introduction to *The Ruins of Detroit*, by Yves Marchand, Romain Meffre, Robert Polidori, and Thomas J. Sugrue. Göttingen: Steidl, 2010.

Marks, Laura U. "Loving a Disappearing Image." *Cinémas: Revue d'études cinématographiques* 8, no. 1–2 (1997): 93–111. doi: 10.7202/024744ar.

Marx, Karl. "Comments on James Mill." In *Karl Marx and Frederick Engels, Collected Works*, vol. 3, *Marx and Engels: 1843–1844*. New York: International Publishers, 1975.

Marx, Karl. *Economic and Philosophic Manuscripts of 1844*. 1932. Translated by Martin Milligan. Revised by Dirk J. Struik. Marxists Internet Archive. 2009. https://www.marxists.org/archive/marx/works/download/pdf/Economic-Philosophic-Manuscripts-1844.pdf.

McAuley, James. "France Mandates Masks to Control the Coronavirus. Burqas Remain Banned." *Washington Post*, May 10, 2020. https://www.washingtonpost.com/world/europe/france-face-masks-coronavirus/2020/05/09/6fbd50fc-8ae6-11ea-80df-d24b35a568ae_story.html.

McClanahan, Annie. *Dead Pledges: Debt, Crisis, and Twenty-First-Century Culture*. Stanford, CA: Stanford University Press, 2017.

McClintock, Anne. "Family Feuds: Gender, Nationalism, and the Family." *Feminist Review* 44 (Summer 1993): 61–80.

McCurry, Justin. "Miss Landmine Beauty Pageant Cancelled in Cambodia." *Guardian*, August 3, 2009. https://www.theguardian.com/world/2009/aug/03/miss-landmine-pageant-banned-cambodia.

McGrath, Jason. "Apocalypse, or, the Logic of Late Anthropocene Ruins." *Cross-Currents: East Asian History and Culture Review* 10 (March 2014): 113–19. Accessed November 21, 2019. https://cross-currents.berkeley.edu/e-journal/issue-10.

McLarney, Ellen. "The Burqa in Vogue: Fashioning Afghanistan." *Journal of Middle East Women's Studies* 5, no. 1 (Winter 2009): 1–23.

McNay, Lois. "The Trouble with Recognition: Subjectivity, Suffering and Agency." *Sociological Theory* 26, no. 3 (September 2008): 271–96.

McQuaid, Cate. "At Mass MoCA, Artist Cauleen Smith Offers Visions of Black Resilience." *Boston Globe*, August 29, 2019. https://www.bostonglobe.com/arts/2019/08/29/mass-moca-artist-cauleen-smith-offers-visions-black-resilience/4AkfdpHNINClUq5PeAobRJ/story.html.

Meekosha, Helen. "Decolonising Disability: Thinking and Acting Globally." *Disability and Society* 26, no. 6 (2011): 667–68.

Meister, Robert. *After Evil: A Politics of Human Rights*. New York: Columbia University Press, 2011.

Menon, Nivedita. "Between the Burqa and the Beauty Parlor? Globalization, Cultural Nationalism, and Feminist Politics." In *Postcolonial Studies and Beyond*, edited by Ania Loomba, Suvir Kaul, Matti Bunzi, Antoinette Burton, and Jed Esty, 206–29. Durham, NC: Duke University Press, 2005:

Mercer, Stewart W., and Rhona MacDonald. "Disability and Human Rights." *Lancet* 370 (August 18, 2007): 548–49.

Mermin, Liz, dir. *The Beauty Academy of Kabul*. Wellspring Media, 2004.

Meskell, Lynn. *The Nature of Heritage: The New South Africa*. Chichester, UK: Wiley, 2012.

Mill, John Stuart. *Inaugural Address to the University of St. Andrews*. 2nd ed. London: Longmans, Green, Reader, and Dyerm, 1867.

Miller, Chanel. *Know My Name: A Memoir*. New York: Viking, 2019.

Mingus, Mia. "Moving toward the Ugly: A Politic beyond Desirability." Keynote speech at Femmes of Color Symposium, Oakland, CA, August 21, 2011. https://leavingevidence.wordpress.com/2011/08/22/moving-toward-the-ugly-a-politic-beyond-desirability/.

Mitchell, Katharyne. "Pre-Black Futures." *Antipode* 41, no. S1 (2009): 239–61. doi: 10.1111/j.1467-8330.2009.00724.x.

Mitchell, Larry. *The Faggots and Their Friends between Revolutions*. Illustrated by Ned Asta. New York: Calamus, 1977.

Mitchell, W. J. T. "Imperial Landscape." In *Landscape and Power*, edited by W. J. T. Mitchell, 5–34. Chicago: University of Chicago Press, 1994.

Moallem, Minoo. *Between Warrior Brother and Veiled Sister: Islamic Fundamentalism and the Politics of Patriarchy in Iran*. Berkeley: University of California Press, 2005.

Mohanty, Chandra Talpade. *Feminism without Borders: Decolonizing Theory, Practicing Solidarity*. Durham, NC: Duke University Press, 2003.

Momaya, Masum. "Miss Landmine Cambodia Pageant: Provocative Art or Pejorative 'Project'?" *Gender across Borders*, August 2, 2010. http://www.genderacrossborders.com/2010/08/02/12848/.

Moon, Whitney. "Reclaiming the Ruin: Detroit's Second Coming?" *Places* 21, no. 1 (2009): 36–41. https://escholarship.org/uc/item/1952g26n.

Moore, Andrew. *Detroit Disassembled*. Bologna: Damiani/Akron Art Museum, 2010.

Moore, Richard O. *Take This Hammer (the Director's Cut)*. Featuring James Baldwin. Produced by the KQED Film Unit. 1963. Bay Area Television Archive, August 2013. https://diva.sfsu.edu/collections/sfbatv/bundles/216518.

Moran, Dominique, Judith Pallot, and Laura Piacentini. "Lipstick, Lace, and Longing: Constructions of Femininity inside a Russian Prison." *Environment and Planning D: Society and Space* 27 (2009): 700–720.

Morris, Regan. "How Tippi Hedren Made Vietnamese Refugees into Nail Salon Magnates." BBC News, Los Angeles, May 3, 2015. https://www.bbc.com/news/magazine-32544343.

Morrison, Toni. *The Bluest Eye: A Novel*. 1970. New York: Vintage, 2007.

Morton, Thomas. "Something, Something, Something, Detroit." *Vice*, July 31, 2009. https://www.vice.com/en/article/ppzb9z/something-something-something-detroit-994-v16n8.

Moss, Jeremiah. *Feral City: On Finding Liberation in Lockdown New York*. New York: W. W. Norton, 2022.

Moten, Fred. "Blackness and Nothingness (Mysticism in the Flesh)." *South Atlantic Quarterly* 112, no. 4 (2013): 737–80. doi: 10.1215/00382876-2345261.

Moten, Fred, and Saidiya Hartman. "The Black Outdoors: Humanities Futures after Property and Possession." Conversation at Duke University, October 6, 2016. https://humanitiesfutures.org/media/black-outdoors-fred-moten-saidiya-hartman-duke-university/.

Mothersill, Mary. *Beauty Restored*. Oxford: Clarendon, 1984.

Moyn, Samuel. *Human Rights and the Uses of History*. London: Verso, 2014.

Moyn, Samuel. *The Last Utopia: Human Rights in History*. Cambridge, MA: Belknap Press of Harvard University Press, 2010.

Murdoch, Iris. "The Idea of Perfection." In *The Sovereignty of Good*, 1–44. London: Routledge, 1970.

Musée Rodin. "Cambodian Dancer." Accessed September 24, 2017. http://www.musee-rodin.fr/en/collections/drawings/cambodian-dancer.

Musée Rodin. "Rodin and the Cambodian Dancers." Accessed September 24, 2017, https://www.musee-rodin.fr/en/musee/expositions/rodin-and-cambodian-dancers.

Mydans, Seth. "Cambodian Leader Resists Punishing Top Khmer Rouge." *New York Times*, December 29, 1998. https://www.nytimes.com/1998/12/29/world/cambodian-leader-resists-punishing-top-khmer-rouge.html.

Mydans, Seth. "Miss Saigon, U.S.A." *New York Times*, September 19, 1993. https://www.nytimes.com/1993/09/19/style/miss-saigon-usa.html.

Myerson, Collier. "Where Have All the Flowers Gone?" *New York Magazine*, April 17, 2020. https://nymag.com/intelligencer/2020/04/how-do-you-buy-flowers-during-the-coronavirus.html.

Naimou, Angela. *Salvage Work: U.S. and Caribbean Literatures amid the Debris of Legal Personhood*. New York: Fordham University Press, 2015.

Nam, Hoai. "Ao Trang by Hoai Nam." 2009–present. https://www.aotrang.com/.

Nap Ministry, The (@thenapministry). "Y'all keep hollering about this New World. . . ." Instagram, May 9, 2020. https://www.instagram.com/p/B_-RPI6F9p_/.

Napolitano, Janet. "Remarks Prepared by Secretary Napolitano to New York City First Responders." September 10, 2010. https://www.dhs.gov/news/2010/09/10/remarks-prepared-secretary-napolitano-new-york-city-first-responders.

Nash, Jennifer C. "Writing Black Beauty." *Signs* 45, no. 1 (Autumn 2019): 101–22. doi: 10.1086/703497.

Nealon, Jeffrey T. *Alterity Politics: Ethics and Performative Subjectivity*. Durham, NC: Duke University Press, 1998.

Neavling, Steve. "Detroit Illegally Overtaxed Homeowners $600M. They're Still Waiting to Be Compensated." *Detroit Metro Times*, April 14, 2022. https://www.metrotimes.com/news/detroit-illegally-overtaxed-homeowners-600m-theyre-still-waiting-to-be-compensated-29800877.

Nehamas, Alexander. *Only a Promise of Happiness: The Place of Beauty in a World of Art*. Princeton, NJ: Princeton University Press, 2007.

Nelson, Dean. "A $1M Bad Hair Day in Kabul." *Sunday Times*, July 15, 2007. https://www.thetimes.co.uk/article/adollar1m-bad-hair-day-in-kabul-g7p57d7xlxw.

Neocleous, Mark. *War Power, Police Power*. Edinburgh, Scotland: Edinburgh University Press, 2014.

Neocleous, Mark. "Resisting Resilience." *Radical Philosophy* 178 (March/April 2013): 2–7. https://www.radicalphilosophy.com/commentary/resisting-resilience.

New York Times Editorial Board. "The Last Steel Column." *New York Times*, May 30, 2002. https://www.nytimes.com/2002/05/30/opinion/the-last-steel-column.html.

Ngai, Sianne. *Our Aesthetic Categories: Zany, Cute, Interesting.* Cambridge, MA: Harvard University Press, 2015.

Ngai, Sianne. *Ugly Feelings.* Cambridge, MA: Harvard University Press, 2005.

Nguyen, Martina Thucnhi. "Wearing Modernity: Lemur Nguyễn Cát Tường, Fashion, and the 'Origins' of the Vietnamese National Costume." *Journal of Vietnamese Studies* 11, no. 1 (2016): 76–118. doi: 10.1525/vs.2016.11.1.76.

Nguyen, Mimi Thi. "The Biopower of Beauty: Humanitarian Imperialisms and Global Feminisms in the War on Terror." *Signs: Journal of Women in Culture and Society* 26, no. 2 (Winter 2011): 359–83.

Nguyen, Mimi Thi. "Diasporic Erotic: Love, Loss, and the Copy." *Camera Obscura* 28, no. 1 (2013): 68–101. doi: 10.1215/02705346-2016960.

Nguyen, Mimi Thi. *The Gift of Freedom: War, Debt, and Other Refugee Passages.* Durham, NC: Duke University Press, 2012.

Nguyen, Mimi Thi. "The Hoodie as Sign, Screen, Expectation, and Force." *Signs* 40, no. 4 (Summer 2015): 791–816.

Nguyen, Mimi Thi. "Minor Threats." *Radical History Review* 122 (May 2015): 11–24.

Nguyễn Ngạc and Nguyễn Văn Luận. *Un siècle d'histoire de la robe des Vietnamiennes.* Saigon: Direction des Affaires Culturelles, Ministère de la Culture de l'Education de la Jeunesse, 1974.

Nguyen, Phuong Tran. *Becoming Refugee American: The Politics of Rescue in Little Saigon.* Urbana: University of Illinois Press, 2017.

Nguyen T. Tan-Hoang, dir. and producer. *Cover Girl: A Gift from God.* 2000. Video essay.

Nguyen, Trung Phan Quoc. "The Labor of Absolution: National Detritus and the Op-Ed Form of the Vietnamese Refugee." *Critical Ethnic Studies* 6, no. 1 (Spring 2020). https://manifold.umn.edu/read/the-labor-of-absolution-national-detritus-and-the-op-ed-form-of-the-vietnamese-refugee/section/19566799-6a7e-416a-9fae-3df25cf7875a.

Nguyen, Vinh. "Refugeetude: When Does a Refugee Stop Being a Refugee?" *Social Text* 139, no. 2 (June 2019): 109–31. doi: 10.1215/01642472-7371003.

Nietzsche, Friedrich. *On the Genealogy of Morals.* Translated by Walter Kaufmann and R. J. Hollingdale. 1967. New York: Vintage, 1989.

Nikpour, Golnar. "Claiming Human Rights: Iranian Political Prisoners and the Making of a Transnational Movement, 1963–1979." *Humanity: An International Journal of Human Rights, Humanitarianism, and Development* 9, no. 3 (Winter 2018): 363–88.

Nir, Sarah Maslin. "The War Is Fake, the Clothing Real." *New York Times*, June 23, 2010. https://www.nytimes.com/2010/06/24/fashion/24close.html.

Nixon, Rob. "Of Land Mines and Cluster Bombs." *Cultural Critique* 67 (Fall 2007): 160–74.

Norindr, Panivong. *Phantasmatic Indochina: French Colonial Ideology in Architecture, Film, and Literature.* Durham, NC: Duke University Press, 1996.

Not a Wolf. Twitter, February 1, 2021, 11:35 a.m. https://twitter.com/sickofwolves/status/1356294995246940160.

Nussbaum, Martha C. *Women and Human Development: The Capabilities Approach*. Cambridge: Cambridge University Press, 2000.

Nuttall, Sarah. "Introduction: Rethinking Beauty." In *Beautiful/Ugly: African and Diaspora Aesthetics*, edited by Sarah Nuttall, 6–29. Durham, NC: Duke University Press, 2006.

Olalquiaga, Celeste. "El Helicoide: Modern Ruins and the Urban Imaginary." In *Materializing Memory in Art and Popular Culture*, edited by László Munteán, Liedeke Plate, and Anneke Smelik, 29–44. New York: Routledge, 2017.

O'Malley, Pat. "Resilient Subjects: Uncertainty, Warfare and Liberalism." *Economy and Society* 39, no. 4 (2010): 488–509. doi: 10.1080/03085147.2010.510681.

Ong, Aihwa. *Buddha Is Hiding: Refugees, Citizenship, the New America*. Berkeley: University of California Press, 2003.

Oppenheim, James. "Bread and Roses." *American Magazine* 73, no. 2 (December 1911): 214. https://hdl.handle.net/2027/uc1.b3065192?urlappend=%3Bseq=232%3Bownerid=9007199273017114–250.

Packard, Cassie. "Martha Rosler Tackles the Problem of Representation." *Hyperallergic*, October 16, 2014. https://hyperallergic.com/155794/martha-rosler-tackles-the-problem-of-representation/.

Paik, A. Naomi. *Rightlessness: Testimony and Redress in U.S. Prison Camps since World War II*. Chapel Hill: University of North Carolina Press, 2016.

Panagia, Davide. *Poetics of Political Thinking*. Durham, NC: Duke University Press, 2006.

Parker, Andrew, Mary Russo, Doris Sommer, and Patricia Yaeger, eds. *Nationalisms and Sexualities*. New York: Routledge, 1991.

Pendleton, Kimberly. "Captivated: Sex Trafficking, U.S. Evangelicals, and the Promise of Rescue." PhD diss., George Washington University, 2018. ProQuest (10743368).

Perkins, Maureen. *The Reform of Time: Magic and Modernity*. London: Pluto, 2001.

Perri, Christina. "A Thousand Years." Track 6 on *The Twilight Saga: Breaking Dawn—Part 1: Original Motion Picture Soundtrack*. Atlantic Records, 2011.

Peycam, Philippe. "The International Coordinating Committee for Angkor: A World Heritage Site as an Arena of Competition, Connivance and State(s) Legitimation." *SOJURN: Journal of Social Issues in Southeast Asia* 31, no. 3 (2016): 743–85.

Phim, Toni Samantha [Toni Shapiro-Phim], and Ashley Thompson. *Dance in Cambodia*. New York: Oxford University Press, 1999.

Phu, Thien. "Thien Phu Sets Record Straight for Colleague." December 12, 2014. http://thienphu-vietsinger.blogspot.com/2014/12/.

Piccini, Angela. "Profane Archaeologies: Erotic Ruins and a Case for Pornography." *Journal of Contemporary Archaeology* 1, no. 1 (2014): 29–33.

Pigg, Stacy Leigh, and Vincanne Adams. "Introduction: The Moral Object of Sex." In *Sex in Development: Science, Sexuality, and Morality in Global Perspective*, edited by Vincanne Adams and Stacy Leigh Pigg, 1–38. Durham, NC: Duke University Press, 2005.

Plato. *The Dialogues of Plato*. Translated by Benjamin Jowett. Oxford: Oxford University Press, 1892.

Plato. *Statesman. Philebus. Ion.* Translated by Harold North Fowler, W. R. M. Lamb. Cambridge, MA: Harvard University Press, 1925. doi: 10.4159/DLCL.plato_philosopher-ion.1925

Price, Uvedale. *An Essay on the Picturesque, as Compared with the Sublime and the Beautiful*. London: J. Robson, 1794.

Puar, Jasbir. *The Right to Maim: Debility, Capacity, Disability*. Durham, NC: Duke University Press, 2017.

Puar, Jasbir K., and Amit Rai. "Monster, Terrorist, Fag: The War on Terrorism and the Production of Docile Patriots." *Social Text* 20, no. 3 (Fall 2002): 117–48.

Quiray Tagle, Thea. "After the Apocalypse, Where Do Ghosts Reside?" In *Where Do You Want Ghosts to Reside?*, curated by Azin Seraj and Zulfikar Ali Bhutto. San Francisco: Southern Exposure, February 2020. Exhibition catalog.

Ramaswamy, Sumathi. "Introduction: The Work of Vision in the Age of European Empires." In *Empires of Vision: A Reader*, edited by Martin Jay and Sumathi Ramaswamy, 1–22. Durham, NC: Duke University Press, 2013.

Ramos Orta, Yuliana M. "Trashed Beauty: Abjection and Burned Females in Mariana Enríquez's *The Things We Lost in the Fire*." *Revista de Estudios de Género y Sexualidades* 45, no. 1 (Spring 2019): 127–40. doi: 10.14321/jgendsexustud.45.1.0127.

Rancière, Jacques. "Aesthetic Separation, Aesthetic Community: Scenes from the Aesthetic Regime of Art." *Art and Research* 2, no. 1 (Summer 2008): 1–15. http://www.artandresearch.org.uk/v2n1/pdfs/ranciere.pdf.

Rancière, Jacques. *Dissensus: On Politics and Aesthetics*. Edited and translated by Steven Corcoran. London: Bloomsbury Academic, 2010.

Rancière, Jacques. *The Emancipated Spectator*. Translated by Gregory Elliott. London: Verso, 2009.

Rancière, Jacques. *The Philosopher and His Poor*. 1983. Edited and with an introduction by Andrew Parker. Translated by John Drury, Corinne Oster, and Andrew Parker. Durham, NC: Duke University Press, 2003.

Rancière, Jacques. "The Thinking of Dissensus: Politics and Aesthetics." In *Reading Rancière: Critical Dissensus*, edited by Paul Bowman and Richard Stamp, 1–17. London: Continuum, 2011.

Rancière, Jacques, and Davide Panagia. "Dissenting Words: A Conversation with Jacques Rancière." *Diacritics* 30, no. 2 (2000): 113–26.

Raymundo, Emily. "Beauty Regimens, Beauty Regimes: Korean Beauty on YouTube." In *Fashion and Beauty in the Time of Asia*, edited by S. Heijin Lee,

Christina H. Moon, and Thuy Linh Nguyen Tu, 103–26. New York: New York University Press, 2019.

Razack, Sherene H. *Dark Threats and White Knights: The Somalia Affair, Peacekeeping, and the New Imperialism*. Toronto: University of Toronto Press, 2004.

Reddy, Chandan. *Freedom with Violence: Race, Sexuality, and the US State*. Durham, NC: Duke University Press, 2011.

Reddy, Vanita. *Fashioning Diaspora: Beauty, Femininity, and South Asian American Culture*. Philadelphia: Temple University Press, 2016.

Redfield, Peter. "Doctors, Borders, and Life in Crisis." *Cultural Anthropology* 20, no. 3 (August 2005): 328–61.

Reed, Julia. "Extreme Makeover." *Vogue*, November 2003, 464–72, 510.

Reindl, J. C. "How Detroit Lost Its Title as 'Ruin Porn' Capital." *Detroit Free Press*, August 16, 2018. https://www.freep.com/story/news/local/michigan/detroit/2018/08/16/detroit-ruin-porn/979984002/.

Reinhardt, Mark, Holly Edwards, and Erina Duganne, eds. *Beautiful Suffering: Photography and the Traffic in Pain*. Williamstown, MA: Williams College Museum of Art, 2007.

Reuters Staff. "U.S. Foreclosure Image Is 2008 World Press Photo." Reuters, February 13, 2009. https://www.reuters.com/article/us-photography/u-s-foreclosure-image-is-2008-world-press-photo-idUSTRE51C2MU20090213.

Ribot, Marc, and Tom Waits. "Bella Ciao (Goodbye Beautiful)." Track 3 on *Songs of Resistance 1942–2018*, by Marc Ribot. Brooklyn, NY: Strange Weather, 2018. MP3.

Rich, Frank. "The Spoils of War Coverage." *New York Times*, April 13, 2003. https://www.nytimes.com/2003/04/13/arts/the-spoils-of-war-coverage.html.

Richmond, Oliver P., and Jason Franks. "Liberal Hubris? Virtual Peace in Cambodia." *Security Dialogue* 38, no. 1 (2007): 27–48. doi: 10.1177/0967010607075971.

Rodriguez, Favianna. "Migration Is Beautiful Artist's Statement." 2018. https://favianna.com/artworks/migration-is-beautiful-2018.

Roelofs, Monique. *The Cultural Promise of the Aesthetic*. London: Bloomsbury, 2014.

Roenigk, Emily. "5 Reasons Poverty Porn Empowers the Wrong Person." ONE, April 9, 2014. https://www.one.org/us/blog/5-reasons-poverty-porn-empowers-the-wrong-person/.

Roitman, Janet. *Anti-crisis*. Durham, NC: Duke University Press, 2013.

Rose, John Mallory. "A Process Evaluation of the North Carolina BEAUTY and Health Project." PhD diss., University of North Carolina at Chapel Hill, 2009. ProQuest (AAI3366414).

Rose, Steve. "Here's What Could Be Lost If Trump Bombs Iran's Cultural Treasures." *Guardian*, January 6, 2020. https://www.theguardian.com/artanddesign/2020/jan/06/the-iranian-cultural-treasures-targeted-by-trump.

Rosler, Martha. *The Bowery in Two Inadequate Descriptive Systems*. 1974–75. https://www.martharosler.net/the-bowery-in-two-inadequate-descriptive-systems.

Rosler, Martha. "In, Around, and Afterthoughts (On Documentary Photography)." 1981. In *Martha Rosler, 3 Works*, 61–93. Halifax, Nova Scotia: Press of the Nova Scotia College of Art and Design, 2006.

Roth, Michael S. "Irresistible Decay: Ruins Reclaimed." In *Irresistible Decay: Ruins Reclaimed*, edited by Michael S. Roth, Claire L. Lyons, and Charles Merewether, 1–24. Los Angeles: Getty Research Institute for the History of Art and the Humanities, 1997.

Roy, Ananya. *Poverty Capital: Microfinance and the Making of Development*. New York: Routledge, 2010.

Roy, Arundhati. *The End of Imagination*. Chicago: Haymarket, 2016.

Roy, Arundhati. "Is There Life after Democracy?" *Dawn*, July 5, 2009. https://www.dawn.com/news/475778/is-there-life-after-democracy.

Roy, Parama. *Indian Traffic: Identities in Question in Colonial and Postcolonial India*. Berkeley: University of California Press, 1998.

Rucker, Philip, and Robert Costa. "'It's a Hard Problem': Inside Trump's Decision to Send More Troops to Afghanistan." *Washington Post*, August 21, 2017. https://www.washingtonpost.com/politics/its-a-hard-problem-inside-trumps-decision-to-send-more-troops-to-afghanistan/2017/08/21/14dcb126-868b-11e7-a94f-3139abce39f5_story.html.

Rushdie, Salman. "Fighting the Forces of Invisibility." *Washington Post*, October 2, 2001. https://www.washingtonpost.com/archive/opinions/2001/10/02/fighting-the-forces-of-invisibility/5ef65046-32ed-4888-ad3c-f009d4347e64/.

Russo, Michael S. *The Problem of God and the Meaning of Life*. New York: SophiaOmni, 2019.

Ryan, Dermot. "'The Beauty of That Arrangement': Adam Smith Imagines Empire." *Studies in Romanticism* 48, no. 1 (Spring 2009): 101–19.

Ryzewski, Krysta. "No Home for the 'Ordinary Gamut': A Historical Archaeology of Community Displacement and the Creation of Detroit, City Beautiful." *Journal of Social Archaeology* 15, no. 3 (2015): 408–31. doi: 10.1177/1469605315601907.

Ryzewski, Krysta. "Ruin Photography as Archaeological Method: A Snapshot from Detroit." *Journal of Contemporary Archaeology* 1, no. 1 (2014): 36–41. doi: 10.1558/jca.v1i1.7.

Sabbatical Beauty. "About Us." Accessed July 19, 2018. https://sabbaticalbeauty.com/pages/about-us.

Safransky, Sarah. "Greening the Urban Frontier: Race, Property, and Resettlement in Detroit." *Geoforum* 56 (2014): 237–48.

Samudzi, Zoé. "Paradox of Recognition: Genocide and Colonialism." *Postmodern Culture* 31, no. 1 (2020). https://doi.org/10.1353/pmc.2020.0028.

Santayana, George. *The Sense of Beauty: Being the Outline of Aesthetic Theory*. 1896. New York: Dover, 1955.

Sartwell, Crispin. *Six Names of Beauty*. New York: Routledge, 2004.

Scarry, Elaine. *On Beauty and Being Just*. Princeton, NJ: Princeton University Press, 1999.

Schafer, Eric. "Romance Lives: The Ao Trang Calendar." *Asia Africa Intelligence Wire*, August 2003. accessmylibrary.com/coms2/summary_0286-24289275_ITM.

Schaffer, Kay, and Sidonie Smith. *Human Rights and Narrated Lives: The Ethics of Recognition*. New York: Palgrave Macmillan, 2004.

Schiller, Friedrich. *On the Aesthetic Education of Man: A Series of Letters*. 1794. Translated by Reginald Snell. New York: Continuum, 1965.

Schlund-Vials, Cathy J. *War, Genocide, and Justice: Cambodian American Memory Work*. Minneapolis: University of Minnesota Press, 2012.

Schneiderman, Rose. "Votes for Women." *Life and Labor*, September 1912.

Schor, Naomi. *Reading in Detail: Aesthetics and the Feminine*. New York: Methuen, 1987.

Schulenberg, Stefan E. "Disaster Mental Health and Positive Psychology—Considering the Context of Natural and Technological Disasters: An Introduction to the Special Issue." *Journal of Clinical Psychology* 72, no. 12 (2016): 1223–33. doi: 10.1002/jclp.22409.

Schuller, Kyla. *The Biopolitics of Feeling: Race, Sex, and Science in the Nineteenth Century*. Durham, NC: Duke University Press, 2018.

Schweik, Susan M. *The Ugly Laws: Disability in Public*. New York: New York University Press, 2009.

Scott, David. *Omens of Adversity: Tragedy, Time, Memory, Justice*. Durham, NC: Duke University Press, 2014.

Sears, Clare. *Arresting Dress: Cross-Dressing, Law, and Fascination in Nineteenth-Century San Francisco*. Durham, NC: Duke University Press, 2015.

Sedgwick, Eve Kosofsky. "Paranoid Reading and Reparative Reading, or, You're So Paranoid, You Probably Think This Essay Is about You." In *Touching Feeling: Affect, Pedagogy, Performativity*, 123–51. Durham, NC: Duke University Press, 2003.

Sekula, Allan. "The Body and the Archive." *October*, vol. 39 (1986): 3–64.

Seligman, Martin E. P. *Flourish: A Visionary New Understanding of Happiness and Well-Being*. New York: Free Press, 2011.

Sellars, Peter. Foreword to *Beyond the Apsara: Celebrating Dance in Cambodia*, ix–xi. Edited by Stephanie Burridge and Fred Frumberg. London: Routledge, 2010.

Semaan, Celine. "What Self-Care Looks Like in a Refugee Camp." *Cut*, May 15, 2018. https://www.thecut.com/2018/05/what-self-care-looks-like-in-a-refugee-camp.html.

Shakespeare, William. *Romeo and Juliet*. Edited by René Weis. London: Bloomsbury, 2012.

Shapiro-Phim, Toni. "Mediating Cambodian History, the Sacred, and the Earth." In *The Routledge Dance Studies Reader*, 3rd ed., edited by Jens Richard Giersdorf and Yutian Wong, 262–73. New York: Routledge.

Sharpe, Christina. "Beauty Is a Method." *e-flux Journal* 105 (December 2019). https://www.e-flux.com/journal/105/303916/beauty-is-a-method/.

Sharpe, Christina. *In the Wake: On Blackness and Being*. Durham, NC: Duke University Press, 2016.

Shaviro, Steven. *Without Criteria: Kant, Whitehead, Deleuze, and Aesthetics*. Cambridge, MA: MIT Press, 2009.

Shell, Marc. *Money, Language, and Thought: Literary and Philosophic Economies from the Medieval to the Modern Era*. Baltimore: Johns Hopkins University Press, 1982.

Shih, Elena. *Manufacturing Freedom: Sex Work, Anti-Trafficking Rehab, and the Racial Wages of Rescue*. Berkeley: University of California Press, 2023.

Shing, Elaine Z., Eranda Jayawickreme, and Christian E. Waugh. "Contextual Positive Coping as a Factor Contributing to Resilience after Disasters." *Journal of Clinical Psychology* 72, no. 12 (2016): 1287–306. doi: 10.1002/jclp.22327.

Sicardi, Arabelle. "A Practical Beauty Guide to Fighting Fascism." *Racked*, December 5, 2016. https://www.racked.com/2016/12/5/13800638/practical-beauty-guide-fighting-fascism-protest-makeup.

Sicardi, Arabelle. "The Queer Person's Guide to Feeling Beautiful in an Ugly World." *Out Magazine*, March 17, 2019. https://www.out.com/commentary/2019/3/17/queer-persons-guide-feeling-beautiful-ugly-world.

Sicardi, Arabelle. "The Year in Ugliness." *Hazlitt*, December 11, 2017. https://hazlitt.net/feature/year-ugliness.

Siebers, Tobin. *Disability Aesthetics*. Ann Arbor: University of Michigan Press, 2010.

Sims, Benjamin. "Resilience and Homeland Security: Patriotism, Anxiety, and Complex Systems Dynamics." *Limn* 1 (January 2011). https://limn.it/articles/resilience-and-homeland-security-patriotism-anxiety-and-complex-system-dynamics/.

Sisavath, Davorn. "The US Secret War in Laos: Constructing an Archive from Military Waste." *Radical History Review* 133 (January 2019): 103–16. doi: 10.1215/01636545-7160089.

Slaughter, Joseph. "Hijacking Human Rights: Neoliberalism, the New Historiography, and the End of the Third World." *Human Rights Quarterly* 40, no. 4 (November 2018): 735–74.

Slaughter, Joseph. *Human Rights, Inc.: The World Novel, Narrative Form, and International Law*. New York: Fordham University Press, 2007.

Sliwinski, Sharon. *Human Rights in Camera*. Chicago: University of Chicago Press, 2011.

Smith, Adam. *The Theory of Moral Sentiments*. 1759. Edited by Knud Haakonssen. Cambridge: Cambridge University Press, 2002.

Smith, Marquard, and Joanne Morra, eds. *The Prosthetic Impulse: From a Posthuman Present to a Biocultural Future*. Cambridge, MA: MIT Press, 2006.

Smith, Martyn. "Why Write Beautifully about Climate Crisis?" *Edge Effects*, July 9, 2019. https://edgeeffects.net/elizabeth-rush-rising.

Smith, Zadie. *On Beauty*. London: Penguin, 2005.

Sobchak, Vivian. "A Leg to Stand On: Prosthetics, Metaphor, and Materiality." In *The Prosthetic Impulse: From a Posthuman Present to a Biocultural Future*, edited by Marquard Smith and Joanne Morra, 17–42. Cambridge, MA: MIT Press, 2006.

Solnit, Rebecca. *Orwell's Roses*. New York: Viking, 2021.

Solomon-Godeau, Abigail. "The Legs of the Countess." *October* 39 (Winter 1986): 65–108.

Sontag, Susan. *On Photography*. New York: Farrar, Straus and Giroux, 1977.

Sontag, Susan. *Regarding the Pain of Others*. New York: Farrar, Straus and Giroux, 2003.

Spillers, Hortense. "Mama's Baby, Papa's Maybe: An American Grammar Book." *Diacritics* 17, no. 2 (Summer 1987): 64–81.

Spindler, Amy M. "Style; O Fashion, Where Art Thou?" *New York Times Magazine*, October 21, 2001. http://www.nytimes.com/2001/10/21/magazine/style-o-fashion-where-art-thou.html.

Spivak, Gayatri Chakravorty. *A Critique of Postcolonial Reason: Toward a History of the Vanishing Present*. Cambridge, MA: Harvard University Press, 1999.

Spivak, Gayatri Chakravorty. *The Post-colonial Critic: Interviews, Strategies, Dialogues*. Edited by Sarah Harasym. London: Routledge, 1990.

Springer, Simon. *Cambodia's Neoliberal Order: Violence, Authoritarianism, and the Contestation of Public Space*. London: Routledge, 2010.

Stacey, Jackie. "The Global Within: Consuming Nature, Embodying Health." In *Global Nature, Global Culture*, edited by Sarah Franklin, Celia Lury, and Jackie Stacey, 97–145. London: Sage, 2000.

Stanfill, Francesca. "Fashion or Folly?" *Town and Country*, March 2002, 154.

Stanley, Eric. *Atmospheres of Violence: Structuring Antagonism and the Trans/Queer Ungovernable*. Durham, NC: Duke University Press, 2021.

Steiner, George. "Night Words." *Encounter* 25, no. 3 (1965): 14–19.

Steiner, George. "On Difficulty." *Journal of Aesthetics and Art Criticism* 36, no. 3 (1978): 263–76.

Stendhal. *On Love*. 1822. Translated and with an introduction and notes by Philip Sidney Woolf and Cecil N. Sidney Woolf. London: Duckworth, 1915.

Stewart, Susan. *On Longing: Narratives of the Miniature, the Gigantic, the Souvenir, the Collection*. Durham, NC: Duke University Press, 1993.

Steyerl, Hito. "In Defense of the Poor Image." *e-flux Journal* 10 (November 2009). https://www.e-flux.com/journal/10/61362/in-defense-of-the-poor-image/.

Steyerl, Hito. "A Thing Like You and Me." *e-flux Journal* 15 (April 2010). https://www.e-flux.com/journal/15/61298/a-thing-like-you-and-me/.

Stiker, Henri-Jacques. *A History of Disability*. Translated by William Sayers. Ann Arbor: University of Michigan Press, 1999.

Stuart, Julia. "Beauty and the Burqa." *Independent*, September 1, 2004. https://www.independent.co.uk/news/world/asia/beauty-and-the-burqa-542676.html.

Stuelke, Patricia. *The Ruse of Repair: US Neoliberal Empire and the Turn from Critique*. Durham, NC: Duke University Press, 2012.

Tadiar, Neferti X. M. "Life-Times of Disposability within Global Neoliberalism." *Social Text* 115, vol. 31, no. 2 (2013): 19-47.

Tama, Mario. "Rio De Janeiro Prison Hosts Inmate Beauty Pageant." Getty Images. November 24, 2015. https://www.gettyimages.com/search/2/image?events=593418935.

Tate, Trudi. "*Mrs Dalloway* and the Armenian Question." *Textual Practice* 8, no. 3 (1994): 467-86. doi: 10.1080/09502369408582206.

Taussig, Michael. *Beauty and the Beast*. Chicago: University of Chicago Press, 2012.

Tarlo, Emma. *Clothing Matters: Dress and Identity in India*. Chicago: University of Chicago Press, 1996.

Taylor, Diana. "The Politics of Passion." *e-misférica* 10, no. 2 (2013). https://hemisphericinstitute.org/en/emisferica-102.html.

Terry, Jennifer. *Attachments to War: Biomedical Logics and Violence in Twenty-First-Century America*. Durham, NC: Duke University Press, 2017.

Thompson, James. *Performance Affects: Applied Theatre and the End of Affect*. London: Palgrave Macmillan 2009.

Thompson, Krista A. *An Eye for the Tropics: Tourism, Photography, and Framing the Caribbean Picturesque*. Durham, NC: Duke University Press, 2007.

Tolentino, Jia. "The Year That Skin Care Became a Coping Mechanism." *New Yorker*, December 18, 2017. https://www.newyorker.com/culture/cultural-comment/the-year-that-skin-care-became-a-coping-mechanism.

Tompkins, Kyla Wazana. "Sweetness, Capacity, Energy." *American Quarterly* 71, no. 3 (September 2019): 849-56. doi: 10.1353/aq.2019.0058.

Tongson, Karen. "Empty Orchestra: The Karaoke Standard and Pop Celebrity." *Public Culture* 27, no. 1 (2015): 85-108. doi: 10.1215/08992363-2798355.

Traavik, Morten. "Miss Landmine Beauty Pageant Helps Landmine Victims." In *Beauty Pageants*, edited by Noël Merino, 67-71. New York: Greenhaven, 2010.

Traavik, Morten. *Miss Landmine: Landmine Survivors' Fashion—Cambodia 2009*, no. 2 (2009). https://web.archive.org/web/20100620072400/http://miss-landmine.org/cambodia/tl_files/misslandmine/pdf/Miss_Landmine_Cambodia_lores.pdf.

Traavik, Morten. "Miss Landmine Manifesto." 2008. Accessed July 19, 2022. http://traavik.info/works/miss-landmine-angola.

Treen, Robin. Introduction to *Ao Dai: A Modern Design Coming of Age*, 2–4. San Jose, CA: San Jose Museum of Quilts and Textiles, 2006. Exhibition catalog.

Troeung, Y-Dang. *Landbridge [Life in Fragments]*. Toronto: Alchemy (Knopf Canada), 2023.

Troeung, Y-Dang. *Refugee Lifeworlds: The Afterlife of the Cold War in Cambodia*. Philadelphia: Temple University Press, 2022.

Tsing, Anna Lowenhaupt. *Friction: An Ethnography of Global Connection*. Princeton, NJ: Princeton University Press, 2005.

Tsing, Anna Lowenhaupt. *The Mushroom at the End of the World: On the Possibility of Life in Capitalist Ruins*. Princeton, NJ: Princeton University Press, 2015.

Tuchman-Rosta, Celia. "From Ritual Form to Tourist Attraction: Negotiating the Transformation of Classical Cambodian Dance in a Changing World." *Asian Theatre Journal* 31, no. 2 (Fall 2014): 524–44.

"Tuol Sleng Image Database." Genocide Studies Program, Yale University, 2022. https://gsp.yale.edu/case-studies/cambodian-genocide-program/cambodian-genocide-databases-cgdb/tuol-sleng-image-database.

UK Cosmetic Toiletry and Perfumery Association. "Faces of Science." Catie. Accessed August 4, 2016. http://www.catie.org.uk/downloads/fos_selfesteem.pdf.

Um, Khatharya. *From the Land of Shadows: War, Revolution, and the Making of the Cambodian Diaspora*. New York: New York University Press, 2015.

UNESCO. "Angkor." UNESCO World Heritage Centre, 1992. https://whc.unesco.org/en/list/668/.

United Nations, Department of Public Information. *Agreements on a Comprehensive Political Settlement of the Cambodia Conflict: Paris, 23 October 1991*. January 1992. https://peacemaker.un.org/sites/peacemaker.un.org/files/KH_911023_FrameworkComprehensivePoliticalSettlementCambodia.pdf.

United Nations High Commissioner for Refugees. "Flight from Indochina." In *The State of the World's Refugees 2000: Fifty Years of Humanitarian Aid*, 79–103. January 1, 2000. https://www.unhcr.org/3ebf9bad0.html.

United Nations, Office for Disaster Risk Reduction (UN/ISDR). *Living with Risk: A Global Review of Disaster Reduction Initiatives*. Vol. 1. Geneva: United Nations, 2004. https://www.unisdr.org/files/657_lwr1.pdf.

US Commission on Obscenity and Pornography. *Report of the Commission on Obscenity and Pornography, September 1970*. Washington, DC: US Government Printing Office, September 1970.

US Department of Homeland Security. *The 2014 Quadrennial Homeland Security Review*. 2014. https://www.dhs.gov/sites/default/files/publications/2014-qhsr-final-508.pdf.

US Department of Homeland Security, Cybersecurity and Infrastructure Security Agency. *National Infrastructure Protection Plan: Partnering to Enhance Protection and Resiliency*. 2009. https://www.cisa.gov/sites/default/files/publications/national-infrastructure-protection-plan-2009-508.pdf.

US Department of Justice. "Lawfulness of a Lethal Operation Directed against a U.S. Citizen Who Is a Senior Operational Leader of A-Qa'ida or an Associated Force." 2011. Accessed July 2018. https://en.wikipedia.org/wiki/020413_DOJ_White_Paper.

US Department of State. "State Department Launches Global Cultural Initiative." September 25, 2006. Archived July 11, 2008, at Archive.org. https://web.archive.org/web/20080711080112/http://www.america.gov/st/washfile-english/2006/September/20060925152441jmnamdeirfo.3944361.html.

US Department of State, Bureau of Democracy, Human Rights and Labor. *Report on the Taliban's War against Women*. November 17, 2001. https://2009-2017.state.gov/j/drl/rls/6185.htm.

US Department of State, Bureau of Political-Military Affairs. "To Walk the Earth in Safety." Office of Website Management, Bureau of Public Affairs. Accessed November 23, 2016. https://2009-2017.state.gov/t/pm/rls/rpt/walkearth/index.htm.

US Homeland Security Council. *National Strategy for Homeland Security*. October 2007. https://www.dhs.gov/xlibrary/assets/nat_strat_homelandsecurity_2007.pdf.

US Trump Administration. *National Security Strategy of the United States of America*. December 2017. https://trumpwhitehouse.archives.gov/wp-content/uploads/2017/12/NSS-Final-12-18-2017-0905.pdf.

Vang, Ma. *History on the Run: Secrecy, Fugitivity, and Hmong Refugee Epistemologies*. Durham, NC: Duke University Press, 2021.

Vasseleu, Cathryn. "Material-Character Animation: Experiments in Life-Like Translucency." In *Carnal Knowledge: Towards "New Materialism" through the Arts*, edited by Estelle Barrett and Barbara Boldt, 155–69. London: I. B. Tauris, 2009.

Vergara, Camilo José. "American Acropolis: The End of an Era in Detroit." *Metropolis*, April 24, 2017. https://metropolismag.com/viewpoints/american-acropolis-the-end-of-an-era/.

Vuong, Ocean. *On Earth We're Briefly Gorgeous*. New York: Penguin, 2019.

Walker, Kara. *A Subtlety, Or the Marvelous Sugar Baby*. Presented by Creative Time. Domino Sugar Factory, Brooklyn, NY, 2014. https://creativetime.org/projects/karawalker/.

Warner, Michael. *Publics and Counterpublics*. Seattle: Zone, 2002.

Waters, John, dir. *Female Trouble*. New Line Cinema, 1974.

Weissman, Terri. "Bankrupt, but There's a Whole Foods." *Scope*, October 2013. https://www.scope-mag.com/2013/10/bankrupt-but-theres-a-whole-foods/.

Wells, Kate. "Detroit Was Always Made of Wheels: Confronting Ruin Porn in Its Hometown." In *Ruin Porn and the Obsession with Decay*, edited by Siobhan Lyons, 13–30. New York: Palgrave Macmillan, 2018.

White, Armond. "Grand Detroit Hotel." *National Review*, April 11, 2014. https://www.nationalreview.com/2014/04/grand-detroit-hotel-armond-white/.

Whitlock, Gillian. "The Skin of the *Burqa*: Recent Life Narratives from Afghanistan." *Biography* 28, no. 1 (Winter 2005): 54–76.

Wilk, Richard. "Connections and Contradictions: From the Crooked Tree Cashew Queen to Miss World Belize." In *Beauty Queens on the Global Stage: Gender, Contests, and Power*, edited by Collen Ballerino Cohen, Richard Wilk, and Beverly Stoeltje, 217–32. New York: Routledge, 1996.

Williams, A. R. "ISIS Smashes Priceless, Ancient Statues in Iraq." *National Geographic*, February 27, 2015. https://www.nationalgeographic.com/culture/article/150227-islamic-militants-destroy-statues-mosul-iraq-video-archaeology.

Williams, Linda. *Hardcore: Power, Pleasure, and the "Frenzy of the Visible."* Berkeley: University of California Press, 1989.

Williams, Linda, ed. *Porn Studies*. Durham, NC: Duke University Press, 2004.

Williams, Timothy, and Abeer Mohammed. "What Not to Wear, Baghdad-Style: Fashion Rules Begin to Change." *New York Times*, June 5, 2009. https://www.nytimes.com/2009/06/06/world/middleeast/06iraq.html.

Wintour, Anna. "Editor's Letter: Lipstick and Power." *Vogue*, November 2003.

"Women in Angkorian History—Past and Present: A 12th Century Bas-Relief and Princess Bopha Devi." *Cambodge Aujourd'hui*, July–August 1962, 46.

Women in the World Staff. "Maximum Security Prison in Brazil Hosts an Annual Beauty Pageant for Inmates." *New York Times*, June 13, 2017. http://nytlive.nytimes.com/womenintheworld/2017/06/13/maximum-security-prison-in-brazil-hosts-an-annual-beauty-pageant-for-inmates/amp/.

Wong, Winnie. *Van Gogh on Demand: China and the Readymade*. Chicago: University of Chicago Press, 2013.

Wood, Nicholas, dir. *The Royal Ballet of Cambodia: Robam Khbach Boran*. UNESCO, Navigator Communications, and Cambodia: Ministry of Culture and Fine Arts, 2008. DVD. https://www.unesco.org/archives/multimedia/document-3752.

Woolf, Virginia. *Mrs. Dalloway*. New York: Harcourt, Brace and World, 1925.

Wynter, Sylvia. "Rethinking 'Aesthetics': Notes towards a Deciphering Practice." In *Ex-iles: Essays on Caribbean Cinema*, edited by Mbye B. Cham, 237–79. Trenton, NJ: Africa World, 1992.

Wynter, Sylvia. "Unsettling the Coloniality of Being/Power/Truth/Freedom: Towards the Human, after Man, Its Overrepresentation—An Argument." *CR: The New Centennial Review* 3, no. 3 (Fall 2003): 257–337. doi: 10.1353/ncr.2004.0015.

Yablon, Nick. *Untimely Ruins: An Archaeology of American Urban Modernity, 1819–1919*. Chicago: University of Chicago Press, 2009.

Yoneyama, Lisa. *Cold War Ruins: Transpacific Critique of American Justice and Japanese War Crimes*. Durham, NC: Duke University Press, 2016.

You Can't Shoot Us All: On the Oscar Grant Rebellions. Accessed August 19, 2022. https://ruinsofcapital.noblogs.org/files/2014/11/youcantshootusall.pdf.

Zambrana, Rocio. *Colonial Debts: The Case of Puerto Rico*. Durham, NC: Duke University Press, 2021.

Zoya, with John Follain and Rita Christofari. *Zoya's Story: An Afghan Woman's Struggle for Freedom*. New York: HarperCollins, 2002.

Zuo, Mila. *Vulgar Beauty: Acting Chinese in the Global Sensorium*. Durham, NC: Duke University Press, 2022.

Zylinska, Joanna. "Photography after the Human." *Photographies* 9, no. 2 (2016): 167–86. doi: 10.1080/17540763.2016.1182062.

INDEX

Abandoned America (Christopher), 147
Abbas, Asma, 26, 167–68
Abu-Lughod, Lila, 70, 86
Adorno, Theodor, 9, 13, 30, 149, 204
aesthetics: of bare life, 108; of beauty pageants, 131–37; deprivation of, 78, 162–68; education and, 87–93, 225n81, 227n110; of historicity, 31, 38–39, 58–63; imperial norms and, 76–77; politics of, 3–4; of resilience, 190–97; rightfulness-rightlessness tension and, 113; right to beauty and, 106–7; of ruin porn, 140–43, 147–48, 158–61, 239n10, 239n14; self-sovereignty and, 32
affect theory, presence of beauty and, 19
Afghanistan: promise of beauty in, 81–86; secret salons in, 81–82; US troop levels in, 98–99; US withdrawal from, 100–101
Afghan women: catch-up framing of, 96; transnational advocacy for, 86–87, 225n75; visibility of, 93; war and narrations of, 79–86
Agamben, Giorgio, 113, 115, 157–58, 232n39
agency, living beautifully as, 188–97
Agent Orange, 125
Aguilera, Christina, 189
Ahmed, Leila, 79, 80

Ahmed, Sara, 14, 79, 97–98, 193
America First initiatives, 178
American Ruins (Vergara), 147
American Society for Aesthetics, 149
amputees, in Miss Landmine beauty pageant, 120–26
Andry, Soofiya, 210n18
angel of history (Benjamin), time and, 171–74, 183
Angelus Novus (Klee), 171, 183
Angkor Cultural Village, 119
Angkor Wat: as heritage site, 117–20, 233n57, 234n69, 234n72; Miss Landmine beauty pageant photos at, 120–21, 123; state and international agencies' contestation of, 235n75
antipolitics, beauty as aesthetic for, 136–37
ao dai (Vietnamese long dress): calendar girls in, 55–63; erotic aesthetics of, 221n110; exhibitions of, 64–68, 220n102; historical changes to, 215n7; performativity in pageants of, 47–54, 215n10; photographs of, 219n73; Vietnamese sovereignty and, 40–41
Ao Trang (white dress) calendar, 55–63; erotic aesthetics of, 218n60; grid in, 60, 66, 219n83
Apel, Dora, 182, 246n39

Aradau, Claudia, 244n4
Archaeology of Knowledge, The (Foucault), 53
ARC Hub, 235n88
Arendt, Hannah, 7, 16, 113, 136, 232n38
Arfaoui, Meryem-Bahia, 60
Argentina: Dirty War in, 206–8; Ford Motor Company in, 144
Aristotle, 7
Arneil, Barbara, 232n46
ARTICLE 22, 187–88
Art Workers' Coalition, 43, 216n15
aspara dance (Cambodia), 118–19, 234nn65–67, 235n78
Asta, Ned, 201
Atanasoski, Neda, 74–75
atrocity, pornography and, 150–51, 158–61
Atuahene, Bernadette, 164, 243n130
austerity, resilience as rationalization of, 193–94
"Authorization for Use of Military Force," permanent war and, 76–77
awareness campaigns, humanitarian use of, 128
Awkward-Rich, Cameron, 203

Baedan, 138
Balfour, Ian, 112–13
bare life: aesthetics of, 108; human rights and, 113, 115–16
Barghouti, Mourid, 25
Barnard, Rita, 14, 89
Barthes, Roland, 45, 57, 63
Beardsley, Monroe, 149
"Beautiful" (Aguilera music video), 189
Beautiful Trauma (Fogg), 189
beauty: Afghan war and framing of, 81–86; civilizational thinking and, 78–79; crime as, 199–208; crisis and, 2–3, 15–17, 26–27, 45–47, 149–56; Detroit ruination and, 164–68; fraud and frivolity in, 149–50; genres of, 5–12; habitus and, 94; history and, 68–69; humanitarian diminishment of, 72–74; as human right, 104–7; inadequacy of, 142–43; instrumentalization of, 73–74; as life force, 12; as moral compass, 88; permanent war and, 77; politics of aesthetics and, 34–35; postconflict salvage paradigm of, 116–17; presence of, 18–28; promise of, 3–5, 12–17, 20; rights after rights and, 137–38; ruin porn and failure of, 168–70; Scarry on, 88–92; sexual autonomy and social liberation linked to, 83–86; ugliness and, 152–56
Beauty and the Breast campaign, 22
BEAUTY (Bringing Education and Understanding to You), 22
beauty of the arrangement, political effects of, 72–74
beauty pageants: ao dai pageants, 47–54, 215n10; liberal democratic aesthetics and, 32–33
beauty regimens, resilience and, 184–85, 246n52
Beauty Academy of Kabul, The (documentary), 86–93; aesthetics and education in, 94–95; copy as theme in, 97–98; makeover allegory in, 93–98; shaming in scenes of, 96. See also Kabul Beauty School
Beauty without Borders, the Body and Soul Wellness Program, 86–87, 95
Becher, Bernd, 244n137
Becher, Hilla, 244n137
Beddawi refugee camp, 230n8
"Beneath the Burqa" (*Vogue* magazine), 92–93, 223n27
Beneath the Veil (documentary), 81
Benjamin, Walter, 27, 54, 60, 143, 171–74, 183
Berger, Alan, 147
Bergson, Henri, 60
Berlant, Lauren: on bargaining and resilience, 185, 192; on beauty and sovereignty, 41; on crisis ordinariness, 29–30, 179–80; cruel optimism of, 17, 192, 196; intimate public of, 224n71; on love and desire, 56, 212n66; politics of aesthetics and, 4, 35, 133; promise of beauty and, 17, 20, 24
Bhungalia, Lisa, 101
Biden, Joseph, Afghanistan withdrawal and, 100–101
biopower, beauty and, 22, 94–95, 213n87
Bishop, Claire, 128, 238n139
biyuti, Filipino queer theory of, 10–11, 130, 202
Black, Paula, 95
Blackness: beauty and, 38–39; urban ruination and, 164–68
"Blk FMNNST Loaner Library, 1989–2019" (Smith), 186
Bloom, Leyna, 8
Bluest Eye, The (Morrison), 9
body: in *Ao Trang* calendar photographs, 57–63; government control of, 94; as property, 236n94

Bourdieu, Pierre, 94, 227n106
Boutopoulou, Alexander, 249n97
Bowery in Two Inadequate Descriptive Systems, The (Rosler), 168
Bracke, Sarah, 177
Brass Bombshell, 187
British *Sunday Times*, 87
broken windows, policing and, 155–56
Bronfen, Elisabeth, 219n89
Brown, Bill, 58, 154
Bryant, Ma'Khia, 36
Buck-Morss, Susan, 242n90
Bui, Keva X., 114
Bui, Thi, 45
Burke, Edmund, 78, 123
burqa: categorization of humanity and, 80–86; disclosure and recognition and, 92–93; French ban on, 226n100; as justification for war, 83–86; Orientalization of, 79; Western criticism of, 81–83
Bush, Barbara, 24
Bush, George W., 70–71
Bush, Laura, 71
Butler, Judith, 20, 65, 72
Butler, Octavia, 186

Cadava, Eduardo, 63, 112–13
calendar girls, 55–63
Cambodge Aujourd'hui (magazine), 119
Cambodia: antipersonnel landmines in, 103–4; court dancers of, 118, 234nn65–67, 235n76, 235n78; genocide in, 108–11; heritage preservation in, 117–20; independence won by, 118–19; Miss Landmine pageant in, 33, 104–7; postgenocide aesthetics in, 126–28; terror and repair in, 109; US loans to, 230n21; US bombing of, 42–43
Cambodian Genocide Program (Yale University), 235n82
Cambodian Mine Action Centre, 126
Cambodian Royal Ballet, 119, 127, 234n67
Cambodian School of Prosthetics and Orthotics, 235n88
Cambodian syndrome, 111
Cambodia Trust, 235n88
Camp, Jordan, 156
Canicoba, Camila, 131
capitalism: beauty and, 9–10, 22–23, 97; resilience as tool of, 194–97; ruins and, 33–34, 145–48
capital projects, Detroit renewal and, 144–48, 165–68

"Case against Economic Disaster Porn, The" (*New Republic* essay), 161
Castile, Philando, 2
causality, crisis and, 42
Centers for Disease Control and Prevention, 195
Central Intelligence Agency (CIA), secret Sahara base of, 100–101
Chakravartty, Paula, 145–46
chemical warfare, repair and ruin and, 108, 125
Cheng, Anne Anlin, 9, 124
Chicago Tribune, 100
Chödrön, Pema, 190
Choi, Franny, 198
Chow, Rey, 59, 65, 98, 108, 157–58, 193
Christianopoulos, Dino, 198, 249n97
Christian Science Monitor, 84
Christopher, Matthew, 147, 161
Chuh, Kandice, 3–4, 7, 12, 35
Chumbawamba (band), 158
City Beautiful movement, 162–63
civic body, governmentality and, 47
civilizational thinking, beauty and, 78
Civil Rights Memorial (Montgomery, Alabama), 112
Clifford, James, 116–17, 247n62
climate change: capitalism and, 139–40; resilience and, 174–75, 194–97
Clutario, Genevieve, 94
Coalition to End Gender Apartheid in Afghanistan, 225n75
Cohen, Leonard, 27
Cold War: permanent war and, 75–77, 176; US ascendancy after, 99; Vietnam and, 43–47
Colebrook, Clair, 73
collectivity, in *Ao Trang* calendar photographs, 57
colonialism: beauty and, 94–95; burqa and, 80–81; credit and debt in, 145–48; environmental sustainability and, 139–40; heritage preservation and, 117–20; mimicry of, 97–98; promise-violence of, 90–91; ruination and, 145–48; time and, 60; urban ruination as, 164–68; Vietnam beauty pageants and, 40–41
Comprehensive Soldier and Family Fitness Program, 175–76, 245n13
"Confessions of a Ruin Pornographer" (Christopher), 161
Constand, Andrea, 2
Cooper Jones, Chloé, 29

copy: aesthetic education and, 96–97; beauty and, 31, 39–40; historical preservation through, 48–54; mortality in, 63, 68–69; narrativization of crisis and, 50–54; original in relation to, 64–68; seriality and, 55, 66–68
costuming, categorization of humanity and, 80
Cottom, Tressie McMillan, 9
counterinsurgency measures: civilian agency conscription and, 86–87; US commitment to, 101
court dancers (Cambodia), 118–19, 126–27, 234nn65–67, 235n76, 235n78
Cousins, Mark, 152, 154
Cover Girl: A Gift from God (Nguyen video), 48
COVID-19 pandemic: beauty regimens during, 184–85; conspiracy theories during, 176–77; resilience training during, 195
Craik, Jennifer, 227n106
Crawford, Ann Caddell, 217n42
credit, ruination and, 145–48, 161–68
crime, beauty as, 199–208
crisis: of 2008, 145, 155–56; absence of freedom framed as, 74–75; beauty and, 2–3, 15–17, 26–27; credit and, 146–48; as event of knowledge, 42–47; living beautifully and, 189–97; Miss Landmine pageant and, 126; ordinariness of, 29–30, 178–81; of partial presence, difference and, 66–68; resilience and, 174–81, 189; ruins and, 33–34, 148–49, 159–61; as style, 181
Critique of Judgment (Kant), 182
Customs and Culture of Vietnam (Crawford), 217n42

Dabashi, Hamid, 9
Dalena (performer), 48–54, 218n53, 218n55
danger, liberalism and culture of, 176
Dango, Michael, 181
Danseuses cambodgiennes anciennes et modernes (Groslier), 118
Danto, Arthur, 7, 78, 162, 225n81
Dean, Carolyn, 141, 150, 159–61, 240n52
death, ruination and, 143
debt: ruination and, 145–48; state violence and, 156; urban property theft and, 164–68
Declaration of Independence, 90–91
De Gaulle, Charles, 234n69
Deleuze, Gilles, 65–66

democracy, pageants and aesthetics of, 131–37
demolition, aesthetic deprivation and, 162–68
Department of Homeland Security (DHS) (US), 177–78
Derrida, Jacques: on aesthetics and history, 59; on copy and preservation, 50, 52–53; on crisis and beauty, 16; on debt and death, 199; on precarity of beauty, 182; promise of beauty and, 19, 22, 27
"Destroying Detroit (in Order to Save It)" (*GQ* magazine), 164
Detroit, Michigan: aesthetic deprivation of, 78, 162–68; bankruptcy filing by, 145; failure and pornography in, 157–61; ruination aesthetics and, 143–48; ruin porn and, 33, 141–43, 158–61; subprime mortgage crisis in, 146
Detroit Disassembled (Moore), 147
Detroit Free Press, 165
Detropia (documentary), 147
Deva, Norodom Buppha, 118–19
Diana (Princess of Wales), 229n4
Diaz, Robert, 10–11, 130
Dick, Alexander, 225n81
difference: repetition and, 65–66; understanding through, 67–68
Difference and Repetition (Deleuze), 65–66
Di Giovanni, Janine, 90
Diotima (seer and priestess), 87
disability, human rights and, 113–14, 232n46
Disability-Adjusted Life Year (DALY), 236n93
Disorder (Kaplan), 205
distribution, beauty and, 91
District Detroit entertainment center, 165
Dolven, Jeff, 191
Donoghue, Denis, 28
Dove, Rita, 30
Dubin, Nina, 145
Du Bois, W. E. B., 11, 38, 201
Dudziak, Mary, 75
Duffield, Mark, 108
Duong, Natalia, 125

Easy Beauty (Cooper Jones), 29
Eco, Umberto, 28–29
École de arts cambodgiens, 118
École française d'Extrême-Orient, 117
ecological resilience, 189
Edensor, Tim, 162

education, aesthetics and, 87–93, 225n81, 227n110
Edwards, Lee R., 184, 203–4
Eisenhower, Dwight D., 144
Elias, Norbert, 94
Eliyahu, Amichai, 213n100
Eng, David L., 61–62, 190
Enriquez, Mariana, 206–8
Ensler, Eve. *See* V
environmental disaster, resiliency and, 176–77
error, fear of, Scarry's discussion of, 89–92
Esmeir, Samera, 113
Evans, Brad, 85, 194
event of knowledge, crisis as, 43–47
Ewing, Heidi, 147
Exposition Coloniale, 118

Faggots and Their Friends between Revolutions, The (Mitchell), 201
failure, pornography and, 157–61
Fanon, Frantz, 27, 79
Farewell to Arms, A (Hemingway), 189
Farrell, Amy, 225n75
Farrokhzad, Forough, 29
Fassin, Didier, 73
Feingold, Stan, 125
Fekkai, Frédéric, 95
femicide: beauty pageants and, 131; patriarchal violence and, 207
Feminist Majority newswire, 83
feminist theory: beauty in, 66; colonialism and, 92; woman and nation in, 60–61
Femmes of Color symposium, 9
Feral Houses (Griffioen), 148
Ferlinghetti, Lawrence, 24
Ferreira da Silva, Denise, 145–46, 156
Ferris, Emil, 7
finance capital, US transition to, 144–45
Fischer, Sibylle, 108
Fleishmann, T, 18
Fogg, Rebecca, 189
Ford, Christine Blasey, 2
Fordlandia (Brazil), 144–45
Ford Motor Company, 144
foreclosure, ruination and, 155–56
Foucault, Michel: on beauty and politics, 73; beauty and work of, 6, 203; biopower theory of, 94–95; on crisis, 15; on living dangerously, 176; on original and copy, 64; on preservation, 53
Frecuencia Latina, 131
freedom: *Ao Trang* calendar and images of, 62–63; beauty linked to, 84–86; human rights and, 113–14; imperial ambition and, 74–75; in Kabul Beauty School, 97–98
Freud, Sigmund, 154
Frueh, Johanna, 186
"Fuck Your Lecture on Craft, My People Are Dying" (Hindi), 149

Gandhi, Evyn Lê Espiritu, 43
Garland-Thomson, Rosemarie, 132
Gaynor, Gloria, 189
Gaza: poetry and, 9; bombing of, 25, 196; civil defense volunteer in, 202
Gebara, Ivone, 27–28, 29
gender: copy as, 65; Islam linked with, 222n33
gender-based violence, war on terror and, 71–72
General Motors, 144
genocide: beauty pageants for survivors of, 130–31; in Cambodia, 108–16, 235n82; post-Nuremberg definition of, 111–12
genres of the human, Western culture and, 78
German South West Africa, genocide campaign in, 130–31
Ghosh, Amitav, 117
Gigante, Denise, 7
Gill, Tiffany M., 23
Gilmore, Ruth Wilson, 9
Gilpin, William, 123
Global Burden of Disease Study, 236n93
Gonzalez, Vernadette Vicuña, 83
Gonzalez-Torres, Felix, 18
Gordon, Avery, 206
governance: population control through, 94; postconflict policies, 116–20; resilience rhetoric and, 177–78
Grady, Rachel, 147
Grande, Ariana, 189
Grandin, Greg, 144, 239nn18–19
Grant, Oscar, 169–70
Grauel, Terri, 95
Grewal, Inderpal, 35
Griffioen, James, 148
Groslier, George, 118, 234nn65–66
Grosz, Elizabeth, 115
Guantánamo, Haitian detainees in, 22

habitus, beauty and, 94
Haeberle, Ron, 216n15
Hannah, Lesa, 184–85
Hantz, John, 165–66

Harlow, Barbara, 231n34
Harney, Stefano, 166
Hartman, Saidiya, 27, 30, 186, 202
Harvey, David, 144–45
Hauser, Gaylord, 26
health advocacy campaigns, beauty and, 22–23
Health Project, 22
Heatherton, Christina, 156
Hedren, Tippi, 22, 212n83
Hemingway, Ernest, 189
Henry Ford Cancer Institute, 165
Henry Ford Performance Center, 165
heritage: Cambodian postwar aesthetic and, 126–28; destruction of world heritage sites, 21; imperial preservation of, 116–20
Hickey, Dave, 72–73
hijab. *See* burqa
Hindi, Noor, 149
Hirschkind, Charles, 221n13
historicity: aesthetics of, 31, 38–39; in *Ao Trang* calendar photographs, 58–63; beauty and, 40–41, 45–47, 204–8; crisis and, 44–47; heritage and, 116–20; resilience and, 174–81; ruination and, 157–61
History of Beauty (Eco), 28–29
History of Sexuality, The (Foucault), 72
Hoa Hau Ao Dai pageant, 215n7
Holling, C. S., 189
Holt-Gimenez, Eric, 166
homosexuality, beauty and, 38
Hong, Christine, 108
Honneth, Axel, 136
House Is Black, The (documentary), 29
housing crisis, urban renewal and, 163–68, 240n31
Howell, Alison, 175–76
Huerta, Dolores, 8
humanitarianism: awareness campaigns and, 128; beauty pageants and, 132–37; gender-based violence and, 71–72; right to beauty and, 104–7; war-making and, 108–9
humanities scholarship, beauty and, 225n81
humanity: aestheticization of, 79–86; human rights and concepts of, 112–14; rights of, 138
human rights: Eurocentrist concept of, 233n50; juridico-institutional structures and, 112–16, 232n39, 232n45; as political violence, 86; politics of resilience and, 194–97; promise of beauty and, 105, 115–16

Human Condition, The (Arendt), 7
Hume, David, 78, 209n9
Hun Sen, 33, 110, 230n20
Hunt, Lynn, 231n32
Hurricane Katrina, crisis coverage of, 193

identification, image and, 63
imperialism: beauty aesthetics and, 74–77; burqa as justification for, 83–86; Detroit and, 144–45; heritage preservation and, 117; permanent war and, 100–101; ruination and, 143–44
Inaugural Address to the University of St. Andrews (Mill), 87–88
"In Baghdad, Hemlines Rise as Violence Falls" (NPR news segment), 84–85
Independent (British newspaper), 79
Indigenous dispossession, Detroit and, 143–44
industrialism, beauty and, 21–22
infrastructure, resilience and, 174
Interboro Partners, 166
Intergovernmental Panel on Climate Change, 194
International Coordination Committee for the Safeguarding and Development of the Historical Site of Angkor, 233n57
international law, US rejection of, 98–99
International Monetary Fund, 177
International Security Assistance Force in Afghanistan, 98–99
In the Wake (Sharpe), 186
Ion (Plato), 218n54
Iraq: promise of beauty in, 84–86; US troops in, 99
ISIS, destruction of cultural sites by, 99
"I Will Survive" (Gaynor song), 189

James, Robin, 189
Jameson, Fredric, 150, 195
Jarmusch, Jim, 148
Johnson, Barbara, 37, 50, 54, 64
Johnson, Lyndon, 149
Joseph, Miranda, 22–23
justice: genocide and, 110–16; promise of beauty and, 101–2; Scarry on, 90; transitional justice, 222n22

Kaba, Mariame, 205
Kabul Beauty School, 31, 73, 77–79, 86–87; civilizational criteria at, 96; closing of, 99–100; global feminism and neoliberal rationality and, 225n75, 228n122; ungovernable students in, 97–98. *See*

also The Beauty Academy of Kabul (documentary)
Kang, Simi, 194
Kant, Imanuel, 5, 7, 9, 23, 52, 78, 88, 181–82, 230n17
Kaplan, Caren, 35
Kaplan, Leslie, 205
Katz, Cindi, 165
Kazanjian, David, 61–62
Kennedy, John F., 144
Kerman, Piper, 211n48
Kermode, Frank, 188
Khalili, Laleh, 77
Khmer Ballet, 234n69
Khmer Rouge: genocide by, 33, 42–43, 104, 109–15, 235n82; postwar aesthetic forms and, 126–28; salvaged culture of, 117–20
Kinney, Rebecca, 164
kintsugi, 186
Kipnes, Alexander, 28
Kish, Zenia, 145
Kissinger, Henry, 114
Klee, Paul, 171, 183
Klein, Melanie, 190
knowledge, crisis as event of, 42–47
Know My Name (Miller), 2, 186
Ko, Dorothy, 61
Kolko, Gabriel, 144
Koren, Leonard, 185
Koselleck, Reinhart, 44
Kossamak, Princess, 118–19
Kracauer, Siegfried, 51
Krauss, Rosalind, 60, 66, 219n83

labor activism: beauty and, 202–3; pageants for, 130
Lancet (journal), 113
landmine picturesque, 123; reparative aesthetics and, 186–88
landmines: in Cambodia, 103–4, 235n88; as environmental terror, 108–9; human rights and, 113–16; Miss Landmine beauty pageant and, 121–26
lapsed worlds, ruination and, 143
Larasati, Rachmi Diyah, 127
Leary, John Patrick, 141, 157, 194–95
Lefebvre, Henri, 29
legal personality: humanitarian aesthetic and, 136–37, 232n35
Leno, Mavis, 225n75
Leonard, Zoe, 10, 202–3
Leroy, Justin, 145
Levinas, Emmanuel, 92, 113

liberal democracy: appearance of rights and, 112; beauty and, 91–92; Kabul Beauty School and, 97–98; pageants and aesthetics of, 131–37, 237n114; resilience ideology and, 179–81; war in name of, 74–77, 83–86
Lieu, Nhi, 215n10, 217n43
l'Illustration (magazine), 118
Lim, Bliss Cua, 59, 63
Lim, Shirley Jennifer, 97
living beautifully: agency of, 188–97; crisis and, 34, 181–88, 246n39; as relief and resource, 173–74, 245n25; repair of objects and, 184–88
Living Beautifully with Uncertainty and Change (Chödrön), 190
living dangerously: aesthetics of, 181–88, 246n39; resilience and, 175–81
Lon Nol regime, 110, 230n21
Loos, Adolf, 115
Lorde, Audre, 185
Los Angeles Times, 78–79
Lose Your Mother (Hartman), 186
lost civilizations, ruination and, 143–44
Louisiana Justice Institute, 193
love, crisis-disturbance and allegories of, 56
Loveless, Natalie, 205
"Loving a Disappearing Image" (Marks), 57–58
Lowe, Lisa, 35, 75, 94
Loy, Mina, 4, 20
Lupton, Christina, 225n81

Macaulay, Rose, 143
Mahmood, Saba, 97, 221n13
Manalansan, Martin, 10, 129, 202
Manning, Erin, 55
Marchand, Yves, 147–48, 159, 242n95
Marks, Laura, 57, 63
Martin, Trayvon, 156
Marx, Karl, on property, 154–55
Marxism, 225n81
materiality, beauty and, 90
McClanahan, Annie, 34, 139, 154–55
McClintock, Anne, 126–27
McDermott, Patrice, 225n75
McGowan, Shane, 239n10
McMaster, H. R., 71
McNamara, Robert, 144
McNay, Lois, 136
media coverage: of Afghan women, 81–86; of Hurricane Katrina, 193; of ruination, 140–42

Médicins sans frontières, 86
Meffre, Romain, 147–48, 159, 242n95
memory, *Ao Trang* calendar photographs and, 59–63
Menon, Nivedita, 82
Michigan Central Station (Detroit), 147, 162
military violence, US imperial ambition and, 74–77
Mill, John Stuart, 87–88
Miller, Chanel, 1–2, 186
Mingus, Mia, 9
Minh-ha, Trinh T., 186
Mirror, Mirror on the Wall (Hauser), 26
Missing Pieces, The (Lefebvre), 29
mission civilisatrice (France), 117
Miss Landmine (Angola) pageant, 229n3
Miss Landmine (Cambodia) pageant: as aesthetic form, 129–37, 172–74; cancellation of, 126–28; creation of, 33, 104–7; humanitarian awareness campaigns and, 128, 132–37; logistics of, 229n3; photographs of, 120–26; prizes for winners of, 229n7; right to beauty and, 120
Miss Landmine (documentary), 125–26, 129
Mitchell, David, 125
Mitchell, Katharyne, 167
Mitchell, Larry, 199, 201
Mitchell, Paul, 95
Mitchell, W. T. J., 147
Moallem, Minoo, 47, 78, 81, 92–93
Mohanty, Chandra Talpade, 224n54
Moon, Whitney, 163
Moon Waxes Red, The (Minh-ha), 186
Moore, Andrew, 147
Morrison, Toni, 5–6, 9, 14, 186
Moss, Jeremiah, 170
Moten, Fred, 1, 7–8, 166
Mothersill, Mary, 26
Moyn, Samuel, 114
Mrs. Dalloway (Woolf), 183–85
Murdoch, Iris, 5
Mushroom at the End of the World, The (Tsing), 175
Muslim Cham minority (Cambodia), 110
Mutu, Wangechi, 182
Myerson, Collier, 197–98
My Favorite Thing Is Monsters (Ferris), 7
My Forbidden Face (documentary), 82
My Lai Massacre, 43, 216n15

Naimou, Angela, 113, 232n35
Nam, Hoai, 55, 59
Namibia, Miss Genocide pageant in, 130–31

Nap Ministry, 196
Napolitano, Janet, 179
narrative prosthesis, 125
Nash, Jennifer, 27–28
National Association for the Advancement of Colored People (NAACP), 129–30
National Geographic (magazine), 126
National Infrastructure Protection Plan, 178
National Security Strategy, 178
national sovereignty: beauty and, 40–41; war and suspension of, 75–77; woman and, 60–61
Nealon, Jeffrey, 52, 217n49
Nehamas, Alexander, 23
Neocleous, Mark, 178, 194
New Republic (magazine), 160
New Yorker (magazine), 184
New York Times, 80, 84, 95, 147, 163–64
Ngai, Sianne, 10, 31–32, 66, 192
Nguyen, Martina Thucnhi, 40
Nguyen, Trung Phan Quoc, 43–44
Nguyen, Vinh, 43
Nguyen Cat Tuong, 31, 40, 215n7
Nguyen T. Tan-Hoang, 48, 52
Nietzsche, Friedrich, 15, 167, 192, 211n65
Nikpouer, Golnar, 233n50
Nixon, Rob, 229n2
nonpersons, categorization of, 79
normativity, Miss Landmine pageant and, 126
Norodom Sihanouk (king of Cambodia), 119
Norwegian People's AID, 134
nostalgia, in *Ao Trang* calendar photographs, 59, 219n74
nudity, human rights and aesthetics of, 115–16
Nuttall, Sarah, 12

Oasis Rescue, 100
Obama, Barack, 99
objects of beauty, 28–36, 213n87; nostalgia and, 59–60; resilience and repair of, 184–88
O'Connor, Patricia, 87
Olalquiaga, Celeste, 143, 147
On Beauty and Being Just (Scarry), 28, 31, 38–39, 88–92
"On Difficulty" (Steiner), 150–51
On Earth We're Briefly Gorgeous (Vuong), 37–39
Only Lovers Left Alive (film), 148, 159
"On National Characteristics So Far as They Depend upon the Distinct Feel-

ing of the Beautiful and the Sublime" (Kant), 78
Oppenheim, James, 1, 202
order, beauty and, 89
ornamentalism, 9; humanitarian diminishment of, 72–74; human rights and, 115n16; resilience and, 196–97; of rights, 137–38
Orwell's Roses (Solnit), 9

pageants, political aesthetics and, 130–37
Paik, A. Naomi, 113
Palais d'Exposition (1931), 117, 123
Panivong Norindr, 122
Parable of the Sower (Butler), 186
Paris Peace Accords (1991), 104, 109–11
PARSA organization, 228n120
Peirce, Charles Sanders, 18
performativity, of ao dai, 65–68
permanent war: chemical warfare and landmines as, 108, 125; liberal imperialism and, 74–77; resiliency ideology and, 175–81; surveillance and policing and, 176; time and, 100; war crimes and, 231n23. *See also* war-making
Persephone (Stravinsky), 120
personhood: beauty linked to, 92–93; human rights and, 113–16; resilience and, 175–76
Philippines, US occupation of, 94
Philosophy of Manufacturers; or, an Exposition of the Scientific, Moral, and Commercial Economy of the Factory System of Great Britain, The (Ure), 21–22
Phim, Toni Samantha (Toni Shapiro-Phim), 119, 127
photography: of Cambodian genocide, 235n82; of ruination, 147–48, 150–56, 168–70, 244n137
Phu, Thien, 218n53
Plato, 5–6, 30, 87
poetic list, 28–29
police violence, urban ruination and, 167–68
politics of aesthetics, 3–4; beauty pageants and, 130–37; permanent war and, 183–85; promise of beauty and, 34–35; right to beauty and, 106–7; ruins and, 145–48, 172–74
pop music, damage and resilience in, 189–90
pornography: debt and, 156; failure and, 157–61; ruination and, 140–42, 149–56, 158–61

postructuralism, 225n81
power: aesthetics and, 4; human rights and institutions of, 112–13; resilience and, 174
presence of beauty, 18–28
preservation: copy as, 48–54; heritage preservation, 117–20
President's Commission on Obscenity and Pornography, 149
prisons, beauty pageants in, 130
promise of beauty: crisis and, 12–17; defined, 3–5, 20; judgment as, 199–208; living dangerously and, 180–81; permanent war and, 101–2; politics of aesthetics and, 86–87; ruin porn and failure of, 168–70; survival and, 172–74
"Promotion of Virtue and the Prevention of Vice #1—Nineveh Province, The" (ISIS video), 25–26
property: ruination and alienation of, 153–56; urban renewal and theft of, 164–68, 240n31
prosthetics industry: beauty and, 33; in Cambodia, 235n88; Miss Landmine pageant and, 124–26
public assembly, beauty pageant as, 133–37
public land, urban renewal and theft of, 164–68

queer Pinoy beauty pageant, 129

racial politics: aesthetics and, 9; beauty pageants and, 129–30; humanity and, 79–81; resilience and, 193–97; urban ruination and, 164–68
Rancière, Jacques, 3–4, 11, 35, 113, 128, 150, 204, 250n15
Ratana, Heng, 126
Rawls, John, 90
Raymundo, Emily, 94
Razack, Sherene, 132
real estate development, urban ruination and, 164–68
reason: Kant's discussion of, 182; resilience and, 192
recognition, as humanitarian aesthetic, 135–37
Red Dawn (film), 148
Reddy, Vanita, 6
Redfield, Peter, 86–87
Reed, Julia, 82

refugees: *Ao Trang* calendar and images of, 62–63; barriers for Vietnamese refugees, 220n90; beauty and cosmetology courses for, 230n8; camps, beauty in, 13–14; capitalism and, 139–40; Vietnam war and crisis of, 43–47
refugeetude, Nguyen's theory of, 43
Reid, Julien, 85, 194
renewal, ruin as prerequisite for, 162–68
repair and reparation: aesthetics of, 181, 186–88; Agent Orange and, 125; counterinsurgency conscription of, 93–94; living beautifully and, 190–91; Miss Landmine beauty pageant narrative of, 122–26; technologies of, 230n15; warmaking and, 108–9
Report on the Taliban's War against Women (US State Department), 70–71
resilience: aesthetics and, 186–88, 194–97; COVID-19 pandemic conspiracy theories and, 176–77; crisis and, 174–81; exploitation of, 193–97; failure of, 197–98; living beauty as, 188–97; subjectivization and, 190–91
resistance, resilience and, 194–95
revitalization, capitalist promise of, 164–68
Ricoeur, Paul, 151
rights after rights, promise of beauty and, 137–38
right to have rights, promise of beauty and, 134–37
Rising: Dispatches from the New American Shore (Rush), 26
risk society, 173–74, 245n25
Road to Resilience campaign, 176–77
RoboCop (film), 148
Rodin, Auguste, 118, 127
Rodriguez, Debbie, 96, 100
Rodriguez, Favianna, 27
Roelofs, Monique, 9
Roitman, Janet, 15, 44, 74, 178
Roosevelt, Franklin D., 144
Roosevelt Park (Detroit), 162–63
Rosler, Martha, 168
Roth, Michael, 239n14
Roy, Ananya, 146
Roy, Arundhati, 27, 140
ruination: beauty of, 182; capitalism and, 33–34, 139–40; characteristics of, 143–44; chemical warfare and, 108, 125; failure and, 157–61; images of, 168–70; industry ruins and, 162–68; representations of, 140–42; uncanniness of, 155–56

Ruin Lust (Tate Modern exhibition), 147
ruin porn: aesthetics of, 140–43, 147–48, 158–61, 239n10, 239n14; failure of beauty and, 168–70
Ruins of Detroit, The (Marchand and Meffre), 147, 159
rule of law: beauty and, 91–92; genocide and, 111; promise of beauty and, 105
Rush, Elizabeth, 26
Rushdie, Salman, 88
Ryzewski, Krysta, 141, 162

Sabbatical Beauty, 185
salvage, rescue of beauty as, 116–20
Samudzi, Zoe, 111
Santayana, George, 209n9
Sarkozy, Nicolas, 226n100
Sartwell, Crispin, 38
scarcity, aesthetics of, 162
Scarry, Elaine, 6–7, 13, 20–21, 28, 30–31, 38–39, 88–92, 143, 216n31, 225n81, 226n85
Schiller, Friedrich, 88
Schlunnd-Vials, Cathy J., 111
Schneiderman, Rose, 202
Scott, David, 100, 180
Sears, Clare, 241n80
security, resilience ideology and, 174, 177–78
Sedgwick, Eve, 7, 151, 186–87
Sekula, Allan, 122
self-care, resilience and, 184–85
self-sovereignty, aesthetic education and, 32
Seligman, Martin E. P., 175
Sellars, Peter, 120
Senses of Style (Dolven), 191
September 11, 2001, attacks: liberalism and, 88; normalization of crisis and, 179–81
sexual assault, by college athletes, 1–2
shadow archive, Miss Landmine beauty pageant and, 122
Shah, Saira, 81
Shakespeare, William, 9
Sharpe, Christina, 45, 186
Shaviro, Steven, 18, 52
Shell, Marc, 146
Sicardi, Arabelle, 11–12, 20, 199, 201
Sims, Benjamin, 174
Sisowath (King of Cambodia), 118
Six Names of Beauty (Sartwell), 38
Slaughter, Joseph, 81, 232n45
slave trade, credit and debt in, 145–46
Sliwinski, Sharon, 103, 112
Smeal, Eleanor, 225n75
Smith, Adam, 87, 90

Smith, Cauleen, 185–86
Smith, Jaden, 8
Smith, Martin, 26
Smith, Zadie, 225n81
Snyder, Sharon, 125
social arrangements, beauty and, 31–32
social order, promise of beauty and, 73–74, 95–98
Socrates, 87
Soleimani, Qasem, 99
Solnit, Rebecca, 9, 25
Song Kosal, 135
Sontag, Susan, 132, 160
Sopheap, Dos, 126, 229n7
Southeast Asia: capitalism and war in, 144; chemical warfare in, 108; history of war in, 109–10
Speaking of Beauty (Donoghue), 28
Specters of Marx (Derrida), 199
Spillers, Hortense, 115
Spivak, Gayatri Chakravorty, 44
Stanfill, Francesca, 70
statelessness, crisis of, 43
Stay Beautiful / Stay Alive campaign, 22
Steiner, George, 150–51
Stendahl, 13
Stewart, Kathleen, 4, 35
Stewart, Susan, 68
Steyerl, Hito, 48, 51
Stravinsky, Igor, 120
Stuelke, Patricia, 93, 195–96
s-21 Cambodian torture and execution center, 122
style: crisis as, 181; living beautifully and, 191–97
Suau, Anthony, 155
sublime: emptiness and, 162; heritage sites and, 99; Kant's discussion of, 78, 181–82; landmine picturesque and, 149; living dangerously and, 181; promise of beauty and, 9, 183; violence and, 149
subprime mortgage crisis, 149, 153–56, 176–77
Subtlety, or the Marvelous Sugar Baby, A (Walker), 9
Sula (Morrison), 186
Sunday Beauty Queen (documentary), 237n117
supplement, Derrida's logic of, 50
sustainable development, resilience and, 174–75
symmetry, beauty and, 90
Symposium, The (Plato), 5, 87

Tadiar, Neferti, 146
Tagle, Thea Quiray, 198
Talavera Bruce prison, beauty pageant in, 130
Taliban: civilizational thinking about, 79; destruction of cultural sites by, 99; disintegration as legacy of, 172–73; Trump negotiations with, 99
Tama, Mario, 130
Taussig, Michael, 6
Taylor, Breonna, 167
Taylor, Charles, 136
Taylor, Diana, 135
"Thank U Next" (Grande), 189
Things We Lost in the Fire (Enriquez), 206–8
Thompson, James, 24
Thompson, Krista, 123, 133
Thomson, Ashley, 119
time: angel of history (Benjamin) and, 171–72, 183; beauty and, 39–40, 172–74; calendar and aesthetics of, 60–63; disability and illness and, 236n93; history and, 179–81; living beautifully in, 188–97; permanent war and, 100; promise of beauty and, 96; ruination and, 147–48
Time Is the Thing a Body Moves Through (Fleishmann), 18
Todd, Helen, 202
Tolentino, Jia, 184
Tompkins, Kyla Wazana, 4
Tongson, Karen, 52
Traavik, Morten, 104, 128–30, 132–34, 229n6
transitional justice, 222n22
transitional regimes: imperialism and, 75–77; justice and genocide and, 110–11; postconflict policies, 116–20
transnational social movements, warmaking and, 86–87
Trump, Donald, 71, 97–98; Soleimani assassination and, 99
truth and reconciliation commissions, 111
Tsing, Anna Lowenhaupt, 144–45, 175
Tu Luc Van Doan (Self-Reliance Literary Group), 40
Tuol Sleng prison, 122
2014 Quadrennial Homeland Security Review, The, 178

ugliness, perceptions of, 152–56
unheimlich (uncanny), 154
United Community Housing Coalition, 167
United Nations, hybrid Cambodian tribunal, 110–11, 231n24

United Nations Educational, Scientific, and Cultural Organization (UNESCO), 21, 119, 239n11

United Nations Transitional Authority (Cambodia), 109, 119

United States: chemical warfare in Southeast Asia by, 108; demand for Cambodian reparations by, 230n21; environmental violence by, 230n12; war in Cambodia and, 108–10

Universal Declaration of Human Rights, 109, 231n32, 231n34

urban planning, ruination and, 162–68, 243n115

Vagina Monologues, The (V), 82–83
van Munster, Rens, 244n4
Vergara, Camilo José, 147–48
V (Eve Ensler), 82–83
Victoria Hand Project, 235n88
Vietnam: anticolonialism and beauty in, 40–41; Cambodian occupation by, 104, 110, 119; crisis as knowledge in, 42–47
Vietnamese diaspora, memory and beauty for, 52–54
violence: aesthetic deprivation and, 162; beauty and, 8–9, 85–86, 206–8; debt and, 156; resilience and, 190–97
Vogue (magazine): Afghan secret salons coverage in, 81–82; "Beneath the Burqa" feature in, 92–93, 223n47; on Kabul Beauty School, 77, 95, 97, 99
vulnerability, embrace of, 178–81, 186–88
Vuong, Ocean, 8, 29, 31, 37–39, 48

Wabi-Sabi for Artists, Designers, Poets, and Philosophers (Koren), 185–86
Walker, Kara, 9, 239n14
war crimes trials, 108–11; permanent war and, 231n23
war-making: beauty pageants for survivors of, 130–31; civilian agency conscription and, 86–87; crisis narratives and, 42–47, 74–77; gender-based violence and, 71–72; landmines and, 108–9; Miss Landmine beauty pageant and, 121–26; promise of beauty and, 74; US global supremacy and, 99. *See also* permanent war

Warner, Michael, 133, 237n131
war on terror. *See* permanent war; war-making
War Powers Act, 99
"War Is Fake, the Clothing Real, The" (*New York Times*), 80
Washington, Tracie, 193
we, concept of, beauty and, 24–25
Weissman, Terri, 166
"What Not to Wear, Baghdad-Style: Fashion Rules Begin to Change" (*New York Times*), 84
Wilk, Richard, 25
Williams, Randall, 86
Wilson, Charlie, 144
Winfrey, Oprah, 83
Wintour, Anna, 77
Without Criteria (Shaviro), 18
Wojnarowicz, David, 10, 202–3
women, Third World texts by, 224n54
Woolf, Virginia, 149, 183–85
World Bank, 144, 177, 236n93
World Disability Day, 126
World Economic Forum, 177
World Health Organization, 236n93
world heritage sites, beauty and, 21
world targets, permanent war and, 108
Wynter, Sylvia, 4, 78

Yablon, Nick, 163
Y-Dang Troeung, 103, 114, 231n28
"Year That Skin Care Became a Coping Mechanism, The" (Tolentino), 184
Yoneyama, Lisa, 114
You Can't Shoot Us All: On the Oscar Grant Rebellions, 169

Zahir, Ahmad, 86
Zambrana, Rocio, 156
Zhang Yimou, 59
Zuo, Mila, 12
Zylinska, Joanna, 148, 240n43